Integrating Islam

Integrating Islam

Political and Religious Challenges in Contemporary France

Jonathan Laurence

Justin Vaisse

BROOKINGS INSTITUTION PRESS
Washington, D.C.

Library of Congress Cataloging-in-Publication data
Laurence, Jonathan.
    Integrating Islam: political and religious challenges in contemporary
France / Jonathan Laurence, Justin Vaisse.
        p.   cm.
    Includes bibliographical references and index.
    ISBN-13: 978-0-8157-5150-2 (cloth: alk. paper)
    ISBN-10: 0-8157-5150-8 (cloth: alk. paper)
    ISBN-13: 978-0-8157-5151-9 (pbk.: alk. paper)
    ISBN-10: 0-8157-5151-6 (pbk.: alk. paper)
    1. Muslims—France—Cultural assimilation. 2. Muslims—France
—Political activity. 3. Muslims—France—Socialization. 4. Islam
—France. 5. Islamic fundamentalism—France. 6. Islam and politics
—France. 7. France—Politics and goverment. I. Vaisse, Justin.
II. Title.
DC34.5.M87L38 2006
305.6'970944—dc22   2006018347

2 4 6 8 9 7 5 3 1

The paper used in this publication meets minimum requirements of the
American National Standard for Information Sciences—Permanence of Paper for
Printed Library Materials: ANSI Z39.48-1992.

Typeset in Minion

Composition by Cynthia Stock
Silver Spring, Maryland

Printed by R. R. Donnelley
Harrisonburg, Virginia

To Rachel and Marie

Contents

PART III
The Politics of Islam in France and Europe

Foreword

The debates surrounding the integration of Muslims in Europe and France have aroused enormous passions in Europe and beyond. The underlying reason for such a strong interest is not merely the future of millions of people, but the fundamental challenge of defining what is known as French, European, and indeed Western identity. Yet despite the high stakes, the debates always center solely on "Islam"—a poorly defined concept.

For what, in fact, is being discussed and debated under that label? Muslim populations living in France (and elsewhere in Europe) are generally assumed to act within one of three contexts. Islam is either portrayed as a foreign culture, defined essentially by "Arab" or "Muslim" values as purportedly propagated by North African immigrants; or as a religion, often a fundamentalist one; or as a geopolitical force, in reference to the crises in the Middle East, the *umma,* and Islamist terrorism. Yet one possibility is rarely considered: that in France these populations of real men and women have their own distinct dynamics that will ultimately give form to a unique French Islam. Muslims in France, like those elsewhere in Europe, are individuals who collectively make up what is less a coherent community than a diverse population that is slowly but surely making the transition from being immigrants to being citizens— however remote the meaning of citizenship may have become for them.

The great strength of Jonathan Laurence and Justin Vaisse's book is to describe these dynamics in a precise and comprehensive manner. The authors consider these populations as they are, not as a function of abstract political considerations that elsewhere often degenerate into clichés. Their book constitutes a formidable tool for understanding the issue of Muslim integration in France.

The evolution of the Muslim population living in France reflects the evolution of French society in general. *Integrating Islam* is not a study of a group closed in upon itself, nor is it a simple demographic comparison of distinct population blocs. Indeed, the authors point out the myths and exaggerations that surround even the question of the number of Muslims in France. Rather, it is a detailed look at the way in which the interaction of Muslims and mainstream French society winds up changing both parties in the process. Their mutual influence serves as the working hypothesis of the book, allowing an exploration of the relationship of French residents, both Muslim and non-Muslim, to religion—and to the famous French *laïcité*—and of their political culture, their social and economic practices, and their daily lives.

For many, the question is whether French society is becoming more Islamic, or whether Muslims are becoming more French. But those who pose that question first need to define "Frenchness" in a country that has always been deeply divided—politically, philosophically, religiously, and ideologically. If the debate on the future of European Muslims is sometimes poorly expressed, it is not merely because it omits one part of the issue at hand—that is, French, European, and Western identity—but also because the concept of Islam carries with it a lot of ideological baggage. A number of "infernal couples" are common in the West, which, in their easy linking of complex phenomena, seem to connect Islam to all of the problems of our era: Islam and immigration, Islam and conflicts in the Middle East, Islam and terrorism, Islam and the social exclusion in the *banlieues,* Islam and the "clash of civilizations."

The first "infernal couple" is that linking Muslims and immigrants. There is no question that throughout western Europe, Islam took root in the aftermath of a massive labor migration that involved mostly Muslim populations (especially from North Africa, Turkey, and South Asia) and that took place in a short period of time (1960–90). That was not the case in North America or Australia, where immigration has been a continuous, long-term process involving various social classes and in which Muslims have always been a small minority. The correlation between Muslims and immigrants in Europe means that Muslims are overrepresented in the most excluded parts of society: in tough neighborhoods, among the ranks of the unemployed, and in prisons. Successful integration of Muslims is often impeded in such socioeconomic conditions. Moreover, even if not all Muslims in Europe are the product of recent migration, and even if all immigrants clearly are not Muslim, there is a constant association of Islam and immigration in the mind of the public and of politicians, which continues to have a negative effect on the generations that have emerged from this migration—but who are not migrants themselves.

The second "infernal couple" associates Islam with the crises in the Middle East. European Islam is seen as an echo chamber of the conflicts in that region, and Muslims often are seen as the fifth column of a coherent geostrategic entity called "the Muslim World" or "the Middle East." Therefore, for example, a constant stream of newspaper articles termed the November 2005 urban unrest in France as the "intifada of the *banlieues*," even though a closer examination of those events would have revealed the complete absence of Palestinian flags, references to the wars in Iraq and elsewhere in the Muslim world, or even symbols of Islam. Similarly, one would notice that the protests in France in early 2006 over the Danish caricatures of Mohammed were sparsely attended and quite peaceful overall. Even the anti-Semitism that one can observe in the *banlieues* is much closer to classical European anti-Semitism, as evoked by the theme of the rich Jew in the work of Pierre-Joseph Proudhon, than it is to Islamic anti-Judaism. European Muslims are much more detached from the Middle East than is commonly assumed, and they also exhibit a consistent refusal to be held hostage by regimes and political movements from the Arab or Islamic world.

Indeed, the distance between French Muslims and those in the Middle East is increasingly apparent. It is illustrated, for example, by the campaign led by the Union des Organisations Islamiques de France (UOIF) (Union of Islamic Organizations of France) during elections for the Conseil Français du Culte Musulman (CFCM) (French Council of the Muslim Religion) in 2005. The UOIF presented itself as the sole truly French Islamic movement, in contrast to its competitors, which it presented as tied in various degrees to different Arab or Muslim governments. Indeed, it was the French authorities who sustained the link between French Islam and the "countries of origin" by encouraging the success of the Fédération Nationale des Musulmans de France (FNMF) (National Federation of Muslims of France), a group supported by Morocco, in the CFCM elections.

Even though there is undoubtedly some feeling of solidarity toward the peoples of the Middle East among French Muslims, that solidarity amounts to very little in political or monetary terms. No visible demonstration of support for Palestine has brought together more than a few thousand Muslims in France. There are no real networks for fundraising, nor are there any mass organizations whose defining mission is to support political causes in the Middle East. The French and other European branches of major Islamic organizations (for example, Milli Görüs and the Muslim Brotherhood) are increasingly autonomous with respect to their parent organizations, largely because their needs, constituencies, and perspectives are quite different. The issues of Palestine and Iraq do not dominate Muslim political conversation in France or Europe. European Muslims are preoccupied by much more immediate concerns related to their place in society. Indeed, it would be quite absurd to demand that a European Muslim take a position on anti-Semitic caricatures in Egypt, for example, because that would be to assign him membership in the very transnational community that is so often said to impede his integration into Europe.

From that point of view, the authorities in France should return to the letter and the spirit of the process that culminated in the creation of the CFCM in 2002. They should no longer subcontract Islam in France to political and religious institutions from the Middle East, whether North African consulates or the Al Azhar University in Cairo. Rather, they must encourage leadership roles for French citizens, whatever their religious tendency. The criterion should not be whether such leaders are "moderate" or "conservative," but rather whether they are "French" as opposed to "Middle Eastern"—especially if their connections are more political than religious.

The third "infernal couple" links Islam with terrorism. This is a consistent image, even though all serious studies of the formation of terrorists in Europe show that the process is more likely to be the result of alienation, isolation, and generational crisis than of the importation of disputes from abroad. Young terrorists most often are westernized and apparently well integrated. They act because their relations with the society around them, including their families and other Muslims, have ruptured. They occupy a political niche of radical opposition to the system that is unique to western Europe (manifested, in earlier forms, as the Baader Meinhof Gang in Germany, the Red Brigades in Italy, and Direct Action in France), with jihad now replacing revolution and *umma* replacing the proletarian masses. Their religious training is weak—they are activists and, above all, rebels without a cause who have found a universal ideology in militant Islam at the very moment when the Marxism of the extreme left has all but disappeared among the socially alienated in Europe.

The fourth "infernal couple" is between Islam and social exclusion. The *banlieues* are relevant here once more, not as a fifth column from the Middle East but as a ghetto that supposedly is becoming slowly Islamicized. It is true, on one hand, that those who have failed to integrate tend to create forms of de facto community isolation at the local level, through the establishment of ethnically homogeneous enclaves, arranged marriages, religious schools, or other means. But, on the other hand, there is also a new category of individuals—those who have risen up the socioeconomic ladder and have tended to leave the harshest neighborhoods, while retaining and sometimes rediscovering their Muslim faith. One can see the emergence of a new middle class of doctors, teachers, entrepreneurs, and other professionals among the second- and third-generation descendants of immigrants. The number of students of immigrant origin is steadily rising in France's Grandes Écoles. Sciences Po's initiative to create special places for students from socioeconomically depressed neighborhoods was particularly welcome in this respect.

This middle class, which represents the future of Muslims in France, is usually ignored by the political parties. When they do pay attention, rather than embracing these individuals, the authorities make them the object of new forms of creeping discrimination. For example, young teachers and bank employees of Muslim origin are systematically appointed to work in difficult neighborhoods. It is all too easy to send back to the ghetto those who just managed to get out.

A fifth "infernal couple" associates Islam and "Islamic values" by placing them in opposition to Western values, in an inevitable clash of civilizations. The best example of this in the French context is the alleged incompatibility of Islam and the concept of *laïcité*. But to speak of the problem of the compatibility of Islam and *laïcité* (or democracy) is to make two assumptions. The first is that all Muslims will think and act as Muslims unless they explicitly distance themselves from Islam, and the second is that *laïcité* is a culture, a system of values or ideology that must be shared by all. Yet neither the French political system—which recognizes only individuals, not groups— nor the legal understanding of *laïcité* as codified in French law pretends to know the religious beliefs of citizens. Rather, it simply demands acceptance of the common rules of the game. The campaign being led to demand that Muslims distance themselves from Islam presupposes the very thing that it seeks to denounce, namely that religious sentiment necessarily leads to a lack of national identity and ethnic separatism.

It is not Muslims who are attacking the legal edifice that defines the separation of church and state in France. Banning the headscarf and other religious symbols in public schools required a new law in 2004 precisely because French courts did not believe that the 1905 law that established the separation of church and state could be used to systematically ban headscarves unless their presence could be tied to problems with public order or proselytism. The sole criticism that the large Muslim organizations in France make of the 1905 law is that it does not allow for public financing of the construction of new prayer spaces of any religion, which poses particular problems for Islam. Indeed, French Muslims have many problems financing their prayer spaces—

which offers further proof that there is neither a common sentiment of religiosity nor a mad rush toward building prayer spaces. The faithful masses are slow to open their wallets.

In fact, the more general debate regarding the compatibility of Islam and the West takes for granted the premise of the "clash of civilizations": that religions are, fundamentally, a set of mutually incompatible political cultures. Immigrants, therefore, are seen as carriers of their culture of origin unless they explicitly alter their system of reference, abandon their faith, or reform it. To replace the word "clash" with the word "dialogue" would be to acknowledge the victory of those who support the "clash" theory because it would mean accepting their flawed premises. They argue that the political culture of immigrants and of Muslims more generally is irreconcilably foreign and non-western. Thus all recent problems involving Muslims are interpreted as a manifestation of the clash of civilizations—the protests over Danish publication of the Mohammed cartoons, the 2005 riots in the *banlieues,* the murder of Ilan Halimi in France—even though such problems are actually the result of the loss of cultural reference points and the resulting search for a new identity. The European model, after all, is not solely one of democracy, tolerance, and freedom of expression. It also includes gang culture (pertaining, for example, to clothes, rituals, violence, slang, and music) and, more generally, to consumerism, machismo, and anti-Semitism. In Europe, Islamic fundamentalism is usually the product of a process of alienation and deculturation rather than the ultimate expression of Islamic culture.

Many commentators speak of the necessity of reforming Islam as a condition of integration. But the forms of religiosity that are visible among observant Muslims in France, even the fundamentalist forms, are actually quite similar to the forms of religiosity that one can observe in contemporary Christianity. It is the same insistence on rebirth, on individual faith, and on personal well-being and self-realization. A good example of this is the veiled girls in schools who take up the feminist slogan "My body is my business." This religiosity aims to create a community of faith that is distinct from traditional communities, that rejects traditional religious institutions and cultures, and that insists on respect for values (on respect for life, for example, in the context of opposition to abortion) more than adherence to traditional norms or law. The return of the religious is taking place strictly within the context of modern Western societies.

Moreover, all religious reaffirmation is not necessarily fundamentalist in nature. One can see various forms of religiosity developing, including the renovation of traditional Sufism in a modern context. The religious symbols of French Islam have left the ghetto of their traditional culture, attaching themselves instead to all that defines modern society: Mecca Cola, Dawah-wear, Islamic rap, and halal pizza and fast food.

Even in their protest movements, French Muslims are asking to be inte-grated on an equal basis, as illustrated by the Danish cartoon affair. The pub-lication of cartoons depicting the Prophet Mohammed touched a nerve with many French Muslims. But it did so not so much because of theological ques-tions regarding the representation of the Prophet, but because depictions of Mohammed as a terrorist highlighted the frequent failure of European soci-ety to distinguish between Islam and Islamist terrorism.

The question therefore is truly one of integration: French Muslims who get involved in politics are not creating their own political parties; rather, they are asking the big parties to open their doors and place them in good positions on party lists—a demand that meets a fair amount of resistance among established French politicians.

This noteworthy book by Jonathan Laurence and Justin Vaisse leaves behind a theoretical sociology of immigration and refuses to engage in the often fruitless debate on Islam as an abstract concept. The authors rely on solid documentation to study actual Muslims who live in France. Their pru-dently optimistic conclusions do not fall into the trap of cliché, excessive sympathy, or political correctness. By emphasizing the complex phenomena of integration and discrimination, they shed light on the mix of identities and the subtle evolution of identity among French Muslims. In so doing, they also point out the difficulties that many in France have in fully understand-ing the environment in which they find themselves and the changes taking place around them. Laurence and Vaisse make considerable progress in advancing the debate in France and elsewhere, an accomplishment that deserves acknowledgment.

OLIVIER ROY
Dreux, France
June 2006

Acknowledgments

We would like to thank Phil Gordon, Peter Singer, and Jeremy Shapiro of the Brookings Institution, who encouraged us to write this book and kept us on track. We also would like to thank Brookings's Center on the United States and Europe (CUSE) and its Saban Center for Middle East Policy for their support of our research and writing. Several interns at the CUSE helped prepare the manuscript for publication: Sarah Moller, Ruxandra Popa, Nicolas Séjour, Severine Wernert, and Tom West. Martin Schain, Roger Norum, and Alek Chance read earlier versions of the manuscript and offered helpful advice. Valérie Amiraux, Olivier Roy, Peter Skerry, and Jim Steinberg provided especially valuable comments on a final draft. We relied on Amanda Cause, former assistant director of the CUSE, for her expert assistance and good cheer.

We were fortunate to have many stimulating conversations about Islam and French politics while conducting our research. For that we would like to thank Alain Boyer, Khadija Bourcart, Sylvain Brouard, Claire de Galembert, Jean-Marc Dreyfus, Hakim El ghissassi, Art Goldhammer, Jean Pierre Guardiola, Peter Hall, Stanley Hoffmann, Yoshiko Herrera, Riva Kastoryano, Ruud Koopmans, Farhad Khosrokhavar, the late Rémy Leveau, Nonna Mayer, Vianney Sevaistre, Paul Statham, Xavier Ternisien, Patrick Weil, and, in particular, Olivier Roy. Jeremy Shapiro gave us guidance in drafting the section on the French antiterrorism apparatus. We also would like to acknowledge all who agreed to be interviewed by us, many of whom are cited in the text. Finally, we are grateful to Eileen Hughes of the Brookings Institution Press for her patience and skill in editing this book.

While we benefited greatly from the insight and advice of many individuals, we take sole responsibility for any errors. The views presented here also are ours alone and should not be attributed to L'Institut d'Études Politiques de Paris, the French Foreign Ministry, Boston College, or the Brookings Institution.

Integrating Islam

Introduction

France is now home to an estimated 5 million persons of Muslim origin, in a total population of 61 million.[1] Roughly half of those individuals are French citizens. While France has integrated numerous waves of immigrants in the past, this new segment of the population, which traces its direct or indirect origins to former French colonies in North Africa and sub-Saharan Africa and to Turkey, poses new and daunting challenges, much as recent immigration does in neighboring European countries. Because of the size of France's Muslim population—the largest in western Europe—and because of France's secular sensibility and its all-encompassing definition of citizenship, which aims to subsume other racial, ethnic, or previous national identities, the French experience with Islam is a particularly noteworthy example of the encounter of Islam and the West. The French "melting pot" has made Frenchmen out of peasants, to paraphrase the title of Eugen Weber's 1977 book, as well as of Catholics, Protestants, Jews, Italians, Poles, Portuguese, and many others.[2] If organized Islam can demonstrate the ability to coexist with *citoyenneté* and *laïcité*—the French brands of citizenship and separation of church and state—that development would be a fortuitous one for both Islam and the government at a time of international and intercultural tensions. This comprehensive study of Islam in France sounds an optimistic note, suggesting as it does that the much-maligned French model of integration—viewed as too permissive by some, too repressive by others—offers some approaches that are worthy of emulation or, at the very least, that merit closer study than they have been given in the past. American discourse regarding Islam in France and Europe has tended to be pessimistic and sometimes amazingly alarmist, at times echoing the old diatribes of Jean-Marie

Le Pen's Front National (FN) (National Front), which mainstream political elites rejected so forcefully in the 1980s and 1990s.[3] In political rhetoric and media commentary, observers from the United States have tended to favor and emphasize an "Islamist" framework for understanding contemporary political dynamics and instability, from Indonesia to Baghdad to the suburbs of Lyon.

The news coverage of the urban riots that erupted on the outskirts of most major French cities in November 2005 is a good case in point.[4] To be sure, the riots—the largest instance of social unrest in France since 1968—represented a major upheaval for French society. They demonstrated the government's failure to eliminate entrenched poverty and unemployment in the bleak housing projects where the latest waves of immigrants have flocked. They also brought into focus the reality of daily discrimination against young French citizens of Arab, African, and Turkish origin. The riots, however, were anything but religious in nature. Many of the participants did come from Muslim backgrounds, as did the two youths whose deaths were at the center of the unrest and many of those whose property was damaged or destroyed. But they had no religious agenda and, even more telling, no political agenda. Muslim religious associations, both mainstream and fundamentalist, tried in vain to play a mediating role and to quell the violence, some issuing press releases and others going door to door to urge an end to the unrest. But their inability to contain the violence over three weeks illustrates that in this case they were not the problem and that indeed they were somewhat irrelevant to the local political equilibrium.[5]

Last but not least, the actual believers in and practitioners of Islam in France—who, in every opinion poll, affirm both their overall satisfaction with their daily lives (except for complaints of discrimination) and their desire to integrate more fully—not only stayed away from the riots but watched them in despair, anxious about the image problem that the rioters were creating among the general population. Still, some American journalists wrote breathlessly about "Islamists taking the streets of Paris"[6] and the advent of a "distinct form of jihad."[7]

More generally, many political commentators and even U.S. officials have ignored the preponderant reality of the day-to-day, peaceful observance of Islam in Europe and have chosen instead to view the activities of Muslim political and religious networks through a monochromatic lens.[8] It is presumed that European Muslims in general seek to undermine the European rule of law—and the separation of religion and state—in order to create a society apart from the mainstream, whether by imposing headscarves on young girls, campaigning for gender segregation in public institutions, defending domestic abuse as a cultural prerogative, or supporting terrorism. In foreign policy circles, American observers tend to paint a portrait of a homogeneous and mobilized community the likes of which Muslim leaders can only dream. Thus, in 2005 a counterterrorism expert told a U.S. House subcommittee the patently false tale that "at least half of the female Muslim population [in France] wear the veil. . . . In some municipalities, the figure is about 80 percent."[9] An article in *Commentary*, similarly, reported that "there are dozens of 'ungovernable' areas in France: Muslim-dominated suburbs, mainly, where the writ of French law does not run and into which the French police do not go."[10] According to Bernard Lewis's darkest predictions regarding the "reverse colonization" currently under way, France and Europe will soon be "Islamicized," by the end of this century at the latest.[11] Other commentators have announced the birth of a mutant continent called Eurabia, "hostile in equal measure to the United States and Israel," and they warn that native Europeans will soon face the prospect of "dhimmitude" (minority status in Islamic tradition) in their own country.[12]

Too often, anecdotal political commentary verging on caricature replaces serious analysis. Writing about Islam in Europe, Thomas Friedman, the *New York Times* columnist, tells how he "spent Friday morning" querying two girls wearing headscarves during his visit to Paris: "They got all their news from Al Jazeera TV . . . the person they admired most in the world was Osama bin Laden . . . they saw themselves as Muslims first and French citizens last, and all their friends felt pretty much the same."[13] So much for a complex analysis of the views of the 15 million Muslims living in the European Union. The author of a recent *Foreign Affairs* article warns that "Europe's angry Muslims" form "an internal colony whose numbers are roughly equivalent to the population of Syria" and predicts that, in contrast to the identity of "the jumble of nationalities that make up the American Latino community," the Muslim political identity in Europe is "likely to be distinct, cohesive, and bitter."[14] But there is scant support for such an outlook. Indeed, some academic researchers have noted the persistent difficulties facing European Muslim leaders who hope to encourage collective action, and they puzzle over Muslims' lack of mobilization in the face of headscarf bans and occasionally repressive antiterrorism legislation.[15] Alarm over these purported trends should be tempered by several factors that are consistent throughout the countries of the European Union: the influence of political Islamic organizations over Muslim populations is limited; less than half the Muslim population fulfills both citizenship and age requirements for voting in national or local elections; and Muslims who can vote are divided along ethnic, national, ideological, socioeconomic, and religious lines and therefore do not make up anything like a unified bloc. But in today's highly polarized atmosphere, would-be Cassandras appear bent on describing a state of crisis.

This is not to say that there are no problems. France has spawned dozens of would-be terrorists and jihadis and hundreds of violent anti-Semites. Concern over proselytism led the government to ban headscarves in public schools and to deport dozens of imams and radical activists (around one a month between fall 2003 and fall 2005), and it is in the full throes of a struggle to navigate the diversity of contemporary French society.[16] The government has turned to a proactive policy agenda, ranging from positive discrimination in higher education to recognition of the Muslim religion as a fact of daily social and political life through the establishment of the Conseil Français du Culte Musulman (CFCM) (French Council of the Muslim Religion). Policies promoting recognition and acculturation in France are no more or less cynical than comparable government policies in other Western democracies such as the United States, where the budding civil rights movement (and the threat of violence and unrest in urban centers) contributed to a gradual opening of the American political arena in the 1960s and 1970s.

Another Point of View

Given the nature of headlines on the topic, Americans might be forgiven if they have a gloomy and somewhat monolithic view of Islam in France and Europe. The research presented in this book makes clear that the situation is too complex to be reduced to a cartoon, and it already is too well documented by researchers and analysts to be a matter of speculation and opinion. This book makes extensive use of French scholarship on Islam in France, though there are still gaps in existing statistics and fieldwork that will be mentioned later. The chapters synthesize the best available official statistics and both published and unpublished studies, elaborated on by the authors' personal interviews with French politicians, bureaucrats, and Muslim leaders. By providing a methodical and detailed account of the reality of Muslim life in France, the book shows that the situation is not nearly as dire as sound bites typically suggest. Indeed, in some ways, the "French way of Islam" gives cause for optimism, more so than Islam in many other European or extra-European contexts.

On the religious front, we find that a "French Islam" is increasingly replacing the "Islam in France" that has developed over the last thirty to forty years. We offer evidence on the emergence of various types of expression of Muslim religious, political, and cultural identity that are all at home in—and largely at peace with—French society. In no way has that growth been painless, and there surely will be many more opportunities for foreign columnists to offer snapshots of disgruntled young radicals, bearded Islamists, racist behavior, and social ills of all sorts—images that may, to some extent or another, always be part of the picture of Islam in Europe. But the positive trend that we find is confirmed by the ongoing process of mutual adaptation on the part of the French state and Muslims in France. The concrete data and analysis gathered in this book offer material for reflection on the religious and political evolution of Islam outside the traditional areas of the Muslim world, of what Olivier Roy calls "globalized Islam."[17]

Despite serious and sometimes spectacular problems and enduring challenges for the French republic, the integration of persons of Muslim origin in French society is, on the whole, going in the right direction. There is little reason to subscribe to the conventional view of an increasingly fractured society in which immigrants and citizens of Muslim origin form anti-Semitic hordes on the verge of imposing shari'a law. Adopting a long-term perspective, this book offers a tour of the actual conditions in which French Muslims live and work, pray, and participate in French politics. Slowly but surely, as with any comparable process of historical significance—whether the integration of Protestants or Jews or of other immigrant groups in France—the process of integration of Muslims in France is under way. This is a tale of several generations, of false starts and small successes. We pay special attention to the French state's recent development of public policies to encourage the integration of Islam, noting, where data are available, how they have fared. This is by no means an unqualified success story, but our findings are in line with a 2005 State Department poll that drew modest but nonetheless substantive conclusions: "Large majorities of Muslims in France voice confidence in the country's government, feel at least partly French, and support integrating into French society."[18]

The word "integrating" in the book's title is as much a description of what Muslims are doing as it is of the political imperative guiding policymaking in recent years. There is, of course, no essence of Islam to be integrated. Islam is constructed and constantly transformed by changing practices all over the world; it is what Muslims make of it. One of the points that the book tries to convey is that in France, as elsewhere, there are dozens of ways to be Muslim. This book portrays a dynamic Muslim civil society, innovative if sometimes insufficient government policies, and encouraging signs of integration. Not only is the state finally paying attention, but there are early signs that Muslims in France are rising to the occasion, from participating in the French Council of the Muslim Religion to slowly joining the ranks of administrators and politicians.

Focus and Content of This Volume

One of the difficulties of this book derives from its aim of comprehensiveness. Religion and culture are only two of the many dimensions of the new and massive Muslim presence in France. As the urban riots of November 2005 demonstrated, social and economic problems, which are common among many children of immigrants, are a key factor, as are domestic and international politics and public policies. So why should we have focused on Islam rather than, for example, the aftermath of Arab, African, and Turkish immigration in France? Why make religion a central dimension of our work?

First, there is an internal logic to our choice of focus. The religious dimension of the lives of the newcomers and their children and grandchildren has been growing in importance relative to other dimensions. The sociological literature on Muslims in France has documented three consecutive phases of political evolution of immigrants and their children.[19] There was "the Arab immigrant" figure of the 1970s, who asked for improved rights (for example, visas and residence permits) and respect for foreign workers. Next, in the wake of the first victories of the extreme-right National Front in the early 1980s, came the "civic *beur,*" who fought racism and discrimination with a secular, left-leaning agenda but encountered a disappointing response from public authorities and a stubbornly discouraging social and economic environment. Last to arrive—and heralded by the first headscarf controversy at a high school in Creil in 1989—was the "Muslim citizen," who asserted the right to a Muslim religious and cultural identity, often arguing that it is possible to be a good Muslim and a good citizen at the same time.[20] In recent years, public policies have focused increasingly on the religious dimension, fueling the perception of "immigrants," "second-generation immigrants," "Arabs," and *beurs* (a term derived from *Arabes* designating children of Arab immigrants, born and raised in France) as Muslims, first and foremost. And recent research has shown just how much integration and minority issues are intertwined—rightly or wrongly—with the question of Islam in the perceptions of many French, whether Muslims or not.[21]

Although this book refers to the French experience, there has been an overall trend, in the context of globalization, toward the reassertion of religious and cultural identities throughout the world.[22] That is the second reason why this book focuses on French Muslims rather than on immigrants or Arabs in France. And though we concentrate on France, we think it tells readers something about what is a global issue of historic significance: the contemporary encounter between Islam and the West. Certainly, at least, it is a European and an American issue. The subject often is dealt with in the abstract, when research should consist primarily of in-depth studies of specific circumstances. This book offers one such specific consideration of the French case, organized in three parts.

Part 1: Being Muslim in France

In the course of a few decades, from the 1960s to the 1990s, a large number of immigrants coming mainly from North Africa, sub-Saharan Africa, and Turkey settled in France, substantially increasing the diversity of the country's ethnic and religious makeup. As the French population expanded from 50 million to more than 60 million between 1960 and 2000, the number of nominal Catholics actually fell, from 48 million to 42 million.[23] In the same forty-year period, the Muslim population grew tenfold, from 500,000 to 5 million. In the Paris suburb of Seine-Saint-Denis, for example, the proportion of foreign residents increased from 2 percent to 19 percent, and now one-third of all residents there are Muslim.[24] This population is more likely than others to suffer social disadvantages such as discrimination and unemployment, which contribute to poor integration and its negative effects. An extreme consequence of such social ills was seen with the eruption of the urban riots of November 2005; though not religious in nature, the riots were a striking reminder of the poor living conditions of certain populations of immigrant origin, many of them Muslim.

French Muslims constitute a very diverse community, divided along lines of national origin, ethnicity, and degree of religious piety. In the four chapters of part 1, a clear overview is given of the implications of that diversity. The data in chapter 1 demonstrate that certain indicators of cultural integration, such as intermarriage and the use of French at home, have quickly risen over time, while educational attainment and unemployment rates still leave room for improvement. In addition, the information presented on controversial issues like fertility rates and patterns of religious observance suggests a less alarming scenario than those often portrayed in the media. Chapter 2, meanwhile, examines the recent trend toward re-Islamization in civil society as well as discrimination, Islamophobia, and racism, which have led to bitterness among some French Muslims. In chapters 3 and 4, the number and kinds of mosques and prayer spaces are reviewed in detail and profiles are sketched of several religious leaders and the main Muslim organizations that compete for votes in the French Council of the Muslim Religion.

Part 2: From Muslims into French Citizens: Muslims and Public Policy

The uniquely French approach to managing diversity defies simple characterization. The three chapters in part 2 discuss the last several decades of policy responses to the challenge of integrating Muslims and Islam into the social and institutional context of French politics. The chapters methodically examine integration policies, whether they explicitly target Muslims or not, and explore their origins. Criticism of French integration policies toward Islam and Muslims has sometimes been unfair: the state is portrayed either as phobic with regard to religion or as overly accommodating. But we argue that the assumption that the French government is prone either to "eradication" or "surrender" is misplaced.

Chapter 5 focuses in depth on the government's creation of the French Council of the Muslim Religion. Some observers loudly criticized the state-led "institutionalization" of Islam in state-church relations as being fraught with pitfalls and dangers. Several recent reports written for the U.S. foreign policy community characterized such examples of state-Islam dialogue as naïve attempts to build a "Muslim church" and warned that the inclusion of Islamists in government-sponsored forums is likely to backfire.[25] This book suggests that such a pessimistic outlook is premature and does not grasp the limited ambitions of the council: it is intended only to "represent" religious (that is, mosque-attending) Muslims, through the associations that run their prayer spaces, in the domain of state-church relations, not in social or political affairs. The inadequate physical state of prayer spaces and the lack of enough properly trained imams in France had permitted an "underground Islam" to develop that was clearly unfavorable to integration. By establishing the French Council of the Muslim Religion, the French government has taken responsibility for seeing that Muslims have official representatives who can negotiate, for example, to ensure that Muslims have respectable conditions for the practice of Islam, from the *banlieues* to prisons to city centers; with the help of these leaders, the French government is attempting to shape an Islam "of" and not simply "in" France. Chapter 6, which deals with the headscarf ban in primary and secondary public schools, explores the French government's reasoning in taking that drastic measure as one element in a wider effort to combat extremism and proselytism while reasserting the traditional sanctity of the French schoolroom.

Frustration with the slowness of electoral institutions to reflect new social *realities* has also led various French governments to pursue sociopolitical integration by other means, as discussed in chapter 7. Officials have appeared keen to create success stories and positive role models for second- and third-generation immigrants by routing some of the best and brightest students onto the fast track to educational and socioeconomic advancement. Affirmative action and the "diversification" of French politics are discussed in the context of recent efforts to employ minority candidates in government positions and to make university admissions policies more favorable to minority applicants. Still, the urban riots of 2005 illustrate the persistence of the problem of poverty and the lack of upward mobility in the neighborhoods where many French of Muslim background can feel stranded and marginalized.

Part 3: The Politics of Islam in France and Europe

In the initial roundup that followed the September 11 attacks, France was the allied country with the greatest number of citizens held prisoner in Guantanamo Bay—and the only one with a citizen facing conspiracy charges related to the hijackers' attacks. The Israeli government accused France of being host to the "worst anti-Semitism" in the West, and one major American Jewish organization took out full-page newspaper advertisements bidding France "Adieu" and urging a travel boycott (around 2 million Americans have nonetheless continued to visit France each year). One American study found that more terrorists of French nationality had been arrested or killed between 1993 and 2004 than the combined total of Pakistani and Yemeni terrorists.[26] The popular American television series *24* featured a U.S. counterterrorism operation against an Islamist cell whose masterminds held meetings on the outskirts of Lyon. France's Muslim population is viewed as a further irritant in French-American relations because some suspect that France's "pro-Arab" stance is intensified because the government is increasingly beholden to Muslims at home.

Chapters 8 through 10 assess the overall significance of the Muslim influence in three hot-button areas: French foreign policy in the Middle East, the rise of anti-Semitic incidents, and terrorist recruitment, while the book's final chapter examines Muslim organizations in the European context. Chapter 8, on electoral politics and foreign policy, explains the absence of a "Muslim vote" and points to studies showing that French Muslims and non-Muslims tend to see the world in similar ways. There is no evidence that French foreign policy would look much different if there were no Muslim minority in France. Chapter 9, on anti-Semitism, reviews the most recent data on attacks on synagogues and individuals perceived to be Jewish and discusses the specifics of French Muslims' resentment toward (and relations with) Jews. Chapter 10 explores common factors in known cases of terrorist recruitment of French Muslims and examines the failure of integration and the social alienation common in those instances of radicalization. The concluding chapter discusses organized Islam in Europe and briefly reviews how France measures up against neighboring countries that have also created policies to integrate Muslim citizens through religious accommodation and political representation.

Conclusion

Even though this volume addresses social, political, and economic issues, its predominant focus on religion entails some clear disadvantages. Many of the challenges of integration—perhaps most of them—have nothing to do with Islam or a putative "Muslim culture" (which, in that abstract form, does not exist) and everything to do with the poor social conditions and lack of educational capital of recent immigrants and their children and grandchildren. That is precisely what the urban riots of November 2005 brought to the forefront of national and international debate over the integration of Muslims in Europe. Using the "Muslim angle" for this book is also unfair to the hundreds of thousands of French residents of Muslim background who do not wish to be considered Muslims. Many of them may not be believers, they may wish to keep their personal beliefs private, or they may simply want be considered "French," as French political culture prefers. Or they may want to project some other identity or affiliation. By referring to "French Muslims" in nonreligious contexts, this book admittedly succumbs to the convenience of shorthand and so emulates the recent trend among policymakers and community activists, though in the interest of providing clear reference points for the discussion of Islam in France.

Just as religious freedom was a founding principle of the United States, freedom *from* religion is an equally strong fundament of the French republic. That is not quite the same as the separation of church and state, which is a more recent development. Instead, it was born during the French Revolution of the desire—reinforced during the Third Republic in the late nineteenth century—to keep the Catholic Church out of politics and education and to stake out a realm of civic culture that belonged uniquely to the state. Public schools, in particular, became known informally as "citizen factories." The French republic is not hostile to religious belief per se, although it is innately prickly toward organized religion. Because of its sensitivities regarding the presence of religion in the public sphere, the state's goal has been to "privatize" religious affiliation, and Islam has been no exception.[27]

The contemporary French experience with integrating Islam may have lessons to offer other European and U.S. policymakers. French administrators have acquired a wealth of experience with and awareness of Muslim minorities and the nature of their connections with the Arab-Muslim world. The French government has spent nearly twenty years confronting a complex network of transnational Muslim organizations active in France and elsewhere, and it has recently made progress in creating conditions to encourage the emergence of moderate Muslim elements and, simply, average French Muslim citizens. Beyond a better understanding of the actual living conditions and political behavior of French Muslims, this book attempts to offer a comprehensive and substantive view of how this important minority has fundamentally changed—and has been changed by—French politics.

Being Muslim in France

PART

I

1 | The Steady Integration of France's Most Recent and Largest Minority

Outside observers of Islam in France often paint a picture of a homogeneous Muslim community that is fast gaining on the "native" French population, one whose religious allegiance stands in stark contrast with its secular environment. The rate of expansion of this community—and its perceived drift away from mainstream French society—has been the subject of much speculation and political maneuvering, both by ambitious Muslim leaders and by the extreme right in French politics. The Front National (FN) (National Front) party once printed on its campaign posters the startling and inaccurate prediction that "France will be a Muslim country by 2020."

In France, which has approximately 5 million residents of Muslim descent, Islam is the "second religion," following Catholicism, and it has more adherents than the next three non-Catholic minorities combined: Jews (600,000), Protestants (800,000), and Buddhists (150,000–500,000). But to understand what that number means, it is important to establish first the basic characteristics of the French Muslim community. As the data presented in this chapter make clear, any assumption of homogeneity is misguided. Instead, Muslims in France hail from a wide range of nations, although most came from North Africa (Algeria, Morocco, and Tunisia, known as the Maghreb). Among residents of Muslim background, the degree of self-declared affiliation with Islam does not differ significantly from the degree of self-declared affiliation with Catholicism among French people of Catholic background (around 66 percent in both cases).[1] Among self-declared Muslims, the rate of attendance at mosques also is similar to that of self-declared Catholics at churches, although daily religious observance (for example, private prayer, abstinence from alcohol, fasting during Ramadan, and so forth) is somewhat more pronounced in the Muslim group.[2] And although the fertility rate of immigrant women who have come to France from Muslim countries is still higher than the national average, there is statistical evidence of acculturation in that the rates tend to converge over time as immigrant women adapt to their new economic and social situations.

Despite their ethnic and national diversity, what Muslims in France increasingly do have in common is their "lived experience," which includes the bitterness of exclusion as well as successful efforts to integrate. That experience forms the basis of an emergent "French Muslim" identity. The integration of the latest wave of immigrants into the fabric of French society has seen progress, even though more troubling problems have occurred than with previous waves (for example, enduring ghettoization in housing projects and related violence) and new issues linked to religion and identity have arisen that did not exist before. But the attention devoted to these problems should not overshadow the long-term trends toward integration, described at length below.

Muslims, Immigrants, or Arabs? Counting a Diverse Minority

The first Muslims came to France centuries ago, following the occupation of Spain by the Moors in the eighth century. Some settled on the outskirts of Toulouse and even as far north as Burgundy, and there are remains of an eighth-century mosque in Narbonne. In 732, Charles Martel fought back the Muslim invaders at the famous—and partly mythological—Battle of Poitiers (also called the Battle of Tours).[3] Some Muslims fleeing the Spanish Reconquista and, later, the Inquisition settled in Languedoc-Roussillon and in the Basque country, as well as around Narbonne and in the Béarn.[4] By the fifteenth century, the expansion of sea trade brought the French into contact with Islam in the Ottoman empire, in West Africa, and in the Indian Ocean. With imperial expansion, France became a "protector" or colonizer of many territories with majority Muslim populations, as in Egypt (1798), Algeria (1830), West Africa (1880), Tunisia (1881), Morocco (1912), and Syria and Lebanon (1920).

The greatest number of Muslims immigrated to France during the contemporary era, in the wake of the colonial wars of independence (1954–62). Their presence in France today can be traced back to the end of this period of decolonization, when many Muslims were officially recruited for labor, but much of the immigration was spontaneous. The oil crisis and economic

Table 1-1. *Foreigners of Various Origins Living in Metropolitan France, as a Percent of All Foreigners*

Origin	1900	1920	1940	1960	1980	2000
Europe	98	90	90	72	44	40
Africa				20	42	41
Asia			2	4	10	15
Other					1	5

Source: Mouna Viprey, "L'insertion des jeunes d'origine étrangère" ["The integration of youth of foreign origin"] (Paris: Conseil économique et social, July 2002), p. 122.

downturn of 1973–74 led the French government to end large-scale labor migration from North Africa, but the reunification of families became a continuing source of immigrants during the late 1970s and early 1980s. Family reunification from all countries grew from 55,000 a year in the late 1960s to 81,000 in 1973, before decreasing over time to about 25,000 in 2004. The arrival of foreign spouses, meanwhile, increased from 23,000 in 1990 to more than 60,000 in 2004.[5] Those years saw a shift from a largely single male population to one consisting of nuclear and extended families. Table 1-1 shows the growth of foreign populations of various origins in France over the twentieth century.

Estimates in the Absence of Census Data

The French republic considers ethnic and religious affiliation a private matter and therefore keeps no such official statistics on citizens of immigrant origin. The last census that indicated respondents' religion was taken in 1872, and a 1978 law restricts official recordkeeping regarding racial and ethnic data.[6] The precise number of Muslims is thus the subject of some controversy and considerable confusion. It has been estimated that there are between 3.65 million and 6 million residents of Muslim descent living in France, equivalent to roughly 6 to 10 percent of the general population. Though France's Muslims represent 123 different nationalities, nearly three-quarters are from the countries of the Maghreb: Algeria, Morocco, or Tunisia. The national census does count the total number of immigrants, which includes everyone born outside France to non-French parents (Muslims and non-Muslims). But even naturalization statistics are taboo, and immigrants' date of arrival in France was removed from the 1975 census.[7]

In the absence of official figures, widely divergent estimates of the Muslim population have circulated, many of which are politically motivated. The highest approximations (from 6 million to as high as 8 million) have been propagated both by the extreme-right National Front, in order to alarm "traditional" French citizens over what it perceives as excessive immigration and the corresponding threat to French identity, and by Muslim associations with a political interest in inflating the number of Muslims that they claim to represent. The lowest estimates have been provided by researchers such as Michèle Tribalat, a demographer at Institut National d'Etudes Démographiques (INED) (National Institute for Demographic Studies), who has suggested that the government and the public pay too much attention to Muslims per se and thereby encourage Muslims to identify foremost with the Muslim community instead of with France and French society in general.

Tribalat, using large-scale sampling techniques on data collected in the 1999 census (which includes detailed information on three generations of family for more than 380,000 adults), concluded that 24 percent of the population living in France was either foreign-born (4.3 million) or had at least one foreign parent (5.5 million) or grandparent (3.6 million). Foreigners, of course, include people from countries that are members of the European Union, like Spain, Portugal, and Italy.[8] Of these 13.5 million "persons of foreign origin," 22 percent (3 million) come from the Maghreb, 5 percent come from sub-Saharan Africa, and 2.4 percent from Turkey. Extrapolating from those figures and partly adjusting for religious diversity (especially for sub-Saharan Africans, half of whom are Christians or Animists), Tribalat offers an estimate of 3.65 million as the number of "potential Muslims"—French residents who, given their origin, are highly likely to declare themselves Muslim.[9] However, that figure dates back to 1999 and leaves out converts to Islam (generally estimated at 50,000) and illegal immigrants (perhaps 50,000 to 150,000 at any given time), many of whom are potential Muslims.

The estimates in table 1-2 of the Muslim population in France have been calculated by different sources over the last fifteen years. It should be noted also that these estimates generally count the number of "potential Muslims" or "persons of possible Muslim origin," not the number of believers in Islam and even less the number of observant Muslims. This book uses the 5 million figure as its point of reference for the number of persons of Muslim background living in France, since that number has emerged as the consensus among Muslim community representatives and government officials and will remain valid for a few years. However, it should be noted that the most scientific estimates available—such as those of Michèle Tribalat and Alain Boyer—point to the lower levels.

Systematic polling regarding religious beliefs—including polls carried out on a regular basis by the Observatoire Interrégional du Politique (OIP)

Table 1-2. *Various Estimates of the Muslim Population in France*

Source	Date	Methodology	Estimate
Bruno Etienne[a]	1989	Census on immigrants from Muslim countries and French citizens with origins in Muslim countries, plus converts and illegal immigrants	Approximately 2.5 million
Haut Conseil à l'Intégration[b]	1993	Census on immigrants from Muslim countries and French citizens with origins in Muslim countries, plus converts and illegal immigrants	Approximately 3 million
Secrétariat des Relations avec l'Islam[c]	1996	Census on immigrants from Muslim countries and French citizens with origins in Muslim countries, plus converts and illegal immigrants	4.2 million
Charles Pasqua[d]	1996	Unknown	"5 million Muslims, 1 million practicing Muslims"
Michel Gurfinkiel[e]	1997	Average of different press and academic sources	"Over 3 million and quite probably over 4 million"
Jean-Pierre Chevènement[f]	1998	Unknown	"Approximately 4 million persons of Muslim culture"
Alain Boyer[g]	1998	Census on immigrants from Muslim countries and French citizens with origins in Muslim countries, plus converts and illegal immigrants	4.15 million
ADRI[h]	2000	Unknown	5 million
Rémy Leveau[i]	2001	Average of different sources	3.5 to 5 million
Xavier Ternisien[j]	2002	Average between different press and academic sources	Between 4 and 5 million
Nicolas Sarkozy[k]	2003	Unknown	"5 to 6 million Muslims"
Michèle Tribalat[l]	2004	New data from a special study of the 1999 census using a sample of 380,481 people with questions on the country of origin for three generations	3.65 million for 1999
Ministry of Foreign Affairs website[m]	2004	Unknown	Between 4 and 5 million

Source: Authors' compilation from various sources, listed below.

a. Bruno Etienne, *La France et l'islam* [*France and Islam*] (Paris: Hachette, 1989).

b. Haut Conseil à l'Intégration, "L'intégration à la française" ["The French model of integration"], UGE 10-18 Documents, 1993.

c. In Catherine Barthélémy, Marie-Bruno Laugier, and Christian Lochon, "L'islam en Europe" ["Islam in Europe"], *Les dossiers du Secrétariat pour les relations avec l'islam* [*Dossiers of the Secretariat for Relations with Islam*], no. 1 (March 1996) (study associated with the Catholic diocese of Paris).

(Table continues)

Table 1-2 (*continued*)

d. Minister of the interior (political right), on French TV (7 sur 7), see "Une quatrième personne est décédée des séquelles de l'explosion dans le RER" ["A fourth person has died after the explosion in the RER"], *Le Monde,* December 10, 1996.

e. Michel Gurfinkiel, "Islam in France: The French Way of Life Is in Danger," *Middle East Quarterly* 4, no.1 (March 1997). Gurfinkiel is editor in chief of *Valeurs Actuelles,* a conservative weekly.

f. Minister of the interior (political sovereigntist, left), "L'islam en France" ["Islam in France"], *Esprit,* November 1998.

g. Alain Boyer, *L'Islam en France* [*Islam in France*] (Paris: Presses Universitaires de France, 1998). Boyer is a civil servant and expert on Islam in France. His estimates are still the most widely used.

h. ADRI (Agence pour le Développement des Relations Interculturelles) estimate, in Luc Gruson, *Le point sur l'islam en France* [*All you need to know about Islam in France*] (Paris: La Documentation française, 2000).

i. Rémy Leveau, "France: changements et continuité de l'islam" ["France: Changes and continuity in Islam"], in Rémy Leveau, Khadija Mohsen-Finan, and Catherine Wihtol de Wenden, *L'islam en France et en Allemagne: identités et citoyennetés* [*Islam in France and Germany: Identity and citizenship*] (Paris: La Documentation française, 2001). Leveau is an expert on Islam in France.

j. Xavier Ternisien, *La France des mosquées* [*The France of the mosques*] (Paris: Albin Michel, 2002).Ternisien is a journalist at *Le Monde.*

k. Minister of the interior (political center-right), quoted in Gilbert Charles and Besma Lahouri, "3.7 millions de musulmans en France" ["3.7 million Muslims in France"], *L'Express,* December 4, 2003.

l. Michèle Tribalat, "Le nombre de musulmans en France: qu'en sait-on?" ["The number of Muslims in France: What do we know?"] *Cités,* hors-série [special issue] (Paris: PUF, 2004). Tribalat is a demographer at INED (Institut National d'Etudes Démographiques).

m. See www.diplomatie.gouv.fr/culture/france/ressources/letour/fr/texislam.html.

(Interregional Center for Policy Studies), a network of local research groups in partnership with the Conseils Régionaux (regional councils), and by the CEVIPOF, a Paris think tank specializing in political issues—do not provide good figures either. Polls result in estimates in the range of 1 million Muslims or fewer, a number that is obviously far too small.[10] Such results can be explained by three factors. First, the CEVIPOF polls (but not those of the OIP) draw on people who are registered voters, and it is generally estimated that half of the people of Muslim origin in France are not French citizens (and half of those who are do not yet fulfill the age requirement to vote). The second factor is the likely underenrollment of French Muslim citizens on voter registration lists. The third factor is the reluctance of Muslims to declare themselves as such to pollsters. However, that reluctance has been diminishing in recent years. In the CEVIPOF's 2001 poll, twice as many people described themselves as Muslim as in 1998, and that increase clearly cannot be explained by the growth of the Muslim community through immigration or new births alone.[11] This reaffirmation of religious identity will be dealt with in greater detail in chapter 3.

Geographic as well as ethnic diversity makes it difficult to speak in sweeping terms about "the" Muslim population. As shown in figure 1-1, the North

Figure 1-1. *Muslim Population in France, by Origin*

Number

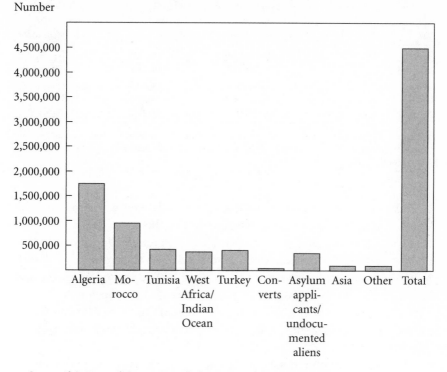

Source: Alain Boyer, *L'islam en France* [*Islam in France*] (Paris: PUF, 1998).

African majority is divided among subpopulations with distinct cultural and religious identities. The 2 million or so French residents of Algerian descent, for example, fall into two major groups:

—Arab and Berber *harkis* and *Français musulmans* (French Muslims), who served as colonial administrators and foot soldiers, and their French-born children and grandchildren

—The descendants of mostly Arab labor migrants recruited in the decade following decolonization (1962–73).

It is interesting to note that perhaps only half of France's 5 million Muslims are of Arab descent. The rest are Algerian or Moroccan Berbers (800,000); immigrants from Turkey, West Africa, islands in the Indian Ocean, or Asia; or French converts to Islam.

The largest Muslim population centers in France are Paris, Marseille, and Lyon and their outlying suburbs (*banlieues*). Muslims typically form between

Table 1-3. *French Cities with the Largest Muslim Populations*

City	Approximate number of Muslims	Total city population	Muslims as percent of local population
Paris	1,700,000	11,000,000	10–15
Marseille	200,000	800,000	25
Lille	200,000	4,000,000	5
Lyon	150,000	1,200,000	8–12
Roubaix (Lille)	50,000	100,000	50

Source: ADRI (Agence pour le Développement des Relations Interculturelles) estimates, in Luc Gruson, *Le point sur l'islam en France* [*All you need to know about Islam in France*] (Paris: La Documentation française, 2000).

10 and 15 percent of the metropolitan area population (except in Marseille, where one in four residents is Muslim, and in the small northern city of Roubaix, where the ratio is one to two). The greatest concentration is in the Paris region (Ile-de-France), which is home to 35 to 40 percent of all French Muslims. Fifteen to twenty percent of Muslims live around Marseille and Nice (in the Provence-Alpes-Côte d'Azur region); Lyon and Grenoble (Rhone-Alpes) are home to another 15 percent; and 5 to 10 percent live around Lille (Nord-Pas de Calais).[12] Table 1-3 ranks the French cities with the most Muslims.

The age distribution of the population of Muslim origin is skewed toward youth, as seen in tables 1-4 and 1-5. In part because of an initial divergence in Muslim and non-Muslim fertility rates, as much as half of the Muslim population in France is under twenty-four years of age. Indeed, one study showed that approximately 1.5 million French children live in immigrant families from Muslim countries. This population thus makes up a significant minority in French schools. It is estimated that 20 percent of sixth-grade students, for example, live in immigrant households; 10 percent have two immigrant parents, and another 10 percent have one immigrant parent.[13]

Projections and Comparisons with Other European Countries

Of the approximately 15 million Muslims who currently live in the European Union, France is home to the largest number, equal to around one-third of the total (see table 1-6). Germany follows with 3.3 million, Britain with 1.6 million, and Italy and the Netherlands with as many as 1 million each.[14] The below-replacement fertility rates among nonimmigrant populations throughout western Europe have raised alarm that "native" populations are

Table 1-4. *Number of Children Living with Immigrant Parents of Selected Nationalities*

Country	Number of children
EU countries	930,094
Portugal	428,894
Italy	165,722
Spain	169,330
Algeria	551,560
Morocco	501,939
Tunisia	188,778
Africa[a]	242,070
Turkey	144,183
Other	526,368
Total	3,084,992

Source: Mouna Viprey, "L'insertion des jeunes d'origine étrangère" ["The integration of youth of foreign origin"] (Paris: Conseil économique et social, July 2002).
a. Former French territories.

Table 1-5. *Largest Populations of Children of Immigrants, by Département*

Département	Number	Percent of all children[a]
Alpes-Maritimes	45,818	19.3
Bouches-du-Rhône	84,959	17.2
Haut-Garonne (Toul)	35,564	13.5
Gironde	33,707	10.2
Moselle	44,914	15.4
Bas-Rhin	45,824	26.4
Haut-Rhin	37,047	18.6
Rhône	95,015	21.2
Paris	142,340	33.3
Yvelines	91,786	21.4
Hauts-de-Seine	102,980	27.2
Seine-Saint-Denis	199,497	27.2
Val-de-Marne	105,832	30.6
Val-d'Oise	108,253	29.6
France	2,312,035	14.4

Source: "L'accueil des immigrants et l'intégration des populations issues de l'immigration," Rapport au Président de la République ["Welcoming immigrants and integrating populations of immigrant origin," Report to the President of the Republic], Cour des Comptes, November 2004, p. 427.
a. Children to twenty-four years of age.

Table 1-6. *Approximate Muslim Populations and Prayer Spaces, Selected Countries, 2003*[a]

Country	Largest groups, by national origin (first- and second-generation immigrants)		As percent of total immigrant population	As percent of total population[b]	Prayer spaces
Germany	Turkey	2,600,000			
	Sunni	2,100,000			
	Alevi	500,000			
	Bosnia	283,000			
	Iran	125,000 (Shiite)			
	Morocco	109,000			
	Afghanistan	86,000			
	Pakistan	60,000 (Ahmadi)			
	Palestine	60,000			
Total		3,300,000[c]	40	3–4	2,300
France	Algeria	1,750,000			
	Morocco	950,000			
	Tunisia	425,000			
	Turkey	407,500			
	West Africa/ Indian Ocean	375,000			
	Asians	100,000			
	Other	100,000			
Total		5,000,000[d]	75	7–8	1,600
United Kingdom	Pakistan	750,000			
	Bangladesh	200,000			
	India	150,000			
Total		1,500,000–2,000,000[e]	40	3–4	1,000
Italy	Morocco	227,616			
	Albania	233,616			
	Tunisia	60,572			
	Senegal	47,762			
	Egypt	44,798			
	Pakistan	30,506			
	Bangladesh	32,391			
Total		700,000–1,000,000[f]	75	1-2	450
Spain	Morocco	240,000			
	Algeria	20,000			
	Senegal	16,000			
	Pakistan	13,000			
	Gambia	10,000			
Total		350,000–800,000	30	1-2	400

Country	Largest groups, by national origin (first- and second-generation immigrants)		As percent of total immigrant population	As percent of total population[b]	Prayer spaces
Holland	Turkey	284,679			
	Morocco	247,443			
	Suriname	35,638			
	Iraq	28,502			
	Somalia	26,050			
	Iran	17,432			
	Pakistan	15,115			
	Afghanistan	15,020			
	Egypt	12,272			
	Other	48,000			
Total		750,000–950,000	75	5-6	400
Total in the EU-25[g]	15–17 million				

Sources:

Germany: Beauftragte der Bundesregierung für Ausländerfragen, "Bericht über die Lage der Auslaender in Deutschland" [Federal Commissioner for Foreigners' Issues, "Report on the Status of Immigrants in Germany"], August 2005; France: Alain Boyer, *L'islam en France* [*Islam in France*] (Paris: PUF, 1998).

United Kingdom: Timothy M. Savage, "Europe and Islam: Crescent Waxing, Cultures Clashing," *Washington Quarterly* 27 (Summer 2004): 25–50; Fourth National Survey of Ethnic Minorities conducted in 1997 by the Policy Studies Institute in London by Tariq Modood; Nico Landman, "Islam in the United Kingdom," in *Islam, Europe's Second Religion: The New Social, Cultural, and Political Landscape*, edited by Shireen Hunter (Praeger: Westport, 2002), for figure on number of prayer spaces.

Italy: Roberta Aluffi Beck-Peccoz and Giovanna Zincone, eds., *The Legal Treatment of Islamic Minorities in Europe* (Leuvent: Peeters Press, 2004); Caritas-Migrantes, *Dossier Statistico* 2002 and 2004 (Rome: Caritas).

Spain: High estimate of total population is from a Spanish Justice Ministry official, quoted in Renwick McClean, "Spain Considers Financing for Major Religions," *New York Times,* August 3, 2004; low estimate is from Bernabe Lopez Garcia and Ana I. Planet Contreras, "Islam in Spain," in Hunter, ed., *Islam, Europe's Second Religion;* Nieves Ortega Pérez, "Spain: Forging an Immigration Policy," Migration Information Source, Washington, Migration Policy Institute.

Holland: U.S. Department of State, "International Religious Freedom Report 2004"; Nico Landman, "Islam in the Benelux Countries," in Hunter, ed., *Islam, Europe's Second Religion.*

Total: The number of prayer spaces is from "International Religious Freedom Report 2005" (www.state.gov/g/drl/rls/irt/2005/51571.htm).

a. All totals are approximate. See table 1-2 for additional sources.

b. Citizens and noncitizens; percentage estimates from Farhad Khosrokhavar, *L'islam dans les prisons* [*Islam in the prisons*] (Paris: Balland, 2004).

c. Including naturalizations and converts. Of 2.3 million immigrants of Turkish origin, 1.9 million still hold only Turkish citizenship; around 750,000 are German citizens.

d. Around 3,000,000 are French citizens. Only half are of voting age, including those of North African descent.

e. Around 800,000 are British citizens.

f. Around 50,000 are Italian citizens.

g. The twenty-five members of the European Union.

shrinking across the continent—and that has led to intense debate regarding the level of immigration that will be required to maintain the workforce and social welfare systems. But France, because of its comparatively higher total fertility rate, depends the least on immigration. Just 20 percent of its population growth comes from immigration, while the corresponding figure is 50 percent in Ireland, 70 percent in the United Kingdom, 82 percent in Spain, and 97 percent in Italy.[15] France (along with Ireland) thus appears to be less plagued by the general European problem with population replacement. The French population is actually predicted to grow, under some projections, to 75 million in 2050 (from today's roughly 61 million, or 63 million including overseas territories), which would make France the largest nation among the twenty-five current members of the European Union. The fertility rate of the immigrant population accounts for part of that growth, but the relatively higher fertility rate of French women of French origin makes up the bulk of the growth differential with countries like the United Kingdom, Italy, and Germany—all of which are expected to experience a steady need for immigrant labor (and welfare state contributions) as their national fertility rates fall and life expectancy continues to grow.

There are three ways that legal immigration to France—one source of a growing Muslim population—takes place today: through family reunification and marriage, immigration of high-skilled labor, and application for political asylum. Net legal immigration to France in the first two categories stayed relatively consistent throughout the 1990s, at between 100,000 and 120,000 people a year. Africans (mostly from the Maghreb) represented around 60 percent of the new arrivals, EU nationals accounted for 20 to 25 percent, and Asians (mostly from China) for about 18 percent. The rest were non-EU Europeans, or they were from the former USSR or the Americas.[16] However, the annual rate has not been perfectly stable; in 2002 and 2003 net legal immigration rose to 156,000 and then peaked at 173,000, including approximately 60,000 foreigners who became residents by marrying French citizens in each year.[17] These figures do not include adult asylum applicants (90,000 in 2003, including minors), who are allowed to stay in France until they receive a hearing (only 15 percent of cases were successful in 2003). Most applicants for asylum in 2003 hailed from Turkey (15 percent), China (10 percent), or Congo (10 percent), and the highest acceptance rates were for applicants from Rwanda, Ethiopia, Bosnia, Tunisia, Russia, and Burundi.[18]

Finally, there is considerable debate about annual *illegal* migration to France.[19] Statisticians estimate it to include from 10,000 to 20,000 individuals, replenishing a stable population of at least 60,000 *sans papiers* (undocumented aliens), many of whom are from China and Southeast Asia.[20] But Nicolas Sarkozy, the minister of the interior, has said that the real figure might be closer to a total of 300,000 *sans papiers*, with 80,000 entering France every year (although often they are en route to the United Kingdom).[21] There has been speculation that the countries of the Maghreb, where unemployment can reach 40 percent, will remain a source of potential illegal immigration in coming years. (President Jacques Chirac was greeted with cries of "Visas!" during his 2003 state visit to Algeria.) The French government has pursued a policy that is strict with regard to interdicting illegal entrants at the country's borders, but it has regularly granted amnesty to long-time illegal residents. However, a law passed in summer 2003 gives mayors the power to enforce the provisions of short-term visas (including by ordering the deportation of violators), aiming thereby to improve administrative efficiency and so keep tourists and short-term employees from overstaying their welcome. New measures also were taken in 2005 to restrict the terms of family reunification, and a comprehensive immigration bill in spring 2006 proposed to end the automatic naturalization of *sans papiers* after ten years of residence (see chapter 7).[22]

The other way in which the Muslim population in France will continue to grow long after the end of mass immigration is, of course, through births on French soil. The fertility rate of Tunisian, Moroccan, and Algerian women living in France has been in decline since 1981, but it is still between 2.57 (for Algerians) and 2.9 (for Moroccans) children per woman; this is higher than that of French women overall, whose rate is 1.94 per woman.[23] With native European populations shrinking at current birthrates, some studies suggest that the Muslim population could double to 20 percent of the total French population by 2020, which would represent a real increase to about 8 million total. However, that estimate does not take into account the decreasing fertility of Muslim women living in France, which makes such a dramatic increase unlikely.[24]

Figures 1-2 and 1-3 document only a slight decrease in the fertility rate of foreign women living in France between 1989 and 1999, but the data, from the Institut National de la Statistique et des Études Économiques (INSEE) (National Institute of Statistics and Economic Studies) also show fertility to be closely tied to length of residence in France. In other words, the longer immigrant women live in France, the fewer children they have; their fertility rate approaches that of native-born French women. Women who arrived in France between 1980 and 1990 exhibit a far lower fertility rate than women from the same country who arrived in France between 1990 and 1999.[25] That

Figure 1-2. *Fertility Rates of Foreign Women Living in France*

Children per woman

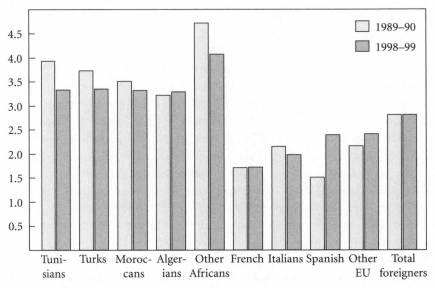

Source: All data in this figure were taken from Françoise Legros, "La fécondité des étrangères en France: une stabilisation entre 1990–1999" ["Immigrant fertility: Stabilization between 1990 and 1999"], Cellules statistiques et études sur l'immigration [Office for Statistical Analysis and the Study of Immigration], *INSEE Première* no. 898 (May 2003).

suggests that the experience of living in France decreases the number of children that a woman will have. Since new immigration accounts for an ever-smaller percentage of the overall Muslim population, this minority is not expected to continue to grow at a significantly faster rate than the overall French population over time.

In 1999, foreign women gave birth to 75,000 children in France, 6,000 fewer than in 1990. The 75,000 children include 26,866 born to women from North Africa (10,854 to Algerian, 12,879 to Moroccan, and 3,111 to Tunisian women); North African women thus accounted for 36 percent of births to foreign mothers in 1999 (down from 44 percent in 1990 and 53 percent in 1982).[26] By way of comparison, 669,683 children were born to French women in 1999. Although the fertility rates of women of foreign origin is still somewhat higher than the French average, these data show that immigrants adapt to local norms (and, perhaps, to the cost of living) soon after arrival. The change may reflect acculturation, a reaction to living in close quarters, the

Figure 1-3. *Average Immigrant Fertility Rates, 1991–98*

Children per woman

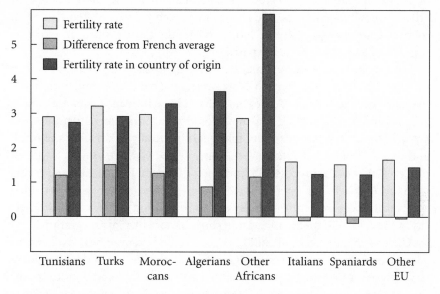

Source: Laurent Toulemon, "La fécondité des immigrées: nouvelles données, nouvelle approche ["Immigrant fertility: New data, new approach,"], *Population et Société,* no. 400 (April 2004).

entry of women into the workforce, or improved socioeconomic status compared with that in their homeland, where extra children might have been welcomed as eventual contributors to household income.

The Economic and Social Gap

The term "integration" has been the nonpartisan mantra of generations of French politicians and social workers, and it is the key word—and the key solution—in a host of interrelated challenges, from social unrest to anti-Semitism, emanating from the settlement of new immigrant populations. But the term itself is somewhat problematic. First, it lacks a clear definition or corresponding set of accepted sociological characteristics that would make it a scientifically useful metric. Many observers have instinctively looked to changing cultural, social, or demographic indicators, such as immigrants' use of the French language at home, number of children, children's performance at school, sources of income, national origin of friends and associates, and so forth. Others use available poll data on declared feelings of belonging to the national community or even on degree of declared patriotism—and conversely, for first-generation immigrants (that is, those who left their country of origin for France), the degree of nostalgia for their homeland. But if such criteria were applied to specific groups of French citizens of French origin, such as Catholics or extreme-left activists, they also would be likely to respond in a less than perfectly patriotic fashion.

Second and more important, some *beurs* (as second-generation Arab immigrants are called in French slang), reject the concept of integration as a matter of principle. After all, they have always lived in France, they are French citizens, and they do not see why they should have to transform themselves in any way or reach out to a society that ought naturally to consider them full and equal members. Furthermore, some see *intégration* not as a formal process—that is, the process of becoming full-fledged French citizens, attaining a certain level of prosperity, and engaging in political activities—so much as a cultural requirement that really means something like "check your identity at the door." To them, integration sounds more like "disintegration."

The visible differences of children of immigrants cannot be considered an adequate measure of their integration; after all, the few who do wear *jellabas* or headscarves may actually be better integrated in social and political terms than their parents, who may dress in a European fashion but may socialize exclusively with fellow immigrants and barely speak French. Finally, the desire to integrate in French society is something of a double paradox: not only have most *beurs* always lived in France, but because of racism and discrimination many also have been denied the very opportunities—in terms of good jobs and well-situated housing, for example—that would help them integrate. That reinforces and perpetuates a vicious cycle of failure and exclusion. Social scientists and politicians, therefore, should employ the word "integration" with caution. Here, it is used to describe the degree of difference between the Muslim community and the rest of the French population with regard to the main economic, social, and political indicators, as well as the process by which (and the extent to which) those differences are being reduced.

Although it might seem otherwise, France has a long history of integrating foreign populations.[27] Beginning in the nineteenth century, it became a country of immigration—not of emigration, like Germany, the United Kingdom, and Italy—receiving waves of Poles, Belgians, Italians, Spaniards, Portuguese, and East Europeans, including Jews (especially in the 1930s). That occasionally led to xenophobic rhetoric in politics and even to mob violence, especially during times of economic crisis. For example, there were anti-Italian riots in the 1880s and 1890s, with several Italians killed at Aigues-Mortes in 1893, and anti-Semitic violence followed the unrest surrounding the Dreyfus affair several years later. It could be said that each generation of immigrants was deemed "unable to integrate," especially religious, working-class families from southern countries like Italy, Portugal, and Spain. The same has been said of Arabs today, but today that claim is accompanied by a new set of arguments that emphasize their non-European and non-Christian heritage. Muslims' culture and religion are viewed as being qualitatively different from those of previous immigrants. In addition, the part that trade unions and the army played earlier in integrating immigrants has been drastically reduced, and the famous assimilating power of the French public education system has been chastened by recent problems in the schools (see the discussion below on "the school gap"). It has been argued, moreover, that the economic stagnation of the urban peripheries is more entrenched than during previous slumps.

The Unemployment Problem

Like most immigrants in industrialized countries, the Muslims who came to France during the second half of the twentieth century have endured lasting economic and social hardships. They first had low-level jobs, predominantly in the industrial sector, when they arrived in the 1960s and early 1970s. Their situation became more difficult as the abundant, stable jobs of the postwar boom disappeared in the economic downturn of the 1970s and 1980s. That helps explain why the economic and social indicators for this population have been so unfavorable. Immigrants have experienced higher unemployment than the rest of the population; a higher incidence of accidents on the job; housing problems, such as being isolated in large, high-density housing projects on the outskirts of big cities that were slowly deserted by native French families; problems at school; and high levels of crime and unrest. Those problems have been reinforced by the economic situation in France, especially the stagnant job market, and they failed to improve in the 1990s. Meanwhile negative stereotypes and racism have continued to take their toll.

Although the integration of Muslim immigrants and their children into French society and their overall situation have not improved as fast as for previous waves of immigrants, substantial, if largely invisible, progress is nonetheless being made. This somewhat paradoxical situation can be assessed with the help of statistical indicators.

In addition to the constructive influence of traditional nuclear family structures, three pillars of French society helped immigrants to integrate in the between-war and early post–World War II period: the public school system, military service, and the workplace. However, today schools have been increasingly confronted with social problems and have lost some of their integrative capacity. Obligatory military service for men was discontinued at the end of the 1990s. Though high levels of military and state-supported employee recruitment play a role in getting some immigrants or second-generation immigrants into the army and the workforce, the job market displays some troubling trends.[28]

Unemployment, however, remains the biggest obstacle to integration and the biggest impediment to advancement for immigrants and their children and grandchildren, whom it affects disproportionately. There is no doubt that the worst enemy of integration is the difficulty of entering—or, more precisely, the incredible delays in entering—the national workforce. Jean-Paul Fitoussi, a well-known economist, illustrates the problem by evoking the image of people waiting in long lines in front of a counter at which jobs in different categories are being offered. The effects of discrimination are amplified by the length of the waiting line: the longer one waits, the more disaffected one becomes.[29] The urban riots of November 2005 had many causes, but they had a lot to do with unemployment. The unrest was both a direct result of the idleness of many youth of immigrant origin and an indirect result of the creation of a vicious cycle in which because these young people have little hope of getting a good job in the future, they have no real incentive to succeed at school and therefore become less employable. It is no wonder, under such conditions, that many observers, from those in the U.S. press to Nicolas Sarkozy, have called for drastically opening the job market by doing away with many of the regulations that protect the French social model and workers' job security but that are now accused of indirectly impeding integration (see chapter 7).

The unemployment rate of populations of immigrant origin is generally twice the rate of the overall population, and that rate is even higher among youth of North African origin.[30] In 1999, foreigners represented 8.6 percent of the working population but made up 15 percent of the unemployed; moreover, while 22 percent of all immigrants were unemployed, only 13 percent of the French workforce was. Foreign women were even more adversely affected—their unemployment rate was 25 percent.[31] (It should be noted that statistics on immigrants and foreigners pertain only to noncitizens and first-generation immigrants. Since most French Arab youth were born in France and already have French citizenship, they are not included in figures on foreigners and immigrants.)

Part of the difference in unemployment rates is undoubtedly due to differences in skill level, since low-skill jobs are the most adversely affected by a weak economy and immigrants tend to hold low-skill jobs.[32] Two-thirds of immigrants are low-skilled workers. Low-skilled workers are especially present

Figure 1-4. *Percent of Self-Declared Muslims and Catholics in Selected Occupations*

Percent

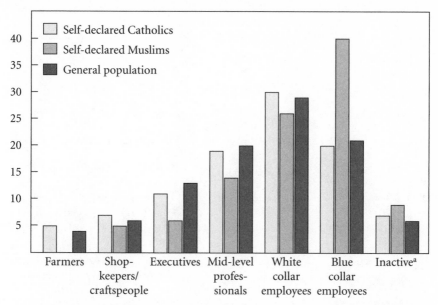

Source: Poll (1998–2001) by the Observatoire Interrégional du Politique [Interregional Center for Policy Studies] in partnership with the Conseils Régionaux [regional councils], in Claude Dargent, "Les musulmans déclarés en France: affirmation religieuse, subordination sociale, et progressisme politique ["Self-declared Muslims in France: Religious affirmation, social subordination, and political progressivism"], *Cahier du CEVIPOF* no. 34 (February 2003).

a. The Inactive category does not include the unemployed, who have been assigned to their former job category. "Inactive" persons have never held a job and stay at home. Among Muslims, 85 percent of them are women.

in the construction industry and domestic services (*services aux particuliers*)—both have a 15 percent immigrant workforce—and in the automobile industry and service jobs in offices (*services aux enterprises*), where 10 percent of employees are immigrants.[33] Figure 1-4, which looks at self-declared religious affiliation (rather than citizenship status or national origin), shows that Muslims are twice as likely as the rest of the population to be concentrated in the "worker" category.

But even at similar skill levels, foreigners are more likely than the general population to be unemployed. In 2002, the rate of unemployment for immigrants with a college degree (16 percent) was still twice that of natives with a college degree (8 percent).[34] Also, Algerian immigrants and youth of Algerian

Figure 1-5. *Percent of Unemployed Fifteen- to Twenty-Nine-Year-Olds,*
by Origin

Percent

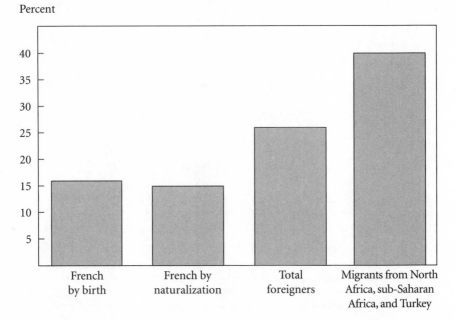

Source: Dominique Andolfalto and others, *L'état de la France 2002* [*The State of France 2002*]
(Paris: La Découverte, 2001).

origin under the age of thirty who held a high school diploma had an unemployment rate of 32 percent while the rate was just 15 percent for French
youth in the same category.[35]

Furthermore, the unemployment problem disproportionately affects foreigners from predominantly Muslim countries. Italian, Portuguese, and
Spanish immigrants experience rates that are lower than the French average,
while immigrants from Turkey, North Africa, and Africa have higher-than-
average rates. Unemployment is worst for the youngest immigrants, that is,
those between fifteen and twenty-nine years of age. There are signs that the
unemployment phenomenon, meanwhile, is not linked simply to a stagnant
economy. Data for the fifteen- to twenty-nine-year-old category showed that
while unemployment among young people of French origin gradually
dropped over time from 25 percent to 18 percent, the decrease among non-
EU foreigners was less, from 46 percent to 37 percent (see figure 1-5).[36]

The antiracism organization SOS Racisme (see chapter 2) conducted a
study that pointed to one potential cause of the problem. It looked at the

Figure 1-6. *Percent of Unemployed Workers in Selected Categories, by European and Non-European First Names*

Percent

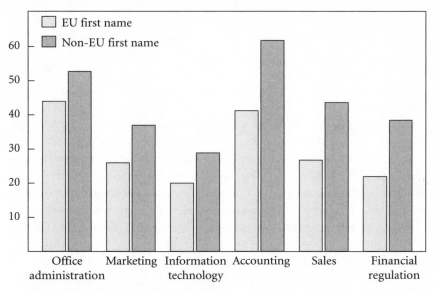

Source: Samuel Thomas, "Rapport d'analyse des affaires recentes de discriminations a l'embauche poursuivies par SOS Racisme" ["SOS Racisme report on recent instances of discrimination in hiring"] (Paris: SOS Racisme, March 2005).

records of two major employment agencies—Michael Page and Page Intérim—and examined the success rate of 20,000 job candidates in six separate employment categories.[37] Using a somewhat imprecise methodology, they drew the candidates' names from those of the 264,000 job seekers in the agencies' databases. The study showed that those with "non-European" first names were, on average, one and a half times as likely to be unemployed in every category, adding further impetus to policy proposals that the agencies should distribute anonymous resumes (see figure 1-6), without names and addresses, to potential employers (see chapter 7). Samuel Thomas, the report's author, observed that candidates with non-European names were especially likely to face unemployment in sales and accounting.

Housing Problems and the Ghetto Phenomenon

Recent immigrants and their descendants tend to concentrate in public housing projects that were built in the 1960s and 1970s in low-rent neighborhoods; in France, these projects are located on the urban outskirts, known as *banlieues* or *cités*. Approximately 6 million people live in these areas, of whom 33 percent are under the age of twenty (only 23 percent of the general population fall in that category).[38] The local nonimmigrant French populations and successful immigrants alike tend to abandon these neighborhoods as soon as their incomes allow. Nonetheless, it is not technically accurate to speak of them as "ghettos," since no area is occupied exclusively by immigrants of a single ethnic origin or religion. The proportion of residents of North African origin may be very high, but it is never all inclusive; other Africans, Turks, and nonimmigrant French live alongside Arabs and Berbers from Algeria, Morocco, and Tunisia.

Something rather like a "ghetto phenomenon," however, based on the sheer concentration in the *banlieues* of individuals who have failed to integrate, is indeed a reality. These neighborhoods are marked by poverty, welfare dependence, black markets, broken families, and single mothers. Fathers have lost some of their importance in the family because often they do not work or are absent. The ghetto phenomenon generates a specific alternative culture similar to that in many other places in the world, including the United States; in fact, when Hollywood movies are dubbed into French, African Americans are made to speak with an accent from the *cités*.[39] In these neighborhoods one finds a mix of everyday violence, gang-type social systems (although organized, powerful Los Angeles–style gangs are not a factor in France), an indigenous code of conduct and honor, the assertion of "masculine" identity, and an emphasis on territoriality (outsiders, therefore, are not welcome, and young men rarely venture far from their own *cités*). It was these *cités* and not the *banlieues* in general—and certainly not the city centers (with the exception of Lyon)—that erupted in flames in November 2005.[40]

More than one-quarter of all public housing is located in the Paris region, although other important urban centers also have large immigrant populations—for example, Rhone-Alpes (around 10 percent of public housing); Nord-Pas de Calais (7 percent), and Provence-Alpes-Cote d'Azur (6 percent).[41] Foreign nationals are much more likely than the general population to live in such housing projects, which are called *habitations à loyer modéré* (HLMs). Of the general French population, 17.6 percent live in these subsidized units, while roughly 50 percent of all North African immigrants, 37 percent of other African immigrants, and 36 percent of Turkish immigrants reside in such housing.[42] Of the 4.2 million households living in French public housing, just over 700,000 are immigrant households (17 percent of all HLM households); Algerians account for 158,253 (3.8 percent), Moroccans for 119,756 (2.9 percent), Tunisians for 45,858 (1 percent), and Turks for 34,819 (0.08 percent).[43]

Département 93 (the North Paris suburb of Seine-Saint-Denis) provides a snapshot of life in the *banlieues*. Nearly a half-million foreigners live in this former industrial center, more than in any other *département* (administrative district). Whereas recent naturalizations have had the effect of lowering the number of Algerian citizens by nearly 10 percent, the number of Turkish and Chinese nationals, by contrast, are growing fast—by 27.8 percent and 16 percent respectively between 2002 and 2003.[44] Eighteen percent of this *département*'s 1.38 million residents live below the poverty line (5.5 percent more than residents of the Paris region at large). The conditions in which first-generation immigrants live can be very poor indeed: nearly one-fifth of them have no hot water at home (versus 7.9 percent of the general French population), and a quarter of the housing units have either no indoor bathroom or shower (versus 12.2 percent of French housing overall).[45] Though some new businesses have recently moved into the *banlieue* of Saint-Denis, the income of about 60 percent of the households there and in nearby Aubervilliers and Bobigny is low enough to be exempt from income tax (the average exemption rate in the greater Paris region is 35 percent).[46]

A report by the Renseignements Généraux (RG), the police agency that monitors radical groups in France, warned in summer 2004 that half of the "sensitive neighborhoods" that they had studied with a high Muslim population showed worrying signs of "community isolation" (*repli communautaire*) from national social and political life. These areas were home to "large numbers of families of immigrant origin"; they had developed networks of ethnic businesses, community associations, and prayer rooms; and they showed evidence of higher rates of polygamy, anti-Semitic and "anti-Western" graffiti, and wearing of non-Western and religious apparel than other neighborhoods.[47] The study was not conducted in a scientific manner, and its authors did not claim to produce any definitive statistics; they sought only to discern, in their words, "trends based on local examples." They found that 300 neighborhoods (with roughly 1.8 million inhabitants) fit the description of isolated communities: "In ghettoized neighborhoods, families of immigrant origin acquire social and cultural handicaps," the report found. "These populations conserve cultural traditions that result in endogamy and the maintenance of traditional ways of life and parallel institutions for social regulation and conflict resolution." Furthermore, the report indicated that residents of European origin were moving out on a large scale and that traditional French businesses were closing. The RG had painted a portrait of a ticking "time bomb," said *Le Monde*.[48] A 2004 report by the Haut Conseil à l'Intégration, however, gauged the number of "ultrasensitive neighborhoods" to be 50 percent less than the DST's assessment, or about 200.[49]

The physical concentration of residents of foreign background in one area can lead to feelings of isolation and ultimately may reinforce a community-based identity. The *banlieues*—and more precisely the *cités*—have suffered a declining quality of life and higher unemployment and crime rates than the rest of the country. Speaking of the challenges of the *cités*, the Ministry of Urban Affairs noted in 2003 that unemployment in the housing projects was four times higher than the national average, sometimes reaching as high as 42 to 44 percent.[50] (The rate is compounded by the fact that the resident population is much younger than the national average.) If the issue of community isolation is not addressed, ghettos may slowly develop. But increasingly specialized initiatives undertaken by the Ministry of Urban Affairs throughout the past decade suggest that there is a growing awareness of that danger (see chapter 7 on French policy responses).

The School Gap

Children of immigrants do as well as or better in their course work than children of French parents of the same socioeconomic class.[51] That is both good news and bad news, however: more than two-thirds of immigrant children are from a working-class background, and like their nonimmigrant socioeconomic counterparts, they do not have high success rates overall. According to a study cited in *Le Monde,* in the best-performing high schools an average of 29 percent of the student body were children of professionals and 26 percent were children of teachers; in the worst high schools an average of 39.2 percent of the student body were children of workers and 33.4 were children of nonworking parents. Forty percent of high schools (598 schools) met the study's standard for "best-performing"; 13 percent (189 schools) were classified as "least well-performing."[52]

High levels of unemployment, especially in the French Arab/Muslim community, perpetuate a cycle of negative feedback. That and children's low level of self-confidence and their skepticism regarding the equality of the opportunities that they are offered has led to underachievement and a lower rate of educational advancement. That assessment was confirmed after the urban uprisings of November 2005 by the fervent debates among the French political class regarding the appropriateness of expanding affirmative action within the educational system.[53]

Some school districts with a large concentration of immigrant children experience intense educational problems. In the Créteil district outside Paris, for example, the high school graduation rate is 71.8 percent, markedly lower than the national average of 80 percent, and a declining number of students graduate with any type of honors.[54] Studies have found that the level of student achievement breaks down along class lines. "The massive presence of an underprivileged student population weighs negatively on any school," said one study, "just as the best schools enroll the students of the highest social categories."[55] That assessment would be an obvious challenge for any government wishing to promote equality. Several policies have been adopted in certain areas targeting concentrations of immigrant families and thus, implicitly, Muslim populations.

According to Michèle Tribalat, in the 1990s just 15 percent of the children of Algerian immigrants received a university degree, and 23 percent received no diploma at all; the figures were 23 percent and 13 percent, respectively, for the children of French parents.[56] If one focuses only on self-declared Muslims, both citizens and noncitizens, rather than solely on the immigrants in Michèle Tribalat's 1995 data, the problems appear in a roughly similar light.[57] The result of that gap between Muslims and the general population in level of education is a commensurate gap in professional status, as shown in figures 1-7 and 1-8.

The Crime Gap

Many poor neighborhoods, and especially housing projects (*cités*) in the *banlieues*, are plagued by a high rate of criminal behavior, often involving small-time drug dealing. Riots have erupted in these places, especially after incidents involving the police, as was the case in late October and November 2005, when 10,000 cars were set ablaze in a matter of weeks. One of the reasons that rioters gave journalists for their rage was that Nicolas Sarkozy, the minister of the interior, had vowed to rid the *cités* of the *racailles* (rabble). "*Racailles*" is a term frequently used by the inhabitants of the *cités* themselves to refer to local delinquents, but they resented it when it was used by Sarkozy, who promised to clean the troublemakers out with a Kärcher, a well-known brand of high-pressure water hose.

While the rate of felonies, such as murder, has been stable or even in decline in France in recent years, minor delinquency has risen.[58] Unemployment has had a destabilizing effect on families and often translates into weak motivation at school among children in families with an out-of-work parent. A study by Sebastian Roché and Monique Dagnaud of juvenile delinquents in Grenoble, in the department of Isère, found that they had common experiences of poverty, parental alcoholism, and problems at school. Two-thirds of minors judged in criminal court there had a father born abroad (50 percent from North Africa), and 60 percent had a mother born outside France.[59]

Figure 1-7. *Level of Diploma and Religious Affiliation, Eighteen- to Thirty-Four-Year-Olds*

Percent

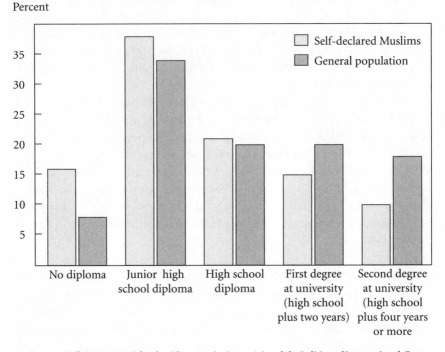

| | No diploma | Junior high school diploma | High school diploma | First degree at university (high school plus two years) | Second degree at university (high school plus four years or more) |

Source: Poll (1998–2001) by the Observatoire Interrégional du Politique [Interregional Center for Policy Studies] in partnership with the Conseils Régionaux [regional councils], in Claude Dargent, "Les musulmans déclarés en France: affirmation religieuse, subordination sociale, et progressisme politique ["Self-declared Muslims in France: Religious affirmation, social subordination, and political progressivism"], *Cahier du CEVIPOF* no. 34 (February 2003).

As a result of the alienation and desperation stemming from such socio-economic handicaps, persons of Muslim origin constitute a majority of the French prison population. According to Farhad Khosrokhavar, a noted sociologist and expert on Islam who has done a great deal of field research in prisons, they make up as much as 70 to 80 percent of inmates in prisons located on urban peripheries, even though they usually constitute just 15 percent of urban populations.[60] It should be noted that the French penitentiary system, while running at capacity, has enough space for only 60,000 inmates, reflecting an incarceration rate of less than 1 per 1,000 residents; it is drastically smaller than the system in the United States, which has an incarceration rate of 7 per 1,000 residents.[61] French authorities do not report crime rates by

Figure 1-8. *Percent of Muslims and of General Population in Selected Job Categories*

Percent

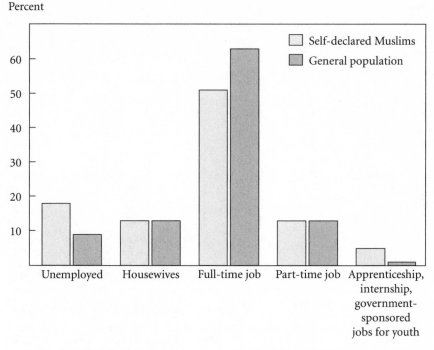

Source: Poll (1998–2001) by the Observatoire Interrégional du Politique [Interregional Center for Policy Studies] in partnership with the Conseils Régionaux [regional councils], in Claude Dargent, "Les musulmans déclarés en France: affirmation religieuse, subordination sociale, et progressisme politique ["Self-declared Muslims in France: Religious affirmation, social subordination, and political progressivism"], *Cahier du CEVIPOF* no. 34 (February 2003).

ethnic or religious group, but it is estimated that around 40 percent of prison inmates in France have a father born abroad, including 25 percent with a father from North Africa. Muslims are greatly overrepresented in prisons and within the eighteen- to twenty-four–year-old age group in particular: they make up only 8.5 percent of that age cohort in France, yet 39.9 percent of all prisoners in the cohort. Those who have a French father, in contrast, account for 75 percent of all eighteen- to twenty-four-year-olds in France yet make up just 38.8 percent of prisoners in that age group.[62] Indeed, Khosrokhavar finds that prisoners with a North African father outnumber prisoners with a French father by 9 to 1 for the eighteen- to twenty-nine-year-old group and by 6 to 1 in the thirty- to thirty-nine-year-old group.[63]

Figure 1-9. *Victims and Perpetrators of Serious Crimes, by National Origin*[a]

Percent

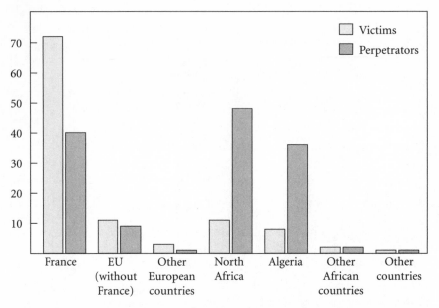

Source: Study by Sebastian Roché and Monique Dagnaud, reported by Nathalie Guibert, "Selon une étude menée en Isère, deux tiers des mineurs délinquants sont d'origine étrangère" ["According to a study in Isère, two-thirds of juvenile delinquents are of foreign origin"] in *Le Monde*, April 16, 2004.

a. One or both parents born abroad.

The Grenoble study by Roché and Dagnaud found that integration problems are partly to blame for elevated crime rates but also that crimes involving young Muslims are prosecuted more vigorously than those of their peers, which leads to a slight distortion of the available statistics. The study's authors concluded that "we are faced with a justice system that concentrates its energies on youth of foreign origin." Youth of immigrant origin may also lose some faith in the justice system given that it does not always protect them from crime in equal measure either. Prosecution of racist acts against citizens of North African origin, for example, has been rare (see figure 1-9). Although hundreds of incidents were reported, just seven cases were brought to court in 1999, twelve in 2001, and twenty-nine in 2002.[64] One *Le Monde* article concluded, "How could these young people not perceive a biased conception of justice?"[65]

Acculturation and Changing Social Practices

The existence of neighborhoods afflicted by poverty and the professional and educational difficulties encountered by immigrant youth does not mean that integration is not getting better overall. In a major study conducted at the beginning of the 1990s, Michèle Tribalat found that a majority of immigrants increasingly—and almost exclusively—spoke French. Mixed marriages (between immigrants and French citizens) were on the rise, the fertility rate among immigrant women was approaching that of French women, and the religious practices of immigrants were not that different from those of the French. In other words, despite their religious and ethnic diversity, recent immigrant populations are undergoing the same process of integration as previous immigrants—despite perceptions of the opposite (which were, of course, present with regard to other immigrant groups too) and spectacular demonstrations of specific problems (like the November 2005 riots). In 2002, 41 percent of French respondents thought that "most immigrants have a culture too distinct from the French to be able to integrate into French society," while 54 percent rejected that statement.[66]

The immigrant population as a whole has shown increasing mastery of the French language, which plays an important role in acculturation since there is no other legally or informally used language, as is the case with Spanish in the United States. Fully 77 percent of the children of Algerians speak only French with their parents (compared with 79 percent of the French children of Spanish immigrants), and when just one parent is of foreign origin, those figures jump to 92 percent and 94 percent respectively.[67]

Many sociologists have measured integration through exogamy rates, the degree of marriage outside the community. Exogamy has been portrayed, in part, as a function of continuity in traditional family structures, and it has even been linked to the imposition of headscarves on young girls—that is, to how tightly "immigrant families control the sexuality of their daughters."[68] The greater the degree of individualism—and the right, therefore, to marry whomever one wants—the argument goes, then the less family and social structures are likely to be transmitted from generation to generation. Forced marriages in immigrant families are not unknown; it is thought there are as many as 70,000 such arrangements in France, and the government recently raised the age of consent from fifteen to eighteen years of age.[69] But a 2005 poll found that 79 percent of Muslims were, in fact, "comfortable with people of different religions dating or marrying" and that 59 percent "would not object if [their] daughter married a non-Muslim."[70] Another large-scale poll,

Table 1-7. *Origin of Spouse of Algerian Immigrants and of Individuals Born in France to Algerian Parents*[a]

	Origin of spouse (percent)		
Gender of immigrant/individual	Native French	Immigrant	Born in France to immigrant parents
Male			
arrived in France after age 15	20	73	7
arrived in France before age 16	25	54	21
born in France to Algerian parents	50	17	33
Female			
arrived in France after age 15	10	85	5
arrived in France before age 16	14	77	9
born in France to Algerian parents	24	47	29

Source: Michèle Tribalat, *Faire France: une grande enquête sur les immigrés et leurs enfants* [*Making France: A large-scale study of immigrants and their children*] (Paris: La Découverte, 1995).

a. First marriage, civil or otherwise. The figures are lower when only civil marriages are counted.

conducted by Vincent Tiberj and Sylvain Brouard in 2005, showed similarly that 32.3 percent of persons of North African or Turkish origin (including 60 percent of self-declared Muslims) would disapprove if their daughter married a non-Muslim man and 14.7 percent would disapprove if their son married a non-Muslim woman (the difference in attitudes may be explained by the assumption that a woman will adopt her husband's religion and culture). In contrast, 18 percent and 19 percent of French persons of French origin would disapprove if their son or daughter, respectively, married a Muslim woman or man.[71]

Statistics suggest that intermarriage, the most intimate form of integration, is well under way. Among the younger generations, as many as one-quarter of Muslim women are married to non-Muslim men and half of young Muslim men cohabit with non-Muslim women (see table 1-7).[72] Turks in Germany also had far lower rates of exogamy—by a factor of two to three for men and ten to fifteen for women—than Algerians raised in France.[73] Mixed marriages between an immigrant (or child of immigrants) and a native French person (born in France to French parents) are more frequent with Spanish or Portuguese immigrants than with North Africans, although the incidence varies according to the country of origin, from Morocco (33 percent of mixed marriages) to Tunisia and sub-Saharan Africa (44 percent and 45 percent respectively).[74] Such marriages are slightly more prevalent among the more educated classes of society, native French and immigrant, and less frequent with women of foreign origin than with men. Between 1975 and 1990, the proportion of births to a couple consisting of an Algerian father and a French mother increased from 12.5 percent to 19.4 percent, and the rates were similarly high for births to a French father and an Algerian mother (rates were lower for Moroccans and Tunisians, who were more recent immigrants at the time the study was conducted).[75]

The proportion of immigrant women who work outside the home—an important factor in the acculturation process—is comparable to that of French women. In 1999, the employment rate for immigrant women was 57.1 percent, compared with 63.1 percent for French women (in 1982, the rate was 41 percent, compared with 54 percent).[76] Differences exist among immigrants of different origins: Turkish women, for example, are much less likely to work outside the home than women from sub-Saharan Africa.

Intergroup socializing is another indicator of the degree of integration. Public housing projects tend to close immigrants off within their own neighborhoods, as they do French natives. Their isolation can be explained as much by the geographical distance of the projects from the city center—they are in the suburbs, not in the "inner city"—as by a community's tendency to stick together. Social visits take place among networks of acquaintances, after all, who often are people who live or work in the same place. For immigrant populations living outside housing projects, social intermixing is more likely to take place, both among groups of foreigners and with native French.

Thus, writes Michèle Tribalat, "when young people of Algerian origin live in a nonimmigrant neighborhood, neighborly relations with people of the same origin are much less common; their frequency is the same as among young people of Portuguese origin.[77] The proportion of young people of Algerian origin who maintain close ties exclusively to other Algerians drops from 25 percent in community neighborhoods (where Algerians make up a majority of the inhabitants), to 11 percent in immigrant neighborhoods (where immigrant populations are diverse), and to just 7 percent in nonimmigrant neighborhoods. It is nonetheless worth mentioning Tribalat's observation that "even in nonimmigrant neighborhoods, neighborly contact with native French is clearly less prevalent among young people of Algerian origin (around one-third) than among those of Spanish or Portuguese origin (around half)." But the 2005 poll conducted for the U.S. Department of State found that only 30 percent of French Muslims preferred to socialize with people of the same ethnic and religious background, while 36 percent of the French public did. Almost all French Muslims claimed to have non-Muslim friends: 61 percent said that they had "many" French friends, and 36 percent said "a few"; 9 percent and 36 percent said the same, respectively, of Jewish friends; and 79 percent said they had "a few" or "many" friends of African descent.[78]

Tribalat also mentions some more personal indicators, like the type of food prepared by immigrants when they have guests. Such habits can be a useful (if anecdotal) benchmark for measuring degree of acculturation, and, in fact, the evidence shows an evolution across generations. The proportion of the population of immigrant origin that prepares "ethnic" food when entertaining guests is high among the first generation—35 percent of Algerians and 25 percent of Portuguese—but their children do not carry on those traditions. Only 6 percent of the children of Algerian immigrants and just 4 percent of the children of Portuguese prepare traditional dishes for guests.[79]

But Do They Feel French?

A less oblique measure of integration is Muslims' attitudes toward French institutions and French identity, as well as their articulation of a "desire" to integrate. On October 6, 2001, an ominous event unfolded. In a long-planned public relations initiative, France faced Algeria in a "friendly" soccer match that was supposed to celebrate the renewed friendship between the two nations. Contrary to script, however, some young immigrant soccer fans booed the national anthem, threw objects at two government ministers, and—once the French lead had reached 4 to 1—ran onto the field of the Stade de France (some of them waving Algerian flags), forcing the cancellation of the game. The impression conveyed by the game's spectacular ending was not the one desired by its organizers. Indeed, the event occurred on the very site where the multicultural dream team of Zinedine Zidane had triumphed in the World Soccer Cup of 1998, inspiring an idealized image of France as a *"black-blanc-beur"* nation. French public opinion suffered a profound shock, and the event was credited with bringing new voters to Le Pen's Front National party, which was victorious in the first round of presidential elections in April 2002. "Where are the *beurs* going?" asked the cover of *Le Nouvel Observateur*, above photographs of second- and third-generation immigrant youth invading the soccer field. More generally, this event was heralded as a demonstration of the ultimate failure of integration among the young—and of their contempt for France as represented by its symbols (its flag, its representatives, and its national anthem).

In poll after poll, however, self-declared Muslims and, more generally, French of African and foreign origin continue to declare their profound desire to integrate, their attachment to France, and their generally optimistic outlook, which is markedly more optimistic than that of other groups. The U.S. State Department poll taken in 2005, for example, indicated that 68 percent and 65 percent of self-declared Muslims had confidence in local and national government respectively. And at least as many had confidence in the judicial system (56 percent) and even in the police (54 percent) as in Muslim religious leaders (56 percent). Eighty-nine percent expressed confidence in the public schools, while 51 percent did so for the (practically nonexistent) Islamic schools. Even while reporting widespread discrimination, they voiced a favorable overall opinion of France (95 percent favorable and 5 percent unfavorable).

Another promising indication of lasting integration is self-declared Muslims' opinion of French democracy and their optimism for the future compared with the attitudes of adherents of other religions. The OIP study conducted between 1998 and 2001 found that fully 69 percent of Muslims thought that French democracy was functioning well; in comparison, 58 percent of Catholics and 63 percent of Protestants did. The same poll reported that 21 percent of Muslims were "very optimistic" about France's future, more than twice the number of Catholics (8 percent) and Protestants (9 percent).[80] Last but not least, the large-scale study conducted by Brouard and Tiberj in 2005 confirmed that optimism, this time among French of African and Turkish origin in general (62 percent believed that democracy was functioning well in France, while only 56 percent of the French population in general did). Finally, it showed that among these "recent French," feelings of closeness with other French people were significantly higher (85 percent) than feelings of closeness with other Europeans (56 percent), people from the same religious group (71 percent), or people of the same national origin (77 percent). Interestingly, the widespread feeling of closeness with other French people was even higher among self-declared Muslims (90 percent) than among survey respondents in general, and in both cases, it was slightly higher than among the general population (84 percent). Finally, looking for signs of community-mindedness (such as having a political agenda for minority rights or feelings of being left out by mainstream society), Brouard and Tiberj found only a tiny minority (4 percent) who fit that description.[81]

So which picture is more accurate: the one painted by the events at the soccer match on October 6, 2001, and the urban riots of November 2005, which tend to indicate a failure of integration and a rejection of France itself, or the many statistical indicators that consistently show Muslims' strong desire to integrate or an already high level of integration?

This paradox can be reconciled by studying geographical and social differentiation. On one hand, there has clearly been a failure of integration in the *cités*, home to a young population that has little hope for the future, little education, and that does not consider itself fully French. These are the young people who boo the national anthem and burn cars and schools in their own neighborhoods. On the other hand, in the background, millions of people of Muslim descent are undergoing the process of integration into French society, and it is this overwhelming majority that responds to pollsters, not the teenagers from the *cités* (although some surveys have targeted school-age respondents).[82] The task, of course, is to determine which social process—alienation or acculturation—will prevail in everyday life and in the media and the political sphere and whether the first is strong enough to undermine the second. The only certainty is that both aspects of integration exist in France today, and they are likely to do so for years to come.

2 | Patterns of Exclusion and Inclusion in French Society

Unlike its neighbors, France has long been a country of immigration rather than emigration. Since the mid-nineteenth century, France has welcomed numerous waves of immigrants—from southern and eastern Europe and from former colonies—and incorporated them into its social and political fabric. In this respect, it has more in common with the United States than with other European countries. The process of integration, which has never been easy, has followed a pattern: each new wave of immigrants encounters strong and even violent resistance from "native" (or recently integrated) residents and accusations of the cultural and sociological incompatibility of their mores with the ideals of the French republic—before, despite such protestations, eventually being successfully integrated.

Recent immigrants from North Africa are facing the same challenges as previous immigrants, except that they tend to accumulate even more negative points with respect to acceptance by French society. They come from a different continent, they are predominantly of a different religion, and they have inherited strong negative stereotypes, some forged centuries ago. Those stereotypes translate into acts of racism and everyday discrimination, impeding the path to integration. This chapter gives specific attention to "Islamophobia" and to the debate over whether, beyond the mixed feelings within the French population about Islam as a religion, Muslims per se are targeted in a fashion that is distinct from the way that other immigrants and Arabs are treated. Last, it discusses positive forces that balance rejectionist tendencies somewhat by favoring inclusion and blending.

Layers of Negative Stereotypes

Many observers are keen to insist on the novelty and specificity of contemporary difficulties with populations of Arab and Muslim origin. But it should be recalled that the acceptance of immigrant and religious minority populations by French society has never been a calm and peaceful process. Anti-Italian racism, for example, claimed many victims, who were injured or killed during riots in the south of France at the end of the nineteenth century. At around the same time, anti-Semitic sentiment culminated in the Dreyfus affair and incidents of violence against Jews. The 1930s were another period of tension due to increasing immigration, notably of Jews from eastern Europe, and the Vichy regime (1940–44) institutionalized anti-Semitic policies. Several historical and international factors, however, complicate matters with regard to the substantially larger group of North Africans who began arriving in the 1960s.

People of North African origin carry the burden of the long history of tumultuous relations between France and the Arab-Muslim world, beginning with the military threat posed by the Saracen and Ottoman armies against Europe as well as by the Crusades. In all those instances, Muslims were the enemy. In the nineteenth century, the European powers considered Muslim countries as places to be "civilized"—especially Algeria, which was colonized after harsh military campaigns in the 1830s and 1840s and thereafter was periodically prone to violent uprisings and repression. Algerians were perceived as backward, at sea in a theological Middle Age and weakened by huge lags in science and technology. Ernest Renan, a late-nineteenth-century French intellectual, wrote, in the spirit of the times, that "Islam is the heaviest chain humanity hath ever borne."[1] The first North African workers to arrive in France after World War I were viewed through that prism of backwardness, and they were considered indolent and incompetent workers, even more so than were Italian, Spanish, or Portuguese workers.[2]

The situation worsened around mid-century, when the Algerian War (1954–62) engendered a whole new set of negative stereotypes. Predominant representations of "the Arab" in that period portrayed a cowardly, bloodthirsty brute, the throat-slitter or the terrorist (because of bomb attacks in public places, primarily in Algiers). Immigrant workers in Paris who protested in favor of Algerian independence on October 17, 1961, were seen in that light, and they were suspected of constituting a fifth column of the Front de Libération Nationale (FLN), a group of Algerian pro-independence guerillas, in France. The national memory of the violent crackdown on the protesters, scores of whom drowned in the Seine River, was essentially repressed for nearly forty years. The realization that the Republic was ill-prepared to assimilate 10 million poor Algerian Muslim citizens played a role in President Charles de Gaulle's decision to grant independence to Algeria. (The alternative to independence was to continue to maintain French Algeria, with a very high birthrate on the Algerian side and a profound imbalance in economic conditions that would create constant pressure on Algerians to migrate to France.)

A new round of negative stereotypes followed in the 1980s and 1990s, when the rise in Iran of political Islam—whose goal was to create an Islamic state—and the violence associated with it (in Egypt, Afghanistan, and Syria, among other places, but most of all in Algeria) gave rise to the image of the fanatical and radical Muslim, ready to seize power by any means necessary.[3] The return to terrorism by a wide range of groups—whether Palestinian nationalists, the Algerian Armed Islamic Group (GIA), or al Qaeda—led to a shorthand equation of negative views: Arab = Muslim = religious zealot = terrorist.

The dramatic increase in North African immigration in the 1970s and 1980s and the problems that came with it—especially crime and ghettoization in the suburbs as well as the rise of the extreme right—had the effect of increasing everyday racism, to which polls bear witness. The "North African" suburbs, which had been the domain of largely communist working families until the mid-twentieth century, took the place of the skid rows (where the "dangerous classes" of yesteryear resided) as the primary social menace in the French imagination.[4] A "culturalist" vision (which emphasizes the role of cultural factors in social life) has cast public debate in terms of Islamic fundamentalism, Islamic terrorism, or Islamic backwardness, which has in turn been fused with an image of youth associated with crime, drugs, violence, and the counterculture, with its hard-to-understand slang and other antisocial characteristics. In short, what is depicted, on one hand, as "a foreign threat to Western civilization" also doubles in rhetorical terms as a "domestic threat" in the crime-ridden suburbs, where any child is seen as one who could grow up to be a fundamentalist or terrorist, wearing a headscarf or planting a bomb. A glance at recent book titles in fashionable French bookstores supports that impression: even serious academic studies, such as *France's Islamist Sickness* or *The Islamists Are Already Here,* play on such alarmist scenarios to attract the public's attention.[5] The Arab/Muslim "enemy," in one popular mythology, has infiltrated the heart of French society. That conviction often is expressed in breathless terms—in the words of one observer, "France, as a

Figure 2-1. *Declared Antipathy in Personal Feelings toward Selected Minorities, 1990–2003*[a]

Percent

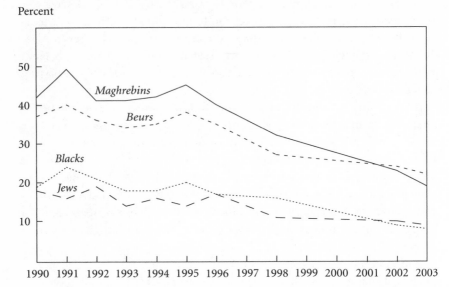

1990 1991 1992 1993 1994 1995 1996 1997 1998 1999 2000 2001 2002 2003

Source: CSA–*Le Figaro* poll, "Le suivi du racisme et de l'anti-sémitisme en France" ["The trajectory of racism and anti-Semitism in France"], April 2, 2003 (www.csa-tmo.fr/dataset/data2003/opi20030402b.htm).

a. Mild and strong antipathy were factored into the total.

historic nation, is at risk of dying because of the plethora of immigrants that it cannot assimilate or even integrate"—and it is echoed by credulous or like-minded observers abroad.[6]

Of course, most people do not mindlessly accept negative stereotypes. Such wholesale claims are generally the preserve of the extreme right, which in any case is forced to temper its remarks because of laws prohibiting incitement to racial hatred.[7] The resulting situation can be observed in the feelings of the French public about selected minorities: the French opinion polls cited in figure 2-1 show that antipathy toward people of North African origin, while decreasing, is still twice as high as that toward blacks and Jews. That finding was supported by a 2005 U.S. State Department poll, which found that 88 percent of the general French public had a favorable view of Jews (versus 12 percent unfavorable) but that just 64 percent had a favorable view of Muslims (versus 35 percent unfavorable).[8]

Beginning in 2004 and 2005, a fierce debate about the French colonial legacy emerged in close connection with integration issues, for several reasons.

First, enough time had elapsed since decolonization that the primary executors of French policies in North Africa were no longer in office. Just as it had taken more than thirty years before an honest debate about the collaboration of the Vichy regime with Germany could emerge (and the discussions remained heated for at least a decade thereafter), it took a generation for public debate about the Algerian War—indeed for any reconsideration of colonization in general—to develop. A second reason was the recent rise in activism on the part of the children and grandchildren of immigrants, many of whom trace their origin to former French colonies, bear the burden of discrimination, and resent their current social situation. For example, the black stand-up comic Dieudonné revived the issue of slavery in the media, calling for more recognition of the importance of slavery in French history, although his repeated anti-Semitic remarks about the responsibility of Jews in the slave trade had the effect of discrediting him as an interlocutor in these matters. Les Indigènes de la République (the Republic's Natives), a coalition formed in early 2005 of activists of immigrant origin and others from the overseas territories, accused France of being a "postcolonial state." The Indigènes argued that residual signs of a colonial mind-set are abundant, from the headscarf ban of 2004 (see chapter 6) to the social situation in the *cités,* especially housing discrimination and zoning, and the persistence of racial discrimination. Third, the French National Assembly passed an amendment on February 23, 2005, containing a provision stating that the "school curriculum should recognize in particular the positive role of the French presence overseas, notably in North Africa." This amendment—which was inserted by parliamentary deputies for the benefit of specific local constituencies of *harkis* (see chapter 1) and *pieds-noirs* (French citizens living in Algeria before independence)—triggered an uproar among many French of immigrant origin, from the overseas *département* Antilles, and also among many historians who were eager for a public reckoning with the past.[9] In his 2006 new year's address, six weeks after the 2005 riots, President Jacques Chirac announced that the amendment would be rewritten.

It is difficult to predict how the opening of this debate will affect integration in the future. On the one hand, more frank political discussion will encourage historical research on the colonial past and slavery. An immigration museum, loosely based on Ellis Island in New York Harbor, has long been in preparation and is projected to open in Paris in 2007 in a building that once hosted the great colonial exhibition of 1931. Its mission is to chronicle the history of the millions of French families of foreign origin, to emphasize the importance of immigration in the development of modern

France, and also to offer facilities for families and others to conduct immigration-related research. On the other hand, a minor competition for space and attention in history textbooks has developed among groups of victims (descendants of slaves, former colonized populations, former inhabitants of Algeria expelled from their homes, and so forth). That could have the effect of reinforcing negative stereotypes and provoking a backlash among the general population, which feels that today's France is being unfairly held responsible not only for its current shortcomings but for past inequities in which it had no role.

It should be noted that negative views of immigrants, Arabs, and Muslims gained ground after the November 2005 urban riots, confirming, at least momentarily, the fear of a "white backlash."[10] A poll taken by the CSA Institute for the Commission Nationale Consultative des Droits de l'Homme (CNCDH) (National Advisory Commission on Human Rights) just one week after the end of the riots indicated that people willing to declare themselves racist had jumped to 33 percent from 25 percent in November 2004. Fifty-six percent (versus 38 percent in 2004), thought that there were too many foreigners in France; 55 percent (versus 46 percent in 2004) thought that there were too many immigrants.[11]

Aside from racist stereotypes, there is another type of rejection worth mentioning, which could be described as the French republic's "allergic reaction" to Islam. This is not rooted in the defense of any ethnic identity; it is instead a reaction to Islam as a basis for the formation of a political identity among populations of North African origin. The allergy originates on the old-fashioned republican left and republican right—not the extreme right. It is a reaction to the perceived threat of the nascent Muslim "community" to the Republic's democratic foundations and to its definition of citizenship, first and foremost with regard to *laïcité*—the religious neutrality at the foundation of France's church-state bargain (see chapter 6). Its rejection of Muslims' demands for religious recognition in the public sphere—and for what is perceived as special privileges for their religion—is based not on the defense of race, blood, Christianity, or even "Frenchness." It defends instead the strong national political identity forged during the Third Republic (1871–1940), which is especially well symbolized by the secularization of the schools, where citizens are to be educated free of religious and political influences. That helps to explain the particular focus on the question of headscarves in public schools, which resonates with fierce battles from the past, especially from the 1880s through the 1910s. Then, the French republic wrested public education from the hands of the Catholic Church, going so far as to ban "teaching religious congregations" from public employment. Indeed, photographs from that era show veiled women being expelled from schools, but they were nuns employed as teachers, not Muslim students. From this perspective, Muslims today are seen as challenging basic tenets of French republican culture and identity by reopening a barely healed debate on the place of religion in the classroom—or they are accused of promoting the return of religious obscurantism against the ideal of progress (whether construed as science and reason or the emancipation of women). The question of religious observance for a new minority group, moreover, raises the hackles of republican-minded officials who fear the onset of multiculturalism, whereby rights would be granted to minorities, undermining the French political ethos of an indivisible national community.

To some extent, such fears can be linked to a more general anxiety about aspects of modern culture and the risk of the dilution or disappearance of French identity in a globalized world. In their book *The French Challenge*, Philip H. Gordon and Sophie Meunier showed how France successfully adapted its economy to new international conditions, even while French public opinion—from the philosopher-farmer José Bové to the pro-Tobin tax ATTAC (Association pour la Taxation des Transactions pour l'Aide aux Citoyens) (Association for Transaction Taxation to Aid Citizens) movement—largely rejected globalization.[12] Trade, culture, and identity were inextricably linked, and French leaders therefore had to show their willingness to "tame globalization" by protecting the French film industry (in the name of "cultural diversity"), traditional French agriculture, and the French language. This resulted in a particular form of schizophrenia that the authors called "globalization by stealth." European integration and the rise of regionalism also threatened the nation-state, which stands as the central pillar of French republican identity.

In this context, the arrival of Islam—apart from any questions of nativism, racism, or Islamophobia—was bound to be seen with suspicion. Reasserting French *laïcité* against Anglo-American–style multiculturalism—most notably through the headscarf ban in primary and secondary schools—was also a way to reaffirm the authority of the state and the traditional political identity of the French republic. Jacques Chirac, himself a traditionalist in terms of political culture, was particularly inclined to reassert French *laïcité* against Anglo-American multiculturalism, while his rival Nicolas Sarkozy, representing a more modern persuasion, was prepared to revise traditional models, such as by retooling the 1905 law separating church and state or by introducing a modicum of affirmative action.

A long-standing tradition of anticlericalism in France also complicates the picture of the country's general cultural reception of Muslims and Islam. The satirical newsweekly *Canard Enchaîné*, for example, has shown no signs of abandoning its long-honored practice of freely criticizing religions, whether Catholicism or Islam or any other. Its attitude, however, is not well received by many Muslims, who feel aggrieved given the minority status of Islam. Catholicism, which is the religion of the majority of French people, is seen as making a fairer target. However, it is sometimes difficult to determine where political considerations end and where cultural or ethnic ones begin. The noble defense of *laïcité*, the Republic, and modern mores can mask basic cultural and even ethnic prejudices. Olivier Roy, an expert in Islam, recounts a revealing anecdote from his hometown, Dreux, where there is a sizable Muslim minority. In 2003, during the debate over headscarves in public schools, he picked up a political flyer that contained ominous language about the wearing of headscarves, equating it with Islamism and appealing for its outright rejection. He writes that given the rhetoric employed, he first thought that it was a flyer of the Front National (FN) (National Front), France's extreme-right party, but then discovered that it originated with a very secular, liberal local group close to the Socialist Party.[13]

It should also be noted that along with negative images, positive stereotypes about Muslims also appear in public debate, especially on the left. This sometimes seems like a reflexive political correctness that excuses any offense by young people of Muslim origin from the *banlieues* because of the socioeconomic difficulties that they face, as was seen during the urban riots of November 2005. This bears some resemblance to the double standard adopted toward—or the benefit of the doubt accorded to—American blacks among some U.S. liberal elites during the 1960s. The subsequent reaction of some French public intellectuals, like Alain Finkielkraut, against any standards of political correctness, also bears a resemblance to the reaction to liberalism of the first generation of American neoconservatives in the second half of the 1960s, who warned of liberalism's excesses (Daniel Patrick Moynihan, Norman Podhoretz, Nathan Glazer, and so forth).[14] In a newspaper interview, Finkielkraut proposed a hypothetical example that illustrated this point of view:

> Imagine that you're running a restaurant, and you're antiracist, and you think that all people are equal, and you're also Jewish. In other words, talking about inequality between the races is a problem for you. And let's say that a young man from the suburbs comes in who wants to be

a waiter. He talks the talk of the suburbs. You won't hire him for the job. It's very simple. You won't hire him because it's impossible. He has to represent you and that requires discipline and manners, and a certain way of speaking. And I can tell you that French whites who are imitating the code of behavior of the suburbs—and there is such a thing—will run into the same exact problem.[15]

This sort of loaded observation has shown some political traction: a mayor of a Paris suburb recently said "you could put a Peugeot factory here, but so long as the youth still show up chewing gum with a backwards baseball cap and torn jeans, they are not going to get hired."[16]

Within the ranks of the French left, a struggle is taking place between the antiracist/anticolonialist wing on one hand and the antitotalitarian wing on the other. The former focuses on discrimination in French society and tends to be indulgent vis-à-vis young people of foreign origin; the latter denounces the risk of Islamism and the dangers it poses to liberal values like tolerance of homosexuality, feminism, and even free speech.[17]

Beyond the realm of stereotypes, there is an esteemed community of specialists who have concrete, academic knowledge of the Islamic world and of Muslim immigration in France. They carry on a tradition that can be traced back to the group of experts who accompanied Napoleon's expedition to Egypt and to the "Arab offices" that were part of military organizations during the conquest of Algeria. These specialists have represented the humane side of the French state, informed about and respectful of their subjects. The Maréchal Lyautey, a high-ranking French officer in early-twentieth-century Algeria and Morocco, embodied this other kind of colonialist, never viewing the "civilizing mission" as a crushing takeover but as an occasion for mutual acquaintance and reciprocal enrichment (unlike, for example, General Bugeaud, who was named governor general of Algeria in 1841).

In the military and academic contexts, French orientalism blossomed, offering an alternative to negative stereotypes of Islam. This tradition has produced contemporary experts on the Muslim world and Muslim immigration in France—such as the late Rémy Leveau, Olivier Roy, Gilles Kepel, Vincent Geisser, Valérie Amiraux, Catherine Wihtol de Wenden, Jean-Luc Richard, Farhad Khosrokhavar, Franck Frégosi, Jocelyne Césari, and many others—whose analysis, especially of political Islam, serve as reference points for government analyses the world over.[18] But academics' view of Islam has never been influential enough to shape collective perceptions of Muslims among the native French population, which often are rather close to the negative images mentioned. That fact certainly hinders the further integration of Muslims in France. As Catherine Wihtol de Wenden has argued, Muslims continue to make good progress in culture and society, but that has had surprisingly little effect on the predominance of negative stereotypes.[19]

Racism and Active Discrimination

Racism and Islamophobia should be viewed in the historical context just described. As is evident in boxes 2-1 and 2-2, many French Muslims are victims of discrimination and hate crimes. Discrimination is not limited to rhetorical attacks by the nationalist extreme right, which has consistently gained 15 percent or more of the vote in presidential elections and is one of the strongest extreme right-wing factions in Europe. There is also daily discrimination and the racist content that circulates on Internet sites based in France. The negative images and stereotypes evoked above may prevail to varying degrees in the minds of many native French (consciously or not) without ever slipping into overt racism or Islamophobia, but they nonetheless add to the discrimination suffered by Arabs and Muslims. Some government officials, however, still painted a rosy picture as recently as one year before the 2005 riots: in the summer of 2004, Nelly Olin, the deputy minister for equal opportunity, said that "in many French cities there is no discrimination and everyone is treated the same way."[20] Incidents of racism against North Africans were long undercounted and therefore "underestimated," according to one report by the Haut Conseil à l'Intégration.[21] Racist acts and threats have greatly increased, and they certainly constitute an important obstacle to the integration of populations of Arab origin in France.[22]

Incidents motivated by Islamophobia and anti-Semitism are discussed later, but it is possible to make a couple of observations about the data in figure 2-2. First, a correlation seems to exist between the surge in racist threats (and to a lesser extent racist acts) and election years (1995 and 2002). At a time of generally increased political activism—in particular, the pasting of political posters and distribution of political literature in public areas—there may be more opportunities for altercations between members of the extreme right and Muslims. On the other hand, anti-Semitic incidents have been most commonly correlated with events in the Near East, at least up until 2004 (see chapter 9). Second, figure 2-2 combines acts and threats, but incidents of racism are, proportionally, slightly more violent than incidents of anti-Semitism (28 percent physical assaults versus 20 percent, respectively, in 2004). That fact reflects in part the better recording of anti-Semitic than racist threats (see chapter 9). Accordingly, there are more serious incidents of

Figure 2-2. *Racist and Anti-Semitic Incidents, 1994–2004*[a]

Number

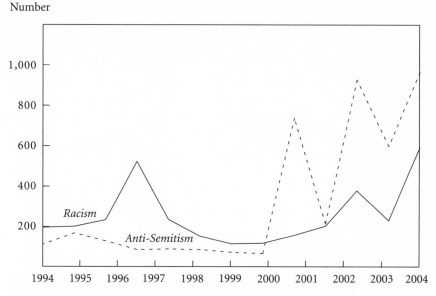

Source: Commission Nationale Consultative des Droits de l'Homme (CNCDH) [National Advisory Commission on Human Rights], "La lutte contre le racisme et la xénophobie 2004" ["The fight against racism and xenophobia 2004"].
a. Acts and threats combined.

racism (twelve dead and 124 injured for 1994–2004) than of anti-Semitism (one dead and ninety-five injured for the same period), although the Jewish minority is much smaller than the Arab/Muslim minority. However, that distribution may be reversed if current trends continue. Third, Corsica accounts for almost one half of violent racist acts, while 23 percent are attributed to the extreme right, 5 percent are attributed to extreme "Jewish defense" groups, and 24 percent are not attributed. The finding for Corsica reflects its strong regionalist sentiment, which rejects everything that is not Corsican, in addition to racism (acts of Corsicans against French people from the continent are not counted as racist).

The French population is aware of the level of racism that exists in French society, and a large majority (88 percent to 90 percent since the early 2000s) consistently judges racism to be "very" or "somewhat" prevalent. It also believes that "North Africans" and "Muslims" are the first targets of racism (before "immigrants" in general, "blacks," "Jews," and so forth).[23] That view—

Table 2-1. *Opinion of the Number of Foreigners, Immigrants, and Muslims in France* [a]

	Foreigners		Muslims	Immigrants	
Response	2002	2004	2003	2002	2004
Not large enough	1	2	1	1	2
Too large	42	38	40	51	44
As it should be	27	25	22.5	22	22
Indifferent	27	31	32	22	28
Don't know	3	4	4.5	4	4

Source: BVA opinion polls in the 2003 and 2004 annual reports of the Commission Nationale Consultative des Droits de l'Homme (CNCDH) [National Advisory Commission on Human Rights].

a. Survey question: "In general, would you say that in France today the number of (a) foreigners, (b) immigrants, and (c) Muslims is not large enough, is too large, or is just as it should be, or you are indifferent?" Figures represent percentage of responses of 1,010 respondents from the general population.

and the accompanying desire to see acts of racism and anti-Semitism punished with greater severity—is nonetheless combined with a marked preference for seeing immigration stop or recede, as shown in table 2-1 by the percent of respondents who believe that the number of foreigners, immigrants, and Muslims in France is "too large."

That particular stance—increasing tolerance vis-à-vis immigrants but ambivalence vis-à-vis immigration—is taken by a growing majority of French, who consider immigration to be a source of cultural enrichment (74 percent in 2004) and believe that a democracy should be judged on the way that it integrates its minorities (80 percent) but nevertheless want the flow of immigrants to stop. But behind the apparent convergence of the figures shown in table 2-1 lie very different opinions: people who think that the number of immigrants or foreigners is too high cite reasons like unemployment, the burden on the welfare state, housing problems, and security issues. But people who think that the number of Muslims is too high (that question was asked in 2003 only) mention "the threat to French identity" first (29 percent), then unemployment (28 percent), insecurity (22 percent), and social cohesion (22 percent).[24]

In more recent times, two factors seem to have hardened perceptions of immigration and immigrants. First, economic considerations appear more important than ever: in the late 2005 polls, respondents were more prone to link immigration and unemployment than they were in previous years. There is no doubt that aside from basic xenophobia and racism, competition for jobs, social services, or even media attention can explain in part the hostile sentiments among the population that can trace its roots in France further back over the last two centuries. Second, urban riots have led to a more xenophobic view of foreigners, immigrants, and Muslims, as mentioned.[25]

One of the consequences of the persistence of racism and negative stereotypes is the de facto discrimination that the population of North African origin suffers in everyday civil society—whether in the workplace, housing, or social life. As one Moroccan immigrant author put it in a recent satirical novel, "When Samia wants to rent a studio apartment that has been advertised in Paris, she finds upon giving her name that the apartment had in fact been unavailable since September 11."[26] Sometimes, landlords or sellers ask real estate agents to screen out certain potential renters or buyers, and it is not unknown for agents to agree to do so. Unofficial and "invisible" fields are added to databases in order to include characteristics that it is illegal to list (like skin color and regional origin). Even in public housing, cases of blatant discrimination are regularly reported to antiracist groups like SOS Racisme. And some invisible barriers may suddenly appear for applicants of immigrant origin, like an extra safety deposit, a requirement for additional documents, and so forth.[27] The same patterns of discrimination are observed when young people of foreign origin are denied access to bars or nightclubs, which can be a painful experience that has a profound influence on their attitudes toward French society (see chapter 10).[28]

The law and government institutions are, of course, officially "colorblind." Moreover, they punish discriminatory practices observed in the private sector. In the 1990s, for example, a discrimination observation group was created and a toll-free telephone number (114) was set up to take reports of discrimination in general. On November 16, 2001, an antidiscrimination law was passed, and on January 17, 2002, the social modernization law added a section prohibiting discrimination in housing. European Union regulations also contain clauses pertaining to discrimination in housing.

In 2004, a French antidiscrimination agency was established, independent of the government, to provide mediation services and legal advice for victims of ethnic or religious discrimination (among other kinds) in housing, at the workplace, or in entertainment establishments.[29] Such an agency had originally been proposed by the High Council for Integration under Prime Minister Lionel Jospin's government, but the proposal had died early in discussions. Former Prime Minister Jean-Pierre Raffarin's government announced its intention to follow up on the idea on taking office in 2002, but it did not produce full recommendations for two years, in the form of a parliamentary bill creating the Haute Autorité de Lutte contre les Discriminations et pour l'Egalité (HALDE) (High Authority to Combat Discrimination and Promote Equality) in October 2004. It also held a national conference against social exclusion in July 2004.[30]

As discussed earlier, youth of immigrant origin are much more affected by unemployment than are other youth; on average the ratio is 2 to 1. That remains true even when the fact that this population is slightly less likely to have a high-school diploma, which makes it much more susceptible to unemployment, is taken into account. Among youth of immigrant origin, those of North African origin are unemployed more often than others.

Those differences can be explained by two factors. On one hand, compared with the children of Portuguese parents, for example, North African youth command less "social capital," in Pierre Bourdieu's sociological terminology.[31] Therefore they do not benefit from the network of contacts and sense of solidarity available to children of other origins, primarily because their parents may be unemployed themselves, thus making it harder for them to help their children integrate.[32]

On the other hand, they suffer from active discrimination on the job market. In 2004, 74 percent of respondents to a French public opinion poll estimated that some people were slowed in their career because of their origin or skin color (although 90 percent declared that they would accept working under a superior who came from an immigrant background or had a different skin color).[33] Job discrimination has occurred mainly in the areas of retail sales and commerce, which require regular communication and contact with clientele. Employers may justify not hiring North African applicants by claiming that their clients are uncomfortable conducting business with persons of such origin. Some antiracist organizations accused private employment agencies of allowing employers to include *bleu-blanc-rouge* ("blue-white-red," the colors of the French flag) on their list of qualifications sought, an insidious form of discrimination implying that only native French need apply.[34]

As discussed in chapter 1, a study conducted for a temporary employment agency revealed that discriminatory practices were prevalent even among recruiters for jobs: when six resumes with identical qualifications but different-sounding names were submitted for 258 job listings, only 5 percent of candidates with North African names received interviews while 30 percent of those with traditional French names did.[35] Affirmative action has entered the political debate and has made some strides in the private sector, but it remains controversial as a policy option for public employment (see chapter 5).

It should be added that once in a job, workers of foreign origin often find that their career advances more slowly, leading to the de facto ethnicization of the division of labor.[36]

The perception of prejudice in the judicial system and the media focus on Muslim extremism and the "Arab peril" have likely contributed to feelings of disaffection among Muslim youth. When asked by journalists or pollsters, Arab youth complain about their treatment: "The media see an Arab or a Muslim before they see the person," said one high school student in the small town of Charente.[37] "The media want people to believe that girls wear a headscarf to avoid being beaten," added an unemployed twenty-year-old named Kadour. "When a French person is accused of a crime, the papers just give his first name whereas North Africans also get their last name included," said one young man. "Journalists feel free to identify young people as North African," complained another young man, from Angoulême, "but it is forbidden to refer to an intellectual as being Jewish."[38]

A watchdog commission formed by two human rights and antiracist groups along with two lawyers' and judges' unions found that in incidents of police brutality between 2002–04, 60 percent of victims were foreign citizens and "the remaining 40 percent are of French nationality, but with few exceptions their name or appearance would suggest that they are of foreign origin."[39] There has been no official or independent assessment of those claims, but their existence points to the lack of trust between French of foreign origin and the police. Of 200 alleged instances of brutality, nearly half of which took place during identity checks and roughly a quarter during police custody, authorities investigated only fifty.[40]

Islamophobia and the Paradox of Increased Acceptance of Islam in France

The acceptance of Islam as a religion in French society has a mixed and somewhat contradictory record. On one hand, negative attitudes regarding Islam are not rare, and they have recently been on the rise, for reasons related to both domestic and international affairs. On the other hand, over the long term, the French population overall seems to be more comfortable with Islam as a fact of French life and increasingly think that the practice of Islam should be facilitated, for example, by state assistance for construction of mosques.

As shown in figure 2-3, however, Islam nonetheless has the least positive image among religions, and its popularity decreased further from 2003 to 2004. It should be noted, however, that religions in general are not particularly "popular" in France, due to a national political culture in which they are

Figure 2-3. *Image of Selected Religions and Concepts, 2004*

Percent

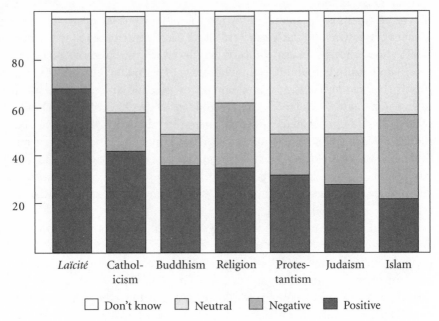

Source: BVA poll in CNCDH 2004 report.

seen as potentially dangerous when they intrude in the public sphere. That perception can be explained by the legacy of the bloody religious wars of the sixteenth century and the Third Republic's struggle against the Catholic Church at the turn of the twentieth century.

This negative image of religion in general (negative opinions on all religions increased from 2003 to 2004) weighs particularly heavily on Islam because of recent geopolitical events involving the persistent threat of Islamism and Islamist terrorism and because of domestic developments. The headscarf ban was largely seen as a necessary reaffirmation and defense of republican and secular principles against encroachment by Islamic values. That view was confirmed by survey questions on whether "the values of Islam" were compatible with "the values of the Republic": only about 30 percent of all respondents answered "yes" in 2002–04, compared with 50 percent to 62 percent who answered "no" (78 percent of self-declared French Muslims said "yes").[41] This mix of domestic and international factors explains, among other things, a general reluctance among the French to see Turkey enter the European Union: in February 2005, clear majorities opposed it.[42]

There is undoubtedly an increasing "irrational fear and total rejection of Islam as a religion, lifestyle, community-building project, or culture," as noted in the CNCDH 2003 report. Does that amount to "Islamophobia"? The term was popularized in a book by Vincent Geisser, in response to Pierre-André Taguieff's concept of "the new Judeophobia." According to Taguieff, anti-Jewish attitudes derived from extreme anti-Zionism, particularly on the extreme left and in Islamist milieux, are increasingly complementing traditional extreme-right anti-Semitism.[43] "Islamophobia" is a catchword that is meant to capture right-wing hysteria about Islam and the generalizing view of Islam as a social and political prison for its believers as well as left-wing excesses in defense of *laïcité*. It is also a direct response to "Judeophobia," since, as Geisser argues, public criticism of Jews is tightly controlled while public criticism of Muslims is less controversial. Indeed, some Muslim leaders have accused politicians of caring little about Islamophobic incidents while showing a high degree of attentiveness to any act of anti-Semitism, but there seems to be little substance to such claims.[44] After two arson attacks on mosques in March 2004, for example, President Chirac "condemned with the greatest severity" such "hateful acts" and extended his "great sympathy" to the victims. And Nicolas Sarkozy, the interior minister, visited both prayer spaces on behalf of the government.

In news media coverage of issues relating to Muslim life in France, the boundary between legitimate criticism of any religion and systematic, negative stereotyping of Islam is sometimes crossed. In recent years, many Muslims took offense at what they considered hateful representations of Islam in a popular novel by Michel Houellebecq and a best-selling polemical essay by Oriana Fallaci. An interview in which Houellebecq called Islam "the dumbest religion of all" even triggered a lawsuit by the Grande Mosquée de Paris (GMP) (Great Mosque of Paris) for incitement to hatred (the court acquitted him).[45] Claude Imbert, a columnist of *Le Point* magazine and member of the High Council on Integration, went on the record twice, stating that "I am somewhat Islamophobic, and I'm not afraid to say so. I'm not alone in thinking that Islam, as a religion, brings forth a whole array of arcane behaviors as well as regularly downgrades the status of women. Islam has calcified ways of thinking and pulled the wool over people's eyes."[46] The French Council of the Muslim Religion and a human rights group, Mouvement contre le Racisme et pour l'Amitié entre les Peuples (MRAP) (Movement against Racism and for Friendship among Peoples), filed suit against two periodicals, *France-Soir* and *Charlie Hebdo,* for republishing Danish caricatures of the prophet Mohammed.[47] In the context of a legal system that bans incendiary hate speech, the question is, of course, whether there are outer limits to legitimate criticism: is it forbidden, for example, to disparage the stoning of women for adultery or the chopping off of hands for theft as prescribed by some texts of Islam? Some critics have taken aim at what they call an "Islamically correct" posture that automatically condones everything Muslim and thereby precludes the free expression of opinion. In this regard, "Islamophobia" presents the same challenge as other concepts, such as anti-Americanism or anti-Semitism—that is, where is the limit between legitimate criticism of U.S. foreign policy and systematic attacks against an unfairly stereotyped America? Between criticism of Israel and attacks on "the Jews"?

If "Islamophobia" is present in the media, it is worth considering whether that attitude is ever converted into violent actions against Muslims. In other words, is there a specific anti-Muslim racism that is distinct from—or that would add its effects to—anti-immigrant xenophobia and anti-Arab racism? The Collective against Islamophobia in France, a group formed by various Muslim associations, found that between October 2003 and August 2004, 118 attacks on Muslim individuals and sixty-four attacks against Muslim institutions (for example, cultural centers or prayer spaces) were reported, including twenty-eight incidents of mosque vandalism and eleven cemetery desecrations. Without knowing the precise nature of those attacks, one can nonetheless observe that they are on the order of the 193 anti-Semitic acts recorded in 2002, although they were directed against a much larger population (neither the anti-Semitic nor the 182 anti-Muslim acts included threats). Half of the targeted Muslim institutions were concentrated in two regions, Alsace and the Paris region, Île-de-France.[48] (See box 2-1.)

However, researchers Nonna Mayer and Guy Michelat find it hard to distinguish between a general rejection of immigrants and Arabs on one hand and any specific targeting of Islam or Muslims on the other. In public opinion polls, indicators of Islamophobia—such as negative views of Islam, the opinion that French Muslims are not completely French, or the refusal to do anything to facilitate the practice of the Muslim religion—often are held by those who also share anti-immigrant, anti-Arab, and anti-Semitic opinions more generally. In other words, Islamophobia is part of a larger ethnocentric and xenophobic view—and traditional republican and *laïc* Islamophobia does not appear in statistics.[49] As far as violent incidents are concerned, it is generally impossible to distinguish between an anti-Muslim and an anti-Arab act when the victim is both Arab and Muslim.

Box 2-1. *Islamophobic Incidents in France, April 2002–June 2004*

Molotov cocktails thrown at mosques in Ecaudin (March 2002) and
Méricourt and Châlons (April 2002)

Letter bomb sent to a mosque in Perpignan (April 2002)

Desecration of a Muslim cemetery in Lyon (April 2002)

Attempted arson of mosques in Belley and Rillieux-la-Pape (December 2002)

Desecration of a dozen prayer spaces with red, white, and blue paint and
another with swastikas (January 2003)

Desecration of tombs in Thiais and Meuse (March 2003)

Arson of a mosque in Nancy (March 2003)

Bomb dismantled in front of prayer space in Nice (March 2003)

Desecration of Muslim tombs in a military cemetery in Haut Rhin
(April 2003)

Arson of a prayer room in Montpellier (October 2003)

Desecration and attempted arson of a mosque in Dunkerque
(November 2003)

Arson of prayer spaces at Seynod and Annecy (March 2004)

Muslim tombs desecrated in Marseille's Canet cemetery and Strasbourg
military cemetery (June 2004)

Shots fired through door at Moroccan imam in Sartène, Corsica
(November 2004)

Shots fired overnight at Mosque in Agen, Acquitaine (January 2005)

Attempted arson of home of regional Muslim council (CRCM) official
outside Strasbourg (January 2005)

Source: Sylvia Zappi, "L'intolérance à l'égard de l'islam passée au crible par la CNCDH"
["Intolerance toward Islam is examined by the CNCDH"], *Le Monde,* November 25, 2003.

In spite of the attention given to Islamophobia and more generally to the
rejection of Muslims, public opinion polls reveal a more nuanced picture of
French attitudes toward Islam over the long term (table 2-2). They indicate
an overall improvement in the image of Islam among the French population,
even in a poll taken just two weeks after September 11, 2001.[50]

Other polls indicate an increasing willingness to see the government facilitate the practice of the Muslim religion: in 2004, 47 percent of respondents

Table 2-2. *Selected Opinions on Islam in France*

Percent

Response	1989	1994	2001	2003
Are you in favor of, opposed to, or indifferent to the building of mosques in French cities when Muslims ask for them?				
In favor	33	30	31	49
Opposed	38	31	22	47
Indifferent/Don't know	26	37	46	4
Would you be against the election of a Muslim mayor where you live?				
Yes	63	55	35	
Are you hostile to the idea of "Muslim" political parties or trade unions?				
Yes	68	70	52	

Source: IFOP poll of October 2001. Data for 2003 are from IPSOS / LCI / *Le Point* poll of May 15, 2003, "Islam, intégration, immigration: l'opinion des Français musulmans" ["Islam, integration, immigration: The opinions of French Muslims"], available on IPSOS website (www.ipsos.fr). "Indifferent" was not an option in 2003 and was replaced by "Don't know."

thought that it was a necessity (versus 41 percent in 2003), and 43 percent thought that the professional and religious training of imams (most of whom are "imported" from the Maghreb or from Egypt, Turkey, or Saudi Arabia) in France was also to be encouraged (versus 40 percent in 2003).[51] These different results indicate a growing acceptance of Islam by the French, including its visible representations (such as mosques), which have traditionally met the greatest resistance, and the encouragement of the normalization and institutionalization of relations between Islam and the state, as with other religions. Such shifts in opinion may indicate a better assessment by French people of "family Islam," which constitutes, for the most part, the practice of their Muslim neighbors and which stands in contrast to the image of Islam presented in the international media.

Continuing improvement in attitudes in the future, however, is by no means guaranteed. The urban riots of November 2005 have taken their toll on public opinion. While organized Muslim organizations were not in any way involved in the riots, a poll taken just one week after the end of the tumult showed deterioration in the image of Islam and Muslims. The opinion that Muslims constitute a separate group went up by 6 points, and the opinion that French Muslims are as French as other people decreased by 11 points, from

77 percent in November 2004 to 66 percent in November 2005.[52] This shows the nexus between integration issues on one hand and the image of Islam on the other, a close connection that has also been revealed by a detailed analysis of systematic polling by Sylvain Brouard and Vincent Tiberj.[53]

Forces of Inclusion and Blending

There also are trends toward inclusion and integration that work against the forces of exclusion and discrimination as well as against the latent or explicit racism prevalent in some segments of the population. In a subtle way, Muslim immigrants' culture and talents have found success in France and transformed French society on many levels, and that fact has contributed to the slow but steady integration process.

First, many neighborhood associations within the Muslim community are trying to foster integration, even in the most underprivileged neighborhoods. Some of these are religious organizations linked to the local mosque, whereas others are social, cultural, or athletic. They take advantage of a 1901 law permitting the formation of civil society associations that was expanded to allow foreigners to create such associations in 1981. There also are more elite national clubs that encourage and promote the achievements of young people of immigrant (though not exclusively Muslim) origin: the Convergences Club; the Averroës Club, created by Amirouche Laïdi in 1997; and the Twenty-First Century Club (Club XXIe siècle), which is a collection of 200 successful young French professionals of foreign origin.[54] This group, headed by Hakim El Karaoui, a speechwriter for then Prime Minister Raffarin (2002–05), who later became an advisor to Thierry Breton, the finance minister, aims to provide "examples of success" for other young people of immigrant origin. Some think tanks have worked on new ideas to fight discrimination and promote integration—the Institut Montaigne has been particularly active in this respect—and some companies, like Peugeot, have led the way (see chapter 7).[55] Religious organizations have promoted interfaith dialogue through ad hoc groups: the Conseil Représentatif des Institutions Juives de France (CRIF) (Representative Council of Jewish Institutions of France) has a Jewish-Muslim committee, the French Catholic Church maintains its Secrétariat pour les Relations avec l'Islam (Secretariat for Relations with Islam), and there is also an Episcopal Commission for Islam.

A good deal of legal footwork is done and major public awareness campaigns are carried out by the "Four Sisters"—LICRA, SOS Racisme, LDH, and MRAP (see box 2-2)—which are national civil society organizations that actively fight racism and anti-Semitism. All of them have a strong universalist

Box 2-2. *The Four Major French Antiracism Associations*

Ligue des Droits de l'Homme (LDH). The oldest of the four organizations, the LDH was created in 1898 in the wake of the Dreyfus affair to fight anti-Semitism. It also led campaigns to defend union leaders in the early twentieth century. In 1922, it created an international branch, the Federation Internationale des Ligues des Droits de l'Homme. In the 1930s, it was active against extreme-right organizations and was instrumental in forming the Popular Front, but it was divided on the question of the war (pacifists versus hawks). After World War II, it fought the repression that accompanied the wars of decolonization and defended civil liberties in France. In the 1980s and 1990s, it was active in favor of immigrant rights. It has always been close to the left side of the political spectrum.

Ligue Internationale contre le Racisme et l'Antisémitisme (LICRA). Created in 1928 after the successful campaign for the acquittal of the murderer of a former Russian official responsible for bloody pogroms in Russia, the Ligue Internationale contre l'Antisémitisme soon incorporated "Racism" in its acronym to reflect its universalist outlook. Joseph Kessel, André Malraux, Léon Blum, Albert Einstein, Sigmund Freud, Bernard Shaw, and many other notable figures were members. LICRA fought actively against Nazism and fascism in the 1930s, and after the war it directed its efforts at the resettlement of victims of the Nazis, especially Holocaust survivors. It has been fighting in favor of immigrant rights and against expulsion of foreigners from the 1970s to the present.

Mouvement contre le Racisme et pour l'Amitié entre les Peuples (MRAP). Created in 1949 and close to the French communist party, the MRAP led legal efforts in the 1950s against collaborationists and residual anti-Semitism from the Vichy period. The association drafted the first proposals for antiracist legislation, which eventually led to the 1972 law. After the large wave of migration from North Africa in the mid-1960s and 1970s, it changed its name (but not its acronym) in 1977, substituting the words "for Friendship among Peoples" for "against Anti-Semitism." It supported the prohibition on maintaining public records of ethnicity in the 1970s.[a]

SOS Racisme. Created in 1984 after the "Marche pour l'Egalité" or "Marche des Beurs" of 1983, "SOS Racisme—Touche pas à mon pote" (or "Hands off my buddy") was created by young *beurs* along with young people of French origin after several racist attacks in order to pursue greater acceptance of youth of Arab origin. It was symbolic of the second age of mobilization, having a purely secular vision of integration that predated the rise of religious identity among younger generations. It rapidly expanded its fight to include the new manifestations of anti-Semitism. It was and remains close to the Socialist Party, and many of its founders (such as Malek Boutih) are now high-ranking party members.

a. Erik Bleich, *Race Politics in Britain and France* (Cambridge University Press 2003).

outlook. They organize demonstrations and conferences, undertake political action at the local and national level against discrimination and xenophobia, and monitor extreme right movements; in addition, since 1985 they have been allowed to join lawsuits as plaintiffs.[56] Their combined campaigns against anti-Semitism helped bring about a 1972 antiracism law, and their reactions to the National Front's advance in the 1980s led to a flurry of legal activity that included revising and updating antidiscrimination laws in 1990 (the Gayssot law) and 2003 (the Lellouche law). There is no exact equivalent of the first amendment in France, and expressing racist or anti-Semitic opinions or denying the reality of the Holocaust are punishable by law.

The Four Sisters sometimes disagree over questions of macro-strategy—for example, on the distinction between racism and anti-Semitism. LICRA and SOS Racisme deem anti-Semitism to be a distinct disease that must be fought with specific tools, whereas LDH and MRAP think that the distinction amounts to communalism and weakens the common fight against discrimination. The latter two also tend to be more sensitive to the Palestinian issue. There are similar disputes over how best to target discrimination against people of North African origin. "At the MRAP, we're mostly secular [*"majoritairement laïcs"*], and we have a critical perspective on religion," said one activist at the association's national conference. "Islamophobia is legitimate, but not anti-Muslim racism."[57] But the MRAP general assembly eventually voted to continue its "fight against Islamophobia" by a vote of 179-0, with twenty-three abstentions.

Aside from civil organizations that actively fight racism and attempt to foster an integration-friendly environment, immigrant culture and immigrants themselves are a growing presence in and influence on French life. Recent contributions to French social and cultural life by individuals of Muslim background range from achievements in the academic sphere to those in the world of sports and entertainment. Such contributions are still disproportionately small, but their visibility has already helped the image of immigrants and is thought to facilitate their social acceptance.

The high point was certainly the World Soccer Cup of 1998, which ended in the victory of the highly diverse French national team. The star players were the children of black and Arab immigrants along with native French players, and the team came to be known as *black-blanc-beur*, a contemporary alternative to the *bleu-blanc-rouge* of the French flag. "Thank you to the overseas territories, thank you to Africa, and thank you twice over to Kabylia," wrote a columnist in *Le Figaro* on July 14, 1998. The multicultural composition of the national team reflected a new France that was able to integrate new talents—*"la France qui gagne"* ("the France that wins")—in stark contrast to the older, uniformly white, team of Germany, for example. Chirac spoke with pride of the "tricolor and multicolor" team; even Jean-Marie Le Pen praised the contribution of French players of North African origin to the national team.[58]

White faces continue to dominate television, to the point that after the urban riots of 2005, President Chirac convened a meeting at the Elysée on November 22 of the CEOs of the major television channels to urge them to increase the ethnic diversity of their journalists, talking heads, and anchors so that they would be more representative of French society. A black anchor was subsequently announced by TF1, the major French network, for the prime time news program in summer 2006. However, even before that, some *beurs* and blacks had been slightly more visible in several programming niches—for example, news programs and reality shows—especially on TF1 (the most popular network) and M6 (a network with a younger audience). Nagui, the talk-show host on Canal Plus and then on France 4, is of Egyptian origin. Kamel Ouali, of Kabylian origin, is a well-known choreographer on TF1's reality show *Star Academy*. Some observers have remarked that viewers rarely vote for minority characters to win the jackpot on game shows (in 2004 only the reality show *Le Chantier,* on M6, saw a minority victory: a gay couple that included a black man won a contest to build a house). But the overall picture is still one of a France that does not offer many major positions—like the news anchor slot for a prime time news program—to the children of immigrants, although France 3 now has a black anchor for *Soir 3,* which airs at 11:00 p.m.

In the sphere of sports, Zinedine Zidane, the top scorer on France's 1998 soccer team, was born in Marseille to Algerian parents. He has become a major cultural figure and role model, joined in the league of superstars by athletes from the Antilles or former French colonies such as Marie-Josée Pérec, Stéphane Diagana, and Djamel Bouras, who won the gold medal in judo for France at the 1996 Olympics.[59] In a late 2005 survey, of all political, show business, and sports personalities, the French preferred first of all Yannick Noah, a former tennis player of Cameroonese and French origin (and the father of U.S. college basketball star Joakim Noah), and second, Zinedine Zidane. The French recording industry has also become a locus of integration. Alongside rap groups from the *banlieues*, there is raï music from the Maghreb, an extraordinarily popular crossover genre sung in a mix of Arabic and French. Singers like Cheb Mami and Khaled laid the groundwork at the 2004 music festivals of Bobigny and La Villette for contemporary stars like Rachid Taha and Faudel, while Khaled, Taha, and Faudel performed in a sold-out show at the Bercy venue in 1998, signaling their definitive arrival on the

Paris scene. Nicolas Sarkozy even invited Faudel to perform at his inauguration as party leader of the Gaullist UMP—originally known as the Union pour une Majorité Présidentielle (Union for a Presidential Majority) and now known as Union pour un Mouvement Populaire (Union for a Popular Movement)—in November 2004. Walking through the tunnels of the Paris metro, one sees large posters advertising entertainers and one-man-show comedians of North African origin, such as the ubiquitous Smaïn, Jamel Debbouze (who co-starred in *The Adventures of Amélie Poulain* and was the highest paid French actor in 2002), Ramzy, and Gad Elmaleh. Trends in popular tastes thus reveal a consistent public appetite for ethnic diversity in the realm of entertainment, an indication of the degree to which the French public has been changed by France's colonial legacy.

In addition, in contemporary French intellectual life, luminaries of Arab origin have played a visible role in the public debate over immigration and religion. Hanifa Cherifi and Dounia Bouzar—from the French ministries of education and justice, respectively—frequently weighed in as experts on religious expression and headscarf wearing among French Muslim youth. Mohammed Arkoun, an Algerian-born Islamic scholar of Berber origin, Abdelwahab Meddeb (Tunisia), and Malek Chebel (Algeria) all have published extensively in French on theological reform in Islam. The late Franco-Algerian Abdelmalek Sayed, a sociologist who studied North African populations, was proposed in 2006 as the first-ever Arab namesake of a public school in France.[60]

French Islam is also now part of the regular fare of newspapers and television programming. The holidays of Ramadan and Aïd al-Adha are announced in the media and accompanied by special reports on the evening news. The media are addressing questions of integration more frequently and in an increasingly open way, and although they sometimes deal in stereotypes, the expanded coverage contributes to the process of social normalization. The urban riots of November 2005 constituted a real shock to public opinion, and they have resulted to some extent in a "white backlash." However, at the same time they increased awareness of the living conditions of the hundreds of thousands of residents in the *cités*, most of them French citizens, and, most important, of the extent of discrimination in everyday life. The number of news reports on the subject increased markedly following the riots, and such popular narratives are now impossible to ignore. Time will tell which of the two effects—backlash or increased awareness—will prevail or whether they will simply coexist, producing conflicting results.

3

From Religion to Identity: 1,001 Ways of Being Muslim

Just as there are many ways to be a Catholic, Protestant, or Jew, there are many ways to be a Muslim. Belonging to the Islamic *umma,* or "community," can be a matter of religious piety, of course, but it is more often relevant as an element of one's cultural background or personal identity. Arab Muslims in France are increasingly defining themselves as Muslims rather than as Algerians, Moroccans, or Arabs. But their identification with Islam can be based on familial or community bonds rather than on adherence to a rigorous Islam imported from the Arab world. The religious obligations of Muslims, as outlined in the "five pillars" of Islam, include affirming that Allah is God and Mohammed His prophet, saying daily prayers, fasting during the month of Ramadan, making a pilgrimage to Mecca (*hajj*), and giving alms. The extent to which Muslims living as a minority in the diaspora fulfill those obligations is one useful indicator of how obligated and able to do so individuals feel when living outside of Muslim lands (*dar al Islam*).

Although this book refers throughout to "Muslims," what is actually meant are those individuals who, by dint of their national origin or ancestry, are of Muslim culture or sociological background. This population, of course, includes many secular-minded citizens who would object to being classified primarily as Muslims. In that respect, the book's main theme is itself a concession to viewing integration problems from a religious perspective. That is not the only possible standpoint from which to view this population, whose members have multiple, layered identities and affiliations. Indeed, speaking almost exclusively about religion tends to reify the process of re-Islamization by limiting members' options for self-definition to "Muslim" rather than

Figure 3-1. *Ethnic Origin of Muslims in France*[a]

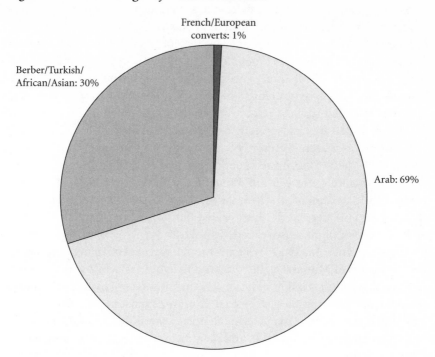

French/European
converts: 1%

Berber/Turkish/
African/Asian: 30%

Arab: 69%

Source: Authors' compilation.
a. French/European converts = 50,000 individuals; Berbers, Turks, Africans, and Asians = 950,000; Arabs = 4,000,000. Figures are approximate.

including, for example, "Arab," "Berber," "Kabylian," "immigrant," or even just plain "French" (See figure 3-1).[1]

After several phases of political mobilization around the nonreligious commonalities discussed below, however, there are signs of the gradual emergence of a clear community identity. Poll respondents have increasingly stated that they "feel Muslim" first and then French (or male or Parisian, and so forth). That was what sociologists Vincent Geisser and Khadija Mohsen-Finan found in their study of Muslim and non-Muslim students in several French high schools in 2001–02, and it was also a central finding of the U.S. Department of State poll in 2005 that reported that 34 percent of respondents (all of whom were self-identified Muslims) felt Muslim first and then French, versus 21 percent who felt French first, then Muslim. (Thirty-three percent said "both equally" and 5 percent said "only Muslim.")[2]

But although the intensification of outward indicators of Muslim identity may lead to some demands on public authorities, such as for the construction of mosques and the creation of Muslim schools, it does not necessarily translate into more frequent religious practice. In 2005, French adults of African or Turkish origin, for example ("potential Muslims," in sociological terminology), were not markedly more mosque-going than French Catholics were church-going: 22 percent versus 18 percent of those groups, respectively, said that they attended services once a month. Among "potential Muslims," 20 percent said that they had no religion, versus 28 percent of French adults.[3] Muslims did appear, however, to be more observant in their daily life. The CSA poll of March 2003 on religion in France revealed that 38 percent who described themselves as Muslim declared that they prayed every day, compared with 13 percent of all self-declared Catholics and 39 percent of regular church-goers (28 percent of Muslims said that they never prayed, compared with 38 percent of all self-declared Catholics).[4] French authorities estimate that between 8 percent and 15 percent (though recent statements have settled on 10 percent) of Muslims regularly attend religious services and that in reality, despite what polls might indicate, less than 5 percent (around 150,000 to 250,000) attend a mosque each Friday.[5] (Although mosque attendance is not a formal requirement in Islam, its incidence is a fair indicator of the intensity of intracommunity socialization and identification, especially among men.) That is roughly the same proportion as that of French Catholics who attend mass once a week (9 percent), according to the CSA poll.[6] A large study undertaken by Sylvain Brouard and Vincent Tiberj in 2005 on the population of African and Turkish origin provides further data: 43 percent of respondents said that they prayed every day; 77 percent said that they never drank alcohol (even though Brouard and Tiberj suspect, from personal interviews, that that figure is exaggerated), and 80 percent said that they fast during Ramadan. Younger respondents, in particular, tended to declare high levels of observance whether they were actually more observant or not, as shown in the study by Geisser and Mohsen-Finan.[7]

Interestingly, this slightly higher level of observance is true of *all* French citizens of foreign origin, including Christians, when compared with those who can trace their family back more than two generations in France.[8] A negligible number of Muslim children are enrolled in religious schools, compared with sizable percentages of their Jewish (more than 25 percent) and Catholic peers.[9] That is due for the most part to the current dearth of Muslim schools: there are only three in all of France, one of which is on the island of La Réunion in the Indian Ocean. Another potential sign of piety, among women, of course, is the headscarf. One should remember that despite the enormous symbolic weight of the *affaire du foulard,* which first made headlines in 1989, no more than a few thousand girls ever actually came to school wearing a headscarf, even in the years before the 2004 school ban on conspicuous religious symbols (see chapter 6).[10]

There are significant differences in observance across nationalities and ethnic groups. The data on piety reveal that there is more to religious identity than collective observance, especially since Muslim prayer need not be conducted in a house of worship. Even if Muslims do not visit prayer spaces frequently, they do respond the most positively to the question of religious faith: in one poll taken in the 1998–2001 period, 95 percent said that they were "believers," compared with 82 percent of Catholics and 78 percent of Protestants.[11] That result is confirmed when one examines the beliefs and identities of Muslim students.

Religious Observance, Mosque Attendance, and Islam at School

Mosque attendance is a valuable proxy for the degree of identification or interaction with organized Islam, since prayer spaces are the center of religious life and of explicitly Muslim social activities. Of those who claimed to be "observant believers," it is interesting to note that around one-third did not pray five times daily but did claim to observe Ramadan. Another 2 percent considered themselves observant believers but observed neither daily prayers nor Ramadan.[12]

In recent years, younger self-declared Muslims have tended more than older Muslims to assert their religious identity in their daily life as well as in polls.[13] In various polls, including those conducted by the Institut Français d'Opinion Publique (IFOP) (French Institute of Public Opinion) and by the Observatoire Interrégional du Politique (OIP) (Interregional Center for Policy Studies) in partnership with the French regional councils in 1998–2001, young self-declared Muslims (less than twenty-five years old) tended to declare higher rates of practice than the next age group (twenty-five to thirty-five-year-olds). That marks a reversal of the situation in past decades. Claude Dargent explains that this is not linked to declining practice rates among older Muslims, but rather to a generational effect discussed below. (See table 3-1 and figures 3-2, 3-3, 3-4, and 3-5 for some indicators of religious observance by subgroup and geographical area.)

Given the mythology that has arisen around the national education system's capacity to integrate new generations of young French citizens, schools

Table 3-1. *Friday Mosque Attendance*[a]

Percent

Response	1989	1994	2001
Yes	16	16	20
No	83	84	79

Source: "L'Islam en France et les reactions aux attentats du 11 septembre 2001" ["Islam in France and reactions to the attacks of September 11, 2001"], Institut Français de l'Opinion Publique, HV/LDV No. 1-33-1, September 28, 2001.

a. Survey question: "Do you go to the mosque on Friday?" Results as a percentage of respondents of Muslim origin.

have been at the forefront of institutional France's encounter with Islam. The Renseignements Généraux, the domestic intelligence service, reported in July 2004 that teachers in some suburbs had encountered students who had adopted a "radicalized religious practice" and openly questioned the materials presented in history and science courses or refused to participate in school

Figure 3-2. *Religious Belief and Practice among Muslims in France, 2001*

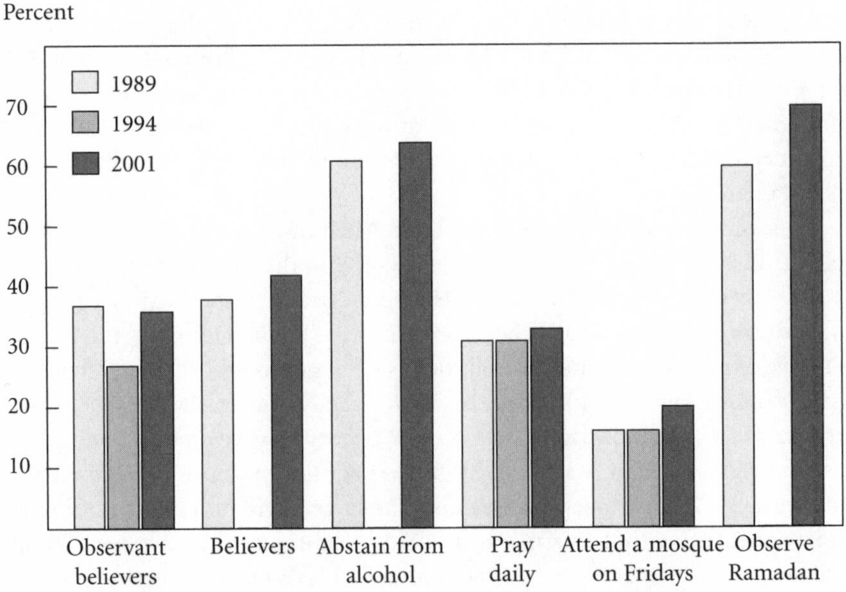

Percent

Source: Claude Dargent, "Les musulmans déclarés en France: affirmation religieuse, subordination sociale, et progressisme politique" ["Self-declared Muslims in France: Religious affirmation, social subordination, and political progressivism"], *Cahier du CEVIPOF,* no. 34, February 2003; and "L'Islam en France et les reactions aux attentats du 11 septembre 2001" ["Islam in France and reactions to the attacks of September 11, 2001"], Institut Français de l'Opinion Publique, HV/LDV No. 1-33-1, September 28, 2001.

Figure 3-3. *Fasting among Muslims in France*[a]

Percent

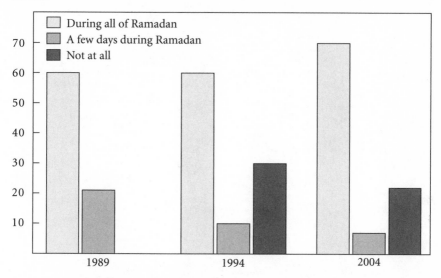

Source: Claude Dargent, "Les musulmans déclarés en France: affirmation religieuse, subordination sociale, et progressisme politique" ["Self-declared Muslims in France: Religious affirmation, social subordination, and political progressivism"], *Cahier du CEVIPOF*, no. 34, February 2003; and "L'Islam en France et les reactions aux attentats du 11 septembre 2001" ["Islam in France and reactions to the attacks of September 11, 2001"], Institut Français de l'Opinion Publique, HV/LDV No. 1-33-1, September 28, 2001.

a. Survey question: "Have you fasted this year?" Results in percent of the population of Muslim origin.

sports. The only "radical" religious practices were apparently limited to observance of *halal* (Muslim religious dietary restrictions) and fasting during Ramadan, though there were some cases of boys pressuring girls to wear the headscarf.[14] The tone of the report, however, was consistent with earlier warnings from some education professionals. In 2002, a collection of teachers' testimonials about schools in the *banlieues* was published under an ominous title: *The Lost Territories of the Republic.* The book claimed, for example, that in such schools it was impossible to teach material about the Holocaust because of the objections of rowdy students of North African origin. Some officials have cast doubt over the accuracy of those testimonials, however, suggesting that the schools involved were not beyond the point of intervention (see chapter 7).

Another, more controversial measure of personal piety or identification with the larger Muslim community is the frequency with which girls of

Figure 3-4. *Mosque Attendance by City, 2002*

BOLD CAPS: 1,000+
Bold caps and lower case: 500–999
Regular: 249–500
Regular italic: 0–249

Source: Hervé Viellard-Baron, "L'espace du religieux dans les banlieues: de la terre de mission aux regroupements communautaires?" ["Religious space in the banlieues: from missionary territory to community-minded groupings?"], in *Les Actes du Festival International de Religion et Géographie* [*Proceedings of the International Festival of Religion and Geography*], edited by Gérard Dorel (Paris: Ministère de l'éducation nationale, 2002).

primary and secondary school age wear a headscarf (*hijab* or *foulard*). Precise numbers are hard to come by, but the Ministry of the Interior has estimated that just 1,254 of roughly 250,000 schoolgirls of Muslim origin did so in 2003, before the passage of the ban; that figure corresponds with a Ministry of Education mediator's estimate of several hundred "conflict" headscarf cases a year at the end of the 1990s.[15] Other expert estimates elicited in testimony to the Stasi Commission were as high as 5,000 girls and increasing; one

Figure 3-5. *Mosque Attendance by City, Detail of the Paris Region, 2002*

BOLD CAPS: 1,000+
Bold caps and lower case: 500–999
Regular: 249–500
Regular italic: 0–249

Source: Hervé Viellard-Baron, "L'espace du religieux dans les banlieues: de la terre de mission aux regroupements communautaires?" ["Religious space in the banlieues: from missionary territory to community-minded groupings?"], in *Les Actes du Festival International de Religion et Géographie* [*Proceedings of the International Festival of Religion and Geography*], edited by Gérard Dorel (Paris: Ministère de l'éducation nationale, 2002).

commission member later said that there were 1,000 veiled girls in the Île-de-France region alone.[16] Even those figures suggest that the challenge that head-scarves pose to a secular school system is of undoubted symbolic importance but hardly epidemic. (The complex issue of headscarves and their signifi-cance to the principle of *laïcité* is discussed in chapter 6.)

Some observers fear the integrative function of national education is also being undermined by the growing influence of Islamic schools, but in fact that has not been the trend.[17] French law allows for state subsidization of teachers' salaries in religious schools following an observation period of three years if the schools operate under a *contrat d'association* (association con-tract) with the state, as long as religious instruction is offered separately from the full national curriculum and the school is open to students of all faiths.[18] But the number of students enrolled in Islamic education in France is tiny, under 200 individuals total. A far greater fraction of Muslim students (10 percent) attend Catholic private schools.[19] As a further measure of comparison, nearly 30,000 children attended Jewish schools in 2002, or 26 percent of all Jewish schoolchildren.[20] Some religious leaders predicted that the headscarf ban in public schools that began in the fall of 2004 would increase demand for religious schools. Indeed, the first private Muslim high school in Lille was conceived to respond to the needs of young women who had been expelled from their high school during an earlier "headscarf affair" in 1994.[21]

But more than ten years later, there are only a handful of Muslim schools in France. The only Muslim high school in France that has an association contract with the state is located in the overseas territory of La Réunion; it was founded in 1990. There is also Averroës, an entirely private Muslim high school in Lille, with forty-six students, and Réussite, a private Muslim junior high school (*collège*) in Aubervilliers, which charges its eighty students annual tuition of €1500, or around US$1,800 (tuition will go down sharply when the school obtains an association contract).[22] Two more *collèges* are currently in planning stages: Ecole Avenir in the Courneuve (Seine-Saint-Denis) and Maison des Enfants in Villepinte. A collective has begun raising funds for a private Muslim high school in Marseille, and the local branch of the Union des Organisations Islamiques de France (UOIF) (Union of Islamic Organizations of France) there also plans to charter a sixth-year class in September 2005. All of these schools aspire to obtain association contracts with the state, like the 95 percent of Jewish and Catholic schools now under contract.

Given the near absence of Muslim religious schools at present, many more can be expected to open in the coming decade. The administrative process of establishing a private school is slow and painstaking, however, and state support through an association contract is not even an option until the Ministry of Education has monitored the school for three years. (Local police closed three clandestine Qur'an nursery schools in 2003–04.)[23] In this light, an increase in the number of Muslim schools and their enrollment of thousands of students would be a sign of normality in a society in which attendance at religious schools is widespread.

Statistics on religious observance, mosque attendance, and Islamic schools do not tell the whole story of individual Muslims' relationship with Islam, of course. On one hand, their religious identity does not appear to be particularly pronounced, and small differences in the piety of Muslims compared with that of the overall French population have tended to diminish over time. But that conceals a growing trend toward self-declared identification with the larger Muslim community. In certain neighborhoods, proselytizing and social activities that employ religious rhetoric—even by nonreligious associ-

Table 3-2. *Approximate Proportion of Prayer Spaces
to Religious Populations in France*

Prayer spaces	Population[a]	Ratio of population to prayer space
500 synagogues	600,000 Jews	238: 1
1,200 Protestant churches	800,000 Protestants	671: 1
43,569 Catholic buildings and churches	45 million Catholics	1,033:1
1,685 Muslim prayer spaces	5 million Muslims	2,967:1

Source: *Administration*, no. 165, October–December 1994 (Paris).
a. Five million is the number of "potential" Muslims, whereas the number of Catholics includes all French citizens who were baptized Catholic.

ations—have led over time to young Muslims' increased assertion of the religious element of their identity (see discussion later in the chapter).[24] In that context, the expression of Muslim social and political solidarity may result, rather than overt piety.

Places of Worship

As an organized religion in France, Islam has a material handicap with regard to the number and condition of prayer spaces. For most Muslims the experience of attending communal religious services often has the feel of practicing an "underground Islam" (*l'Islam des caves*). There are approximately 1,685 Muslim places of worship in France, slightly more than the U.S. total (1,250) for a population of comparable size but much lower than in Germany, where there are 2,300 prayer spaces for around 3.3 million Muslims (see table 3-2).[25] The growth of the Muslim population has been accompanied by a natural increase in demand for prayer spaces. Given the occurrence of prayer times during working hours, Muslims first requested prayer spaces at their place of employment and where they lived. In the 1970s that meant car manufacturing plants and public housing (known by its acronym, SONACOTRA); today that practice extends to the provision of prayer spaces for Muslim employees of Disneyland Paris.

There are just twenty mosques in all of France that can accommodate more than 1,000 attendees; fifty-four are big enough to hold between 500 and 1,000 people. Two-thirds of prayer spaces, however, are converted rooms—"micromosques"—in housing projects, garages, or even basements, whose capacity often does not exceed fifty people. In the most popular prayer spaces, there is regularly a spillover of prayer rugs onto adjoining courtyards or even sidewalks. Thus, at present the typical places of worship are improvised and are not identifiable as mosques from the outside. A local religious businessman, for example, may simply rent a storefront and lay down some rugs. Just 120 spaces have been refurbished as "permanent prayer rooms," and only ten mosques were actually built from the ground up, though that number is expected to rise.[26] The editor of a guide to France's mosques said that only thirty or so basement prayer spaces were still in operation in 2004; he expected that demand for places of worship would lead to a total of 3,000 Muslim prayer spaces over time.[27]

Politicians, bureaucrats, and Muslim leaders alike have deplored the lack of appropriate physical facilities in which to practice Islam. A former director of the Fonds d'Action Sociale (FAS) (Social Action Fund) described the state of Muslim prayer spaces in the following vivid way: "You'll find garages, basements in housing projects, two or three bedrooms in workers' hostels, with torn pieces of carpet on the floor, unheated—it is undignified. For those who wish to practice the religion, it is very humiliating."[28] Half of Marseille's seventy-three prayer spaces, for example, were thought to be without hot water or proper plumbing.[29] "It is indecent that Muslims are constrained to pray in prayer spaces incompatible with their devotion," said Jean-Pierre Chevènement, interior minister from 1997 to 2000. "I am aware of the legal difficulties that undermine state intervention in this area. But I also know the ravages provoked by feelings of humiliation; it would be unjust to let them fester."

As Nicolas Sarkozy would later state, it is not minarets that the French people should fear, but garages and basements.[30] By the end of 2004, however, it was generally estimated that only thirty to fifty prayer spaces of the total of 1,685 were linked to (mostly Salafi) "radical movements."[31] Although the number of radical prayer spaces in the Paris region had increased from seven in 2000 to thirty-two in 2003, the Ministry of the Interior claimed that "targeted operations" in 2003 and 2004—deportations of imams and closings of prayer spaces spearheaded by a special antiradicalism task force—reduced that number to twenty.[32]

Funds from foreign governments and other private donations channeled through the major Muslim organizations often pay the salaries of trained imams and the rent for prayer spaces. In addition, a handful of new mosques have been indirectly subsidized by municipal budgets, such as those in Lyon, Montpellier, Rennes, Colmar, and Creteil, as well as older mosques like the Grande Mosquée de Paris (Great Mosque of Paris). Moreover, under a 1961 law, city governments can grant a *bail emphytéotique,* a ninety-nine-year lease on public space to religious groups in exchange for a symbolic fee of one euro. Municipalities typically have preferred to support modest prayer rooms rather than large mosques, which require consensus among competing influences in the local Muslim community as well as the mosque's neighbors. "We do not want to create a cathedral-like mosque," said a local official in the eighteenth arrondissement of Paris in 2004, where the city hall helped to open two small prayer rooms instead.

Approximately two-thirds (1,126) of the 1,685 prayer spaces are run by formally chartered associations, which are regulated by the 1901 law on associations. They therefore are eligible for subsidies from the Social Action Fund and from local authorities, and they may participate in elections for the Conseil Français du Culte Musulman (CFCM) (French Council of the Muslim Religion), as virtually all (1,121) chose to do in spring 2005.[33] Their eligibility for funding is the result of an early strategy of the Ministry of the Interior to bypass religious funding restrictions. In a 1991 parliamentary report, Philippe Marchand (a Socialist member of parliament and former interior minister) recommended that mayors encourage Muslim associations to register under the 1901 law so that they could receive municipal subsidies.[34] The practical effect of creating 1901 law associations, reliant as they are on city councils for budgetary scraps, is that mosque construction remains vulnerable to politicization by local governments.

New mosque construction proposals seeking zoning approval or local support usually include minarets and amplifiers to broadcast calls to prayer from the muezzin. Those features are the source of much local strife over the visibility and audibility of mosques in the French landscape and the reason why many projects never see the light of day. New mosques have tended to include minarets with an average height of forty feet, but they are always located "in the banlieue, not in the city center."[35] The place of mosques in the French religious landscape is considered by some community leaders to be of great symbolic and practical importance. Dalil Boubakeur, rector of the Great Mosque of Paris, lamented that "when you discourage the emergence of a visible religion, you encourage the more extremist elements, feeding the problem of young people's oppositional relationship to the state."[36]

Under the 1905 law separating church and state, associations can also be recognized as tax-exempt *associations cultuelles* (associations for the practice of religion).[37] The chartering of more mosques under the 1905 law will move the subject out of the domain of local governments, such as elected city councils, and into the legal and administrative realm, which governs about 10 percent of Protestant and Jewish prayer spaces (see table 3-3). While he was interior minister in 1997, Jean-Louis Debré argued that Muslim associations should register under the 1905 law rather than the 1901 law so the state could "verify that foreign money in support of prayer spaces does not arrive stuffed

Table 3-3. *Places of Worship and Muslim Associations*

Place/association	Number
Cultural associations (established under the 1901 law) that administer prayer spaces	1,126+
Prayer spaces without any legal status	400+
Religious associations (established under the 1905 law) with prayer space	46
Cultural/social associations	c. 500
Total	2,000+

Source: Authors' compilations.

in suitcases," thereby making the funding process more transparent and conferring tax-exempt status on donations.[38] However, the 1905 law places restrictions on the nonreligious activities that may take place in the same physical space that the religious sanctuary occupies, and local Muslim associations are reluctant to scale back their numerous social and educational activities in the community, which are seen as an important part of a mosque's functions.[39] And mosques' dependence on foreign money for their imams' salaries and maintenance costs is still very high.[40] Compared with Catholic organizations, therefore, only a handful of Muslim associations (forty-six) have acquired 1905 status ("association for the practice of religion"), but it is worth noting that the same pattern is true of Jewish religious associations (only fifteen of 147) and Protestant religious associations (109 of 1,138).[41]

Some politicians and community leaders have suggested compensating Muslim associations for their late arrival by enabling associations for the practice of religion established under the 1905 law to receive state funds. "Islam has a historical handicap," complained Fouad Alaoui, the leader of UOIF, a major Muslim federation. That could be redressed, he suggested, by "a new openness in 1905 law status that allowed Islam to make up for its late arrival" by using French state funds.[42] Under the 1905 law, after all, the French state subsidizes the maintenance of churches that already were in place in 1905, but there were no mosques in metropolitan France at that time. However, the law does not subsidize the building of new ones, so it would have to be slightly altered to allow for subsidies to build mosques—a change that would have the desirable side effect of limiting the need for foreign financing. The idea of altering the 1905 law to allow for some public funding of mosques has been floated on several occasions by the center-right leader Nicolas Sarkozy and his political allies, but it has been rejected out of hand by other members of his own party.[43] Several leading intellectuals and religious leaders have recently come out in favor of changing the 1905 law, including respected Catholic historian René Rémond and the Protestant Federation. But there are strong forces in favor of the status quo, namely the Catholic Church and most mainstream politicians.[44] Given the sacrosanct status of the 1905 law, any modification would likely have to await Sarkozy's possible accession to head of government or head of state to rally the same kind of political will that President Jacques Chirac brought to bear in passing the law against religious symbols in public schools. Dominique de Villepin, who briefly succeeded Sarkozy at the Ministry of the Interior before becoming prime minister in 2005, pursued the alternative of creating a national foundation to channel all funds arriving from abroad and within France for the purpose of mosque construction, and that is likely to remain the preferred method of financing for some time (see chapter 5).[45]

National Origin and Ethnicity

Religious observance varies with national origin and ethnicity. Available statistics suggest that Muslims from sub-Saharan Africa constitute the most observant subgroup of Muslims in France, while the subgroup of Algerian descent is the least observant (figure 3-6). Around half of Moroccans and West Africans claim to be religiously observant, but only a quarter of Turks and Algerians say the same.[46] But ethnic groups within national groups observe religion differently: in a 1995 study by Michèle Tribalat, Algerians of Berber ethnicity were twice as likely to eat pork or drink alcohol as their Arab compatriots, practices considered *haram,* or forbidden, in traditional Islam.[47] Furthermore, while half of all Algerians said either that they had "no religion" or that they did not practice their religion, two-thirds of Algerian Berbers said the same.[48] This apparent Arab/Berber distinction does not hold across the board, however: Moroccan Berbers are slightly more observant than Moroccans in general.[49]

Overall, the degree of Muslim piety does not appear incongruous in France, where the baptism rate is 84 percent and where 60 percent of Jews say that they attend synagogue on high holy days.[50] One journalist and community activist, Hakim El ghissassi, has suggested that young Muslims, in particular, are in search of a common, visible identity, rather than religious purity: "Seventy percent say that they 'celebrate' Ramadan, not that they 'practice' it. Even those who 'observe' Aïd al-Adha don't actually slaughter a lamb themselves—they get the meat from a butcher or give money to charities."[51] In other words, religious observance often means symbolic fulfillment of cultural and religious traditions, as often occurs among a religious minority in

Figure 3-6. *Friday Mosque Attendance among Muslims in France, by Country of Origin*

Percent

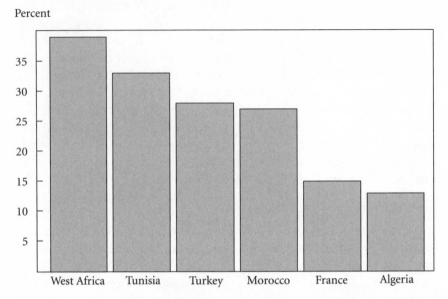

Source: "L'Islam en France et les reactions aux attentats du 11 septembre 2001" ["Islam in France and reactions to the attacks of September 11, 2001"], Institut Français de l'Opinion Publique, HV/LDV No. 1-33-1, September 28, 2001.

diaspora. El ghissassi argues that most French Muslims know that less than 5 percent of meat carrying the "halal" label is from animals that have been slaughtered according to the prescribed religious ritual, and the national department of consumer affairs has even closed some slaughterhouses for fraud.[52] Yet France's 3,500 halal butchers do a brisk business, including 1,250 in the Paris region alone. Muslims generally shop in the same stores as non-Muslims, though a popular supermarket franchise (Franprix) opened a halal branch in Evry in 2002 that did not carry pork and alcohol (it was later pressured to expand its inventory), and a kosher branch of the same supermarket chain opened in Paris in the early 1990s. A Carrefour supermarket opened a halal branch in Marseille a few years before the Evry Franprix.[53]

Re-Islamization and Redefining Citizenship: From Algerians to *Beurs* to Muslims

The local development of Muslim associations in France has taken place amid competition between "homeland" organizations and international Muslim

Table 3-4. *Three Phases of Immigrant Associations*

Generation	Central issue	Label	Typical organization	Event
First (1974–82)	Minority rights	Immigrant activist	Movement of Arab workers	1972 anti-racism law
Second (French-born) 1980s	Integration/ citizenship	Civic *beur*	SOS Racisme/ France Plus	Marche pour l'Egalité et contre le Racisme
Third 1990s	Religious recognition/ community rights	Muslim	Prayer space/ Conseil Français du Culte Musulman	Headscarf

networks active in Europe. French political scientists suggest that three generations of immigrant associations can be distinguished (see table 3-4).[54]

The first generation, in the 1960s and 1970s, was born of the workers' movements and trade unionism of the 1970s. It was largely secular and concerned with legal rights, and it can be described as marking the progression from immigration to citizenship. Home country associations like l'Association des Marocains en France, Association des Travailleurs Tunisiens, and Association des Travailleurs Turcs mobilized the male population around homeland issues and in defense of immigrants' rights (visas, residence permits, and social rights, though occasionally political rights and citizenship, too).[55]

The second generation cut its teeth in the civic-minded *beur* movement, which began in 1983–84 in response to racism, discrimination, and the early electoral victories of the Front National. This generation—which was defined by its willingness to integrate with mainstream French society, its identification with victims of social problems throughout the world, and its left-wing allegiances—could be described as initiating the movement from citizenship to identity.[56]

The third generation has taken up less politicized themes. It could be described as beginning the shift from political to social aims, but it also has exhibited a degree of community isolationism. The French state may have unwittingly reinforced the religious aspect of this latest generation of associations through its pursuit of community leaders to participate in the French Council of the Muslim Religion, the representative body for Islam. The French government's policies did not single-handedly transform the grandchildren of labor immigrants into Muslims, but aspects of that transformation do reflect an official strategy since 1989 to incorporate the myriad

Muslim associations into a formal forum on state-religion relations (see chapter 5).

Re-Islamization—the increased religious consciousness among younger generations—may also be a consequence of social exclusion and economic hardship, along with the fact that often young Muslims learn about their culture of origin from foreign imams (see chapter 4). Re-Islamization is now a well-documented phenomenon. It can be understood as the process whereby French youth of African, Turkish, or Middle Eastern origin turn to Islam in their search for identity—and often, but not always, to a form of abstract and globalized Islam rather than the "family Islam" of their parents. In their 2005 study, Vincent Tiberj and Sylvain Brouard found clear statistical signs of this increased interest in religion. Not only do self-declared Muslims say that they give more importance to religion than before, but a comparison with data collected in the early 1990s by Michèle Tribalat shows clear signs of an increase. In 1992, 30 percent of twenty- to twenty-nine-year-olds with two Algerian parents said that they had no religion, and the figure was twice as high (60 percent) when they were the child of a mixed (Algerian and French) couple. In 2005, less than 15 percent of the same respondents, now thirteen years older (thirty-three to forty-two years old), still said that they had no religion. And in a sample of twenty- to twenty-nine-year-olds in 2005, less than 10 percent, even children of mixed couples, said that they had no religion.[57]

One of the main reasons for re-Islamization has been immigrants' disaffection and disenchantment with the promises of integration. "Under the pretext that integration would occur spontaneously in the republican melting pot, we have ignored the problem," said Nicolas Sarkozy, the minister of the interior. "This strategy has been catastrophic because it denies the cultural and religious identity of Muslims. And an identity denied is an identity that radicalizes."[58] The recent history of immigrant youth from Lyon, to cite one urban area, provides a portrait of the successive phases of the immigrant experience. During the *beur* generation, fifteen young people from the *banlieue* outside Lyon initiated the March for Equality and against Racism, which attracted 100,000 participants, and the leaders had a meeting with President François Mitterrand. More than a decade later, special police forces killed a young French militant Islamist named Khaled Kelkal in a shootout in the Lyon *banlieue* in connection with a wave of bombings over the summer of 1995. Lyon also has become a bastion of the Union des Jeunes Musulmans (UJM) (Union of Young Muslims), a religious association with close ties to Tariq Ramadan, a Swiss scholar and preacher who has offices in a Paris *banlieue* (see chapter 4). In addition, some religiously motivated young men from the Lyon area traveled to Afghanistan throughout the 1990s, and two of the six French prisoners held for a time in the U.S. enemy combatant camp in Guantanamo were from Lyon (see chapter 10 on terrorism).

France's predominantly secular approach to integration and its encouragement of civic identity through the creation of associations under the 1901 law meant that many Muslim religious organizations had to be imported from elsewhere. For practical reasons, French and other European governments uniformly encouraged the involvement of "home countries"—in particular Algeria, Morocco, Turkey, Senegal, and Saudi Arabia—in meeting the religious requirements of immigrants in the early years of their residence in Europe. That involvement has coincided with the revival of Islam's importance in the international sphere since the 1970s, from the Arab-Israeli conflict and the oil embargo through the Iranian revolution, the Soviet invasion of Afghanistan, and the conflict in Bosnia. Saudi Arabian "Muslim diplomacy" was increasingly active, both through private charities and through Saudi Arabia's state-run Muslim World League, as were vehicles of Turkish, Algerian, and Moroccan state-sponsored variants of Islam. Many of even the most secular Muslim states institutionalized aspects of Islamic law to undercut support for Islamist opposition at home, which they subsequently exported to their consulates and embassies in order to inoculate émigré populations that might serve as a base for extremism abroad.[59] French openness to state-sponsored organizations from the Arab-Muslim world—which established mosques, charities, and foreign imam exchanges in France—was also a conscious decision to undercut the potential establishment of radical organizations on French soil.[60]

The reluctance of France and other European nations to formalize their relations with domestic Muslim representatives in the 1980s and early 1990s permitted the expansion of homeland-sponsored religious networks as well as proselytizing activity by nongovernmental organizations (NGOs) that targeted the new populations of immigrant origin in Europe (see chapter 5 on Islamic organizations at the European level). Three currents of re-Islamization can be distinguished:

—neo-fundamentalism, which emphasizes religious observance and reading of the Qu'ran as part of a global *umma* and downplays ancestral traditions (as done, for example, by the Muslim Brotherhood, an international Islamist organization that began in Egypt in 1927).

—Tabligh (based in Pakistan), a simpler and more charismatic brand of religion promoting "apolitical and puritanical" religious practice through obligatory proselytizing: it does not seek to combat secular society, but rather "to carve out a place for the formation of a 'neo-community' with its own ethical and religious norms."[61]

—Salafism, mainly of the Saudi Arabian Wahhabi strand: a literalist and rigorous Islam that aims to imitate the life of the prophet and his first followers (*salaf* means "ancestor"). Hostile to the Tabligh movement, salafists are themselves divided between "jihadist" salafists, who approve of violence as a way of returning Islam to its origins, and "sheikhist" salafists, who follow the rule of Saudi sheikhs and denounce the use of suicide bombing. Salafists in France often place direct calls to sheikhs in Yemen or Saudi Arabia to ask for religious advice on textual interpretation or on social and family life.[62]

Some young people find a safe haven in a religious environment that gives them a moral and spiritual framework within which to live. They find sustenance in the efforts of the numerous Muslim religious leaders who spread a new, distinctly European Islam through speaking tours and the distribution of sermons on audio- and videocassette. On the other hand, solidarity with international Muslim causes has sometimes been reinforced by satellite television from the Middle East, which often broadcasts brutal images of conflict in Palestine, Kashmir, Bosnia, Chechnya, and Iraq. A report by the Ministry of the Interior on "sensitive neighborhoods" noted that although "the integration of North African youth and the secularization of Islam is progressing throughout French society," the activities of salafist or Tablighi Islamist preachers in 200 neighborhoods may be undermining that process. "Radical proselytizing has been successful among young people and even children taken care of by numerous sports or educational associations (nursery schools and Qur'an schools)."[63]

Their practices mark the evolution from a lapsed "home country Islam" tethered to the ancestral cultures of North Africa to a "textual Islam" that relies on interpretation of the scriptures, primarily the Qur'an and selected *hadiths* (writings concerning the sayings and doings of the prophet Mohammed), individualized and adapted to the modern world.[64] Re-Islamization is not young people's discovery of their ancestral roots, since their parents' and grandparents' interpretation and practice of Islam often was mixed with local folklore and custom; furthermore, it constitutes a rejection of the politically sanitized state Islam exported from homeland governments in North Africa and the Middle East.

Re-Islamization of Associations

The dilemma for French youth of Arab origin is that they are not always accepted as French by French society at large, yet they cannot be considered

Algerians or Moroccans. They identify only in a limited way with either the civic *beur* associations or the homeland associations of their parents' native land. They generally know very little of their parents' home country and culture. In addition to its other negative consequences, the experience of racism creates serious identity problems: Who am I? What defines me? Where do I belong? That helps explain young people's increasing identification with Islam: if they are not accepted as Algerian or French, then they may see themselves as Muslims, and they may loyally (though sometimes selectively) identify with all things Muslim—including, for example, the Palestinian cause. If, in addition, they are disenfranchised and oppose the system, they are capable of becoming radicalized, especially if doing so fills a cultural and spiritual void in their lives (see chapter 10 on terrorism). These existential questions are especially important because the young people of immigrant origin now coming of age do not necessarily act as a bridge between their parents and French society, as other second generations had done earlier, thereby providing one source of mitigation of integration problems. Today's youth are themselves in the midst of an identity crisis. In a context in which many young people are victims of economic, social, and cultural exclusion, they may explore their religious identity in a search for their origins and a sense of belonging.

The reappropriation of Islam has taken place in the wake of the perceived shortcomings of the civil rights movement born in the 1983 March for Equality and against Racism. The increased religious presence in the *banlieue* can sometimes be a force for good, occasionally even offering community social services that compete with state social services.[65] Muslim preachers often stress the need for discipline and individual responsibility in their Friday sermons: "To be a good Muslim, one should pick up trash around the neighborhood, carry old ladies' groceries, study, go vote, and so forth."[66] Dounia Bouzar, who has referred to these young Muslim preachers as "the new social workers," gives the example of Amar Lasfar, the rector of the Lille-sud mosque, who during the Lille riots of April 2000 acted as a mediator and facilitated dialogue between the young people and the authorities.[67]

"Islam has helped many young people get away from a life of crime," noted the sociologist Didier Lapeyronnie, who conducted a study of immigrant neighborhoods. "Unlike many politicians, religious leaders speak to them with respect." "Islam has helped us avoid doing stupid things and put us on the right track," said one young man interviewed by Lapeyronnie. But there is frustration with the lack of recognition for Muslim associations: said one individual, "When we picked up garbage in the street to raise money for a field trip, we got two lines in the local paper, which gave an entire page to a vandalized bus stop shelter."[68] Though many researchers have highlighted the positive role of Muslim preachers who help discourage crime and delinquency, the Ministry of the Interior has expressed concern that preachers may also reinforce young people's feeling of victimhood. "Sometimes cultural isolationism is combined with the rejection of Western values to construct a negative identity that mixes homeland culture, neighborhood values, and only the barest knowledge of Islam."[69]

Bouzar, who was a member of the French Council of the Muslim Religion for two years, revisited her earlier scholarship on the religious discourse of "re-Islamizers," worrying aloud that a more pernicious textualism is gaining ground. "I always supported the struggle of Muslim women who used sacred texts to establish their rights, since they undid the male monopoly of speaking in God's name," Bouzar said in an interview. "But undertaking this study opened my eyes to the limits and dangers of looking for ready-made answers in the scriptures, which displaces actual reflection on the text itself."[70] In her examination of twelve "socioculturally Muslim" associations (not prayer spaces), she found that Islam was the "principal reference" used by all leaders to justify their participation in the associations and that they appealed more or less openly to religious teachings in their activities. That was true whether the associations were offering tutoring services or civic education courses or organizing sports events. Even associations that organized co-ed soccer, for example, justified it by referring to the Prophet Mohammed's camel races with his wife Aisha. While associations include men and women, norms of modesty are insisted upon, and "some associations separate boys and girls when swimming from the age of six. One high school teacher complained that "eating halal has become an obsession and a necessity to the point that it is now impossible to do field trips. Before, one felt a desire for integration. Today, we observe a self-imposed isolation and an unhealthy dynamic."[71]

But like any other participant in public debate, Bouzar has her critics: "Bouzar has done what de Villepin [then the minister of the interior] could only dream of," wrote Fouad Immarraine, a founder of the association Approches 92. "She plays into the 'possible nightmare' scenario: an Islamic republic in our *banlieue*," Immarraine complained. "But it is inaccurate to speak of Islamists trying to indoctrinate the youth of our *banlieue* and make them stray from the path of republican integration."[72] French sociologists agree that reality is much more complex: "Residents describe their neighborhood both as a place of solidarity as well as a jungle where people don't talk to one another."[73] Yet there is undoubtedly some truth to Bouzar's assertion that "if there is such a thing as 'too religious' it is only because in some other category there is not 'enough' of something else." Along those lines, Lapey-ronnie noted that "twenty years ago, people [Muslims] still spoke about society and made demands. Today they identify first and foremost with reference to their neighborhood and do not believe that things can change. . . . The reality is an isolationist ghetto mentality, empty of logic."[74]

Re-Islamization and Religious Identification

The trend toward re-Islamization in associations does not appear to have led to a general increase in religious practice. As noted, rates of practice tend to be higher among young Muslims (those under twenty-five years of age) than the next age cohort (twenty-five to thirty-five-year-olds), marking a reversal of the situation of past decades. Dargent explains that that is not linked to declining practice rates among older Muslims, but rather to a generational effect. In recent years, younger self-declared Muslims have tended to emphasize their religious identity more than older ones, in their daily life as well as in their responses to polls.[75] It is worth noting that even nonpracticing and moderately observant Muslims are increasingly defining themselves as "Muslims": witness the "French Council of Lay Muslims" and other secular Muslim associations that compete with "observant" Muslims to establish a looser manifestation of Muslim identity in the public sphere.[76]

Younger generations demonstrate a high degree of identification with Islam, especially with regard to public displays of faith. In particular, young Muslims say that they are committed to making the pilgrimage to Mecca (*hajj*) and to fasting during Ramadan. The number of Saudi visas granted to French residents for travel to Mecca has increased each year since 1996, from 14,000 to more than 20,000 in 2005.[77] Three-quarters of Muslims under twenty-four years of age said that they observe Ramadan and intend to go on *hajj* "in the next couple of years."[78]

Even more significant than the level of declared religious practice, however, is the increase in "personal identification" with Islam. Geisser and Mohsen-Finan's study, discussed earlier, found that religious beliefs were "very important" for 85 percent of Muslim students but for only 35 percent of non-Muslim students (see figure 3-7).[79] A third of Muslim students said that they felt defined most by their religious group, much more than by their skin color (10 percent) or where they lived (11 percent). Only 4 percent of non-Muslim students felt defined by their religion and many more by their gender (24 percent) and place of residence (27 percent). Geisser and Mohsen-Finan concluded that although Islam was practically absent from the concerns of students of

Figure 3-7. *Students' Self-Identified Defining Characteristic*[a]

Percent

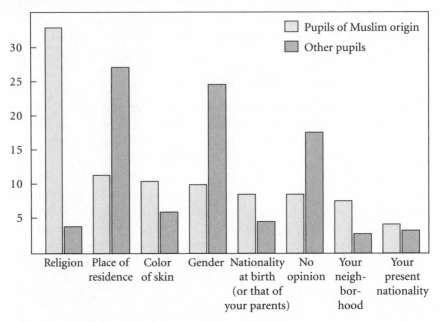

Source: Vincent Geisser and Khadija Mohsen-Finan, "L'Islam à l'école" ["Islam at school"], Institut des Hautes Etudes de la Sécurité Intérieure (IHESI) [Institute of Higher Studies in Internal Security], Paris, 2001.
a. Survey question: "Which element characterizes you the best?"

North African descent up until the 1980s, it has now become a major factor. Islam gives meaning to these students' daily lives and defines their identity in the public sphere. In response to the question: "Out of the following elements, which characterizes you best?" the study's authors found that students of North African origin were much more likely to define themselves by their religion than their non-Muslim classmates.[80]

Mohsen-Finan and Geisser saw those students' growing identification and sense of belonging with Islam as a reaction to their non-Muslim peers, since many of them felt that others viewed them first of all as Muslims. Considering the tendency of many respondents to give idealized answers to the questions of an external observer, the authors strongly doubted that 11.9 percent of Muslim students actually attended a religious service every day, as claimed (compared with 2.5 percent of other students), and they questioned the

25.7 percent who stated that they visited a place of worship every week (compared with 7.4 percent of non-Muslim students). But in general their findings are consistent with other observations of a general trend toward the emergence of a Muslim community identity and hint at the extent to which re-Islamizers may operate on fertile ground.

4 | Islamic Organizations and Leaders in France

There has always been a tension in French politics between the ideal of an unmediated relationship between citizen and state, on one hand (de Gaulle famously denounced political parties as the "dividing forces of the Republic") and, on the other, the right of citizens to form interest groups, whether based on class or a common ideology. Rousseau's legacy of the *volonté générale* (general will) and the Revolution's rejection of feudal society and the guilds of the *ancien régime* culminated in the passage in 1791 of the Chapelier law, which prohibited the creation of civil associations. Yet French governments have recognized the usefulness of civil associations and representative groups since the Waldeck-Rousseau law legalized trade unions in the 1880s, and the right to form such associations was enshrined in law in 1901. Private citizens founded thousands of such "1901 law associations" each year, and by the turn of the twenty-first century there were more than 750,000 civil organizations.[1] The 1905 law separating church and state created a category of associations for the practice of religion (*associations cultuelles*). "Tocqueville's revenge," as one scholar has called it, was France's belated discovery of civil society's utility in achieving certain government goals.[2] As Stanley Hoffmann argued in a seminal study of post–World War II French politics, "French governments need [the] advice of those affected by public policy in order to formulate it and [they need to] cooperate with groups if policy is to be implemented effectively."[3] That governments increasingly turn to civil society to make policy is a trend that has undermined the concept of an indivisible "general will" in fact and in practice, although that has had little impact on theoretical discussions of ideal citizen-state relations.

After the Socialists liberalized association law in 1981, allowing immigrants the same rights as citizens under the 1901 law on associations, the first generation of Muslims in France took full advantage of the civil rights afforded them by the law. Most of the new associations affiliated themselves with transnational networks, whether led by foreign governments or spearheaded by international nongovernmental organizations (NGOs). When planning the Conseil Français du Culte Musulman (CFCM) (French Council of the Muslim Religion) in the late 1990s, French administrators faced an array of more than 1,600 prayer space associations and dozens of elites claiming leadership roles in the Muslim community. A small group of a dozen or so public figures has emerged from this field of national and transnational religious associations. Because these leaders' public statements and private meetings may have repercussions in Muslim countries as well as in France, they can be scrutinized for what they reveal about tectonic shifts within "global Islam." While some of the leaders have been successfully cajoled to participate in national representative bodies, others elude attempts to box them into a single national political framework. The trajectory of Islam's "institutionalization"—as historic a process as the emancipation and recognition of Jewish communities across Europe in the nineteenth century—will depend largely on the international struggle to "represent" Muslims in the administration of religious affairs *and* in public debate. Since policy toward religious communities is made at the national level, the nation-state framework is the right place to look for developments. But since religious networks and theological debates are inherently cross-border phenomena, governments that nurture local interlocutors cannot (and do not) ignore the international implications of their actions.

Approximately 60 percent of Muslim associations in France have joined one of three main umbrella organizations (federations) that, along with their leaders, constitute the public face—and the informal negotiating team—of Islam in France: Algerian-dominated Grande Mosquée de Paris (GMP) (Great Mosque of Paris); Moroccan-dominated Fédération Nationale des Musulmans de France (FNMF) (National Federation of Muslims of France); and the Union des Organisations Islamiques de France (UOIF) (Union of Islamic Organizations of France), which is loosely associated with the Egyptian Muslim Brotherhood. These organizations have "centerpiece" prayer spaces, and they use membership dues and foreign grants to rent smaller spaces (see table 4-1).[4] The aggregate membership of the federations probably does not exceed 10 to 15 percent of Muslims in France, at most; they "represent" Muslims to about the same degree that trade unions can be said to represent French workers. On the other hand, they may represent many of the 8 to 15 percent of observant Muslims who regularly frequent the prayer spaces that belong to the organizations. It should be noted that alongside these major federations, many nonreligious associations have been created to represent immigrants or "secular" Muslims (*laïcs*) in all their social and cultural diversity; these unaffiliated groups claim to speak on behalf of the "silent majority" of people of Muslim origin in France (see chapter 5).

Foreign influence has been most evident in the realm of religious leadership. One of the major difficulties in creating a "French" Islam stems from the fact that most imams were born, raised, and trained in the Arab world—if they were trained at all, which is the case with only around one of every four.[5] Jacques Berque, an expert on North Africa, argued in the 1980s that there could develop a "Gallic Islam, just as there is an Islam of the Maghreb" but that it would require creation of a Muslim theological faculty and seminary to train French imams.[6] Indeed, there have been quantitative and qualitative problems with imams in France, and they contributed to the government's decision to publicly fund civic training seminars for imams at two Paris universities in 2004.

Competing Federations

Immediately after François Mitterrand and his Socialist party came to power in 1981, they passed a law reversing a four-decade-long prohibition on the formation of civil associations by foreigners. This general shift toward civil institutions allowed immigrants to join the proud twentieth-century tradition of French "associationalism." The change gave Muslims—who at the time were still largely foreign-born—the opportunity to charter religious associations to run prayer spaces and cultural organizations to support social and athletic activities.[7] Two new umbrella organizations sprouted up in the early 1980s under Moroccan leadership, in competition with the Great Mosque of Paris, each giving itself an ambitious title: the Union of Islamic Organizations of France and the National Federation of Muslims of France.[8]

In the wake of the birth of this supernova, another federation representing associations of sub-Saharan Africans and citizens from French overseas territories, the Fédération Française des Associations Islamiques d'Afrique, des Comores, et des Antilles (FFAIACA) (French Federation of Islamic Associations of Africa, the Comoros, and the Antilles) appeared and was later joined by a Turkish government–sponsored organization representing Turkish prayer space associations (see discussion of smaller federations below). Successive

Table 4-1. *Muslim Federations and Associations*[a]

Organization	Year established in France	Approximate number of affiliated prayer spaces	Approximate number of total affiliated associations
GMP	1926	200–300	200–300
UOIF	1983	200–250[b]	350–400
FMNF	1985	150–200	500
CCMTF	2000	150	150
IGMG	1998	100–150	100–150
Total		1,685[c]	2,000[d]

Source: The numbers given are based on claims of the associations' leadership and Ministry of the Interior estimates.

a. UOIF (Union of Islamic Organizations of France); FNMF (National Federation of Muslims of France); GMP (Great Mosque of Paris); CCMTF (Coordinating Committee of Turkish Muslims of France); and IGMG (Islamic Community of the National Vision).

b. Only thirty are under direct control.

c. Including about 650 unaffiliated prayer spaces.

d. Including 500 unaffiliated social/cultural associations.

French ministers of the interior have favored different federations over time. First among those that the government has relied on as an institutional interlocutor has been the Great Mosque of Paris. That can be explained in part because the (usually Algerian) leadership was at first viewed as the most representative and eventually as the most amenable to government preferences with regard to organizing Islam in France. The UOIF, in contrast, saw its profile increase when Nicolas Sarkozy was minister of the interior (2002–04 and 2006–), while the FNMF received more attention from then Minister of the Interior Dominique de Villepin in the course of his attempts to streamline theological training for Muslim clerics. The three federations, with all of their intricacies and networks of associations, perform a useful division of labor in terms of satisfying domestic and international constituencies.

Grande Mosquée de Paris

The Grande Mosquée de Paris (Great Mosque of Paris and Muslim Institute and Association of Holy Sites), which controls approximately 14 percent of prayer spaces, is the oldest and most revered Muslim institution in France. The French government constructed this religious sanctuary as a gesture of gratitude to Muslim soldiers of the Empire who died fighting for France in World War I. The mosque was built in the fifth arrondissement of Paris and personally inaugurated by the president of France in 1926. The large complex also includes a *hamam* (Turkish bath), bookstore, and a popular café where many Parisians and visitors go to drink mint tea. Although its first board of directors included Algerians, Moroccans, Tunisians, and Senegalese, it gradually came to be dominated by Algerians in the two decades that followed Algeria's independence.[9] In 1982, the Algerian government took responsibility for the GMP's finances: the mosque and institute currently receive around e750,000 ($914,775) from Algiers each year and perhaps another e100,000 ($121,970) in revenues from certification of halal butcheries in France.[10] The GMP is organized as a federation with five regional muftis, and it controls 250 prayer spaces around France. The rector has authority over 150 imams (around 15 percent of all imams in France), most of whom are "imported" from Algeria in cooperation with the French government. It won only six of forty-one seats in the 2003 elections for the administrative council of the French Council of the Muslim Religion, but two years later its share increased to ten of forty-three seats.

Although it is not the most representative of Muslim umbrella organizations, the GMP is considered the most moderate. Over time, the GMP in France became a de facto "second Algerian embassy," yet it has also served as "a useful bulwark against Islamic radicalism."[11] Its rector, Dalil Boubakeur, a former cardiologist and the son of a previous GMP rector (Si Hamza Boubakeur, 1957–82)—and the first French citizen to hold the post in the GMP's history—is well liked by the French political elite. Jacques Chirac paid him frequent visits while Chirac was mayor of Paris in the 1980s, and he directed municipal subsidies toward upkeep of the mosque, and in June 2004, Chirac personally inducted Boubakeur into the Légion d'Honneur (Legion of Honor). Successive ministers of the interior have turned to Boubakeur as the natural leader of French Muslims since his appointment as rector of the mosque in 1989, and it was easy to understand why when he was named president of the CFCM in December 2002.

Boubakeur has consistently promoted a theological stance that aims to reconcile Islam with Western society, in particular by challenging fundamentalists' self-proclaimed monopoly over Islam and democracy. A 1995 "charter" drafted by the GMP as a framework for formalizing relations between Muslim federations and the French government offered a shari'a-based interpretation of non-Muslim France as *Dar al-Ahd* ("house of covenant"), where Muslims can live their religion freely, and no longer as *Dar al-Harb* ("house of war"), considered enemy territory.[12] He has been an optimist with regard to Islam's ability to adapt to French society: "Islam is a dynamic reality, a religion and a culture that has combined itself with other cultures and that is now combining itself with Western democracy."[13] In the aftermath of September 11 and Osama bin Laden's calls for jihad in the West, Boubakeur spoke publicly of his "wish for a tolerant Islam, humanist, inviting the faithful to live with their times, to accept modernity. . . . We French Muslims say that it is time to stop ideologizing Islam . . . the calls to 'holy war' make no sense."[14]

Boubakeur has met regularly with visiting American Jewish groups and with French Jewish representatives. "We try to create links with French society and keep an open spirit of dialogue with other religions—our hands are outstretched to other religions."[15] He speaks out against anti-Semitism and has made pro-Israel gestures with comments such as "Muslims should see the return of Jews to the promised land of Canaan as God's wish and not as a political act of spoliation."[16] Boubakeur's openness to the intermarriage of Muslims with Jews and Christians earned him sharp criticism from the Armed Islamic Group in 1995.[17] He has been characteristically cooperative with government plans to ban headscarves in public schools, a stance that is somewhat out of step with other federation leaders. But he is not completely out of touch with his constituents. He was opposed to the U.S. invasion of Iraq from the start, believing that it would splinter the post-9/11 coalition in the "war on terror." In a wartime interview with the *Financial Times* soon after the invasion, he came out as a fierce critic of U.S. policy in Iraq.[18]

Boubakeur's coziness with those in power has allowed his rivals to suggest that he is somewhat out of touch with the reality of Islam in France. He has not always helped to counter that suggestion, notably by saying that the practice of Islam in the *banlieues* was "overexcited"; his words may have been reassuring to some, but to others they were an indication of his detachment. Although he is only sixty-five, Boubakeur is said to suffer from ill health. And although Algerians have traditionally served as the French government's official interlocutor for Islam, Moroccan representatives are slowly gaining power and legitimacy because of their numbers, good organization, and relatively greater degree of piety: as one Boubakeur adviser put it, "The Algerians build the mosques and the Moroccans fill them" (see chapter 3).[19] Boubakeur has therefore seen their growing influence on the French Council of the Muslim Religion as something of a threat to the status quo, and he clearly prefers a slow and steady approach to state-Islam relations. He has sometimes behaved erratically in his new function as CFCM president, resigning one Friday during the summer of 2003 only to deny that he had done so two days later, and he later threatened to boycott CFCM elections in 2005 unless the electoral rules were adjusted in the GMP's favor. Since much of the CFCM's claim to stability is invested in his person, that kind of unreliability could become problematic; however, it appears that he has usually struck such obstructive postures more as a bargaining tactic than out of a desire to torpedo the council.

His discomfort with the fact that members of the CFCM are elected is not hard to discern: "We want to create a balance among all the sensibilities of Islam in France, not based just on the voting booth but also on the general will to maintain harmony within the community."[20] On another occasion, Boubakeur targeted the rival Union of Islamic Organizations of France directly, saying that it "represents a reactionary school from tenth-century Baghdad that has been spread thanks to oil money. It is an activist and literal, fundamentalist Islam, which I regret very much."[21] It is undeniable that Boubakeur often tells the French government what it wants to hear, although he seems to recognize that his may be a losing battle: "The Mosquée de Paris preaches the Islam of tolerance—that is our vision, and we will defend it even at the price of our own sacrifice."[22]

Even so, after two years as CFCM president, Boubakeur demonstrated a growing ease with the legitimacy and importance of the Union of Islamic Organizations of France; in March 2005 he courageously took the stage at the UOIF's annual convention, where he might have expected to be booed, and gave a speech promoting Muslim unity and the importance of cooperation on the French Council of the Muslim Religion. He has never made a secret of his ties with the Algerian government, however, which continue to be a source of discomfort for many Muslims of Moroccan origin (as well as for Algerian Islamists who oppose the Algerian government).[23] During his campaign in the 2005 CFCM elections, Boubakeur appeared with an Algerian consul general in Strasbourg and rallied French delegates of Algerian origin to vote for the GMP: "It is not out of nationalism, but rather because of the social reality of special and historic ties between France and Algeria that it is necessary to unite around the GMP."[24]

Union des Organisations Islamiques de France

Headquartered in a defunct factory in the suburbs of Paris, the Union of Islamic Organizations of France is one of the main grassroots forces to be reckoned with in contemporary French Islam. However, it has struggled to retain its influence since pursuing the "clientelist" strategy of seeking state recognition and joining the CFCM.[25] The federation was founded in 1983 as a challenge to the monopoly of the Great Mosque of Paris and as a result of other schisms among "official" Franco-Algerian Islam.[26] The UOIF, which encompasses approximately 250 of the many cultural, religious, and professional civil associations in France, is the French branch of the Federation of Islamic Organisations in Europe (FIOE), which is headquartered in London and has twenty-seven branches across Europe. The UOIF won fourteen of forty-one seats on the administrative council of the French Council of the Muslim Religion in 2003 and eleven of twenty-five of the seats on the Conseils Régionaux du Culte Musulman (CRCM) (Regional Councils of the Muslim Religion); two years later, in the 2005 elections, it won only ten of forty-three seats on the administrative council.[27] It exercises control over approximately 13.5 percent of French prayer spaces (it claims to control 150 prayer spaces but directly owns less than one-third of them). The UOIF also runs a small theological seminary in a nineteenth-century chateau in Burgundy.

The UOIF's current president, Lhaj Thami Brèze, and general secretary, Fouad Alaoui, both were born in Morocco, and both came to France to pursue advanced degrees in Bordeaux; they have held their positions in the UOIF since 1992. Brèze holds a master's degree in political science, and Alaoui is a doctor of neuropsychology. Although the UOIF's two founding presidents were an Iraqi and a Tunisian, its administrative council is now informally known as the "Moroccan axis," counterbalancing the Algerian-dominated Great Mosque of Paris; only one member of the federation's administrative council was born in France.[28]

The UOIF rose to prominence during the first "headscarf affair" in 1989, when it offered legal counsel to the veiled girls who were expelled from schools in Creil and paid for some lawsuits to fight the expulsions. It was a main voice in protests against the government's plan to ban headscarves. These days, it is best known for its annual conference on Muslim life in Bourget, which has grown impressively since the early 1980s; it drew 5,000 attendees in 1999 and 30,000 (including the French minister of the interior) in 2003 and again in 2005. Outside some UOIF prayer rooms, one may find lists of Israeli products to boycott or invitations to donate to Islamic charities, and there is of course a good deal of solidarity with Palestinians on display at the annual Bourget conference. "Concerning the situation in Palestine, the UOIF has neither the mandate nor the power to enter into political complexities," President Brèze said in an interview. "And so we have decided to act on the humanitarian front."[29] But the vast number of participants and associations who attend the UOIF's three-day conference give the overall impression of having successfully integrated into the French religious landscape. They speak French in all its regional dialects, form associations to lobby French administrators, and help raise funds for the construction of prayer spaces and Muslim private schools, in accordance with the laws on religious associations and in the spirit of reducing the influence of foreign donors on Islam in France.

Part of the UOIF's dynamism comes from its rapport with young French Muslims. Star preachers sometimes come to the federation's headquarters to speak of how to be a good Muslim in a non-Muslim country, and their speeches are highly attended. UOIF affiliates include some of the most popular Muslim youth movements, including the Jeunes Musulmans de France (Young Muslims of France) and the Collectif des Musulmans de France (Collective of French Muslims), both of which are also connected to Tariq Ramadan, the charismatic Swiss preacher profiled later in this chapter, although each has put some distance between itself and the other since the UOIF's entry into the CFCM.[30] Another affiliate is Etudiants Musulmans de France (Muslim Students of France), which won 5 percent of votes in the 2004 nationwide university student council elections.

Like the Great Mosque of Paris, the Union of Islamic Organizations of France receives most of its financing from abroad, though Secretary General Alaoui claims that the amount has gone down in recent years.[31] Its representatives go on regular fundraising trips to the Gulf States and to Saudi Arabia, sponsored in part by the French offices of the Muslim World League and by private donors. Alaoui said that Gulf State donations composed only 10 percent of the UOIF's operating budget in 2004, down from 27 percent in 2001. There are conflicting accounts as to whether the organization receives one-third or two-thirds of its financing from foreign sources, but its directors speak openly of their wish to decrease their dependence on foreign funds.[32] The federation maintains a "policy of nonintervention" by its donors in its affairs: the UOIF independently owns and administers the prayer spaces paid for with money from Saudi Arabia or the Gulf States.[33] Moreover, the UOIF has sought to dispel any ambiguity regarding where its sympathies lie, and in 1990 it changed its name to the Union of Islamic Organizations *of* France (rather than *in* France) to affirm its affiliation with its adopted country.

Figures associated with Algerian Islam and the Great Mosque of Paris in particular have painted the UOIF as a Trojan horse for Islamic fundamentalism. "Why cut beards in Kabul if we're cultivating them in the suburbs of Paris?" asked one Algerian rival.[34] A French-Algerian appointee to the French Council of the Muslim Religion—the lone woman representative—even resigned because the UOIF was included, saying "I cannot accept for France that which I fought with all of my might in Algeria." Prominent members of the Socialist Party have also criticized the predominance of the UOIF; Laurent Fabius accused the government of "playing a dangerous game that is less a dialogue than a legitimation of people with an all-or-nothing view of religion."[35] Paris mayor Bertrand Delanoë also asked why "Sarkozy accords so much importance to the UOIF, the most radical force?"[36] Most complaints revolve around the UOIF's reported ties to the Egyptian Muslim Brotherhood (MB), though some have also linked the UOIF to Al-Adl wa Al-Ihsan (Justice and Development Party) in Morocco, which is headed by Sheikh Abd el Salam Yacine.[37] Officially, leaders deny any organizational links with the MB, but Secretary General Alaoui admits that he frequently meets with Syrian Al-Houweidi (a roving ambassador of the MB),[38] and President Brèze once uttered the Muslim Brotherhood phrase "The Qur'an is our constitution" in a newspaper interview, although the UOIF later denied that he had done so.[39] Yusef Al Qaradawi, a Qatar-based spiritual leader of the Muslim Brotherhood who met a controversial reception during a visit to England in July 2004 because of his stated support for suicide bombing in Israel and the insurgents in the Iraq war, was a featured speaker at the UOIF convention in 2000 and is reported to be the federation's preferred fundraiser among Saudi donors. (Al Qaradawi is discussed later in the chapter.) And Hani Ramadan, the director of the Islamic Center of Geneva (and elder brother of Tariq Ramadan), who became infamous for his defense of the literal stoning of adulterers in a *Le Monde* op-ed article, was invited to address the UOIF convention in 2006.[40] But UOIF leaders have sought to quell suspicion by placing themselves firmly under the rule of French law: "No one can say that religious law is comparable to the law of the Republic," insists Secretary General Alaoui.[41]

With the encouragement of the Ministry of the Interior, UOIF leaders have met occasionally with the heads of the Jewish umbrella organization Conseil Représentatif des Institutions Juives de France (CRIF) (Representative Council of Jewish Institutions of France) since 2002. Alaoui participated in a radio debate with CRIF president Roger Cukierman in June 2004: "We need to lift a taboo by having this kind of meeting," Alaoui told Cukierman. "I rely on my religious convictions, on my Muslim religion, to say that sitting down together around a table is a divine religious command." Regarding anti-Semitism in France, Alaoui reported having sent letters to all UOIF imams and association leaders to tell them that "anti-Semitism is condemned by Islam and by Muslims and that one cannot attack a Jew because he is a Jew."[42] One prominent UOIF preacher, however, admitted to having made an anti-Semitic speech, for which he later apologized (see chapter 9 on anti-Semitism). Theologians associated with the UOIF's seminary in Nièvre hold lectures and seminars that pursue answers to the question of how to be a good Muslim while respecting the customs and laws of the West. They also explore responses based on the text of the Qu'ran to the new moral questions and the needs that come with living in modern societies—for example, regarding dispensations for Muslims to get mortgages, to pray at special times, and to choose euthanasia.

Fédération Nationale des Musulmans de France

Based in the working-class suburb of Evry, the National Federation of Muslims of France was founded after association laws were liberalized to allow foreigners to form associations in the 1980s. Today, the FNMF claims to have 500 affiliated associations, which would represent one-quarter of all Muslim organizations in France. The FNMF is the largest Muslim umbrella organization, but it exhibits many internal fractures and is less well organized than the UOIF. It has close ties to the Moroccan government and considers itself the representative of the Islam that dominates the *banlieues*. It controls perhaps only 7 percent of prayer spaces, including fifty in the Paris region, though most FNMF-affiliated prayer spaces are located around Strasbourg, in eastern France. Although it recently experienced a serious leadership conflict that ended up in the French courts, the FNMF is led by Mohammed Bechari, a former student leader of Moroccan origin.[43] Bechari is flanked by two other Moroccans in the positions of vice president and general secretary, although after the organization was criticized for being dominated by Moroccans, a Senegalese, Chérif N'diaye, was appointed doyen on its administrative council. "The FNMF is neither Senegalese nor Moroccan nor Algerian nor Tunisian," N'diaye told a meeting of the council in 2005. "It remains a federation of French Muslims, whether the ambassadors like it or not."[44] In the late 1990s, the FNMF had the support of Martine Aubry, the minister of labor in the Jospin government, in a shift from the preference of previous governments for the Great Mosque of Paris. The FNMF saw its star rise under Minister of the Interior Dominique de Villepin (2004–05), though his predecessors had alternately favored the GMP or the UOIF. Because the FNMF does not already run its own theological seminary (unlike the GMP and the UOIF) and its interests in the area are less entrenched, support of the FNMF was crucial to Villepin's plans to create training programs for French imams.[45]

The FNMF emerged as another dominant force in the French Council of the Muslim Religion, winning sixteen of the forty-one seats open for election in the very first CFCM elections in April 2003 and nineteen of forty-three seats in the June 2005 elections. Its rivalry with the Great Mosque of Paris has been ongoing, especially as the number of observant Muslims of Moroccan origin seems to have surpassed the number of the faithful of Algerian origin in France. It has occasionally banded together with the GMP in an attempt to stymie the rise of the UOIF, and Bechari has proven to be a useful envoy within international political Islamist networks. Bechari appears regularly on Al Jazeera, and he has ties to the Libyan government through Da'wa Islamiya, a missionary association created by Muammar Qaddafi.[46] Sometimes his activities have threatened to undermine the CFCM's fragile internal peace, such as his much publicized visit with former Front Islamique du Salut (FIS) (Islamic Salvation Front) leader Abbassi Madani in Doha as well as with Sheikh Mohammed Hussein Fadlullah (an honorary founder of Hezbollah) as part of an attempt to resolve the crisis involving French journalists held hostage in Iraq in fall 2004. The meeting with Madani, in particular, created serious tensions with the GMP. Bechari takes pains to avoid being painted a fundamentalist: "We do not ask for the application of the shari'a. According to our charter, French Muslims must first obey the law of the Republic. But the Moroccan community is the most observant and therefore the most visible."[47] Bechari has acknowledged the presence in the FNMF of members of the Moroccan Justice and Development Party (Al-Adl wa Al-Ihsan), led by Abd el Salam Yacine. Bechari's international credentials lend him growing personal prestige but also create doubts about the depth of his connections to the French Muslim grassroots, and the lawsuits under way against him suggest he is on shaky ground with the Moroccan authorities.[48]

The National Federation of Muslims of France was initially founded to give a voice to French converts. Its first two presidents were French, and they maintained relations with the Muslim World League (MWL) until 1993.[49] In the mid-1980s, FNMF cofounder Daniel Youssef Leclerc also cooperated with the leader of the Turkish dissident group Milli Görüs (known under its French acronym, UITF) to create a line of halal products; Leclerc later went on to serve as French representative to the MWL. The FNMF's links with the Muslim World League came by way of the construction of the great mosque of Evry (which was built thanks to the MWL's sponsorship) under the mosque's long-time director, Khalil Merroun, who serves as honorary president of the FNMF. Merroun supported the election of current FNMF president Mohammed Bechari on behalf of the Muslim World League. Bechari's participation in a Cairo conference in 1997 sponsored by the Egyptian foreign minister marked his international ascent. He later led a delegation of French Muslims to Baghdad in 1998 to show solidarity with the Iraqis by protesting the international embargo of their country. Bechari has maintained ties with the Moroccan government, which has traditionally viewed the FNMF as a stalwart opponent of the Muslim Brotherhood's purported influence in the Union of Islamic Organizations of France. "There is nothing wrong with a country of origin aiding its community living abroad," Bechari said. "Morocco cannot decide or influence how Moroccan Muslims living in France practice their religion. But the FNMF is in permanent contact with Morocco—we receive donations from there and they also send us imams."[50]

The Moroccan government, meanwhile, in a reflection of its own domestic politics, is reconsidering its relationship with the FNMF. It has reportedly been involved in attempts to replace Bechari as the head of the federation. Ahmed Tawfiq, the religious affairs minister of the Moroccan government, held a meeting in Rabat in summer 2004 to discuss how the FNMF could better "reflect the evolution of the religious situation in Morocco," according to Hakim El ghissassi.[51] The meeting included Nadia Chekrouni, the minister for Moroccans living abroad (one-third of all Moroccans living abroad live in France), along with representatives of Moroccan prayer spaces in Europe, but Bechari was not present. In 2005, Abdallah Boussouf (former rector of the Strasbourg mosque) was appointed instead of Bechari to serve as vice president on the French Council of the Muslim Religion on behalf of the FNMF, along with Abderrahim Berkaoui, an imam in the southern French city of Nîmes.[52] The Moroccan government has also been considering how to shore up the FNMF with the support of Moroccan spiritual brotherhoods that had tended to ally themselves with the GMP.[53] "Integration is our objective," Chekrouni said in an interview. "But that need not constitute a rupture with the mother country. . . . Political representation is one of our priorities, because our strategy is centered on citizenship."[54]

Smaller Federations

There are several smaller federations that represent non–North African Muslims and Islamic associations in France. The French Federation of Islamic Associations of Africa, the Comoros, and the Antilles has been an important partner in the Ministry of the Interior's consultations with organized Islam; it was given control of the organization of the Aïd al-Adha festival, a major Muslim religious holiday marking the end of the annual pilgrimage to Mecca, on the French Council of the Muslim Religion.[55] There also are older organizations that control a small number of important mosques: Tabligh (Faith and Observance), whose French branch was founded in 1972, and the Association des Etudiants Islamiques en France (AEIF) (French Association of Islamic Students), which was established in 1963 and maintains ties with the Syrian branch of the Muslim Brotherhood.[56]

Turkish Islam is another realm where the contest between "embassy Islam" and the political Islamist opposition-in-exile has been particularly visible. Two Turkish umbrella organizations in France each have more than 100 member associations. One is the well-organized Comité de Coordination des Musulmans Turcs de France (CCMTF) (Coordinating Committee of Turkish Muslims of France), the French branch of the Diyanet İşleri Türk-Islam Birliği (DITIB), which represents Diyanet İşleri Başkanliği (DIB) (Turkish Directorate for Religious Affairs) and which gained one seat on the administrative council of the French Council of the Muslim Religion in the 2005 elections. The other is Milli Görüs (National Vision), an Islamist opposition group based in Germany that has a strong organizational presence in the eastern French region of Alsace. Local Milli Görüs branches have emerged as a major organizational force among Turks in France and Germany and elsewhere, principally as the archrival of the DITIB, whose foreign branches are the Turkish government's religious caretaker of Turks abroad.[57] Turkish Prime Minister Recip Tayyip Erdogan stated at a DIB conference in fall 2004 that he hoped that there would soon be a cleric in every Turkish consulate, with at least two religious officers to attend to the needs of Turkish citizens abroad.[58]

The DIB is the quintessential model of an "official Islam."[59] Like the Great Mosque of Paris, the DIB has a secular outlook and actively supports the separation of Islam and the state. Founded in Ankara in 1950, this special agency of the Turkish prime minister's office is responsible for the construction, administration, and staffing of mosques—60,000 clerics are on its payroll—the organization of Qur'an courses, and the publication (and censorship) of liturgy.[60] It underwrites construction, maintenance, and rental of prayer spaces outside Turkey through DITIB offices, staffing them with diplomats from Turkish consulates. The DIB indirectly controls half of all Turkish mosques—about 1,100—in Europe.[61] When its prayer spaces in Europe join the DITIB umbrella organization, the property is transferred to the DIB and is considered sovereign Turkish territory under the control of the Ministry of the Interior. The DIB's mission statement is to "instill love of fatherland, flag, and religion," and a portrait of Kemal Atatürk hangs in the offices or foyers of prayer spaces.[62] The French branch (CCMTF) was established during the late 1990s, when the Turkish population had grown to a critical mass of roughly a half-million, partly in response to the opening of a French office by its rival, Milli Görüs. However, since 2003, the relationship between Prime Minister Erdogan's ruling AKP party and Milli Görüs has been more nuanced than was the case with previous governments.[63]

The Islamische Gemeinschaft Milli Görüs (IGMG) (Islamic Community of the National Vision) was originally linked to the Turkish Refah party through the nephew of Refah founder Necmettin Erbakan. The nephew, Mehmet Sabri Erbakan, was general secretary of IGMG from 1996 to 2002. Its estimated budget of e40 million ($48,672,000) depends on individual contributions from its 20,000 plus members across Europe and private contributions from Persian Gulf countries.[64] Established in Cologne in 1976 as the Türkische Union Europa (Turkish Union of Europe), it underwent several transformations before becoming the IGMG in 1992. There are currently fourteen IGMG branches in Europe, including four in France. The IGMG defines itself in contrast to the DITIBs, which consider themselves foreign organizations operating under diplomatic cover, and which the IGMG views as an obstacle to integration: "We do not wish to be treated as a foreign organization or as a Turkish political party. We see ourselves as a community established in, concentrated on, and developed in the context of Germany and Europe."[65]

Muslim Organizations at the European Level

Transnational Muslim organizations and the diplomatic representatives of Muslim states are increasingly active at the European level. Other religious and ethnic groups and many NGOs and embassies have special annexes in Brussels to take advantage of opportunities to lobby the European Union there. The Saudis have tended to influence debate by way of the Muslim World League, a Mecca-based NGO, and the Turks have used their foreign offices (DITIB) of the Directorate for Religious Affairs (DIB). Another set of equally important actors vying for European Muslims' allegiances are the unofficial (that is, non-state) activists who challenge much of the "official" Islam preferred by homeland governments.

Though Europe's internal borders are increasingly irrelevant in some areas, such as fundraising for prayer spaces, the absence of a European-level religion policy has created little incentive for interorganizational cooperation beyond the nation-state level. There have been ephemeral attempts to create unified, European-level Muslim federations: in December 1996, the Muslim Council for Cooperation in Europe assembled thirteen associations from eight countries, including all the major French federations. The Forum of European Muslim Youth and Student Organisations also was established in 1996 to serve as "a platform for youth organisations to congregate [and] exchange information . . . to work for a better Europe . . . and to develop a

European Muslim identity, via the involvement of Muslim youth . . . highlighting their social responsibilities and contribution to Europe."[66] Dalil Boubakeur, president of the French Council of the Muslim Religion, stated in an interview with the authors the intention of the Mosquée de Paris to embrace a European perspective in organizing Islam: "The idea of Europe has superseded the era of nation-states, and there are now financial networks concerning cultural and religious life across these states. The disparity in national legislation over the financing of religion cannot last, and it will be hard to prevent Muslims in France from benefiting from the flow of finances." But he noted that a cross-border strategy for Europe does not seem possible yet: "We are still waiting for Europe to develop a common vision of all religions," Boubakeur said, "and when we are all better organized we'll discuss if what goes for Muslims in Belgium should also go for Muslims in France, or whether the current situation, governed by national differences, should remain unchanged."[67]

The largest single French Muslim umbrella federation, the Union of Islamic Organizations of France, is itself one of twenty-seven European branches of the Federation of Islamic Organisations in Europe, which is headquartered in the United Kingdom and presided over by Ahmed Al Rawi, an Englishman of Iraqi origin. Another key FIOE member organization is Yusef Al Qaradawi's European Council for Fatwa and Research.

Competing Foreign Influences

Until the late 1980s, successive French governments relied on representatives from embassies and international NGOs to govern and administer Islam associations in France. Apart from the Great Mosque of Paris, which served as de facto interlocutor from the time of Algeria's independence, the civil associations described above saw the light of day only in the mid-1980s. Four major reasons converged to favor interstate solutions to the question of Islam in France:

—the secular pragmatism of *laïcité*
—national security concerns
—ambiguity regarding the permanence of the Muslim minority
—trade relations and ambitions in the Middle East.

The hesitant hand of the secular French state under the 1905 law amounted to an invitation for foreign influence on Islam in France. There was political ambiguity over the permanence of labor migrants' settlement in France, continuing even after labor migration formally ended in 1974. President Giscard d'Estaing had drawn up plans to return migrants to their homes in the late 1970s, and one law promised 1 million centimes (€1,526) to Algerian families that returned home.[68]

During most of the post–World War II era, then, the French government encouraged the involvement of Muslim countries—in particular Algeria, Morocco, Turkey, Senegal, and Saudi Arabia—in meeting the religious needs of immigrants, for practical and diplomatic reasons. In turn, home countries with large emigrant communities have always sought to retain political and religious influence over their expatriate nationals. That policy is partly pragmatic. Moroccans living abroad account for nearly 10 percent of the Moroccan population (approximately 2.5 million) and foreign cash remittances to Morocco make up the largest portion of national GDP after revenues from tourism and the phosphate industry; within the Moroccan government, "remittances were clearly understood to be a key factor standing between relative solvency and economic crisis."[69] In addition, each national brand of Islam is in competition, ideologically, with that of its neighbors as much as with any conception of the West.[70] During the 1960s, Algerian and Moroccan governments supported *amicales*, religious clubs for single male guest workers. The Moroccan government even created a special ministry and several parliamentary seats in 1984 for members of the "emigrant community" in Europe, although their voting rights were restricted in 2003.[71]

The favorable arrangements for home countries also reflect the pragmatism of French and other European governments, which appreciated these states' adeptness at fighting Islamist radicals, since dissidents operating in the relative freedom of Western countries sometimes posed a threat to their regimes from afar. Also, the home states had experience ministering to the religious needs of Muslim populations and could efficiently organize mosque construction, the appointment of trained clergy, repatriation for religious burial, and so forth—all taboo topics in secular, postcolonial France when labor migration ended in 1973.

The usual interlocutor until the late 1980s was the Algerian-dominated Great Mosque of Paris, but increased European dependence on Saudi oil reserves following the oil crisis that year (1973–74) favorably disposed the French government to the arrival of the Muslim World League, which opened a branch in 1976. The Great Mosque of Paris served as a conduit for the moderate Islam promoted by the Algerian government, and government missions from Turkey's Directorate for Religious Affairs supported religious expression deemed compatible with *laïcité*. Morocco and Saudi Arabia exercised religious and political influence over their emigrant populations through special branches of state ministries of religion and foreign affairs and quasi-governmental agencies such as the Hassan II Foundation, created in 1990 by the king of Morocco to maintain "ties of allegiance with Moroccans living abroad" and to encourage "our community abroad to achieve its potential to enrich the development and modernization of Morocco."[72] This foundation does the bidding of the king of Morocco—who is considered a descendant of the Prophet and the religious leader of all Moroccans—in consultation with twelve government ministries. It coordinates with the Ministry for Moroccans Living Abroad (MRE) to appoint teachers of Arabic language and Moroccan culture for service in Europe, including sixty-six in France, seventy-one in Belgium, thirty in Italy, ten in Spain, and two in Germany; it also sent sixty-three preachers throughout Europe for Ramadan in 1995. The foundation had a e15 million ($19,160,548) budget in 1998, of which 75 percent was spent on teaching and administration in European countries.[73] The Saudis work through the foreign offices of Al Rabita al Islamiya al'Alamiya (Muslim World League), a funding source for mosque and education projects around the world (see box 4-1). The competition among governments is quite intense, and it is common to see alliances that would raise eyebrows in any other context—for example, Saudi and Moroccan interests aligned against those of Algeria—and there have also been instances of Saudi-Algerian cooperation (see chapter 5).

Today, private and public funds from the Muslim world to support mosque construction and imams' salaries are channeled to the four largest Muslim federations in France: the National Federation of Muslims of France (FNMF), Union of Islamic Organizations of France (UOIF), Great Mosque of Paris (GMP), and Coordinating Committee of Turkish Muslims of France (CCMTF). The financial stakes are not enormous; they provide perhaps only several million euros each year to support the practice of Islam in France. But the financing of these federations (and of the prayer spaces they manage) has come almost entirely from foreign sources. Throughout the 1980s and 1990s leaders of all major French Muslim umbrella organizations made periodic tours of the Gulf States to raise funds for mosque projects and operating costs. Saudis learned to appreciate the role of French Muslim associations—the UOIF in particular—in influencing Muslim public opinion abroad, for example, when it was necessary to explain the presence of foreign troops on the Arab peninsula before and during the Gulf War.

It is unclear whether such subsidies actually buy much influence, since the French federations enjoy complete organizational autonomy. When alliances do occur between French federations and foreign donors, they are

Box 4-1. *The Muslim World League*

The Muslim World League (MWL) (Al Rabita al Islamiya al'Alamiya) was founded in Mecca in 1962 as an NGO to support Muslim people outside the Muslim world. Its founders, a mix of Wahhabis and Salafists, aimed to undermine the diplomatic dominance of the League of Arab States and viewed the MWL as a religious counterweight to secular nationalist Nasserism. Under its charter its goals were "to make direct contact with Muslim minorities and communities wherever they are in order to keep them informed, to close ranks, and to encourage them to speak with a single voice, in defense of Muslims and Islam." The current president of the MWL is Prince Abdallah bin Abdul Muhsen al-Turki, former Saudi minister of religious affairs. Its fifty-three board members, who come from throughout the world, hold a board meeting each year.

The MWL has 120 offices worldwide and a number of subcouncils and institutions, including regional Islamic councils on each continent (the headquarters of the European council are in London); the World Mosque Council (its European headquarters is in Brussels); and a private Islamic bank, Dar al Mal al Islami (established in Geneva in 1981). Six foreign branches of the league are located in the Arab world, eight on the African continent, five in Europe, and four in Asia. The league's *Bureau d'Organisation de la Ligue Islamique Mondiale* (BOLIM) (Organizational Office of the Muslim World League in France) was opened in Paris in 1976.[a]

The World Supreme Council for Mosques (WSCM) was established to oversee mosque construction and maintenance outside Saudi Arabia. The WSCM provided major financing for mosque projects in Mantes-la-Jolie (€120,000 [$151,488] a year since 1997, plus the salaries for two Moroccan imams); Evry (€9 million [$11,361,600] between 1984 and 1995 and €90,000 ($113,616) a year afterward); and Lyon (€4 million [$5,049,600]). Every year, the WSCM receives ten to twenty funding applications in France, of which it is able to give financial aid to about four or five.[b] The WSCM has also provided major funding to mosques in Madrid, Rome, Copenhagen, Vienna, and Kensington (United Kingdom).[c]

The MWL requested and was denied observer status in the French Ministry of the Interior's consultation process with Islam in 2000 and 2002, but some have argued that the league is indirectly represented in the French Council of the Muslim Religion by delegates from the WSCM-funded mosques of Mantes-La-Jolie and Evry.[d]

a. Rainer Schulze, *Islamischer Internationalismus im 20. Jahrhundert: Untersuchungen zur Geschichte der islamischen Weltliga* [*Islamic internationalism in the twentieth century: An investigation of the history of the Muslim World League*] (Leiden: Brill 1990).

b. Thomas Milcent, "Interview exclusive du Cheikh Abdallah Turki, Secrétaire générale de la Ligue Islamique Mondiale" ["Exclusive interview with Sheikh Abdallah Turki, secretary general of the MWL"], January 1, 2004 (www.oumma.com); Besma Lahouri and Boris Thiolay, "L'argent de l'islam" ["The money of Islam"], *L'Express*, November 21, 2002.

c. "Islamic Centre in Vienna: Beginning of a New Era for Islam in Europe," *Muslim World League Journal* 27, no. 10 (January 2000).

d. Alain Boyer, "La Consultation des Musulmans de France" ["The consultation of French Muslims"], *Regards sur l'Actualité*, no. 279, March 2002; "Abdallah Turki, incontournable mais embarrassant" ["Abdallah Turki, unavoidable but embarrassing"], *France Soir*, October 8, 2002.

often fleeting; both the FNMF and the GMP enjoyed the temporary favor of the Muslim World League before going their own way. The administrations of the most important mosques have changed hands often, even between supposed rivals—for example, from Moroccan to Algerian control. The Al Haramayn foundation, which centralized private donations from Saudi Arabia before the Saudi government dissolved it in June 2004, reportedly offered to buy a school building for €480,000 ($584,000) to establish the first private Muslim middle school in metropolitan France in 2002 (at Aubervilliers). But, according to the school's director, Dhaou Meskine, who is associated with the UOIF's theological seminary, the donation was contingent on having single-sex classes, which Meskine refused. Meskine reportedly accepted a separate €15,000 ($18,250) donation from another Saudi prince, but he claims to have refused donations from the MWL.[74] It is also quite rare for a single government or organization to be the sole contributor or source of income. The central mosques in Evry and Mantes-la-Jolie, for example, received large donations from the Muslim World League. But Evry's mosque was also built with the support of the Hassan II Foundation, which paid for the ceramics and other decorations, and Libya contributed about €300,000 ($365,000) to the construction of Mantes-la-Jolie.[75] The mosques of Evry and Lyon also receive about €100,000 ($121,000) in revenues from their activities certifying halal butchers. King Fahd of Saudi Arabia paid for nearly all the costs of constructing the central mosque in Lyon, but the mosque would never be suspected of Wahhabi ideological influence: its director, Kamel Kabtane, has long been known for his links to Algerian Islam and the Great Mosque of Paris, although he has sometimes been critical of the GMP's rector, Dalil Boubakeur.

Nonetheless, since the beginning of its "consultations" with domestic Muslim organizations, the French government has sought to decrease the involvement of foreign governments while respecting the Republic's restrictions on public financing of religion. That has meant maintaining respectful ties with foreign funding sources while installing domestic controls on the administration of prayer spaces and on religious leaders through the CFCM. Future funding arrangements through the Fondation pour les Oeuvres de l'Islam de France (see chapter 5) may resemble the tripartite solution negotiated by the current government with Saudi Arabia and Algeria, which aims to direct funds toward the more moderate expressions of Islam in France—and thus away from the Muslim World League. The upcoming restoration of the Mosquée de Paris, for example, is being financed by three parties: the city of Paris, which will pay €2 million ($2,415,800); King Fahd of Saudi Arabia, who will pay €1 million ($1,207,900); and the Algerian Ministry of Culture, which will pay e600,000 ($724,740).[76] In a similar fashion, the Mosquée de Clichy will be funded by the municipality of Clichy, the National Federation of Muslims of France, and Morocco's King Mohammed VI.[77]

The Issue of Imams in France

Besides being in short supply, many imams in France today are linguistically and culturally disconnected from the French environment in which they operate. Half are over the age of fifty, only one-third are proficient in the French language, and two-thirds are on welfare.[78] "Imams are in great demand and fulfill their religious and social roles, but they are often discouraged by obstacles in their situation here," said Dhaou Meskine, head of the Conseil des Imams de France (CIF) (Council of French Imams), founded in 1992.[79] He continued, "Many don't have permanent residency, and too often the doors of army barracks, prisons, and hospitals are closed to them." For several successive French ministers of the interior, the creation of French-trained imams has been a main impetus for state support for the organization of French Islam. As Nicolas Sarkozy stated in 2002, "Imams are not adapted to the reality of French society and the needs of Muslims. . . . The current situation leads to clandestine behavior, which leaves room for extremism."[80]

A recent study of thirty imams conducted by a knowledgeable official of the Ministry of the Interior sheds some light on this population.[81] According to Bernard Godard, an adviser to the minister, approximately 1,000 to 1,200 imams are active in France, meaning that only three-quarters of prayer spaces have a dedicated prayer leader (see figure 4-1). Half of the imams are full-time preachers; 10 percent are part-time, and 25 percent are "Khatib imams" ["sermon imams"] who preach only on Fridays. The number has not grown significantly over time (there were 800 imams in 1995), meaning that there has been no discernible "parachuting" of imams into France by radical network or governments in recent years. Nonetheless, almost all imams in France are foreign born. Only one in five imams is a French citizen (most recently naturalized); 30 percent are Moroccan; 20 percent are Algerian; 13.5 percent are Turkish; and 5 percent are Tunisian. There is no standard appointment procedure: imams may be elected by their community or nominated by a mosque or embassy. Just under half are regular salaried employees, paid either by the associations that run the prayer spaces (22 percent) or by foreign countries (12 percent); the rest are volunteers or do not have regular salaries. For the most part, the foreign countries are represented by Turkey (the seventy-five Turkish imams sent by DIB are among the best

Figure 4-1. *Imams in France, by Nationality*

Percent

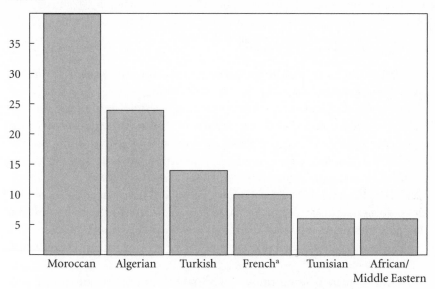

Source: Agence pour le Développement des Relations Interculturelles (ADRI) [Agency for the Development of Intercultural Relations], *Le point sur l'Islam en France* [*All you need to know about Islam in France*] (Paris: La Documentation française, 2000); Amara Bamba, "La formation des imams: le nouveau défi de l'Islam en France" ["Training imams: The new challenge for French Islam"], June 12, 2003 (www.saphirnet.info).

a. Many are recently naturalized Moroccans; this figure was only 5 percent in 1990. Xavier Ternisien, *La France des mosquées* [*The France of mosques*] (Paris: Albin Michel, 2002).

trained but the least francophone) and Algeria (eighty imams).[82] The Moroccan government pays for only two imams, and Saudi Arabia pays for the salaries of about ten former graduates of its theological seminaries.

Nine of the thirty men included in Godard's study had a university degree; five had traditional training "en Zawiya," a Sufi spiritual retreat; and sixteen were autodidacts. Notably, none had graduated from one of the three imam training institutes in France. Among the 300 to 400 imams in France who have received formal training, it is typical to have attended one of three universities abroad: Al Azhar University (Egypt); Al-Qarawiyyin (Morocco); or Al-Zaytûna (Tunisia).[83] Hakim El ghissassi, an expert on Islam in France who has launched several community publications and who also edits a website for Morocco's Ministry of Religious Affairs, describes five categories of imam in contemporary France:

—*civil servant imams* from religious institutes in Algeria, Turkey, or Morocco, who are on the payroll of home country governments

—*charismatic imams,* often self-trained or trained at Saudi, Syrian, or Pakistani universities, who arrive as students or political exiles and who affiliate with UOIF or FNMF prayer spaces and serve as interlocutors for French authorities

—*lecture hall imams,* who are hired by French religious associations to give public presentations and religious instruction

—*working class imams* for whom preaching in a small local prayer space is a part-time vocation and who may receive unemployment checks or welfare benefits

—*second-generation imams,* who were born or grew up in France and attended one of the existing French theological seminaries.[84]

Muslim federations and the French government have placed a high priority on domestic training of native-born French Muslims—the fifth type—so that they eventually can take the place of the "embassy imams" (*civil servant imams* above), who studied abroad, and of the less formally prepared local prayer leaders.

French residents—even those whose parents are native speakers—who want to become imams encounter linguistic obstacles because they cannot always master the classical Arabic required for recitation of the Qur'an.[85] Muslim communities therefore have had to import imams, a task that has involved the foreign ministries of several Muslim countries (for example, Morocco, Algeria, and Turkey) and even the independent initiative of the French Foreign Ministry, through special stipends known as ELCO (the program has been reduced, and there are currently only four ELCO imams in France); the Ministry of the Interior currently works with the GMP to issue three-year visas for several dozen Algerian imams at a time.[86]

There has been surreptitious monitoring of Islamic sermons in France for decades, as part of the state practice of maintaining oversight of civil society and religious organizations in particular. The Renseignements Généraux, the domestic intelligence service, centralizes and analyzes Friday sermons in all of France's prayer spaces, and those imams found to have used objectionable language are invited for a talk with the Brigade Criminelle (Criminal Brigade): "As a result, there is no more radical sermonizing."[87] A handful of imams were deported in the 1990s for exhorting their congregations to violence in sermons, but a study by the Ministry of the Interior of Friday sermons in 2001–02 concluded that "jihad is *not* being preached in French mosques."[88] There were clearly some exceptions to the overall moderation, however, leading the ministry to carry out a small number of highly visible expulsions of extremist Islamist figures between fall 2003 and fall 2005—thirty-four in total, including numerous foreign imams (most Turkish and Algerian), plus an additional eleven imams who were in the process of being deported.[89] This has led to tensions between the Council of French Imams and the CFCM, which was seen as complicit in the draconian measures.[90] The several preachers who were expelled had made public remarks condoning terrorism (including a preacher who had repeatedly praised the 2004 Madrid bombings), domestic abuse, or anti-Semitism. One notorious expulsion case concerned the salafist imam Abdelkader Bouziane in Lyon, father of sixteen and husband of two, whose deportation order was twice reversed.[91] Another occasion for concern arose with the preacher Hassan Iquioussen, who, unlike the others, was born and bred in France. Iquioussen had circulated an audio-cassette of a speech on Palestine in which he made several denigrating remarks about Israel and Jews, and his case raised the question of how to address the question of native-born intolerance, which obviously cannot be resolved with deportation.[92]

The number of scandals involving ill-prepared imams and the government's expulsion of those who had broken the law made it increasingly difficult to avoid addressing the issue of local religious training. "I want French imams who speak French," said Dominique de Villepin, then the minister of the interior, in an interview in December 2004.[93] Plans are now under way to create a semi-official Islamic theological studies and civic education program at two branches of the University of Paris—Sorbonne and Assas—that could eventually be equivalent to theology departments and Catholic institutes in Lille, Strasbourg, and Paris.[94] An 1875 law authorizing churches to open their own universities had led earlier to the creation (or reopening) or five Protestant and five Catholic institutes, which are eligible for partial state subsidies (about 17 percent of their budgets on average). These institutes have more than 25,000 students total in training in theology and religious ministry. But proposals for the Ministry of Education's involvement in the training of imams had repeatedly faltered in the past. In 1996, a group of professors created an informal theological study group under Etienne Trocmé, former president of the University of Strasbourg, in the hope of gaining official status at the Marc Bloch University in Strasbourg. Alsace-Moselle (where Strasbourg is located) is thought of as a good location because it is exempt from the 1905 law prohibiting public financing of religion (see chapter 5). Alternative plans for a theological department under the direction of the Ecole des Hautes Etudes en Sciences Sociales in Paris foundered in 2000 when the Ministry of

Education appeared to lose interest. However, the ministry commissioned a report by Daniel Rivet in 2003 on how to organize cooperation with other universities in order to establish an Islamic theological studies program.

Beginning in fall 2006, candidates for the position of imam in French prayer spaces will be "highly advised" to undertake a two-year university degree program. Currently practicing imams will be asked to take a shorter, six-month course. The course, "Contemporary French Society and Civilization," will cover "civic and legal instruction" regarding religion and the law in France as well as linguistic and theological studies. Readings reportedly include Rousseau's *Social Contract* as well as works by Montesquieu and Ibn Kathir's *Noble Qur'an*.[95]

The first Islamic theological seminaries on French soil opened a decade ago, but they are separately organized by rival federations and have not been successful in finding employment for their few graduates (see box 4-2). The imam institute of the Great Mosque of Paris, which is directed by the former director of the Islamic Institute of Oran (Algeria), has only around sixty students, but it is in the process of expanding. At present, the most important Islamic seminary is the Institut Européen des Sciences Humaines (IESH) (European Institute for Human Sciences), which was opened by the UOIF in 1992 at Saint-Léger-de-Fougerey, in the Nièvre region. The IESH has 150 full-time students in addition to 200 to 300 part-timers who take courses in Arabic language and culture at its recently opened Paris branch, which offers two-year programs. The FNMF also has plans to open an Islamic seminary, called the Institut Avicenne des Sciences Humaines (Avicenna Institute of Human Sciences), in September 2006, where it will train imams in theology and the French language.[96] Bechari, the FNMF's general secretary, traveled several times to the United States to consult with the International Institute for Islamic Thought (IIIT) in Virginia about organizing imam training (the IIIT also has an office in Seine-Saint-Denis).[97] Although the seminaries under discussion are located in France, none can be considered an organic expression of French Islam, given the composition of their advisory boards and the fact that their funding comes almost exclusively from the Gulf States and North Africa. Even the government's attempt to involve the CFCM directly in imam qualification has relied on a foreign component: in fall 2005, Foreign Minister Philippe Douste-Blazy flew to Cairo to ask Al Azhar's Sheikh Mohamed Sayyed Tantawi to coordinate with the CFCM president to train Muslim preachers "to avoid using religion in achieving political purposes."[98]

Many communities still prefer foreign imams to native candidates, because of their presumed religious authority and their advantage in the

---

Box 4-2. *Islamic Theological Seminaries in France in 2006*

Institut Européen de Sciences Humaines (Nièvre), established 1992
—Run by the UOIF
—One hundred fifty resident students and 200 correspondence students in
Europe
—Thirty graduates, including ten women

Institut d'Etudes Islamiques (formerly Université Islamique de France) (Paris),
established 1993
—Founded by a French convert, in cooperation with the FNMF and the MWL
—Offers evening courses to part-time students
—Ten graduates; 150-200 students

Institut de Formation Religieuse et Theologique (Paris), established 1993
—Run by the Great Mosque of Paris
—Inaugurated by Interior Minister Charles Pasqua
—Algerian government withdrew funding in 1995
—Directed by the former director of Islamic Institute of Oran
—Number of graduates unknown; approximately sixty students

University of Paris (Sorbonne and Assas branches), established 2005
—Run by the Ministry of Education in consultation with the Ministry of the
Interior
—Six-month to two-year curriculum on French civilization and religion in
France (not a seminary)
—No graduates to date

Institut Avicenne des Sciences Humaines (Lille), established 2006
—To be run by the Fédération Nationale des Musulmans de France
—No graduates to date

Arabic language; they also are less expensive to employ than French-trained imams.[99] The IESH is thus seen as something of a failure because of its inability to place its graduates in French communities; its imams often are sent abroad, for example, to eastern Europe. The UOIF's president, Lhaj Thami Brèze, has welcomed the government's plans to offer a university degree and said that he would encourage IESH students to attend one of the University of Paris programs: "An imam in France cannot afford to ignore *laïcité* and its history."[100]

The training of imams is of particular importance because the most learned members of the Muslim community will be the ones who eventually release *fatwas* concerning the conduct of Muslims in France—religious rulings on headscarves, animal slaughter, euthanasia, mortgages, divorce, and so forth—in addition, perhaps, to offering religious rulings on activities of geopolitical significance, such as suicide bombing. For that reason, many close to the French government want Muslim immigration to France to amount to an "opportunity for Islam," as Bruno Etienne has put it.[101] Jacques Berque wrote, "We must not miss the chance to synthesize France and Islam. We will offer to Islamic civilization the opportunity to progress by adjusting to modern society, allowing it to take root in an industrialized context where it never has before."[102]

There is already a certain degree of healthy theological debate on the status of Muslims who live as minorities in the West. In addition to its theological seminary in Nièvre (IESH), the UOIF has its own *fatwa* committee (*Dar al Fatwa*), and the federation is also a member of the European Council for Fatwa and Research.[103] The anthropologist John Bowen has reported on exchanges between French religious leaders who enter into debate with Islamic scholars from the Arab world over the acceptability or necessity of mortgages, for example.[104] These French leaders (such as CIF leader Dhaou Meskine and Ahmad Jaballah of the UOIF and IESH) argue that jurisprudence (*fiqh*) and law (*shari'a*) should be adapted to life in France today under the Islamic doctrine of necessity (*darurat*) and the principle that Muslim minorities may sometimes receive dispensation from Islamic law. One religious leader of a very popular mosque (Ad'dawa) in the nineteenth arrondissement of Paris, for example, advocates the "adaptation of scripture's principles or objectives to the conditions of life in a particular society." The rector of the Lyon mosque has said in a similar vein that Islamic jurisprudence "has always seen it as necessary to adapt to local customs." Yet, as Bowen points out, many reject overcontextualization as a dilution of their religion, and view Islam as having a "universal character," no matter where Muslims happen to live. He warns that "to urge that Islam stop at Marseille . . . would force Muslims to embody a non-Muslim version of French life." One former adviser to the Ministry of the Interior said that the French government would have to walk a fine line to avoid creating an official Islam, such as there is in Turkey or Algeria, for example.[105] He evoked French history and the danger that a *clergé réfractaire* (rebellious clergy) could emerge in opposition to the *clergé constitutionnel* (constitutional clergy) such as that created when priests were made civil servants in the nineteenth century. It is important to be realistic about expectations, of course. Even if French-trained imams soon preached in the thousands of mosques and prayer rooms of the country, the relationship between Islam and its clergy is highly individualistic and fundamentally different from that between other religions and their clergy. As one Muslim leader told *Le Monde* in October 2003, "L'imam, c'est le coran" ("The Qur'an *is* the imam").[106]

Competing Visions of a French Islam: Tariq Ramadan, Soheib Bencheikh, and Yusef Al Qaradawi

There is a new generation of high-profile religious leaders in their late thirties and early forties who are incontestably familiar with French culture and values and who are usually French citizens themselves. They are not university professors of theology, although they write numerous articles and books, and their voices can be heard on the hundreds of thousands of audiocassettes of recorded sermons that circulate among observant Muslims. Several stand out on the national level, sometimes overshadowing the presidents and general secretaries of the major federations. "The 'old guys' tend to have grown up in their country of origin, and are from a culture structured by clans that decide the place of the individual," Dounia Bouzar observed in an online chat in June 2005. "But young people born in France have learned how to say 'I'—as in 'I reserve the right to verify what the clan tells me'—and have been raised with a sense of autonomy in modern cities, and so they question a number of traditions."[107] The popularity and tireless touring of two UOIF preachers— Tareq Oubrou (Bordeaux) and Hassan Iquioussen (Lille)—attract large gatherings in Muslim communities around the country. This generation also includes intellectual media darlings such as Tariq Ramadan and Soheib Bencheikh—both of whom stand outside the framework of national Muslim federations—who aim to influence French public debate as well as shape the religious practice of Muslims. Ramadan and Bencheikh are profiled below, as is a third figure worth discussing in this context: Yusef Al Qaradawi, a much older but highly influential and controversial thinker, who is a ubiquitous defender of political Islam in international politics.

Tariq Ramadan is perhaps the best-known Muslim in all of Europe, denounced by some as a radical Islamist and heralded by others as the sole legitimate interlocutor for Muslim youth. Ramadan is very hard to pin down ideologically. He is not affiliated with any federation, although he associates with youth groups that are close to the UOIF (such as the Collectif des Musulmans de France). He has led thousands of prayer meetings throughout France and Europe since 1997, and approximately 50,000 cassettes of his recorded sermons are sold every year. He comes from a line of rigorous Muslim leaders: he is the grandson of Egyptian Muslim Brotherhood founder Hassan al-Banna and the son of Saïd Ramadan, an Egyptian dissident under

Nasser who went into exile in Switzerland and later drafted the charter of the Muslim World League in Mecca.[108] Although he has become an unofficial spokesman for French Islam, Ramadan is actually a Swiss citizen (married to a French woman); he has offices in Geneva and in Paris Saint-Denis as well. He began his career as a high school philosophy and literature teacher, but he was soon hired by the University of Geneva to give lecture courses.

Ramadan is an impressively prolific commentator and essayist on French-language Internet sites like www.oumma.com and www.saphirnet.com; he has written twenty books and more than 700 articles, and 170 of his sermons circulate on audiocassette and on the Internet.[109] He has been drafted as a spokesman for the *altermondialiste* (alternative globalization) movement, which is critical of certain aspects of globalization. In fall 2003, Nicolas Sarkozy debated him live on television, and Ramadan was named a consultant on Islam to the office of the president of the European Commission and, in 2005, to the British government.

Although he has promoted the view that Muslims in Europe live as a minority, or "under contract," and thus are eligible for certain exceptions to Islamic law, Ramadan does not fit neatly into the schemas of the Islamic scholars discussed above. Islam is not "just a religion" since it encompasses aspects of private and public life.[110] He does not seek to adapt *fiqh* to the European context, but argues instead that "Europeans must accept that Muslims believe in universal values." He qualifies that apparently standoffish position with the observation that "a sense of universal transcendence can coexist with a sense of human relativity."[111] Most important, Ramadan argues, is the fact that Muslims are adapting to Europe in the same way that other Muslims have done throughout history in an array of geographical and cultural contexts.

Ramadan is accused of being a "prince of doublespeak": essentially, saying one thing in French and another in Arabic. That accusation was largely discounted by a discursive study undertaken by Khadija Mohsen-Finan in 2003, but in any case Ramadan has made comments that some have found objectionable, including an ambiguous talk about suicide bombers that he held in Malaysia.[112] He wrote a preface for and commented on a collection of fatwas of the European Council for Fatwa and Research, headed by Yusef Al Qaradawi. In an article written for www.oumma.com (which had been rejected by all major French newspapers), Ramadan accused "Jewish intellectuals" (including some non-Jews) in France of having abandoned their "universal values" in defense of Israel and of engaging in identity politics.[113] He defended his finger-pointing by noting that no one hesitates to call him a "Muslim intellectual."

In the eyes of many observers, Ramadan's opposition to the headscarf ban in primary schools confirmed his status as a re-Islamizer. But he claimed that he seeks above all to avoid a Muslim communal withdrawal from mainstream society. He thinks that Muslim girls should be allowed to stay in French schools as they are and not be forced to choose segregated qur'an schools in order to wear the headscarf. He also has argued that lessons on Muslim culture and history as well as the Holocaust should be taught in history classes. Nonetheless, he startled many people in his debate with Minister of the Interior Sarkozy when he insisted that what he advocated was merely a "moratorium" on *shari'a*-inspired stoning of adulterers—as part of his "realistic" strategy for reform—not an outright ban.[114]

Ramadan has emerged unscathed from several allegations of links with terrorists, and he has waged judicial battles against magazines to keep his name clean of any accusations of Islamism. He was briefly banished from French territory between November 1995 and May 1996, on the recommendation of the Egyptian government, "to limit his impact among French youth."[115] The French anti-terrorism magistrate Jean-Louis Bruguière had accused him of facilitating meetings of the Armed Islamic Group during the previous summer's terror wave.[116] Because of the popularity of his speeches, he has had some contact with a couple of figures who later became involved with terrorism (Khaled Kelkal, Djamel Beghal, and a Spanish al Qaeda member).

Ramadan is an avid proponent of Muslim citizen engagement, and his public speaking often focuses on the responsibilities of Muslims in the West to think beyond their own grievances. The Bush administration denied Ramadan a visa to accept an appointment at the Kroc Institute at the University of Notre Dame in 2004, citing the Patriot Act and suggesting that Ramadan represents a public safety risk or national security threat. In an interview for a visa at the American embassy in Bern a year later, Ramadan told U.S. diplomats that he thinks "resistance in Iraq and Palestine is legitimate, but the means utilized are not"; he claims that he was then informed that he may have to wait another two years for his visa.[117] There is no public record of his having endorsed or espoused terrorist activity, and indeed he has called for Muslims in Europe "to work together with police and the state against preachers of hatred."[118] He has also called suicide bombing "contextually explainable," but he prefaced that remark with a condemnation of the practice "because it kills innocent people." In response to rumors in the Muslim world that Israel or the U.S. Central Intelligence Agency was behind the September 11 terrorist attacks, Ramadan told a Malaysian audience: "We know the attackers were Muslim, and we have to admit that. We should say that this is not acceptable and that it is not Islamic, and that those doing these things in the name of Islam are betraying Islamic teachings."[119] Finally, he has made it clear that while criticizing Israel's policies, he accepts the existence of the state of Israel: "The Muslim conscience must speak out and clearly say that anti-Semitism is unacceptable and that Sharon, while oppressive, is not Hitler."[120] Nonetheless, new books are published at a brisk pace that attempt to incriminate Ramadan and reveal him as duplicitous and potentially dangerous, and debate is sure to endure as long as he is active in the public sphere.[121] "Muslims who listen to Tariq Ramadan understand him differently, according to their personal, familial, political, and historical trajectories," Dounia Bouzar has argued. "There are some who use Islam as a social system in competition with mainstream society, and others who acknowledge that there will always be an interaction between his religious message and how they live in reality."[122]

Soheib Bencheikh El Hocine represents an alternative, less fiery vision of Islam in France. Bencheikh is a reform-minded imam who stands squarely in the Republican firmament; he claims to represent "the majority that has privatized its faith: a faith that nonetheless remains Muslim for the important moments in life—the birth of a child, marriage, the coming of death, the loss of a loved one."[123] The son of a former rector of the Algerian-dominated Great Mosque of Paris, Bencheikh is a graduate of Al Azhar University in Cairo and also holds a doctorate in religion from the Ecole Pratique des Hautes Etudes (School of Applied Advanced Studies).

His "base" is actually among elite figures, leading some to accuse him of seeing Islam through a "Paris prism."[124] He was named Grand Mufti of Marseille from 1995 to 2005 (though he had no mosque to go along with the title) by his uncle Dalil Boubakeur, the current rector of the Great Mosque of Paris. And Minister of the Interior Sarkozy named him an expert adviser with full voting rights (*personnalité qualifiée*) on the governing board of the French Council of the Muslim Religion. He favors a top-down approach to organizing Islam, and he has spoken out repeatedly against the Union of Islamic Organizations of France and Tariq Ramadan, whom he considers de facto representatives of the Muslim Brotherhood. He denounces "Wahhabis and Salafists who try to imitate the Prophet's example down to a millimeter," arguing that "this kind of subservient imitation is the root of Islam's marginalization in the modern world."[125]

Bencheikh aims to modernize Islamic divorce, make the headscarf optional, and declare ritual lamb sacrifice on Aïd-al-Adha to be nonobligatory.[126] "Islam's only choice is to espouse the era in which it exists," he argues, "otherwise it will be valid only for societies of previous eras."[127] Though he was appointed as mufti by the Great Mosque of Paris, he is no kinder to the official state Islam of Algeria or other Muslim countries; those expressions of religion, he maintains, "know no citizens, only subjects" and ultimately work against the state's own interest, as in the case of Wahhabism, which has come back to haunt Saudi Arabia. Similarly, he has said that many aspects of Malekite *fiqh*, which is predominant in Algeria, made sense "in an era when life was organized around clans, not housing projects." During the public debate over the Danish caricatures of the prophet Mohammed, he said it was "surreal" to see fellow Muslim leaders "pathetically asking" heads of government to apologize for the publications.[128]

But however alluring Bencheikh's reformism has been to non-Muslims, he has not attracted a popular following. He is a member of the French Council of the Muslim Religion, but he is somewhat marginal within it, given the strong influence of the Moroccan-dominated organizations. Although many French Muslims are unlikely to disagree with much of his worldview, Bencheikh does not receive a great deal of respect because he does not spend time in the neighborhoods where young Muslims live. He projects the image instead of a somewhat out-of-touch elite who inherited his position thanks to family connections and who was maintained as "Mufti of Marseille" not because of his significance within the community but because French politicians find what he says agreeable.[129]

Finally, the Qatari sheikh Yusef Al Qaradawi is an organizational force to be reckoned with: he presides over the European Council for Fatwa and Research (ECFR) (Conseil Européen de la Fatwa et de la Recherche) in addition to the International Association of Muslim Scholars (IAMS), both based in Dublin.[130] Though he has visited France infrequently, Qaradawi, now seventy-seven years of age, travels often to Egypt (he was trained at Al Azhar University there) and throughout Europe as a touring preacher, and he has his own satellite broadcast, *Shari'a and Life*, on Al Jazeera. He was received by London mayor Ken Livingstone in summer 2004 and was a featured speaker at the UOIF's annual convention in Bourget in 2000; he is also on the advisory board of the UOIF's theological seminary in the Nièvre.[131]

French politicians have taken note of Al Qaradawi's influence over the airwaves, both within their own borders and abroad. At one point during the French hostage crisis in fall 2004, President Chirac reportedly asked the Qatari authorities to help tone down Al Qaradawi's appearances on Al Jazeera (the station is based in Doha) and on his Internet site (www.islam-online.net), in which he frequently denounced the French headscarf ban.[132] But Al Qaradawi claims that on two occasions in 2004 and 2005, French foreign minister Philippe Douste-Blazy asked him to appear on Al Jazeera and call for the release of French journalists being held hostage in Iraq.[133] Al Qaradawi is often criticized for his personal (though not the ECFR's) support for suicide bombing as a legitimate act of resistance ("martyrdom operations") and for having spoken of Islam's coming "conquest" of Europe—"not by the sword or by armies, but by preaching and ideology."[134]

The European Council for Fatwa and Research, over which Al Qaradawi presides, is one of the only major European-level organizations with wide-reaching influence.[135] Founded in March 1997 in London and now headquartered in Dublin, the ECFR focuses on the adaptation of Islamic law (*fiqh*) to the realities of the Muslim presence in Europe, or what is called "jurisprudence for the minority." The ECFR functions as a sort of religious think tank, conducting research and issuing legal opinions on the status of Muslims in Europe. The ECFR aims to take "context" into account when setting the guidelines for the observance of Islam in Europe, and no more than 25 percent of the council's members can reside outside of Europe. Decisions are made by absolute majority of thirty-two Muslim scholars (all men), including five sheikhs from France, six sheikhs from Great Britain, and three sheikhs from Germany.

In its first book of fatwas (with a preface written by Tariq Ramadan), the council recommends that Muslims in Europe "work tirelessly to obtain recognition for Islam as religion and all their rights with regard to their civil status in marriage, divorce, and inheritance."[136] In order to accommodate Muslims working in offices, the ECFR has issued rulings that relax the strictness of Friday prayer times, allowing them to pray at 1:00 p.m. instead of the customary 2:00 p.m. during daylight saving time. Another ruling authorized a woman who had converted to Islam to stay married to her non-Muslim husband, and others have approved mortgages for Muslims in non-Muslim countries who were buying a home, even though paying interest is technically forbidden in Islam. A press release from the Federation of Islamic Organisations in Europe (ECFR's parent organization) immediately after the U.S. invasion of Iraq in March 2003 "welcomed the positive change in Western public opinion" (European opposition to the invasion) and stated that any fatwas coming from Muslim councils or Muslim leaders requiring opposition to the U.S. military presence on Muslim land "do not apply to Muslims living in Europe."

The ECFR has clear hegemonic aspirations across the European continent. Yet Qaradawi's council is a "leading, but by no means uncontested authority."[137] Non-Arabic speakers simply do not have access to many of the rulings, though some of the fatwas are available in imperfect English translation on the council's website. One scholar of the ECFR and Muslim authority in Europe observes that it is "difficult to asses the real influence of the ECFR . . . because its communications are in Arabic, [so] most Muslims in Europe have no direct access to them and at best become aware of its fatwas through intermediaries."[138] The ECFR's quest for religious authority is also challenged on several fronts: by the "private" fatwas of local muftis and those called in from abroad by telephone or published on the Internet; by Salafi criticism from within Europe and in the Arab world; and, finally, by the fact that the ECFR is still very much an Arab-language institution, which reduces its capacity to communicate effectively and directly with the majority of European Muslims. The ECFR seems to be somewhat on the defensive recently. Its sheikhs constantly emphasize that their rulings are strictly applicable as *fiqh al aqalliyyat*—minority *fiqh* outside Islamic lands—and thus are not intended to supplement or replace Islamic jurisprudence in the Arab world. It also receives criticism in the other direction, namely, that its thirty-two sheikhs do not know the reality of the younger generations well enough. Although a majority of the sheikhs reside in Europe, none was born a child of immigrants in Europe. In 2005, the UOIF declined to translate and publish the ECFR's second collection of fatwas into French, as it had done with the first.[139]

The French government's consultations with Muslim federations will continue to be the primary arena for formulating policy regarding Islam as the state seeks to address fundamental questions relating to its Muslim citizens' transnational relationships. Can any one institution speak *urbi et orbi* for Islam, whether composed of the sages and sheikhs of the Muslim World League or the thirty-two sheikhs on the European Council of Fatwa and Research? Given the decentralization of authority in contemporary Islam, do any fatwas ever really carry weight uniformly across the "*umma*"?[140] The decision to observe a given fatwa in the West, as Roy has written, is "absolutely personal and voluntary, not the object of coercion."[141] Nonetheless, French and other European religious actors have emerged alongside the reinforced channels of traditional religious authority. The responses of different European nation-states can be observed in their establishment of domestic theological training programs for local imams and the creation of leadership roles for European Muslims in managing their own religious affairs.

*From Muslims into
French Citizens:
Muslims and Public Policy*

5

Liberté, égalité . . . laïcité: Creation of the French Council of the Muslim Religion

The legacy of European colonialism in the Islamic world and the aftereffects of post–World War II immigration are felt throughout Europe—from France, Belgium, the Netherlands, Denmark, and Germany to the United Kingdom, Spain, and Italy. EU member states' stances on religion differ even more than their social policies or tax regulations: some have established state churches (Denmark, United Kingdom); some have mixed "recognition" systems with some public funding of religious communities (Germany and Italy); and some are full-fledged "secular" states (France and Sweden). In contrast to the situation in the United States, where the separation of church and state is formalized in the First Amendment to the Constitution and where religious entities are loosely governed by the laws on nonprofit organizations, religion in continental Europe is nearly everywhere a government affair. National ministers of the interior oversee orderly religious practice, for example, by regulating religious facilities (mosques, temples, churches, and so forth), and ministers of education may supplement clerical training through the national university system. Local governments award funds and permits for construction of facilities, and, where religion is taught in public schools, they entrust religious community associations with religious education. Other matters of religious practice also require state oversight: ritual animal slaughter, establishment of cemeteries, and appointment of state-paid chaplains in the military, hospitals, and prisons.

How are Muslim communities being integrated into the national institutions that govern church-state relations across Europe? When formulating policies that will have an impact on Muslims or on the practice of Islam,

European governments now generally speak to a combination of grassroots organizations, international NGOs, national federations, and the ambassadors of Muslim and Arab states. Each government faces a similar array of three to five domestic federations that have sprung up among its population of immigrant origin, divided along lines of national origin, ideology, and doctrine, much as in France. To this day there is an increasingly outmoded inclination to allow diplomatic representatives from Turkey, Saudi Arabia, Algeria, Morocco, and Tunisia to retain their privileged status as spokespersons for Muslims in Europe. Home governments send imams or money to build and maintain prayer spaces, and sometimes they even handpick the leaders of Muslim associations. Nearly all the few proper mosques that have been built from scratch in Europe have been funded by foreign governments—for example, those of Morocco, Saudi Arabia, Algeria, and Turkey. Nevertheless, European governments have sought to limit foreign government influence on the practice of Islam in their countries. Both the German and French governments have asked the Saudis, for example, to discontinue funding certain schools or organizations and instead to funnel money to moderate and locally based Muslim federations. This is only part of the story of how governments seek to "domesticate" religious practice so that a "homegrown" Islam of France, Germany, Italy, and so forth can emerge; they also have worked through formal political institutions.

All European governments with sizable Muslim minorities (those of Belgium, France, Germany, Italy, Netherlands, Spain, and Austria) have initiated consultations with a broad swath of Muslim religious organizations and prayer spaces, and they have pursued the domestication of Islam as well as of other major religious communities by institutionalizing church-state relations. The institutionalized interactions between Muslims and the state over as long as sixteen years have improved their knowledge of each other and have reduced the degree of formal foreign control over prayer spaces and religious personnel in Europe. Subsequent state accommodations of Islam—in terms of mosque funding, cemeteries, halal slaughter, religious education, and so forth—fulfill genuine material needs for religious practice as well as undercut political Islamists' complaints that Europe is inhospitable or hostile territory, claims that may otherwise be used to gain sympathy among potential followers. The consultations between governments and Muslims are recent, and the emergent Muslim councils are quite young, but they provide a blueprint for state participation and interaction with the major civil organizations and religious leadership of the Muslim minority.

Government efforts to initiate contact with Muslim associations have taken place in a piecemeal fashion, sometimes through local mayoral decrees, court rulings, and one-off deals. Some cities host relatively efficient Muslim councils that act as interlocutors on religious issues, such as those in Bradford and Leicester in the United Kingdom or in Marseille. Councils also have been convened for specific purposes, such as building a mosque or organizing religious education, in Lyon and in Hamburg and North-Rhine Westphalia in Germany. Individual associations have been awarded the right to teach religion in some German states, such as Bavaria and Berlin. Few countries, however, have held formal elections for a national representative council or signed a blanket accord governing state-Islam relations (as they have, for example, with other majority religions and minority religions like Judaism and Buddhism). Only Belgium (1999), Austria (1979), Spain (1992), and France (2003) have officially recognized Muslim councils and given them a representative monopoly on issues of religious practice; Greece alone has a national mufti of equal status with other heads of religious communities. Denmark and the Netherlands both are in the process of creating such councils. The Muslim Council of Britain, which is recognized by the state but does not have a monopoly on representation, excludes extremist groups, and it has proven reasonably successful; the Belgian Islamic Council, however, has erred on the side of state control and has had difficulty finding legitimacy within the local Muslim community.[1] The Italian Ministry of the Interior, which was not extensively engaged in developing an Islam policy until after September 11, opened a dialogue with "moderate" Muslims through the Consulta Islamica (Consultation with Islam) in 2005.[2]

State-Islam Relations in France

The history of state-Islam relations in France over the last three decades can be broken down into roughly two periods of "incorporation" of Muslim immigrants. The first fifteen years (1974–89) were characterized by toleration and minimal accommodation of the religious needs of what had inadvertently become, in a historic settlement, a sizable Muslim population. On the other hand, efforts to place Islam within the framework of national church-state relations over the sixteen years from 1989 to 2005 reflect the government's acknowledgment that Muslim religious leaders should enjoy the same rights and responsibilities as leaders of other religious communities.

In the wake of the oil crisis and the end of mass labor migration in 1973–74, the French tolerated the religious activities of foreign governments and international Muslim organizations in their territory. In that *laissez-faire* era, the French were uncertain of the permanence of the Muslim minority's stay in France, as discussed in chapter 4. A mix of secularist pragmatism, national security concerns, and diplomatic relations with the Arab world influenced French policies toward organized Islam. Increased concern over immigrants' integration into mainstream French society and Islamic radicalism soon put an end to that relatively passive arrangement. In the second period, therefore, the government used domestication and incorporation as instruments to target and transform the transnational characteristics of Muslim populations.[3] The exclusive reliance on foreign representatives in the 1974–89 period undermined integration by legitimizing foreign consular oversight of immigrant populations. It also stifled the burgeoning French Muslim federations and local associations—which often had a political Islamist bent—that had emerged in the 1980s to challenge the outsourcing of responsibility for state-Islam relations.

The government-led creation of the Conseil Français du Culte Musulman (CFCM) (French Council of the Muslim Religion) was an attempt to reduce foreign influence on France's Muslim population. Rather than simply tolerate the existence of Islam *in* France, the government has made it a policy goal to create an Islam *of* France—for example, to provide for domestic financing of prayer spaces and training of religious leaders and to encourage development of local sources of religious authority. The French government has internalized the vision of a Mediterranean "cultural synthesis" that has been promoted by French experts on the Maghreb. In the words of Jacques Berque (the former dean of scholars of the Islamic world) France is "a partially Muslim country" and should assume its *Islamicité;* the Muslims of France should, in turn, assume their *francité.*[4]

Helping Muslim representatives organize has been a politically acceptable way for the French Ministry of the Interior—a cross between the U.S. Department of Justice, Department of the Interior, and Department of Homeland Security—to make contact with local associations and prayer spaces, with the underlying aim of cultivating an organized religion that is more or less at peace with the state. The French government cooperates with the CFCM on appointing chaplains in prisons, designing seminary courses for imams, and regulating the sources of funding for mosques and religious personnel. The heavy state involvement is in part an effort to treat Islam as it does other recognized religions and in part an attempt to redress the religion's institutional "handicap" due to its recent arrival. State arrangements for religious accommodation and representation of Muslims have been modeled on existing arrangements for Jews and Christians. As with many questions regarding

Muslims in France, the government has abandoned its earlier passive and defensive posture in favor of taking an active role in shaping relations with its Muslim residents.

Several recent reports written for the U.S. foreign policy community characterized European consultations as naïve attempts to build a "Muslim church" and warned that the inclusion of Islamists in state-religion relations was likely to backfire.[5] Critics argue that political Islam activists are only temporarily deferring their political aspirations while awaiting numerical superiority and the establishment of an Islamic state: "Islamists may profess a commitment to democracy but only for tactical reasons. . . . [They] never espouse wholeheartedly democracy and its values."[6] Along the same lines, some observers have loudly criticized the institutionalization of Islam in Europe today as being fraught with pitfalls and dangers. Such a pessimistic outlook is premature and does not fully grasp the limited ambitions of Muslim councils: they are intended only to "represent" *religious* (that is, mosque-going) Muslims through the associations that run their prayer spaces—and only in the domain of church-state relations, not in social or political affairs. Most political Islam activists in France appear to be lawful, and in any event their activities fall well within accepted norms of church-state relations in their respective host societies. Muslims' making of religious and cultural claims in response to international and domestic events—whether in the headscarf controversy or during the furor over the Danish caricatures of the prophet Mohammed, for example—have been channeled largely through new and existing institutions, from French courts to the CFCM.

The Republican Ideal of Laïcité *and the Specific Challenge of Islam*

The institutional and political cultures of the Fifth Republic do not present ideal conditions for the official recognition of a newly transplanted religious community. The separation of church and state is viewed differently in the United States and in France. In the United States, religious liberty is one of the freedoms that the nation itself is founded on and the state is restricted from establishing churches and interfering in church activities. In France, on the other hand, it was the late-nineteenth-century state, a progressive and democratic force—and then the Third Republic—that had to be protected against one church in particular, the Catholic Church, whose agenda was socially conservative and antidemocratic. The French, who have a long history of religious violence, are wary of any mixing of religion and politics. In the hope of weakening organized religion's potentially seditious effects, they try to the extent possible to relegate religion strictly to the private sphere and to regulate its entry into the public sphere. This secular outlook was enshrined in the 1905 law separating church and state, imposed amid violence, which prohibits the public funding or official recognition of religious communities.[7] But while there is no state "recognition" (*reconnaissance*) of religions, there is, of course, state "acquaintance" (*connaissance*) with religions in the interest of treating them equitably.[8] The first article of the French constitution states that "France respects all beliefs," and the tenth article of the Declaration of the Rights of Man and Citizen spells out that "no one may be disturbed for his opinions, even religious ones, so long as their expression does not trouble public order as established by the law."

Over the past two centuries, community interlocutors for Catholics, Jews, Protestants, and most recently Muslims have been granted limited powers from the government to address religious issues that are of an undeniably public nature—for example, choosing chaplains to serve in prisons and in the military or establishing religious burial grounds. But although "the Republic engages in dialogue with all associations and religious sensibilities," as the French president acknowledged in a recent speech, "it refuses to recognize community membership as a component of citizenship." Chirac praised state secularism as the last protection against the encroachment of religious communities on the state in a transnational and global world: "We cannot allow ethnic or religious belonging to be constructed as a political act."[9] There has been much debate over whether Islam is in conflict with this private-public divide, since many consider it to be an "all-encompassing" religion that does not distinguish between the spiritual, social, and political spheres.

This chapter explores how the presence of Muslims in France has challenged *laïcité*, forcing it to adapt to the needs of Islam, as well as how Muslims came to depend on foreign sources to meet their basic religious needs. There are indications, however, that the sum total of government action in this area—combined with independent developments within Muslim communities themselves—has laid the foundation for the development of a "Gallic Islam," as Jacques Berque presaged.

The status of Islam suffers from de facto inequality due to its relatively recent implantation in metropolitan France. Divisions within the Muslim community delayed until 2003 the creation of a representative authority equivalent to the Fédération Protestante de France (Protestant Federation of France), the Jewish Consistoire Central de France (Central Consistory of France), or the Conférence des Evêques de France (Conference of French Bishops). The law separating church and state favored those religious communities that were present in 1905, when the law was passed. French secularism bears the imprint of the status quo ante; as Edgar Morin memorably wrote, France is actually a *"catho-laïque"* country.[10] Half of the ten national holidays are Catholic holidays (as are Sundays), although a Ministry of Public Employment memo from 1967 tacitly allows for non-Christian employees to miss work for a specified list of other holidays.[11] Despite its tumultuous relations with the Holy See, there are signs that France still considers itself the "eldest daughter of the Church." On a visit to the Vatican in 1996, then Prime Minister Chirac assured the Pope of France's "fidelity to its Christian heritage, its spiritual and humanitarian vocation, its origins, and the sources of its culture and civilization."[12] Furthermore, on the death of Pope John XXIII and Pope John Paul II, the government ordered all French flags to fly at half mast, an honor reserved for former heads of state with whom France has a special relationship.[13]

In addition, there have been noteworthy exceptions to the 1905 prohibition of public funding for religious purposes. The Ministry of Culture authorized a large subsidy for the Museum of Holy Art in Evry in the 1980s, which in fact paid for renovation of the cathedral in which it is housed. There are various options for the public maintenance of religious buildings, and local taxes may be used for maintenance of religious associations. Much of the Catholic Church's real estate patrimony fell to the care of the French state after the Vatican rejected the 1905 law (it restored diplomatic relations with France in 1924). The French Foreign Ministry offers theology scholarships that attract rabbis, priests, and imams from around the world, and since the reestablishment of ties with the Holy See, the foreign minister has had an adviser on religious affairs. The government also pays the salary of Jewish, Protestant, Catholic, and Muslim chaplains who offer spiritual guidance (and certify halal or kosher meals) for French soldiers, public hospital patients, and prison detainees (as well as the social security benefits of other prayer leaders). In addition, taxes pay teachers' wages at religious schools that have signed association contracts (see chapter 1). And although the central government is barred from directly financing prayer spaces, many mayors have taken advantage of two laws enacted in 1930 and 1961 to enable towns and *départements* to make land grants and ninety-nine-year loans for symbolic sums to support the construction and operation of prayer spaces for religious associations.[14]

Interestingly, there are some areas of France where the law of separation is altogether moot. This is the case in the eastern region of Alsace-Moselle (which includes Strasbourg), which was exempted from the 1905 law separating church and state because it was then part of Germany.[15] Catholic, Calvinist,

Lutheran, and Jewish ministers are all considered civil servants in Alsace-Moselle, and local municipalities subsidize religious infrastructure like theological seminaries and prayer spaces (including the occasional mosque); however, in the 1990s, while Christian and Jewish students received religious instruction, Muslim students were sent to driver's ed class. And in several overseas territories, or *départements et territories d'outre mer* (DOM-TOM), Islam and the French administration also interact smoothly. The island of Réunion, about 500 miles east of Madagascar in the Indian Ocean, was the site of the first French mosque (1903) and the first French Muslim cemetery (1915) outside Algeria, in addition to the first French Muslim high school (1947). On the French island of Mayotte, the state prefect still names the Muslim religious leader (the mufti), and the administration recognizes Islamic law instead of the civil code with regard to polygamy, spousal repudiation, and inheritance rights.[16]

There have been instances of de facto government accommodation of the practical religious needs of Muslims since the mid-1970s. Governments responded first to the demands made on behalf of several hundred thousand Algerians, known as *harkis* and *musulmans français* ("French Muslims"), who had served as municipal employees and soldiers. More than 80,000 such families migrated to France upon de Gaulle's withdrawal from Algeria. Given their status as collaborators in Algeria, their return home was unimaginable, unlike that of more recent labor migrants, who were the object of forced-return policy proposals as late as 1978.[17] Some of these French Muslims took up administrative posts in France, and the often-neglected *harkis* had dependable political allies among other Algerian veterans' groups. The accommodation of their religious needs demonstrates how the French government was able to absorb certain religious demands in the interest of ensuring the equality of this compromised population. Into the mid-1980s, the state secretary for veterans' affairs even chartered flights to Mecca each year so that descendants of *harkis* could make the pilgrimage.

Why Institutionalize French Islam?

"Institutionalizing" Islam as a tool of integration policy—that is, reaching out to Muslims by helping them observe their religious requirements—came about only after the large-scale reunification of families of labor migrants (including half a million family members who arrived in the late 1970s). Among the first gestures toward an integration policy for labor migrants involved providing prayer space and the means for halal animal slaughter. Semi-public enterprises like Renault, the car manufacturer, and SONACOTRA, the public housing system for immigrants, resolved labor and rent strikes in the late 1970s and early 1980s by granting prayer space for workers and residents. In the words of one observer, the 1905 law separating church and state did not envision "the belltowers of the future"—that is, minarets—yet it was increasingly clear to local administrators that official interlocutors would be needed for a variety of practical reasons.[18] Faced with the reality of Muslim observance of Aïd al-Adha—when 30,000 lambs are slaughtered in the Paris region alone—French prefects set up twenty-two special locations for the ritual sacrifice. And with insufficient prayer space in metropolitan areas—and in the interest of minimizing foreign donations—mayors in Marseille, Montpellier, and Paris approved substantial subsidies to build or renovate central mosques between 1982 and 1992. But in most cases, French administrators' hands were tied by the 1905 law, and foreign governments were left to provide for Muslims' religious needs.

By the late 1980s, many politicians and policymakers agreed that Muslims in France had been all but abandoned by the state. The children of North African labor migrants living in suburban housing projects suffered disproportionately from unemployment, there were few economic elites, and no deputies of Muslim origin sat in the National Assembly, even though the number of Muslim voters had already risen to as many as 1 million by then. There were insufficient Muslim prayer spaces and not enough imams; those that were in place were largely foreign-sponsored and did not speak French. In addition, in the late 1980s, Muslim communities in France felt tremors from the first Palestinian *intifada,* the first round of headscarf affairs involving schoolgirls, and the Gulf War. Those responsible for religious affairs at the Ministry of the Interior began to acknowledge that further ignoring the integration of this population would invite its radicalization—or at least encourage its overreliance on the social systems in place in isolated communities.

Given the French government's avoidance of racial or ethnic origin as a criterion of its immigrant integration policies (see chapter 7), religious representation was the sole area where a government office—the Bureau Central des Cultes (Central Office of Religions) of the Interior Ministry—could legitimately pursue contacts with young Muslims as such. With few exceptions, Muslims had not yet succeeded in entering electoral politics or other visible professions, but they were beginning to display more curiosity about their cultural heritage. In the words of Mouloud Aounit, the leader of the Mouvement contre le Racisme et pour l'Amitié entre les Peuples (MRAP) (Movement against Racism and for Friendship among Peoples), the logic is as follows: "I go to the mosque because there, I exist."[19] As Olivier Roy writes, "The state is not engaging in a grand strategy but rather making the observation that the spontaneous organization of Islam in the West is still the mosque, not political parties, unions, or national movements. So there is a 'state-ification' of religious representation, in the sense that the logic of the state is imposed upon believers."[20] That observation contributed to the state's decision to pursue religious policy as the surest approach to symbolic integration. Alain Billon, chief adviser to the Ministry of the Interior in discussions with Muslim leaders between 1997 and 2002, explained that in "the effort to integrate the Muslim religion by way of consultations and by treating its representatives with consideration, we as public authorities *symbolically* demonstrated our desire to integrate the entirety of the population of Muslim origin or culture."[21]

Nicolas Sarkozy, who vigorously pursued state-Islam negotiations for the center-right coalition, directly echoed former interior minister Jean-Pierre Chevènement's words from 1997 upon taking office in 2002: "We cannot ask Muslims in France to respect the values of the Republic if we do not invite them to the table of the Republic. I am of the conviction that a humiliated identity is a radicalized identity."[22] Furthermore, Sarkozy pointedly stated in interviews that

> We are not going to resolve the problem of young people in the *banlieues* just by giving them soccer fields and youth centers. . . . The *banlieues*, like any other cities, need "places of enlightenment" where people gather and respect one another. Places where the values of life and hope are defended. A synagogue, a temple, a church, or a mosque can fulfill this function.[23]

His rhetoric, which placed religion squarely in the public domain, emphasized the aggressive tack the government would take in its pursuit of a Muslim interlocutor. Under Chevènement and later Sarkozy, the Ministry of the Interior would twist the arms of Muslim leaders and test the limits of state secularism in order to establish the French Council of the Muslim Religion. This process overcame the timidity and divisions that had characterized previous efforts to formalize state-Islam relations.

The Long and Bumpy Road to the French Council of the Muslim Religion

The Ministry of the Interior's sixteen years of consultations with Muslim leaders have shared an indirect objective: the social integration of the growing population of North African origin. But ideas about how best to achieve

Table 5-1. *Interior Ministry's Consultations with Islam (1989–2004)*[a]

Interior minister	Consultation	Accomplishments
Pierre Joxe (PS: 5/1988–1/1991)	CORIF	Halal food and chaplains in military; Muslim sections in cemeteries; starting time for Ramadan
Philippe Marchand (PS: 1/1991–4/1992)	CORIF	
Paul Quilès (PS: 4/1992–3/1993)	CORIF	
Charles Pasqua (RPR: 3/1993–5/1995)	CRMF	Charter of the Muslim Religion; halal certification and theological seminary (abortive) entrusted to GMP
Jean-Louis Debré (RPR: 5/1995–6/1997)	No consultation	End of GMP's halal certification monopoly
Jean-Pierre Chevènement (MDC: 6/1997–8/2000)	Al-Istîchara	Juridical Principles and Foundations (*Principes et Fondements Juridiques*)
Daniel Vaillant (PS: 8/2000–5/2002)	Al-Istîchara	Framework Agreement (*Accord Cadre*)
Nicolas Sarkozy (UDF/UMP: 6/2002–4/2004)	CFCM	Composition of governing board; working groups; CFCM/CRCM elections
Dominique de Villepin (UMP: 4/2004–5/2005)	CFCM	French Foundation for Muslim Works; imam training courses at the University of Paris
Nicolas Sarkozy (UMP: 6/2005–)	CFCM	Appointment of national head of Muslim military chaplains

a. PS (Socialist Party); UDF (Center-right coalition, non-Gaullist); RPR/UMP (Center-right coalition, Gaullist); MDC (republican/citizen).

integration underwent a great deal of change. The government of the secular French Republic has recently, gradually, and ironically recognized the nature of integration problems and the relevance of religion as a tool to facilitate the integration of the Maghrebin population. The French government has tried to contain the threat of religious radicalism by loosening its formal ties with organized Islam in Muslim states—whether it is state controlled ("embassy Islam") or percolates up through nongovernment fundamentalist networks ("Islam of the streets").

Though *laïcité* is renowned for its restrictiveness, the Ministry of the Interior's Central Office of Religions was able to initiate a series of forums for dialogue (consultations) between Muslim representatives and the state (see table 5-1). It is in the common interest of both political Islam organizations such as the Union des Organisations Islamiques de France (UOIF) (Union of Islamic Organizations of France) and the French state to free Muslim institutions from the control of foreign governments, and to that extent, the French government is indeed furthering one facet of the political Islamists' agenda. But the interests of foreign governments have never been excluded from the consultations, in part as an institutional check against the threat of an Islamist monopoly. That has made the French government's task rather difficult.

Through the Grande Mosquée de Paris (GMP) (Great Mosque of Paris), Algeria had effectively served as the French government's interlocutor for Islamic affairs since 1978. But by the late 1980s, highly organized Moroccan-led federations like the UOIF and the Fédération Nationale des Musulmans de France (FNMF) (National Federation of Muslims of France) slowly challenged the GMP's monopoly. In addition, changing demographics within the Muslim population led French authorities to tire of the Algerian government's treatment of the Mosquée de Paris, which has been under the financial control of the Algerian government since 1982, as a "second embassy."[24]

The Ministry of the Interior has tried off and on to encourage Muslims to self-organize since 1988, after the GMP was no longer considered a suitable representative on religious matters. Pierre Joxe, twice minister of the interior during the 1980s, was the first to try to end foreign dominance of the GMP— as well as the GMP's dominance over Islam in France. Recognizing that the representatives of Algerian Islam could no longer speak exclusively for French Muslims, Joxe convened a broad range of Muslim leaders to consult on religious needs. In 1989, he asked six community figures to propose nine other representatives, and the fifteen-member Conseil de Réflexion sur l'Islam en France (CORIF) (Council of Reflection on Islam in France) was installed in March 1990. Joxe's idea was never to create a representative council, only a "council of reflection," and the CORIF was never included in the parliament's *Journal Officiel*. The assembled leaders were treated as specialists from whom the administration would seek advice on technical religious questions. But Joxe was under no obligation to follow their advice, and he did not delegate any formal powers of deliberation or implementation to CORIF members. The CORIF was nonetheless able to accomplish the first symbolic measures toward unifying French Islam, such as making halal food available to Muslim soldiers and agreeing, with the aid of the Paris Observatory, on a common starting point for the holy month of Ramadan.

Charles Pasqua, minister of the interior in the mid-1990s, took institutionalization a step beyond the informal advisory role that the CORIF had intermittently played. But preferring a hierarchical power structure that would fit easily into state-religion relations, he relied almost exclusively on the Great Mosque of Paris. Pasqua asked Dalil Boubakeur, rector of the GMP, to organize local associations and mosques into federations, and he granted a monopoly on halal certification to the GMP, which included rights to significant revenues based on the quantity of meat sold. Pasqua also encouraged the creation of a theological seminary at the GMP in 1993—a reversal of the center-left's policy since 1989 of downplaying Algerian influence and broadening the leadership pool beyond the rector and his inner circle. Pasqua chose instead a diplomatic solution that bypassed the heads of local associations in favor of foreign representatives and even encouraged an alliance between the GMP and the Saudi Muslim World League.[25] The Great Mosque of Paris issued a "charter of the Muslim religion" but failed to effectively federate the Muslim associations under Algerian leadership, weakening the rector's position as sole interlocutor. Pasqua's top-down approach allowed for temporary progress toward institutionalizing religious representatives, but after suffering the defection of key participants, that round of consultations quickly lost any hope of being representative of French Islam.[26]

Jean-Louis Debré, Pasqua's successor as minister of the interior, argued that the government was mistaken in trying to create an officially recognized Islam, and state-Islam relations relapsed into a policy of *laissez-faire* between 1995 and 1997. Debré thought that both Pasqua and Joxe had conveyed legitimacy on certain Muslim federations without having the authority to do so, saying that "neither the organizations nor their representative nature can be decreed by the state." Debré took away the GMP's monopoly on halal certification, granting equal accreditation rights (and tax revenues by the kilo) to the Saudi-funded *grandes mosquées* of Lyon and Evry. Under Debré, the Ministry of the Interior remained indecisive and immobile, never moving beyond rhetorical acknowledgment that some representative body to oversee state-Islam relations should exist.

Convincing Muslim federations to work together would require the minister of the interior to roll up his sleeves and get more involved in religious and international networks. Jean-Pierre Chevènement, interior minister under Jospin, reinitiated a "grand forum" of Muslim federations in 1999. That fall, the Ministry of the Interior formally launched "Al-Istîchara" (Arabic for "the Consultation"), complete with a newsletter printed at the ministry's expense on paper tinted green, the color of Islam. Chevènement sent a letter of invitation to six federations, six great mosques, and six experts on Islam (*personnalités qualifiées*) to take a seat "at the table of the Republic."[27] With that invitation, the ministry irrevocably took matters into its own hands, initiating a phase of formal recognition of Muslim associations by the French state, though all the while insisting that the government was only a "witness in good faith" and "facilitator" of contacts among Muslim federations and power brokers. This process set in motion a series of institutionalized meetings regarding the religious needs of Muslims in France. Most important, Chevènement and his two immediate successors, Daniel Vaillant of the Parti Socialiste (Socialist Party) and Nicolas Sarkozy, all signed agreements that structure state-Islam relations and regulate the establishment of a system of sharing responsibilities in a number of technical and symbolic areas:

—"Juridical principles and foundations governing relations between the public authorities and the Muslim religion" (*Principes et fondements juridiques*). All participants signed a founding agreement in January 2001 that regulates their behavior and avows their loyalty to the Republic—"reciprocal recognition" of the state and Islam, in the words of an Interior Ministry official—and a written guarantee to respect the rule of law.[28]

—"Framework agreement" (*Accord cadre*). Participants signed an agreement in May 2001 to form committees to determine electoral districts and voting rules and to draft a statute for the forthcoming CFCM.

—The election of the first French Council of the Muslim Religion in April 2003.[29]

—The establishment of working groups in December 2003 to propose CFCM policies and practices to meet Muslims' religious requirements.

To address technical aspects of Muslims' religious needs, advisers in the Ministry of the Interior maintain close contact with diverse Muslim organizations. While vowing to "accompany" Muslims on their path to representation, the minister took pains to operate within the limits of *laïcité:* the minister's cabinet delegated any organizational activity that it could to a 1901 law association independently run by Muslim leaders. The process that Joxe initiated with the CORIF, though punctuated by several failed attempts to finalize its status, paved the way for Chevènement's Al-Istîchara and, four years later, Sarkozy's negotiation of the CFCM. The CFCM that emerged in 2002–03 reflects the lessons drawn from nearly fifteen years of consultations.

The Ministry of the Interior granted leadership positions on the CFCM to four major Muslim federations—Great Mosque of Paris (GMP), Union of Islamic Organizations of France (UOIF), National Federation of Muslims of France (FNMF), and the Comité de Coordination des Musulmans Turcs de France (CCMTF) (Coordinating Committee of Turkish Muslims of France)— and negotiated a complex electoral scheme based on the square footage of existing prayer spaces. The electorate consisted of 4,042 delegates from around

1,000 prayer spaces who were to vote in indirect elections in the spring of 2003: roughly three-quarters (3,226) of those delegates came from 210 large prayer spaces, while the rest (816) came from 782 smaller spaces.[30] That formula was necessary to convince the UOIF to participate in elections, leading the GMP to complain that the great mosques were being diminished in favor of the small prayer spaces typically affiliated with the other major federations. The general French Muslim population did not designate the "grand electors"; instead, they were nominated by the prayer spaces' boards of directors. It is not necessary to be a French citizen to vote or be elected in the CFCM, and polling stations did not require proof of French nationality for the delegates in the April and June 2003 elections for the CFCM and the Conseils Regionaux du Culte Musulman (CRCM) (Regional Councils of the Muslim Religion).

By minimizing any challenge that even limited elections might pose to the major federations' existing positions, the CFCM reassured the federations that they could participate at little risk to their standing. The Ministry of the Interior also allayed public fears about the new council by guaranteeing before elections that the CFCM's president would be the GMP's personable rector, Dalil Boubakeur, who represents a moderate Islam acceptable to mainstream French society. That preelection deal in 2002 (reconfirmed in 2005)—which also allocated the CFCM's vice-presidencies to members of the UOIF and the FNMF and the CFCM's general secretariat to the CCMTF—was aimed at mitigating the possibility of any unacceptable electoral outcome (especially for the GMP) while securing the participation of all members in the process.[31] After all, Boubakeur had twice delayed elections, in April and May 2002, for fear of finally losing his perch atop French Islam—and, he said, to hold back Islamist organizations that were gaining ground.[32] Sarkozy had been open about his strategy of direct intervention in the CFCM's makeup, saying early on that "minority views will have to be represented by ministerial appointment."[33] With regard to the inclusion of the UOIF, which many have criticized as a fundamentalist group linked to the Muslim Brotherhood, Sarkozy responded:

> I wanted to create an institution that represents the reality on the ground as it really is—from the most moderate to the most engaged. ... I know there are some people who love Muslims so long as they've chosen them according to their resemblance to us. But if tolerance is just about having a dialogue with people who are like you, it quickly reaches its limits![34]

Nicolas Sarkozy gathered his advisers on Islam together with Muslim leaders at Nainville-Les-Roches in December 2002 to negotiate nominations to the bureau éxécutif (governing board) in closed quarters.[35] These occupants of one-third of the sixty seats on the CFCM *conseil d'administration* (administrative council)—including representatives from five great mosques and seven federations and six government-selected experts—were appointed by the Ministry of the Interior. The composition of the governing board thus took into account the reality on the ground and diplomatic sensibilities while paying attention to the CFCM's reception by the broader domestic audience.

Elections for the remaining two-thirds of the seats in the CFCM's administrative council (as well as its general assembly) were held six months after those discussions, in April 2003; the CRCM vote followed in June. Abstention was very low, discounting any perceptions that the ministry's tactics may have been too heavy-handed to ensure the council's legitimacy. Indeed, 80 percent of eligible prayer spaces have voluntarily participated in discussions with the government since Chevènement's Al-Istîchara in 1999. An equal proportion of prayer spaces (992 of 1,126) registered for CFCM/CRCM elections in 2003, and the number increased to 1,221 in 2005.[36] The abstention rate of those registered for elections also was low: 75 percent voted in April 2003, and 85 percent voted in June 2005.[37] The electoral results, shown in box 5-1, did not surprise participants: the federations engaged in electoral alliances with one another and some agreed to refrain from presenting a candidate in several regions where elections were close.[38] The UOIF and FNMF have emerged as new leaders, and the Coordinating Committee of Turkish Muslims of France also performed well, with the aid of the Moroccan and Turkish consulates respectively. The GMP and other Algerian networks, which were less cohesive, did less well in 2003 but recovered somewhat in 2005 (increasing the GMP's share from six to ten seats on the administrative council).[39]

The CFCM elections to date thus have confirmed the GMP's relative decline and the rise of the Moroccans (through the FNMF) and a form of organized political Islam (in the UOIF). But that decline had been noted as early as 1989, when the Moroccan-born leadership of the UOIF took the lead in the first headscarf affair and when the Algerian-led GMP failed to unite the Muslim community during Pasqua's years at the Ministry of the Interior.[40] The Moroccan state proved itself an ascendant force in French Islam with the strong 2005 electoral results for the FNMF (whose share of seats on the administrative council increased from thirteen to sixteen), which it supported. Bruno Etienne observed that the CFCM would likely remain at the center of a power struggle among international forces, both governmental and ideological:

Box 5-1. *The First French Council of the Muslim Religion, 2003–05*[a]

Governing Board		
President Dalil Boubakeur, rector of the Grande Mosquée de Paris		
Vice president Fouad Alaoui, secretary general of the Union des Organisations Islamiques de France		**Vice president** Mohamed Bechari, president of the Fédération Nationale des Musulmans de France
Representatives of the seven largest Muslim federations Invitation et Mission pour la Foi et la Pratique Tabligh et Dawa Il Allah Fédération Française des Associations Islamiques d'Afrique, des Comores, et des Antilles Comité de Coordination des Musulmans Turcs de France[b] Union des Organisations Islamiques de France Fédération Nationale des Musulmans de France Grande Mosquée de Paris	**Six government-appointed experts** Saada Mamadou Ba (academic) Soheib Bencheikh (former Mufti of Marseille) Khaled Bentounès (Sufi spiritual leader) Eric Geoffroy (professor, Sufi convert) Mohsen Ismaïl (theologian) Dounia Bouzar (independent scholar, sole woman on governing board)[c]	**Representatives of the five great mosques** Lyon (affiliated with Grande Mosquée de Paris) Mantes-la-Jolie (affiliated with Union des Organisations Islamiques de France) Evry (affiliated with Union des Organisations Islamiques de France) Al-Islah de Marseille (affiliated with Union des Organisations Islamiques de France) Saint-Denis de la Réunion (unaffiliated)

a. Governing Board (*Bureau Exécutif*) and Administrative Council (*Conseil d'Administration*) of CFCM. Sixty-four members: twenty-three appointed, forty-one indirectly elected.

b. Haydar Demyurek, president of CCMTF, serves as general secretary of CFCM.

c. Bouzar resigned January 2005; she had replaced Betoule Fekkar-Lambiotte.

The next CFCM elections will have to avoid the pressures of Algeria, and to a lesser extent of Morocco and Turkey, concerning the choice of candidates—the French state will have to let Muslims organize their own representation, just like Jews or Protestants. That means the GMP's status will have to be reconsidered.[41]

The visible hand of the state in Muslim affairs—notably, the reconfirmation of the GMP in the CFCM presidency in 2005—has frustrated some purists among the defenders of French *laïcité,* who claim that the CFCM crosses the line separating church and state, as well as critics who say that the elections were about as open and transparent as those in French Muslims' countries of origin. Sarkozy defended his decision to institutionalize relations with Islam by arguing that the real risk lay in not acting, as evidenced by the development of underground Islam in the 1980s and 1990s. "What was the alternative?" he asked:

> Stand by while the *banlieues* radicalize? We have refused to confront reality for forty years. If you find Islam incompatible with the Republic, then what do you do with the 5 million people of Muslim origin living in France? Do you kick them out, or make them convert, or ask them not to practice their religion?[42]

In addition to the role that the Ministry of the Interior played in composing the governing board, two ministerial advisers also attend the board's meetings. Some have criticized their official presence as proof of the CFCM's lack of independence from the government; Michèle Tribalat has argued, for example, that the government long ago abandoned its role as "witness in good faith" or "companion" to the CFCM's consultations.[43] However, one French-born member of the governing board defended the ministry's participation in very strong terms, noting that the CFCM's members had voted in favor of continued ministerial involvement: "Without the technical aid of the ministry, we would be incapable of completing our tasks; we need this help for the first two years of our existence, since the projects are relatively complex, and we need the ministry's accompaniment to open doors in other ministries. I thank the government and the Interior Ministry for this help."[44] The CFCM, Sarkozy has insisted, is the best way of helping an Islam that is compatible with the values of the Republic to emerge.[45] After the April 2003 elections, the CFCM, which is registered as an association under the 1901 law, held its first general assembly in May 2003, one month before the election of regional councils in June.

The CFCM's Official Roles

Although the Ministry of the Interior has taken pains to ensure the CFCM's broadly representative character, the council is limited to representing the Muslim *religion*—not Muslims themselves—in state institutions. The CFCM was never intended to speak for the Muslim population, but rather to give voice to the observant Muslims who frequent prayer spaces and to oversee those spaces. The CFCM's working groups, or *commissions,* make proposals regarding religious practice, narrowly defined (see box 5-2). The government did not ask the CFCM its advice on the headscarf law before or during National Assembly debate, for example, even though individual CFCM leaders were called before the Stasi Commission. (The council's executive board issued a separate press release stating that wearing the headscarf was *"une pre-scription religieuse"*—a religious rule.) As one Interior Ministry adviser involved in the consultations said: "We are interested only in practicing Muslims, not in the Muslim community in general. This concerns only the 10 to 20 percent of Muslims who frequently go to prayer spaces. Our role is to know how these people want to practice their religion in the public sphere."[46]

Box 5-2. *Working Groups* (Commissions) *of the French Council of the Muslim Religion*

Creation of Muslim prayer spaces (Fondation pour les Oeuvres de l'Islam de France)

Association regulations

Imams and training of imams

Chaplains in hospitals, prisons, and the military

Regulation of lamb slaughter for Aïd al-Adha

Audiovisual media (weekly broadcast on France 2 and CFCM website)

Organization of pilgrimage to Mecca (*hajj*)

Religious training of clergy (*Diplome universitaire en études islamiques*)

Membership dues and finances

Juridical statute of the CFCM

Halal certification

Sarkozy noted in an interview that the details of local religious arrangements should be left to local or regional authorities, so as much as possible is settled at the regional level, through the CRCM's twenty-five regional councils, which are analogous to the regional Jewish consistories.[47] The working groups, assemblies, and administrative councils of the CFCM and CRCM deliberate only on questions of religious practice. Their aim is to speak in a unified voice on issues affecting Muslims' observance of rituals and prayer: once consensus is achieved among the members of a given working group—chaired by different federations' leaders in a careful division of labor (and spoils)—a report is issued that includes recommendations to the relevant government ministries: Interior, Agriculture, Education, and even Foreign Affairs. The regional councils, in turn, are a convenient forum for national and local administrators to consult Muslim religious leaders about mosque construction, the starting time of major holidays, the provision of halal food, and so forth.

To a large extent, the Muslim national and regional councils are the equivalent of the Catholic Conférence des Évêques, the Jewish Consistoire Central (1807), and the Protestant Fédération (1905), all of which serve as national and regional interlocutors for the state. The French Council of the Muslim Religion bears little resemblance to the Conseil Représentatif des Institutions Juives de France (CRIF) (Representative Council of Jewish Institutions of France), however, because the CRIF includes cultural and political associations under its umbrella and therefore can act more as an all-encompassing lobbying group. Both CFCM and the Consistoire were created by the French state to act as interlocutors for their members and public authorities, whereas the CRIF was founded by Jewish associations in 1943 without any encouragement from the government. The minutiae of state-religion relations with these Protestant, Catholic, and Jewish representatives are conducted in a similar manner, through regular contacts between the relevant bureaucracies and community officeholders, whether on the subject of chaplains, prayer spaces, Jewish *kashrut,* and so forth.

In addition to the internal ideological tensions that limit the scope of the CFCM's ambitions, the council's activities are institutionally circumscribed in several ways. The working groups are not given sole authority over the projects that they undertake, only the power to make proposals; nor are the working groups the only venue through which the government can pursue policies concerning Muslims in France.

The question of a theological seminary for training imams has been tackled by the Ministry of the Interior and the Ministry of Education in consultation with the CFCM. The government has also addressed the question of financing for prayer spaces in conjunction with the CFCM, but it has not delegated this issue wholesale to the council. In 2005, the Interior Ministry asked the CFCM to participate in establishing the Fondation pour les Oeuvres de l'Islam de France (French Foundation for Muslim Works), which acts as a central depository for foreign donations and funds for cultural activities and for the construction and maintenance of prayer spaces.[48] As with the question of imam training in chapter 4, some federations stand to lose the comparative advantage of the status quo—in this case, private contacts for fundraising abroad. The foundation operates under the control of a board composed of civil servants from the Cour des Comptes (Court of Accounts) along with an observer from the Ministry of the Interior and nominees of the CFCM's four major federations (the GMP, UOIF, FNMF, and CCMTF).[49]

That would not represent a major departure from French *laïcité*. There is already a national Protestant foundation that regroups existing associations; Nicolas Sarkozy's proposal for outright state funding of prayer spaces and revision of the 1905 law would go further by making some French state funds directly available. It has been many years since the need for "transparency" in mosque funding was first evoked—by Interior Minister Jean-Louis Debré's reference to "suitcases stuffed with money"—yet little in the way of transparency has been achieved.[50] Opponents to state interference therefore have found it difficult to object to a change in the current system, which essentially encourages unregulated foreign interference in domestic religious affairs. The foundation would offer private donors a tax break of 60 percent of the donation, similar to benefits under the rules in place for 1905 law associations.[51] Such a foundation would pose a challenge to the CFCM's monopoly over state-Islam relations, especially if a leader who is not also a member of the CFCM headed it.

For the French Council of the Muslim Religion, given the diversity of its members and their competing national and ideological interests, there is no such thing as a wholly uncontroversial task.[52] Nonetheless, progress has been made toward consensus on the designation of religious chaplains in prisons, the organization of the pilgrimage to Mecca, and the certification of halal meat.[53] Currently only a handful of imams work in French prisons, and the number is universally deemed inadequate given the high proportion of inmates of Muslim background.[54] Poorly trained chaplains and the occasional extremist chaplain have created worries about proselytism (see chapter 10). A part-time imam at the Nanterre prison told reporters that only eight Muslim chaplains covered the roughly 20,000 Muslim inmates in the twenty-five prisons in the Paris region of Ile-de-France.[55] Before the advent of the CFCM, regional prison directors would solicit local religious authorities for names of potential chaplains, many of whom were foreign imams and were later rejected by the domestic intelligence service (Renseignements Généraux).[56] Now the CFCM's national chaplains, named by its chaplain commission, prescreen candidates before proposing them to departmental prison directors for employment.[57]

The CFCM's halal commission will make proposals regarding how best to organize the large-scale, lucrative halal meat industry, which produces 300,000 tons of meat each year, about one-third of which is destined for consumption elsewhere in the Muslim world. (Almost half of French exports of halal meat goes to Turkey, Saudi Arabia, Yemen, Qatar, Egypt, and Iran; the other half goes to Europe.) In the 1990s, the privilege of granting the halal imprimatur brought with it a dividend of e0.15 per kilogram of halal meat sold and the right to sell halal slaughter certificates to butchers for e150 ($181.19) each; the CFCM commission will now figure out how to divide those revenues among the participating federations.[58] But there has been a lack of precise regulation in the halal industry in France, leaving consumers vulnerable to being misled by mislabeling. For example, magazine exposés have shown that sometimes pork is stored in supposedly halal freezers, a practice that has evoked sanctions from the consumer protection bureau.

The CFCM's *hajj* working group negotiated a new visa policy with Saudi Arabia for French Muslims planning to make the 2005 pilgrimage, and it set up an information hotline as well as on-site offices in Mecca, Medina, and Jeddah to coordinate activities with French consulates there. Twenty-six thousand pilgrims planned to travel from France in winter 2006, several thousand more than in previous years.[59] French Muslims have avoided abiding by the Saudis' pilgrimage quota, which restricts the number of pilgrims to 1 percent of a country's Muslim population and so would normally allow France only about 50,000 visas (although some leaving for *hajj* from France are not French nationals, they still receive their visa from the Saudi embassy in Paris). The CFCM defends the "religious" interests of French Muslims on *hajj*, though "without taking the place of French diplomatic representatives." The CFCM offices attend to any problems that French Muslims have with private tour operators, the religious requirements of the hajj, accommodations, or medical needs during their visit.[60] It has modeled itself after the "pilgrimage missions" set up by Muslim countries such as Morocco, which sends state representatives to ensure that pilgrims to the holy cities are treated fairly by tour operators. The CFCM grants a "seal of approval" to trustworthy providers of pilgrimage packages, and it plans to finance its services by way of a e10 ($12.50) tax.[61]

Community Mediator? The CFCM's Unofficial Functions

The lion's share of CFCM activity involves the practical regulation of religious observance. Invariably, however, there will be moments when the CFCM is asked to offer the "Muslim community's" view on issues that exceed the bounds of religion strictly defined. During national debates in 2003–04 over the propriety of headscarves in schools, anti-Semitic incidents, the Iraq war, and the French hostage crisis, for example, the council constantly slipped into the role of community spokesperson. Some of the confusion was encouraged by government officials, who suggested the council might play a role in "pacifying" the *banlieues* during times of crisis. In fact, the CFCM played no role in tamping down violence during the riots of October–November 2005, although Boubakeur visited a mosque that had been hit by a tear gas canister and the Union of Islamic Organizations of France issued a fatwa declaring that participation in the widespread arson and destruction did not befit Muslims.[62] Nonetheless, at the beginning of the Iraq War, when many wondered what French Muslims were thinking, Prime Minister Jean-Pierre Raffarin said that the CFCM could play a "moderating role among young people."[63] Along those lines, regional CRCM affiliates planned to create "round tables in the neighborhoods, inviting youth of all religions and nationalities."[64] Some have drawn bold conclusions regarding the CFCM's positive side effects on social integration. Several months after organizing council elections, Nicolas Sarkozy gained enough confidence to make what would later prove to be a spurious argument, especially in light of the unrest of November 2005:

> There has never been as little violence in the *banlieues* as today. Urban violence has gone down by 22 percent since the beginning of the year. Do you think that is a coincidence? Who can't see the relation between an overture to an Islam of France in broad daylight, on the one hand, and the cleaning up of difficult neighborhoods? These two things go together.[65]

If the urgency to find Muslim representatives in the aftermath of September 11 had begun to wane two years after the fact, the impending invasion of Iraq and an increase in anti-Semitic incidents provided a new impetus to follow through on the CFCM. "You must finish creating the CFCM and CRCM quickly," Sarkozy told Muslim leaders in winter 2003, "in order to respond to any violence that might destabilize French society and discredit the Muslim community by throwing it and the Jewish community into opposition."[66]

During Sarkozy's press to organize CFCM elections, Kamel Kabtane, the rector of the Mosquée de Lyon and later the CFCM's treasurer, commented that "Sarkozy thinks the UOIF is best suited to calming the *banlieue* in case of a war in Iraq."[67] Fouad Alaoui, general secretary of the UOIF and vice president of the CFCM, accepted that the CFCM would occasionally have a calming role to play, "if it is a matter of alleviating conflict between religious communities, in order to keep international conflicts from spilling over into France."[68] Indeed, after the American-led invasion of Iraq, a CFCM press release noted French Muslims' "consternation over this aggression, which is contrary to international law," but called for "calm and dignity" as the appropriate response.[69] After President Jacques Chirac announced the bill to ban conspicuous religious symbols in French schools in December 2003, the CFCM again issued a statement urging "calm and serenity" among French Muslims.

The French Council of the Muslim Religion thus may come to be seen as more than just a religious representative body; politicians may expect it to act as an instrument of social order. However, any overplaying of that role would undoubtedly backfire among Muslims, who seem tolerant of the CFCM as long as it sticks to its mandate. Jean-Pierre Chevènement, who jump-started the consultations with Muslim leaders in 1999, cautiously rejected the thesis that the CFCM can play any special mediating role in potential crises. During the Iraq invasion, for example, Chevènement said, "I'm not sure it was the CFCM that kept the *banlieues* calm. I think it was rather the [government's] stern reaction to anti-Semitic incidents and the fact that France had an equitable position [with regard to Iraq], all in all. That prevented any unfortunate mix-ups. France was not seen just trotting loyally behind the United States."[70] That does not speak to what the CFCM's role might be in a scenario in which the French government took a foreign policy position not shared by a majority of Muslims.

But any hopes that the CFCM may have of speaking on behalf of Muslims on political matters risk foundering on its leadership's inherent disunity. It is difficult enough for working groups to reach consensus over rituals and technical matters, and the mix of strong personalities could lead the council toward stalemate. Only after weeks of bickering did the UOIF and the GMP set aside their differences on a common ending date for Ramadan in 2004 and 2005. And both the commission that nominated the national chaplain and the CFCM delegation that visited Saudi Arabia to negotiate pilgrimage visas found their work challenged by the UOIF.[71] Furthermore, while the GMP and FNMF have generally acquiesced to the deportation of extremist imams, the UOIF has objected to the government's methods: in UOIF president Brèze's words: "The state is within its rights to be concerned about what is said in mosques, but if an imam's behavior is against the law, then let the French authorities bring him to court—not expel him."[72]

The major federations, it should be remembered, also had different initial reactions to the headscarf law. Dalil Boubakeur, rector of the Great Mosque of Paris and the CFCM president, recommended an institutional approach to influencing the law's content and application, whereas vice president Fouad Alaoui, of the Union of Islamic Organizations of France, suggested that it was legitimate to use street protests to voice one's opinions. The UOIF later cracked down on a Muslim student organization after it called for demonstrations against the law, replacing the leader with someone more moderate. Even the unified CFCM delegation to Baghdad to free French hostages—which included Fouad Alaoui, Mohamed Bechari, and a representative of the GMP—was undermined by personal initiatives undertaken by individual members and the GMP's lack of enthusiasm for the project. For example, the secretary general of the National Federation of Muslims of France, Mohamed Bechari, annoyed the GMP by meeting with a former Front Islamique du Salut (FIS) (Islamic Salvation Front) leader in Qatar and with an honorary founder of Hezbollah, though he insisted that he did so solely to help the hostages. Sensing that the UOIF's and FNMF's stock was rising thanks to their new international visibility, the GMP later disavowed the Baghdad delegation entirely. Boubakeur stated that "it is not the job of religious leaders to negotiate with governments or terrorists, and it is contrary to *laïcité* because it gives religious leaders a political weight which can easily be misused."[73]

Will the CFCM Survive?

The French Council of the Muslim Religion is prone to internal power disputes, and it is still trying out different methods of reaching consensus while testing the limits of its actual influence over Islam-related policies in France. The CFCM's unity during the French hostage situation and the imposition of the headscarf ban in schools lent the council a new vitality one year into its operation. Its press releases urging the release of the French hostages were given ample coverage by Al Jazeera, and even Jean-Marie Le Pen applauded the delegation's visit to Baghdad. Subsequent disagreements over the CFCM's second elections in 2005, however, cast a shadow over its accomplishments. The Great Mosque of Paris renewed earlier objections to the electoral system, which assigns delegates on the basis of a prayer space's overall square footage, calling it "ridiculous to define one's weight in the community" in that manner. Boubakeur complained that the role of the great mosques has been diminished in favor of the more numerous prayer spaces that belong to the FNMF and UOIF, whom he called "fundamentalists." The National Federation of Muslims of France has been riven with internecine conflict and has, in turn, complained that the regional CRCMs were not yet organized well enough to hold elections (see chapter 4). And the Union of Islamic Organizations of France abruptly resigned from the vice presidency of the CFCM in May 2005 to protest the government's heavy-handedness in appointing a national Muslim chaplain (although it rejoined two weeks later). Following those hiccups—or electoral posturing—the second CFCM elections went ahead in June 2005, two years after the first elections. Of the 5,200 voting delegates, 85 percent participated in 2005, compared with 75 percent of the smaller group of delegates in 2003.[74] In a significant display of unity, CFCM leaders filed suit in February 2006 against a French periodical that reprinted the Danish caricatures of the prophet Mohammed, and they later petitioned President Chirac to pass an antidefamation law.[75] That helped defuse potential protests and projected a more self-assured image of the CFCM as actively defending the interests of religious Muslims in the political system.

Despite the ideologically inclusive nature of the CFCM's administrative council, it should be recalled that the council represents only *prayer spaces* registered under the 1901 or 1905 laws—thereby excluding cultural, sports, or educational associations as well as the 400 or so prayer spaces that do not have association status. Youth movements also are among those absent, because they do not have their own prayer spaces—as are, obviously, secular Muslims (*musulmans laïcs*) and Muslim intellectuals. Secular Muslims may indeed care little about the starting time of Ramadan or guidelines for animal slaughter during Aïd al-Adha. But they are wary of the visible community role seized by practicing Muslims during the creation of the CFCM. Tokia Saïfi, who was the first cabinet member from the *beur* generation, said observant Muslims should not have a monopoly over Islam in the public sphere. "I think as a 'citizen' but also as a Muslim," she said.[76] Saïfi was among the initiators of the Conseil Français des Musulmans Laïques (CFML) (French Council of Lay Muslims), which was soon followed by three other secular Muslim organizations claiming to represent the nonobservant masses. "Islam also belongs to non-practicing Muslims," said Abderrahmane Dahmane, president of the Conseil des Democrats Musulmans de France (Council of Democratic Muslims).[77] This organized reaction to the creation of the CFCM led Nicolas Sarkozy to consider modifying the strictly religious character of the council:

> The CFCM needs to make room for the "cultural" Muslims because Islam is not solely the property of the "believers." It belongs to those who are not practicing but who have received Islam as cultural heritage. . . . However it is not my job to organize nonbelieving Muslims; then one could really accuse me of *communautarisme!*[78]

That is one of the CFCM's paradoxes: as a highly visible institution, it has sometimes appeared to be the only game in town for leaders of Muslim background, and yet the government has insisted that the CFCM's purpose is restricted to handling narrowly defined religious issues. Such ambiguity was evident in Dounia Bouzar's resignation as one of the six government-appointed experts on the CFCM in January 2005: "For twenty years, Muslims have been asked to leave their religion at the border in order to integrate, and now we define them solely by their religion!"[79] Bouzar went on to write, however, that she regretted that the "second and third generations are not represented on the CFCM." While he was minister of the interior, Villepin invited several "lay" Muslim leaders (including Yazid Sabeg, Abderrahmane Dahmane, and Amar Dib) to a meeting to discuss a representative organization for "secular or liberal Islam" along the lines of the Jewish CRIF. Villepin's advisers were quoted as saying that "the CFCM is a good instrument worth keeping, and it should take its place—and only its place—by concentrating on strictly religious activities. It has no business representing the 5 million French Muslims, just the 10 percent of observant Muslims."[80] Villepin's creation of the French Foundation for Muslim Works has been one way of diffusing the concentration of the CFCM's power, as would be the addition of more government-appointed experts to the CFCM's governing board.

There are additional factors that could undermine the council's legitimacy—for example, its exclusion of certain groups, who are free to criticize the CFCM from the outside. Unlike in previous state-Islam consultations in the 1990s, no spot is reserved on the CFCM for *harkis*, the descendants of Algerians who fought for France in 1958–62.[81] Nor does the French policy of *parité* (parity) apply to the CFCM: there are only four women on its sixty-four-member administrative council and one on its governing board. Also excluded from the CFCM are extremist prayer spaces or associations whose commitment to "republican" forms of religion is in doubt, as well as several important mosques that opted out: the Mosquée de Strasbourg, which is associated with the UOIF and the Association des Etudiants Islamiques de

France (AEIF) (French Association of Islamic Students) (see chapter 4); the Mosquée de Bordeaux; the Mosquée de Toulouse (AEIF); the Mosquée de Lille (UOIF); and the Mosquée Adda'wa (AEIF). The Turkish-German association Islamische Gemeinschaft Milli Görüs (IGMG) (Islamic Community of the National Vision) also decided not to participate in the CFCM after a privileged role was given to its official Turkish rivals in the Coordinating Committee of Turkish Muslims of France, although it later softened its stance.[82]

The CFCM's performance as Islam's representative in the public sphere could also affect its chances for survival. The CFCM was seen as having been left out of the loop during the Ministry of the Interior's expulsions of radical imams as well as during the Stasi Commission's hearings and its subsequent decision to ban the headscarf in schools (see chapter 6). That perception was not lost on the council's critics. The CFCM is "not simply a buffer for the wave of anger felt by Muslims in France," wrote one community activist disappointed with its response to the headscarf law. The Muslim leadership could soon find itself "between the hammer of community demands and anvil of the law."[83] Nonetheless, in an April 2003 poll by Ipsos, 81 percent of Muslims thought that the CFCM would help secure adequate recognition of the presence of Muslims and of Islam in France, and 74 percent thought that the CFCM would help Muslims resolve any difficulties that they might have in practicing their religion.[84] Two years later, in 2005, 55 percent of Muslims told pollsters that they had a "great deal" or a "fair amount" of confidence in the CFCM (28 percent had "not very much" or "no" confidence).[85] Hakim El ghissassi, a journalist and publisher, has cautioned against placing too high hopes in the council: "For most young people, the religious question is of secondary importance; their principal concern is their desire for social and economic integration."[86]

6 Intolerance or Integration? The Ban on Religious Symbols in Public Schools

On March 3, 2004, the French Senate gave final approval to a bill prohibiting the wearing of conspicuous religious symbols in public elementary and secondary schools.[1] The law, which went into effect the following September, does not ban the wearing of headscarves or any other conspicuous symbol in public places, in universities, or in private schools, and it did not actually change the status quo, which was established in France by a ministerial decree in 1994. Rather, the law is a narrowly defined reassertion of religious neutrality within French public schools. The law implements one of the recommendations of a special commission on religion in France, appointed by the government and headed by Bernard Stasi, a former member of the European Parliament and now the *mediateur* (ombudsman) of the Republic, which heard hundreds of witnesses between July and December 2003.

Since the issue first arose in sensational media coverage of three schoolgirls' expulsion from a school in Creil in 1989, the headscarf has been the symbolic heart of the problem of integrating Islam in France.[2] "The patent question of whether 'Islamic' headscarves should be accepted in schools," sociologist Pierre Bourdieu wrote at the time, "masks the latent question of whether immigrants of North African origin should be accepted in France."[3] One reason why so much attention has been given to this particular problem is that the public schools have been a political battleground since the French Revolution. The underlying assumption had always been that the schools had the ability to educate and even to create new citizens, away from the antidemocratic and antirepublican influences of the nineteenth-century Catholic Church—hence the enormous stakes involved in the debate. School is where the young citizens of the Republic can interact without religious, sectarian, and commercial influences. In the public school's pure form only knowledge and reason are admitted inside the walls of the classroom.

In the first decades of the Third Republic, especially the 1880s, the school teacher, or *instituteur,* was a heroic figure. Dressed in an austere black uniform and dubbed the *"hussard noir de la République"*—the soldier, or missionary, of the Republic—the teacher taught French children in all regions of France the same language (at a time when many local dialects were still in use), the same curriculum, and the same *laïc* ethos. Eugen Weber describes this process in fascinating detail in his study *From Peasants into Frenchmen.*[4] In the twentieth century, intense political battles were fought around schools as the Catholic Church tried to maintain its right to teach and to offer private schools (1 million demonstrators flocked to the streets of Paris as recently as 1984 to defend subsidies for private—mostly Catholic—schools). In other words, the French have always fought bitter disputes around schools. Schools lie at the very heart of French political identity, and they are the first line of defense of *laïcité.*

Laïcité is intended to defend pluralism, not threaten it. As one philosopher put it recently, French secularism is not anticlerical; instead, it is liberal, in the nineteenth-century sense of the term.[5] And, as a 1989 Conseil d'Etat (Council of State) memorandum says, "Lay values teach students to respect the convictions of others and to substitute communication for mutual caricature; these values are knowledge, a critical spirit, and personal reflection."[6] In the Stasi Commission report, submitted to President Chirac in December 2003, the authors wrote, along the same vein: "To the schools of the Republic are welcomed not merely users [of a service], but students destined to become enlightened citizens."[7] Under the new law, which went into effect in fall 2004, wearing discreet signs (like a small cross, Qur'an pendant, or Star of David necklace) is still allowed. The headscarf ban is undeniably restrictive in nature, and the French reputation for religious tolerance has suffered in the Muslim world (and elsewhere) for it. But this has never been a simple debate, and its twists and turns over the last fifteen years have revealed a society struggling to reconcile a new social reality with a set of relatively consistent secular values.

A Scarf with Many Meanings

Headscarf cases (*affaires du foulard*) have occurred with regularity since 1989, and in an effort to improve on earlier, indecisive rulings from the Council of State and the Ministry of Education, the government proposed and passed the March 2004 law. The law was always considered a symbolic measure, since there had never been an "epidemic" of headscarf wearing. Before a bill was introduced in Parliament, the Ministry of the Interior had reported only 1,254 girls wearing headscarves in French schools in 2003—a fraction of 1 percent of all Muslim girls—down from 2,000 girls in 1994.[8] While there were 300 cases of a Muslim girl refusing a teacher's request to remove her *foulard* in 1994, there were only 150 in 2002.[9] The actual numbers are a point of contention. Private interviews by the Stasi Commission produced accounts of 1,000 headscarf wearers in the Paris suburb of Seine-Saint-Denis alone, plus several thousand in the Alsace region, leading some commission members to estimate that the actual number could be as high as 5,000 to 10,000.[10] It is hard to believe that the estimates of the Ministry of the Interior, the Ministry of Education, and the Renseignements Généraux (the domestic intelligence service) would be so uniformly inaccurate, but both opponents and proponents of the headscarf ban had incentives to state their case in the starkest terms possible.

The headscarf can carry a number of different meanings in a number of different contexts. Often, the headscarf is a simple expression of religious tradition or belief, a sign of respect toward one's family's ancestry and culture. But it also can be a symbol of the "re-Islamization" of women of North African origin, and sometimes parents or other family members may impose it on girls and young women—in some cases at the behest of local religious leaders or even on the promise of stipends from abroad. Headscarf wearing may also be inspired by fundamentalists who are "advancing their pawns" and testing the resistance of France to the proclamation of their values. That is the interpretation of opponents of headscarves in schools and of numerous feminists who reject such proselytizing along with the submission of women that, for them, the headscarf symbolizes. Such opponents argue that public schools should contribute to the liberation of women, not condone their confinement. In their view, it is seen as a subversion of the principle of tolerance to accept the inequality of women as a cultural-religious trait.

In many other cases, the headscarf is a free outward expression of identity during a young woman's exploration of her religious commitment. That is not something imposed by parents on their daughters; it is instead part of adolescence—it relies on conflict to affirm a conviction. The headscarf can be worn without taking parental opinion into consideration—and indeed, even in spite of it. An example of the latter was the October 2003 case of Lila and Alma Lévy, two high-school-age sisters in Aubervilliers. Their stubborn desire to wear a headscarf certainly did not come from their Jewish (nonpracticing) father or from their mother, who was of Algerian Kabyle origin but agnostic and who had been separated from her husband for many years. Nor was it linked, as far as is known, to manipulation by an Islamist group. The young girls patched together their own Islam, mainly with the aid of audiocassettes by Tariq Ramadan. The central issue with the Lévy sisters, according to numerous observers, was their desire to affirm their individuality and to put themselves in the media spotlight by taking an uncompromising position on their right to express their faith. Seen from that perspective, wearing a headscarf is really not much different from wearing a baseball cap sideways or getting one's nose pierced: it is a sign of adolescent self-assertion or rebellion.

In yet another interpretation of headscarf wearing, Dounia Bouzar has shown how the *foulard* can serve, paradoxically, as a means of liberation from familial constraints and a way to avoid the macho rebukes of brothers concerned with their sisters' chastity. In this sense, the headscarf becomes "an instrument of emancipation," protecting young girls from the aggressive behavior of males, both within the family and on the street, and making parents more likely to let their daughters come home late on the subway. In other words, in certain cases, the headscarf can be synonymous with freedom because it allows young girls to leave the *cité* and not remain shut in.[11]

The Stasi Commission

In July 2003, President Jacques Chirac appointed a blue-ribbon commission of nineteen experts to consider the question of *laïcité* in French society. The commission, headed by Bernard Stasi, an old hand on the center-right, drew its members (including two Muslims) from the school system, universities, the civil service, the National Assembly, and the private sector. No official role was granted to the French Council of the Muslim Religion, although Prime Minister Raffarin addressed the council on the matter and all its principal leaders were invited to give testimony (the CFCM later issued a press release in which it said that wearing the headscarf was "*une prescription religieuse*"— "a religious rule").[12] The commission interviewed hundreds of witnesses and concluded its deliberations six months later. It then delivered an eighty-page report that outlined twenty-five proposals, including a ban on conspicuous religious symbols in elementary and secondary schools—the only proposal that was immediately converted into law.[13]

Given the ire that the ban has aroused around the world—from Cairo to Falluja to Washington—and given the relatively small number of girls who ever wore a headscarf to school, it is interesting to consider the reasons why the government chose to act on such an explosive issue.[14] It is equally intriguing to ask how nineteen experts from such different intellectual and religious backgrounds came to a nearly unanimous decision on the matter (18 to 1).[15] Commission members heard testimony from a wide variety of sources regarding increasing re-Islamization among young people in high-risk neighborhoods. In addition, research conducted for the Ministry of the Interior suggested that religion was filling a cultural vacuum in the *banlieue,* to the point that even ordinary physical activities like camping and soccer were being given religious significance (see the discussion of re-Islamization in chapter 3). The ban can thus be seen as part of a larger effort to reduce the further development of certain religious inclinations and to prevent the potential development of dual loyalties among France's Muslim population—a development that the government fears is being stoked by transnational pressures.

The question of overt religiosity had also arisen in some public administration offices. In the Paris mayor's office, for example, some civil servants who have contact with the public start wearing the veil as soon as their trial employment period is up.[16] The heavy media coverage of any instances in which Muslims have demanded male-female segregation—in sex education or gym classes, at public pools, or in hospitals—has enhanced the sense of a brewing challenge. (The Stasi Commission decided to tolerate separate hours for women at swimming pools but rejected demands that only female doctors be allowed to care for women.) The reaction to such demands is almost unanimously negative, at least in debate at the national level. As a conservative former parliamentary majority leader and close ally of Chirac rhetorically asked, "What's next: separate compartments for men and women on public transportation? This could lead to a form of apartheid, contrary to our republican ideals."[17] The French value of individual religious liberty has thus been superseded by the perceived threat to national sovereignty and the French way of life.

The headscarf ban served as a useful symbol of a robust state response, aimed to relieve the transnational pressures exerted on France's youngest, female citizens. The French state considers itself to be doing battle with transnational forces, not with individual consciences, using the instruments at its disposal: it demands a highly visible "sacrifice" on the part of Muslims to achieve republican integration. In this sense, the headscarf law could be seen as the French counterpart to Germany's citizenship law reform in 1999–2000. The German reform affirmed the state's sovereignty over its Turkish population (most of whom were citizens of Turkey), effectively asserting the state's jurisdiction over all its residents.[18] There, the initial government proposal

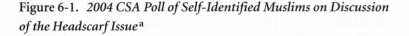

Figure 6-1. *2004 CSA Poll of Self-Identified Muslims on Discussion of the Headscarf Issue*[a]

Percent

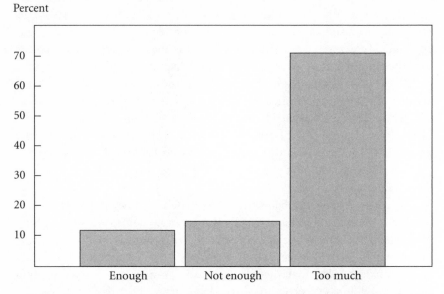

Source: "Les musulmans et la laïcité" ["Muslims and secularism"], poll by CSA/*Le Parisien/ Aujourd'hui en France*, January 21, 2004 (http://www.csa-tmo.fr/data2004/opi20040121b.htm).

a. Survey question: "Do you think that there is too much discussion, not enough discussion, or enough discussion of the question of headscarves in schools?" The question was asked of self-identified Muslims only, not persons of Muslim origin in general.

allowed for dual citizenship, but a petition campaign led to its reversal, forcing German-Turkish youth to decide their own nationality at age twenty-three. In the same way that some French Muslims were reluctant to part with the *right* to wear a headscarf as a matter of principle, many Turks in Germany resented having to choose between their Turkish passport and a German one. For some German Turks, wanting to keep their Turkish passport was not a nationalist claim, just as wanting the right to wear the headscarf is not always a religiously motivated desire. In each case, however, governments sought to bind Muslims to the state by way of a public, cultural sacrifice. By insisting on that kind of choice, governing parties in France and Germany also let voters know that a degree of cultural and political assimilation would be demanded of immigrant populations (see figure 6-1 and table 6-1). That was seen as particularly important in France, where the center-right coalition has sometimes lost as much as 18 percent of right-wing voters to the extreme nationalist

Table 6-1. *2004 CSA Poll of Self-Identified Muslims on Conspicuous Religious Symbols in Public Schools*[a]

Percent

Responses	Favorable	Opposed	No opinion
Total	42	53	5
Gender			
Men	42	51	6
Women	42	56	2
Age			
18 to 24 years	34	65	1
25 to 34 years	39	59	2
35 to 49 years	56	37	7
50 years +	42	44	15
Profession of the head of household			
Managerial or self-employed[b]	47	50	3
Technician/other professional[b]	40	52	8
Company employee[b]	39	61	0
Worker	42	54	4
Retiree/inactive	43	52	5

Source: "Les musulmans et la laïcité" ["Muslims and secularism"], poll by CSA/*Le Parisien/ Aujourd'hui en France,* January 21, 2004 (http://www.csa-tmo.fr/dataset/data2004/opi20040121b.htm).

a. Survey question: "Are you in favor of, mostly in favor of, opposed, or mostly opposed to a law prohibiting schoolchildren from wearing conspicuous religious symbols or clothing?" The question was asked of self-identified Muslims only, not persons of Muslim origin in general.

b. Results based on small samples.

Front National (FN) (National Front) party in national elections, as occurred in April 2002.

The Stasi Commission declined to evaluate specific reasons why individual French girls wore the headscarf and did not conduct any sociological surveys. A simplified narrative became dominant among French officials: foreign radicals are using France as a testing ground for their broader strategy. Headscarf wearing in schools, the officials reasoned, therefore should be examined in terms of such external factors. In something of a logical somersault, the law is actually intended to defend individual schoolgirls' religious freedom by allowing them the freedom *not* to believe. "Muslim girls who do not want to wear the scarf also have a right of freedom of conscience," wrote one Stasi Commission member in justifying his vote for the law.[19] Some witnesses told the Stasi Commission that girls wore the headscarf in response to intimidating schoolboys in their classrooms, or in response to neighborhood pressures generated by a freshly arrived foreign preacher who does not understand the French way of life, or even because some wealthy Saudis paid French Muslim families to send their girls to school wearing the headscarf. The law was therefore not intended as an affirmation of feminist principles— which would have required passing judgment on the religious meaning of the headscarf—but rather as a way of protecting schoolgirls who choose in good conscience not to wear a headscarf. The Stasi report appealed to the European Convention on Human Rights, which allows for limitations on religious expression when public order or the freedom of conscience of others is endangered.

Back to School: The Headscarf Law's Début

As the National Assembly debated the bill banning headscarves in February 2004, there were only a couple of protest rallies, which never gathered more than a few thousand participants—small by Parisian standards. After the bill became law and a follow-up memorandum was issued on how to apply it, Muslim leaders remained split over how strictly to interpret the law and whether to recommend civic disobedience on the first day of school. The fact that Sikh turbans, Jewish yarmulkes, and Christian crosses are included in the French school ban has been of little comfort to many observers concerned that Muslims are unfairly stigmatized and victimized in today's political climate. One French Muslim leader compared the government ban on the headscarf to other "unjust laws" of the past, such as that forcing French Jews to wear yellow stars during the German occupation. In fact, although the CFCM issued a statement indicating that "the law cannot be interpreted as a general and absolute prohibition of all head coverings" in May 2004, there has never been strong opposition to the law among the French Muslim population, whom opinion polls showed to be only slightly against it. (See the January 2004 CSA poll in table 6-1; in the same poll, 69 percent of the general French population was in favor or mostly in favor of the law.)

On the first day of school in 2004, U.S. news crews that had staked out schools in immigrant-heavy neighborhoods in the hope of witnessing an "uprising" were disappointed by the lack of drama. What might have been a very divisive start of the school year unfolded "in the spirit of fraternity," in the words of the education minister. Predictions of mass expulsions of Muslim girls turned out to be off the mark. Only 639 girls appeared on the first day of school wearing a head covering. Of those, all but 100 or so agreed to remove their headscarf within the first couple of days, roughly the same number as that of the so-called conflict cases as in previous years. By October 15, 2004, the Ministry of Education announced that its teachers had managed to persuade all but seventy-two holdouts to forgo their scarf. All told, forty-eight girls were expelled under the law during the first year, most of them in the environs of Strasbourg and Paris (three Sikh boys also were expelled from a school outside Paris), and 143 students left the national education system "voluntarily."[20] This number conceals headscarf-wearing girls who pursued their education elsewhere, such as the handful of students who moved abroad (around sixty-seven girls went to Turkey, Belgium, and England) or who enrolled in Catholic schools.[21] But the attrition has been modest, given the dramatic run-up to the law's application. The following year, on the first day of school in fall 2005, only twelve students arrived at school wearing headscarves—down from 639 the year before.[22] In school districts where scores of girls had worn headscarves to protest the law in 2004—Lille (118 cases) and Montpellier (sixty-one cases)—there were none in 2005. In Strasbourg, where 208 girls came to school wearing a headscarf in September 2004, only one girl defied authorities one year later.

Two factors helped maintain calm. First, as mentioned above, headscarf wearing had never been widespread. After the divisive national debate over the law on religious symbols, the law's failure to incite widespread disobedience reassured the French public that their Muslim compatriots were not, in fact, seeking confrontation. And a small number of school officials have shown willingness to compromise. Parents summoned to a school in Mantes-La-Jolie, for example, negotiated for their daughters' right to wear bandannas between courses and to remove them upon entry in the classroom. And one activist counted a dozen cases of "accommodation" in which girls have been permitted to wear a "discreet headscarf" thanks to flexible local administrators.[23]

Ironically, a significant factor behind the relatively peaceful outcome in French schools was the August 2004 hostage taking of two French journalists in Iraq, whose kidnappers demanded retraction of the French headscarf ban in return for their freedom. After that, even opponents of the law who had organized demonstrations led unanimous calls for all schoolgirls to respect the new law. Muslim leaders denounced this foreign interference in their internal affairs and proved their republican mettle by calling the kidnappers' demands an "odious [form of] blackmail" (Tariq Ramadan) and by proclaiming loudly the phrase "There will be no blood on my headscarf" (Dalil Boubakeur repeated this remark, initially attributed to a French Muslim girl). In the short time leading up to the first day of class, French Muslim leaders achieved communal unity in their unambiguous assertion of respect for the

French rule of law over any religious obligations. In grateful recognition of their support, the government approved a diplomatic mission to Baghdad by three representatives of the recently created French Council of the Muslim Religion to help secure the journalists' release.

The CFCM delegation to Iraq included its two vice presidents (Mohamed Bechari and Fouad Alaoui) and a Grande Mosquée de Paris (GMP) (Great Mosque of Paris) representative. "We cannot leave here without them," they announced in a press conference upon arrival in the Iraqi capital. "Their families are watching us. Show us that you are Muslims like us and give us the hostages."[24] The journalists were not released for several months, but the event forced Muslim leaders out of their sometimes ambiguous stance on Islamists' demands—for example, they had ignored several terrorist threats on jihadi websites after the headscarf ban was passed in spring 2004. The law revealed the depth of integration and nationalization of Islam in France, which led to a public refusal to play into the kidnappers' vision of a uniform, transnational *umma*. French Muslims had refused to be used as pawns in an international terrorist battle. As *Le Monde* editorialized, young Muslim women made the leap in the eyes of others from "victims" to "heroes of the republic." The hostage situation introduced a significant twist that may well determine the legacy of the policy on religious symbols in schools. What had threatened to lead to a grave confrontation between Muslim leaders and French government officials had led instead to a major rapprochement.

The Aftermath of the Law

To many religious observers and civil liberties activists, the ban boils down to a simple question of freedom of expression and religious rights. But to a government concerned with integrating a new, large minority community, the notion of headscarf-wearing school girls undermined a larger effort—not just the effort to sell republican values to its new citizens, but also, in a sense, to sell the "integrate-ability" of the new citizens to the majority population. From that perspective, the reaction of Muslim leaders faced with the choice of following the law or ceding to foreign pressures could not have been more opportune. "This showed that French Muslims are republicans, unlike the Wahhabis from Saudi Arabia," wrote Bruno Etienne, a specialist on Islam in France. "France's Muslims have finally started asking themselves questions about how they relate to the law of the Republic."[25] Under political pressure, Muslim leaders, like the early nineteenth-century Jewish *notables* (elites) before them, have explicitly placed the laws of the Republic above their per-ceived religious obligations by recommending that Muslim schoolgirls obey the law.[26]

The law is likely to lead to the creation of more Muslim confessional (reli-gious) schools, like those of other religious communities, governed by asso-ciation contracts with the state. In such schools, though tuition is subsidized by the state, girls are able wear what they please. After all, the first private Muslim High School in metropolitan France—the Lycée Averroés in Lille—was created for the seventeen young women expelled from high schools dur-ing the first headscarf affairs in the late 1980s and early 1990s.[27] Today, just four private Muslim schools offer courses in all of France, but funding cam-paigns are under way for new schools in several cities.

French Muslim organizations' relative lack of opposition to the headscarf ban has been criticized by Muslims elsewhere. French Muslims have had to face pressure not just from terrorists (for example, from the "Islamic Army in Iraq," which had held the French journalists hostage) but also from fellow Muslim organizations in Europe. Several articles posted on the influential U.K. website Islam Online expressed frustration at French Muslims' lack of opposition to the ban. However, a Muslim Brotherhood leader stated in Feb-ruary 2004 that "our brothers in France will be able to handle this matter however they see fit,"[28] and Sheikh Al-Tantawi of Cairo's Al Azhar mosque ruled in December 2003 that the headscarf ban was an "internal French affair," saying that Muslims in France should obey local laws.[29]

A French Muslim backlash against the law on religious signs is still con-ceivable, especially if some public officials continue to apply it at their per-sonal discretion outside of public schools. There were reports in 2004 of a Muslim man being fired from his job at a municipal swimming pool because of the style of his beard, and there have been isolated incidents of veiled women being refused entry to municipal polling stations, to the Senate gallery, and even to a town hall naturalization ceremony where the women in question arrived to take the oath of French citizenship.[30] Such incidents weaken the French state's argument that it seeks only to protect underage girls from undue religious pressure and send an ambiguous signal to the Muslim population regarding the actual purview of the law.

Such incidents have led Muslim leaders to demonstrate to the grassroots that they are actively defending the religion and that they are not in cahoots with a repressive government. Though the Union des Organisations Islamiques de France (UOIF) (Union of Islamic Organizations of France) was generally cooperative with the headscarf ban during the law's inaugural year, it has shown signs that it intends to challenge the law in the future. "Laws concerning religious neutrality apply to civil servants, not to those who use public services, such as schoolchildren," UOIF secretary general Fouad Alaoui said in a recent interview.[31] Overturning the headscarf ban was a major theme of the UOIF's annual assembly in March 2005. One association published the testimony of schoolgirls who felt humiliated and excluded by the ban, and many other groups collected funds for the private education of Muslim girls. In his keynote speech, Alaoui hinted at the residual rancor within the community: "Our freedoms have been compromised because in our country, the land of human rights, young girls are excluded from the classroom and denied an education simply for refusing to show their ears." One year after the law passed—while calling for respect of the law—Alaoui implied that, for the UOIF at least, the question of headscarves in schools is not closed: "We hope that we will finally be able to debate, in a period of calm, this fundamental question of the coexistence of *laïcité* and Islam."[32]

The headscarf debate may rage yet again. In the interim, it is possible that the government will soften the rigidity of the ban somewhat, and compromises could still be struck during future reviews of the law (as required by an amendment) or in the Ministry of Education's "application memorandum" governing how the law is enforced—perhaps by allowing girls to wear discreet kerchiefs, for example. There is always the possibility that some Muslim organizations may still try to organize displays of civil disobedience during the annual return to school. Should that occur, the government may find that it is a good time to introduce some of the other twenty-four measures proposed by the Stasi Commission, such as courses dealing with the subjective experience of Muslim populations under slavery and colonialism and the creation of school holidays for Muslim holy days.[33]

7

An Assessment of
French Policy Responses

The task of integrating a large, highly visible minority could be seen as one for which the French state is singularly unsuited. French republicanism resists making official reference to either the foreign origin (after the first generation) or the religious affiliation of its citizens, except as it relates to the free exercise of religion. The French government has traditionally rejected U.S.- and British-style minority group politics, especially as institutionalized in the United Kingdom's Commission on Racial Equality or in affirmative action policies in the United States. To try to get data or elicit opinions regarding immigrant populations—or worse, specific "communities"—from a civil servant or politician can be like pulling teeth. Such resistance is at once a drawback and an advantage of French citizenship. The 215-year-old tradition of *citoyenneté* casts the individual first and foremost as a citizen, not as a member of any ethnic, racial, or religious group. However, the state's stubborn faith in the civic education offered through the public schools, military service, and the professions precluded any development of an explicit integration policy for first- or second-generation immigrants.[1]

The French Republic relegates ethnic background and religious affiliation to the private sphere, at least officially: a 1978 law greatly restricts keeping of official racial and ethnic records, and the last census indicating respondents' religion was taken in 1872. To track citizens by race or ethnicity would evoke the crimes of Vichy France, while excessive attention to religious affiliation is seen to threaten the notion of *laïcité*.[2] Such information can be recorded if there is pressing need, however, and polling institutes regularly ask for it (since respondents can, of course, refuse to give it), but a *républicain* political correctness pervades public institutions.[3] During a mini-scandal in 2003 over the national statistical agency's inclusion of "ethnic origin" on a census, President Jacques Chirac declared: "The Republic does not recognize people on the basis of their origin. You are French, and there are French people of all ethnic origins. The idea of checking a box for ethnic identity is scandalous and contrary to the principles of the Republic. It is illegal and immoral."[4]

This philosophy was sustained even after decolonization, when in the 1960s waves of North African immigrants transformed France into the home of Europe's largest Jewish and Muslim populations. On one hand, because of official and culturally ingrained taboos, that approach makes it difficult to measure—not to say promote—the "success" of the descendants of immigrants (or even to count them). But it is beneficial in that French citizenship provides a universal identity that immigrants can readily adopt. In the French view of U.S. political culture, individual members of American minorities are more likely to feel imprisoned than empowered by their group identity. The conflicting loyalties and outright confrontation sometimes seen among communities in the United States—condoned or indeed encouraged by affirmative action policies and institutionalized ethnic lobbying—are believed by the French to weaken the universal bond of citizenship. By extension, the civil organizations in France that stand between citizens and the state have been treated historically "as 'private wills' in a political culture that values the 'general will.'"[5] French policymakers therefore have been generally hesitant to adopt policies explicitly designed to level the playing field because they fear that granting legal status based on group identity perpetuates the very boundaries that undermine a national sense of community.

As discussed in other chapters, French citizenship has not brought about the kind of social advancement and political integration that had been hoped for. Part of the bargain of political participation, of course, is that it translates into representation in the National Assembly. Despite the fact that Muslims represent a growing (yet still small) share of voters—it is thought that between 1.5 and 2 million are French citizens of voting age, although many have not registered to vote—the political representation of recent immigrants has been noticeably weak. The major political parties have fielded few candidates of North African origin, and there has not been a single deputy of Muslim origin in the National Assembly, although two senators were elected in 2004. The lack of representatives contributed to government officials' sense that something had to be done, and they set off in search of community interlocutors in order to emphasize the inclusiveness of the French political system. Policymakers have indeed shifted their attention to the promotion of social and political integration, although it still usually takes place under the cover of socioeconomic policies or policies targeting specific geographic locations—not ethnic policies.

The Diversification of French Politics

When in fall 2003 Nicolas Sarkozy, the minister of the interior, pointed out that his administration lacked a single "Muslim prefect" (department governor), Chirac fired back from an official visit in Tunisia that "it is not acceptable to nominate people on the basis of their origin." However, the lack of a single parliamentary deputy of Muslim or North African origin has been a striking symbol of the lagging political integration of immigrants, and although ethnic quotas are indeed anathema in republican ideology, symbolic appointments are now beginning to be made—and public policies pursued—that appear designed to send a positive signal to French voters of Arab-Muslim origin.

In 2002, Chirac's center-right coalition seized the initiative in recognizing the multi-ethnic nature of French society. Chirac sometimes has contradicted himself in this matter—for example, by claiming to have originated the idea of diversifying the government and ultimately heeding Nicolas Sarkozy's call for diversification by appointing Aïssa Dermouche (a Frenchman born in Algeria) as a prefect in January 2004. In fact, earlier in his term the president had insisted that a citizen of North African origin be appointed as a school chancellor in the Ministry of Education as a "symbol for the Muslim community."[6] And the president's adviser on integration issues has undertaken a review of public employment dossiers, looking for candidates of immigrant origin who may have been overlooked in the past. But tolerance toward raising the profile of immigrant communities in the public sphere should not be interpreted as approval of a U.S.- or U.K.-style system in which well-organized minority group lobbies zealously guard their own group's interests. As Chirac has put it, the Republic can countenance "*communautés*" (communities) but not "*communautarisme*" (communitarianism).

In May 2002, the newly appointed prime minister, Jean-Pierre Raffarin, took a page from former U.S. president Bill Clinton's first term and named a cabinet staff that reflected the diversity of contemporary France. Under Chirac's directions, Raffarin broke the de facto color barrier in national government by appointing two cabinet members of North African origin: Tokia Saïfi, deputy minister for sustainable development, the first *beur* cabinet member, and Hamlaoui Mékachera, deputy minister for veteran affairs, the first Muslim to hold the post.[7] The personal staff of Raffarin's cabinet members also came from an expanded pool of candidates, although they still were largely recruited from France's *grandes écoles*. Hakim El Karoui, a young graduate of Normal Supérieure, penned much of a book by Raffarin that was released before the spring 2002 elections and became one of the prime minister's speechwriters.[8] In addition, Raffarin's adviser on integration issues was Richard Senghor, a graduate of the Institut d'Etudes Politiques (Sciences Po) and a grandnephew of former Senegalese president and poet Léopold Sedar Senghor. All ministers with important portfolios in Raffarin's cabinet—from Dominique de Villepin at Interior, Michèle Alliot-Marie at Defense, Renaud Donnedieu de Vabres at Culture, and Michel Barnier at Foreign Affairs to Nelly Olin, deputy minister for integration—relied on at least one and sometimes several staff members of North African immigrant background.[9]

Following suit, the Socialist Party soon thereafter named Malek Boutih, former head of the antiracist association SOS Racisme, as a national secretary.[10] Another woman brought in by the Socialist Party, Bariza Khiari, eventually became one of the first two French senators of North African origin since the independence of Algeria. The other senator, Alima Boumediene-Thiery, French-born of Moroccan and Algerian heritage, was elected for the Green Party. In radio addresses and stump speeches, Prime Minister Raffarin went out of his way to dispel "the impression among many Muslims that there are different classes of French nationality."[11]

In addition to the appointment of minority candidates to office, many other issues considered of interest to minority voters have received a good deal of government attention. And, interestingly, the predominantly center-right politicians were the ones who found themselves at the forefront of this evolution. Chirac was the first president to recognize the state's responsibility for the deportation of Jews at the Vélodrome d'Hiver during the Vichy regime, acknowledging in July 1996 that "France did not shield her children."[12] And while swearing in eighteen new members of the Haut Conseil à l'Intégration (High Council on Integration)—more than a third of whom were of recent immigrant origin—Prime Minister Raffarin declared that the council reflected "the face of twenty-first-century France, one that carries racial mixing [*métissage*] in its heart."[13]

In addition, Alexandre Dumas, an accomplished author and grandson of a Haitian slave, was given an elaborate funeral at the Panthéon—a prestigious building where national heroes are buried—in October 2002. When President Chirac decreed this posthumous honor—bestowed on only five other authors since 1791—he called attention to Dumas's black heritage, saying that Dumas "embodies the France of the nineteenth century and even of the twenty-first century, in all of its most intimate contradictions."[14] In his eulogy Chirac spoke evocatively of the author's "brown skin, frizzy hair, and mixed blood."[15] Government ministers and literati huddled in the cold while, in a cross-cultural variation on the usual presentation, a black woman dressed as Marianne, the symbol of the French Republic, sitting astride a white horse, bowed her head before Dumas's casket. And on July 14, 2004, Bastille Day, during the culminating rally of a five-week march by a group called Against Ghettos and for Equality, 200 young people from the *banlieue* joined Jean-Louis Debré, the National Assembly president, to unveil a new fresco adorning the frontispiece of the Parliament building. The fresco, entitled "Today's Mariannes," portrayed fourteen young women of different ethnicities in revolutionary garb. Debré, who as a law-and-order interior minister in the mid-1990s was a target of the ire of immigrant rights groups, said that France was a "Republic of mixed races, at home with itself everywhere."[16]

Further adding to the sense that the government was finally taking French society's contemporary diversity into account, the Conseil Français du Culte Musulman (CFCM) (French Council of the Muslim Religion) was installed in the spring and summer of 2003 (see chapter 5). One year later, Chirac personally inducted its president, Dalil Boubakeur, as an officer of the Légion d'Honneur. In addition, the National Assembly passed the Lellouche law in December 2002, which increased legal protections against anti-Semitic and racist hate crimes.[17] And in February 2004, a report written by Bernard Stasi (who also chaired the report on religious symbols in the public schools) laid out the details for the creation of a national agency to monitor and actively fight all kinds of discrimination, especially that based on ethnicity and religion. The new agency would have broad authority to influence all legislation and decrees relating to discrimination. Plans for an "integration ministry," such as that in Sweden, were not acted on, nor were plans to grant third-country nationals (people who are not citizens of an EU nation) the right to vote in city elections. But the sustained activities in these areas of Social Affairs Minister Jean-Louis Borloo and Yves Jégo, a deputy of the Union pour un Mouvement Populaire (UMP) (Union for a Popular Movement), have provided further indication of the conservative majority's interest in the topic. In December 2004, the Haute Autorité de Lutte contre les Discriminations et pour l'Egalité (HALDE) (High Authority for Combating Discrimination and Promoting Equality) was formally instituted by the National Assembly, and it began operations on January 1, 2005.

The national board of the HALDE is composed of eleven members (eight of whom are proposed by the president, prime minister, and two chambers of Parliament), and it has an annual budget of nearly €11 million ($13,353,000). It may be approached directly by any victim of discrimination based on gender, sexual orientation, ethnicity, marital status, name, physical appearance, handicap, political orientation, religion, union membership, and so forth. The authority can launch its own investigations—with the consent of victims—and it was given additional enforcement powers after the social unrest of November 2005. It is expected to attempt to mediate any complaint first, but it may also initiate lawsuits on behalf of victims. Its other mission is to promote equality by encouraging research, supporting private initiatives—for example, the "diversity charters" under which firms pledge to actively recruit minority employees—and launching public campaigns to increase awareness of discrimination. It shares its second mission with a much older and somewhat smaller institution, the Commission Nationale Consultative des Droits de l'Homme (CNCDH) (National Advisory Commission on Human Rights), which was created in 1947 by René Cassin, one of the fathers of the Universal Declaration of Human Rights, and revived in the mid-1980s. Though it lacks enforcement powers, the CNCDH has a played a useful role in fighting discrimination—most notably racism and anti-Semitism—through its annual public report (see chapter 9).

Last, the government enacted a set of "equal opportunity" measures after the unrest of November 2005 to address the dire situation in the *cités,* where many descendants of immigrants live and where the unrest took place. In addition to enhancing the HALDE's powers to fight discrimination, the Ministry of the Interior created six new deputy prefects for equal opportunity (a prefect is usually named by the central government to serve as chief administrator of a *département,* or region), who are responsible for overseeing all the different policies and their budgets. Another new agency ("agency for social cohesion") also may be created to improve coordination, in addition to other small existing public bodies in charge of integration, such as the Fonds d'Action et de Soutien a l'Intégration et à la Lutte contre les Discriminations (FASILD) (Support Fund for Integration and the Fight against Discrimination) and the Agence Nationale de Lutte contre l'Illetrisme (ANLCI) (Agency for the Fight against Illiteracy). Chirac also convened a meeting of major television network CEOs to urge them to increase the ethnic diversity of their journalists and talking heads, and he called for increasing to 30 percent the proportion of students from poor neighborhoods in the highly selective public classes that prepare students to take tests for university admission (*classes préparatoires*).

Under the current prime minister, Dominique de Villepin, who was named in June 2005, the government also has tried to promote new policies aimed at addressing the fundamentals of the integration problem, namely, school and social disaffiliation, the ghetto phenomenon, and unemployment. In addition to injecting nearly €100 million ($120 million) extra into municipal budgets for the funding of civic associations in 2006, the government has stressed the magnitude of the state's efforts, undertaken by Social Affairs Minister Jean-Louis Borloo in 2003, to launch a "Marshall Plan" for the *banlieues.* Its objectives are ambitious: renovation of 400,000 public housing units and replacement of 250,000 of them, among other measures, for a total investment of up to €20 to €30 billion ($24 to $36 billion) over the 2004–12 period. Half of that amount is budgeted for a variety of activities to help guide as many as 800,000 young people toward employment, and it foresees training 100,000 young people from "sensitive neighborhoods" to enter public employment without having to sit for the regular exams. In addition, the government hopes to assign two or more apprentices to all firms that have more than 100 employees.[18] However, the effects of this policy, which has a slight pie-in-the-sky feeling to it, will be visible only over the long term. As far as unemployment is concerned, a new apprenticeship contract has been put in place that allows youth as young as fourteen years of age to start working part-time while studying part-time. Public funds to encourage the employment of young people in "sensitive urban areas" have been increased, and fifteen new "tax-free zones" to encourage business investment in these areas have been added to the existing ones.[19] However, considering how entrenched unemployment has become in France, many economic experts—including Daniel Cohen and Jean-Paul Fitoussi, who are not known for their free market inclinations—remain skeptical about the efficacy of these measures.[20] In their view, nothing short of a radical overhaul of the job market—to increase flexibility in hiring and firing—would ensure integration. Any such overhaul, however partial—Prime Minister Villepin's Contrat Première Embauche (CPE) (New Hire Contract) targeted only workers under the age of twenty-six—is strongly resisted by the trade unions, as attested by the series of anti-CPE strikes and demonstrations coordinated with student leaders in February-March 2006, which forced the government to bury the proposal.

Some of the institution building of the last decade is based simply on the consistent application of the republican principle of equality and recognition of individuals and groups—whether Jewish, Muslim, or of immigrant origin—that are important components of French society. But the trend also reflects a new bipartisan consensus regarding the contemporary state's role in promoting immigrant integration: first, that important religious minorities must be granted institutional representation, and second, that ethnic groups—especially Arabs and Jews—should be protected from acts of discrimination, racism, or anti-Semitism. Moreover, the mobilization of the government after the urban riots of November 2005 was mirrored by an increased awareness of the magnitude of the challenge in French civil society. It is too soon to know, however, whether this increased awareness will have long-term positive effects that would outweigh the short- and medium-term negative effects that a backlash in public opinion against the population of immigrant origin would have.

Affirmative Action, Priority Education Zones, and Military Recruitment

The national government has started quietly giving preferential treatment to members of ethnic and racial minorities, especially in the areas of educational opportunity and public administration. But across the political spectrum, public recruitment efforts have steered clear of establishing any criteria that evoke quotas or suggest that merit may be disregarded. Private firms have been at the forefront of the diversification effort in French society—as summed up in a 2004 report by the Institut Montaigne, a business-oriented think tank—and they seem to be actively trying to foster a neutral, "equal opportunity" environment.[21] A series of proposals targeting discrimination in the professions was spearheaded by a report to the prime minister in fall 2004 that included a dramatic plan to require all firms with more than 250 employees to remove the names from job applicants' resumes so that applicants remain anonymous, identified only by their educational and professional achievements.[22] The report's author began requiring anonymous resumes at his own company (AXA Insurance) in 2005, and soon thereafter the municipality of Lyon set up a trial review of anonymous resumes during service-sector hiring between January and June 2005.[23]

Private companies have begun to see diversity as an asset in developing new markets and international business. Many large companies have publicly affirmed their commitment to having a diverse workforce, while avoiding any discussion of establishing numeric quotas. For example, in 2004 thirty-five companies—including the hotel group Accor, the metal firm Arcelor, AXA, and IBM—voluntarily signed a "diversity charter" pledging to actively recruit minority employees.[24] Two recent conferences demonstrate a further reason why integrating young Muslim professionals in the French workplace is of increasing urgency: if talented *beurs* are stymied in France, they may be forced to look elsewhere. In the spring of 2005, multinational companies with offices in the Maghreb drew 400 French-trained students of North African origin to their recruitment stands at a regional employment fair; one year later, a Moroccan association of students at elite universities organized an event for graduates, urging them to return to the home country, to build "the Morocco of tomorrow."[25]

The recruitment programs promoted by the Institut Montaigne are in their infancy, and the effectiveness at enhancing diversity in French firms has yet to be measured. But the message has spread to various government offices, some of which have begun to call for greater diversity in the administrative ranks. The High Council on Integration and the Institut National de la Statistique et des Etudes Economiques (INSEE) (National Institute of Statistics and Economic Studies) each released studies in 2004 that called for redressing the underrepresentation of ethnic minorities in the civil service.[26] Another report commissioned by the Ministry of the Interior noted that just 5 percent of the 11,000 police officers (*adjoints de sécurité*) and only ten of 1,800 police chiefs (*commissaires*) hired in January 2004 were of North African or African origin.[27] But affirmative action is not the instinctive response to such inequality of most influential policymakers, who prefer more vigorous recruitment—"going to the [minorities] where they are," in the words of the Interior Ministry report—to stating ethnic preferences in the hiring process. Azouz Begag, the report's author, proposed "breaking the taboo around ethnic origins" by aggressively pursuing youth of North African origin and by appointing a "director of equal opportunity" at the ministry. (Chirac later appointed Begag as deputy minister for equal opportunity in 2005.)

The distinction between enhanced recruitment and preference policies is not purely semantic. On one hand, many French officials retain a certain pride in the French ideal of citizenship and the ability of the state to provide its citizens with equal opportunities. "The American republic had two centuries of legal discrimination," the immigration scholar Patrick Weil wrote in *Le Monde*, "and has compiled racial data since the creation of the republic." In France, he continued, "universal access to social protection and public health is guaranteed and our school system assures a minimum of equality in terms of resources and teachers across the national territory."[28] But many politicians have hinted that they have doubts as to whether that guarantee is actually being fulfilled, whether in education or the civil service.

The center-left Jospin government encouraged people of immigrant origin to apply for positions in public administration and law enforcement—most notably in the ranks of the army and the state railroad system. Minister of the Interior Jean-Pierre Chevènement (1997–2000) sponsored exam preparation and language courses so that "youth of immigrant origin" could more easily compete for jobs as police officers. "School is not playing its role in social mobility, which has always been a French tradition," he said. "I want to return to that tradition." But Chevènement did not want his promotion of opportunities for immigrants' children to be confused with affirmative action. "I try to avoid defining people by their origins, since that boxes them in. We must 'de-ethnicize' the way we look at people."[29] He also initiated regional "equality commissions" that would make employers and administrators aware of the need to hire youth of immigrant origin, which were later maintained by succeeding governments, both left and right.[30] While Chevènement acknowledged that his police officer initiative was "80 percent concerned with youth of North African origin," the preparatory courses and examinations were open to everyone. Around 1,000 children of immigrants became police officers in the late 1990s, but Chevènement said that "this was not at all a form of positive discrimination," because police officers were not recruited exclusively in immigrant neighborhoods.[31] Similarly, when President Chirac named Aïssa Dermouche as prefect, he took care to insist that it was not a case of "positive discrimination," since he had no intention of creating quotas.[32]

Nicolas Sarkozy, however, has been a vocal proponent of positive discrimination, which he has dubbed "*real* equality" (*egalité effective*). "Equity is the first value of the republic, not just equality," Sarkozy said in one interview. "There are people and areas that have more handicaps and need to be helped more, in order to compensate for historical, social, or economic inequalities."[33] He claims that his proposals are the "exact opposite of Anglo-Saxon models"—though that statement may slightly misrepresent U.S. policies, suggesting that they are simply quota driven—and that the designation "Muslim," for example, refers to cultural origins, not religion. Sarkozy appeals not to the U.S. experience, therefore, but to the legacy of Charles de Gaulle, who decreed in 1958 that 10 percent of public sector jobs be reserved for Muslims from French Algeria—a population that had, for the most part, sympathized with the French against the independence movement. In support of his argument for a policy shift, Sarkozy also cites priority education zones, which receive additional government support, and the 2000 "parity law," which sets aside 50 percent of all candidacies on political party lists for women: "What is all this, if not positive discrimination?"[34]

Political leaders on the whole reject ascribing group status to individuals, but several developments have led to its acceptance in certain cases. The government's Mattéoli Commission, for example, indemnified individual Jews whose goods and bank accounts were confiscated under the Vichy regime. Yet it also assigned the unclaimed amount of €220 million ($267 million) to the new Fondation pour la Mémoire de la Shoah (Foundation in Memory of the Holocaust)—whose board is partly controlled by Jewish community institutions—to support Holocaust studies and Jewish culture.[35] Therefore the postwar French Jewish community has not been treated exactly the same way as hurricane victims, as one politician put it, but has benefited as a class of victims, regardless of personal suffering during the war.[36] Together with the 2000 parity law, the Mattéoli Commission marked a departure from preference policies developed for historically mistreated or disadvantaged groups that target specific neighborhoods or areas. Such policies included priority education zones, departmental housing policies for disadvantaged populations, and *zones franches* (tax-free business incentive zones) in certain *banlieues*.

The left-wing coalitions under President François Mitterrand in the 1980s pioneered policies designed to better integrate second-generation youth of North African origin. But the Socialist Party, perhaps fearful of a right-wing backlash after the National Front emerged as an electoral force, hewed to a strict "*républicain*" line, using the neutral language of citizenship-based political participation. Any helping hand therefore was wrapped in the guise of policies that targeted specific neighborhoods or areas and could be aimed only indirectly at immigrant youth. At the time, one spoke generally of "*jeunes*" (youth) and "difficult neighborhoods" without mentioning their ethnicity or national origins.[37] After 1981, the Socialists relied on newly founded immigrant associations to complement their urban policies targeting unemployment and poverty. Mitterand's Socialist Party acted as patron of a significant antiracism association—SOS Racisme—born of the 1983–84 second-generation *beur* movement. The government oversaw the disbursal of funds for some social service programs that were to be carried out by the new immigrant associations—for example, through the Direction de la Population et des Migrations (DPM) (Population and Migration Administration), a government agency. Throughout the 1990s the government continued to channel extra subsidies into housing projects in poor neighborhoods, never mentioning the ethnic or religious background of the target populations.

President Mitterrand's main legacy in this domain was the creation of *zones d'éducation prioritaire* (ZEPs) (priority education zones) in 1981, assigning an extra 8 percent of resources to 362 schools in districts that accounted for one-tenth of all primary and secondary school students at the time.[38] Today those districts include 20 percent of all primary and secondary school students; an additional 12,000 teachers and assistants, who receive pay bonuses for the difficulty of their jobs, are assigned to work there.[39] The 1.8 million students concerned are not solely minority students, but ZEPs are designated in areas where, due to a combination of socioeconomic factors, minority students are likely to reside. Sixty percent of junior high school students in ZEPs are the children of workers or unemployed parents, and 27 percent have two parents of immigrant origin.[40] More than a quarter of elementary and junior high school students in the Paris region, in Lille, in Aix-Marseille, and in the French overseas territories attend a ZEP school. In the Paris suburbs of Département 93 (discussed in chapter 1), half of all public schools are in ZEPs, and 3,000 extra jobs were added in 2004 in the local school district of Creteil, on the outskirts of Paris, where some schools are in ZEPs.[41] An additional category of school was created in the 1990s—schools in *zones urbaines sensibles* (ZUS) (sensitive urban areas)—to allow the heads of local school districts further flexibility in allocating funds (more than 95 percent of students who live in a ZUS attend a ZEP school).[42]

Students attending schools in ZEPs are eligible for special scholarships, job placement assistance, and supplementary courses in eight school districts to help prepare them for public employment exams. Many ZEP schools also have access to social services that aim to keep at-risk children from becoming dropouts. Education Minister François Fillon (2002–04) proposed creating special vocational track programs in summer 2004, challenging the tradition, in place since 1975, of offering a single junior high school curriculum for all students. Fillon argued that preparation for professional life would "better respond to the diversity of students and their expectations," and three- or six-hour weekly vocational modules are already offered (on a voluntary basis) in a ZEP junior high school in Val d'Oise. ZEP schools are sometimes stigmatized—ZEP students still underperform the average student in French and mathematics by about 10 percentage points—but it is presumed that their scores would be worse without the extra teachers and resources.[43] And although these schools were long considered to be more violent or unruly than other schools, a 2005 government study found that there was no more vandalism or violence there than elsewhere, an improvement from previous findings.[44]

Emblematic of how times are changing is the way in which recent governments have elaborated on ZEP policies, transforming them into something designed to promote the social advancement of minorities in a more forthright manner.[45] The elite Institut d'Etudes Politiques (Sciences Po) (Institute of Political Studies) in Paris, the premier university for training future top civil servants and executives, signed *conventions d'education prioritaire*

(CEPs) (priority education agreements) with seven ZEP high schools in 2001, and there were thirty-three agreements in 2005. The CEP exempts several students graduating from these high schools from Sciences Po's grueling entrance exam; the admissions process starts with teachers' recommendations alone. Successful applicants are granted a merit scholarship for university tuition and a stipend for living costs in Paris. "Our objective is a public service in the image of society," said Richard Descoings, Sciences Po's director. In another move aimed at increasing diversity, the university's tuition is now fixed in direct proportion to family income, lessening the cost for poorer families. Descoings might also have noted that graduates could well bypass public service and find their way to the private sector instead, as many Sciences Po graduates now do; representatives of several large private companies sit on the CEP's advisory board, including l'Oréal, Accor, and BNP Paribas.[46] The CEP has been a topic of great controversy, with the program's detractors deriding Sciences Po's American-style affirmative action approach, mocking its magnanimous acceptance of "boat people," and describing it with an unkind pun—"*Sciences Pauvres*" ("science for poor people"—or, alternatively, "poor science").[47] The school won legal challenges to the CEP in France's constitutional court, although on the condition that the program undergo regular evaluation and be subject to renewal after a four-year trial phase.[48]

An initial review indicated that the 132 students who were admitted during the four years of the CEP program since fall 2001 successfully integrated into the school's rigorous program of study. Fifteen of the first seventeen students were promoted to the second year, as were thirty of the second group of thirty-three students. Overall, nine in ten CEP students continued on to the second year.[49] Thirty-seven students who had attended ZEP high schools were members of Sciences Po's 2004 graduating class of 360 students. Although ZEPs are established along socioeconomic criteria, ZEP students heading to Sciences Po are frequently second-generation immigrants: about two-thirds have one foreign parent and 55 percent have two foreign parents.[50] After the program's first two years, in which 70 percent of CEP students were young women, the gender imbalance has evened out, to 50/50. The program's review stated that the students had been "perfectly socially integrated" into school clubs and the student government, to which one-third of CEP students were elected as representatives. Sciences Po's branch in Aix-en-Provence also has started to broaden its applicant pool. However, rather than adopting the automatic entry formula of the Paris campus, it offers exam preparation courses for high school students "from difficult backgrounds." In addition, several other schools—Essec, Grenoble School of Management, and the

National Academy of Arts and Professions (Ensam)—have since declared their intention to recruit more students from underprivileged neighborhoods.[51] This recruitment system is technically based on merit, and it rejects actual quotas, simply rewarding those who rise to the top of underprivileged schools.[52]

One final neighborhood- or area-based initiative worth mentioning is the military's recruitment of youth of immigrant origin. With the end of the draft in 2002 and the subsequent crisis in enlistments, suburban ghettos have come to be seen as reservoirs of ambitious and available potential recruits. The military therefore opened recruiting offices in districts with heavy immigrant quotients: Seine-Saint-Denis (Département 93), for example, is the only administrative district with two information and recruitment centers.[53] Military officials hope to use association presidents and social workers in their recruiting efforts, with the aim of signing up 19,000 young people from these neighborhoods. In the words of one top officer, the state wants "to make the words 'army' and 'integration' rhyme once more."[54] The proportion of second- and third-generation immigrants in the armed forces is unknown. One recruiter in Tours said that of 250 recruits in 1999, 4 percent were of North African origin. In 2004, the scholar Rémy Leveau estimated that 10 percent of new recruits were of North African origin, while a 2005 study estimated that between 10 and 20 percent of the army was composed of new soldiers of Muslim background.[55]

Like the U.S. army, the French army promises the children of immigrants a chance to find a profession, to get out of the ghettos, and eventually to attend college. A documentary film by Yamina Benguigui about recruitment in the *banlieue* provides a glimpse of the army's pragmatic views: a lieutenant colonel in charge of recruitment said that "for us, there is no such thing as 'recently French' or 'French for a long time'—there are only Frenchmen." A general added, "We need to look for young people where they are."[56]

There are some indications that the idea of affirmative action is gaining ground with the French public, perhaps due in part to the supportive role played by the popular politician Nicolas Sarkozy.[57] But Sarkozy's plans for the introduction of modest measures of "positive discrimination" met opposition within his own party, especially from President Jacques Chirac, who stated that "skin color, the sound of a name, an accent, or even an address— all of these signs mean nothing in a Republic."[58] In a poll conducted by BVA in 2004, 40 percent of those asked said that they favored "positive discrimination"; the rate increased to 60 percent among those less than twenty-five years of age.[59] French and U.S. perspectives are not always opposed, of course, and future education policies may follow a best practices approach modeled on the experiences of some American universities. The immigration scholar Patrick Weil has proposed that France's *grandes écoles* adopt a system like that of the University of California or of Texas—some of whose campuses reserve spots for the top 5 percent of high school graduates in the state—and grant spaces in preparatory classes for the top high school students from around the country.[60]

Policing Immigrants: The Firm Hand of the Republic

The policies of openness described above suggest that there has been a sea change in attitudes toward second- and third-generation North African immigrants. But the Ministry of the Interior has not forgotten its job description, the primary component of which is to maintain domestic order and security. Although half of the French population of Muslim origin was born in France, there are at least 2 million noncitizens for whom legal problems related to immigration—such as renewal of visas or residence permits—can be an alienating experience. For decades, noncitizens who committed crimes were subject to expulsion after serving their time. This was known as the "*double peine*" (double jeopardy) and was only (partially) abolished in 2003, a move that added to Sarkozy's popularity among the population of Arab origin.

The ministry has redeployed police officers (under the Ministry of Defense) and gendarmerie officers (under the Ministry of the Interior) to immigrant neighborhoods, where undercover units and "anticriminality brigades" recruit informants and work on crime prevention, usually without kid gloves. And although positive action has been taken to support the integration of youth of immigrant origin, new immigrants are still expected to adapt to French norms upon arrival. Early assimilation of the 100,000 to 150,000 (net) legal immigrants who arrive each year is now encouraged through a government program that welcomes them and requires them to sign a "welcome and integration contract" (*contrat d'accueil et d'intégration*), which includes free French language courses and tutoring on their civic rights and obligations in exchange for their affirmation that they are willing to integrate into French society and abide by the law. If they fulfill the terms of the contract, they are given a ten-year residence permit; if not, a one-year renewable permit is issued. This contract, which is now offered in all regions of France, does not include naturalization, but it is a step toward the active encouragement of integration by emphasizing the respective obligations of immigrants and the state.[61]

Although interior ministers no longer use the mid-1990s rhetoric of "zero immigration," illegal immigrants are still the subject of much unwanted attention from the national police. One of Interior Minister Sarkozy's first acts, in 2002, was to close the Red Cross's refugee camp at Sangatte and order the arrest of groups of undocumented migrants who occupied two churches in Pas-de-Calais and in the eleventh arrondissement of Paris. The Ministry of the Interior also introduced fingerprinting for visa requests in order to better control illegal immigration. The central office for the prevention of illegal immigration claimed to have dismantled twelve international smuggling networks in 2003 and fifteen in 2004. In the Pas-de-Calais department, which the Eurostar passes through on its London-Paris route, 312 smugglers were arrested in 2003 and 467 in 2004. The number of deportations of illegal immigrants in 2004 increased by 40 percent and 56 percent compared with the number in 2003 and 2002 respectively, and it rose to more than 20,000 in 2005. The official objective for 2006 deportations was increased to 25,000.[62] More generally, Nicolas Sarkozy has toughened the conditions for family reunification and for the entrance of foreign spouses of French nationals outside of the family reunification provisions—that is, through a wedding contracted abroad *after* immigration to France. In 2004, foreign spouses accounted for more than twice as many immigrants as those who entered under family reunification provisions (see chapter 1).[63]

By the end of 2005, the urban riots had triggered a series of negative reactions from the right—along the lines of "We told you so"—and there were early indications of a public backlash. Allies of Nicolas Sarkozy at the National Assembly began to target immigrants in their speeches, for example, by raising the purported role of polygamous households in the rioting because parents in such households were not in control of their children. Sarkozy himself was accused of exacerbating the unrest by stating his desire to clean the "rabble" (*racaille*) out of the *cités* with a high-pressure water hose. Though his rhetoric mimicked the plain language of many inhabitants who actually live in the *cités* in regard to getting rid of their own rabble, many French of Arab and African origin reacted negatively to the use of such terms by a minister of the Republic. Although they may have strongly disapproved of the riots, they also condemned Sarkozy for using language that they feared might stigmatize an entire population. Sarkozy's strong law-and-order stance, which endeared him to the right-wing of the political spectrum, left a bitter taste in the immigrant community.

It is against this more repressive face of the government that the French left can still offer some criticism—in addition to criticism of the right's heavy reliance in national election campaigns on "security" themes, which some view as code for more protection of "natives" from immigrants and Arab youth. But the right's efforts in this area, notably during the unrest of November 2005, allowed it to reclaim the law-and-order mantle from the extreme right. For example, for three months after the riots the government authorized local officials to ban demonstrations, declare curfews, and conduct police raids at day or night, under the authority of a 1955 law on public order, and Sarkozy threatened to deport any foreigners who had participated in the riots, though there were very few such cases.[64] In addition, the UMP government's immigration and integration bill passed in spring 2006 included tougher conditions for family reunification and the naturalization of illegal immigrants and contained measures tying "selective immigration" (*l'immigration choisie*) to needed skills, though it steered clear of establishing any national quotas.[65] "We must draw some lessons from the riots in the *banlieues* in November 2005," said the UMP parliamentary deputy in charge of presenting and defending the new immigration bill. "We must choose an immigration policy that succeeds through work, and I am unashamed to say that in a context of international competition, France must choose the best."[66] Sarkozy, who promoted the law, even argued that "selective immigration is a rampart against racism."[67]

However, in a televised debate in 2003 with Front National leader Jean-Marie Le Pen, Sarkozy, alluding to his Hungarian heritage, rejected the vision of an "ethnically pure" French citizenry: "With *jus sanguinis*, I wouldn't be French today," he reminded Le Pen. "Admit that that would be a pity!"[68] And Sarkozy and his political allies within the UMP have continually raised the possibility of granting foreigners the right to vote in city (though not national) elections.[69] Sarkozy has shrewdly managed to wave both carrot and stick. In a 2002 opinion poll, 53 percent of Front National voters and 60 percent of the French population as a whole approved of then Interior Minister Sarkozy's performance in office. And Sarkozy also managed to be one of the most popular politicians among young French Muslims, too, at least until the riots of 2005. The challenge of designing integration policies that work—without arousing right-wing extremism or fomenting *communautarisme*—remains a central task for the French government. It is clear, however, that the parameters of French policies toward the country's minorities have changed drastically in the past decades, from a classically republican and "color-blind" approach to something more nuanced. As one long-time ardent opponent of *communautarisme* conceded in a recent interview, perhaps a modicum of multiculturalism is more efficient than an "unapplied French model" of citizenship.[70]

*The Politics of Islam
in France and Europe*

8

The Pursuit of the Muslim Vote and Its Impact on Foreign Policy

The participation of Muslims in French politics has advanced slowly over the past several decades, but in recent years the political parties have greatly increased their appeals for Muslims' electoral support. Some politicians have tried to attract support by appointing more minorities to high-level positions, while party strategists have designed policies specifically to attract Muslim votes. As an abstract concept, the notion of a "Muslim vote" has captivated the imagination of French politicians (many of whom pursue it) and of some French and U.S. critics, who fear that the government is being held hostage by France's Muslim population, which threatens it with electoral punishment (or social unrest) if foreign policy is not to Muslims' liking.[1] But available data indicate that both groups may be disappointed with the political reality, which is somewhat less exciting. There have been noteworthy flirtations with Muslim voters, such as that of some Socialist Party leaders involved with the *altermondialiste* (antiglobalization) movement, who were eager to form an alliance with the followers of Tariq Ramadan.[2] And on the right, policies pursued by President Jacques Chirac and former interior minister Nicolas Sarkozy have at times encouraged speculation that creating a Muslim voting bloc was part of their long-term political strategy. But thus far, none of that has translated into greater institutionalized political power for French Muslims. To take one indicator, just 123 candidates of non-European immigrant origin stood in the 2002 parliamentary elections—the highest number ever, but, in a field of 8,000 candidates, still very small (see table 8-1 for data on elected officials of immigrant origin).[3]

Given the heterogeneity of French Muslims and the variety of their organizational affiliations, they do not make up a bloc of voters that can be easily

Table 8-1. *French Elected Officeholders of Non-European Origin, 2004*

Office	Number of officeholders of non-European origin	Total officeholders
Parliamentary deputy	0	577
Senator	2	321
European Parliament deputy	3	77
Regional councilor	44	1,719
Municipal councilor	c. 1,000	142,000
General councilor (cantons)	32	3,804

Source: "Elus d'origine non-européenne en France métropolitaine" ["Elected officials of non-European origin in metropolitan France"], Suffrage universel (http://users.skynet.be/suffrage-universel/fr/frmiel.htm); Malika Ahmed, "Les arabes et le référendum" ["Arabs and the referendum"], May 18, 2005 (www.sezame.info).

courted. Only half of the 5 million Muslims in France are citizens, and it is estimated that half of those are under the age of eighteen. That leaves only a modest fraction of Muslims who fulfill both citizenship and age requirements and who have registered to vote: about 1.2 to 1.5 million individuals. There is no Muslim political party to speak of, and no single organization can claim to represent a majority of French Muslims, except the Conseil Français du Culte Musulman (CFCM) (French Council of the Muslim Religion), whose statute limits it to religious activities. And as earlier chapters have illustrated, the Muslim community is divided along multiple axes: national origin; length of residence in France; religiousness; school of Islam; socioeconomic status; and, of course, political ideology.

French politicians now pursue likely Muslim voters, however, and each party has actively recruited young Muslim leaders. As discussed in chapter 7, President Chirac's center-right Union pour un Mouvement Populaire (UMP) (Union for a Popular Movement) has taken the lead by appointing minority politicians, thanks in part to the activism of the party's president, Nicolas Sarkozy. Kacim Kellal eagerly accepted a position as a national secretary of the UMP, saying that "Muslims are sick of having a dialogue only with the ministry of police." Kellal also noted, however, that he did not view his nomination as a "naïve act" and insisted that he would not play the role of *arabe de service* (Arab servant).[4] Mouloud Aounit, leader of the Mouvement contre le Racisme et pour l'Amitié entre les Peuples (MRAP) (Movement against Racism and for Friendship among Peoples), observed that "Sarkozy knows he has an electoral springboard here, that the majority of Muslims are French and that they vote."[5] Indeed, during the March 2004 regional election campaign, Sarkozy focused on the problems of integration and bad neighborhoods: "I want to be understood by that France, too, which experiences such difficulties—not just by the intellectual France that just talks about it."[6]

However, Sarkozy's adoption of a rhetorical hard line while he was minister of the interior during the urban riots of November 2005 hurt his image as a sympathetic figure among many young people from the *banlieues,* who felt personally offended by his claim that he would clean the "rabble"out of the *cités* to make life safer for the residents. More generally, many Muslims, while strongly disavowing the riots, resented Sarkozy's language. That was especially true when, in an attempt to appeal to the right-wing electorate, some of his political allies in the National Assembly engaged in the wholesale stigmatization of recent immigrant populations—for instance, by calling polygamy (a violation of French law) and inadequate parental control of children a central reason for the unrest. Interestingly, an unprecedented number of Muslims registered to vote right after the urban riots, in an impromptu campaign led by pop stars and entertainers such as Zinedine Zidane, Mathieu Kassovitz, and Jamel Debbouze.[7] In Clichy-sous-Bois, for example, where the riots started, the number of registered voters almost tripled in the five weeks between the end of the riots (November 15) and Christmas, even though no election was scheduled for 2006.[8] But it is by no means certain that this new engagement in politics will benefit Sarkozy's rivals in the Socialist Party.

Five years of perceived indifference from the center-left coalition (1997–2002) served to alienate a large number of *beurs* from the political left, leaving them open to "poaching" from the right. With the notable exception of the appointment of cabinet members of Muslim origin, however, many of the center-right's initiatives under Chirac-Raffarin-Sarkozy had been proposed during the five years of Jospin's center-left government (especially by his labor and solidarity minister, Martine Aubry, and his interior minister, Jean-Pierre Chevènement).[9] Their proposals were on a relatively smaller scale than later center-right proposals, however, and they often were forced to back down in the face of opposition from the right. As Tokia Saïfi's brother repeated in interviews to curious journalists who descended on the family home in May 2002, "The left promised it and the right delivered it," in reference to his sister's presence in government. Saïfi, the first government minister of the *beur* generation, did not begin her political career on the right. "Today, the left is running after all the children of immigration," she said, "whereas before it took them for granted."[10] In 2004, the Socialist Party had two national secretaries of North African origin: Malek Boutih (for social issues) and Kader Arif (for globalization issues). There are, of course, limits to this new inclusiveness. Kellal, the national secretary of the UMP, predicted "significant resistance" to his senate candidacy.[11] And despite the overtures made by figures on the center-right, which has been in power for four years, Muslims' political preferences still appear to lean heavily toward the left.

Even if Muslims do not make up an electoral bloc that can be rallied to win elections, it is conceivable that the government would steer clear of policies that could alienate them and pursue others that might unify them. After all, politicians' efforts to appeal to Muslims and to convey inclusiveness are not just acts of generosity. But the disproportionately low number of minority candidates fielded by French political parties—and the even lower proportion of Muslim elected officials—make clear that there are limits to their use of this strategy. Parties do occasionally pander, but there is no evidence that it pays off in terms of increased Muslim support (or in preventing urban violence), and there also is no indication that such efforts—or party reactions to Muslim reactions to them—are part of a coherent strategy. The same government that declined military involvement in Iraq, after all, introduced a headscarf ban in schools less than a year later. Poll data show that Muslims care less about foreign policy than other issues, and it is not clear that French foreign policy would be any different if there were no Muslim minority in France.

Muslims do care about France's role in Europe and the rest of the world, of course, and there are signs that they are becoming increasingly politically active. But there is no reason to think that they will express their concerns uniformly. The 2005 French referendum on the European Union constitution provides a good snapshot of the natural divisions in the Muslim community and suggests the limitations of viewing Muslims as a voting bloc (see box 8-1). While some Muslim leaders praised a stronger EU as a better forum for asserting their community's interests, others, like Tariq Ramadan, called for a "no" vote, insisting that the "neo-liberal" treaty perpetuated economic injustice. According to the director of Oumma.com, a heavily visited Muslim news site, "French Muslims are divided 50-50, just like the rest of the French electorate."[12]

A Local Muslim Vote?

The situation is somewhat different on the local level, however, where populations of recent immigrants may be geographically concentrated in a way that could be meaningful in a close election. In recent years there have been several instances of Muslims flexing their electoral muscle—or of having it

---

Box 8-1. *Muslims and the European Union Referendum, May 2005*

Press Release: "Muslims, Europe will be built with us."

Dear Sister, Dear Brother,
There are a multitude of valid arguments to vote "yes" or "no," but one thing is incontestable: whatever the result, the French vote is so influential that Europe's future will be changed by it. Four hundred million Europeans are looking to France, and French Muslims cannot be indifferent to that fact. . . .

(Union des Associations Musulmanes de la Seine-Saint-Denis [Union of Muslim Associations of Seine-Saint-Denis], May 27, 2005)

Press Release: "Three Times 'No' to the European Constitutional Treaty!" [a]

Dignity has a price in Islam—to carry forth the principles of defending the weak and resisting the strong, before humankind and God. The world order crushes millions of lives, and the European constitutional treaty will reinforce the current world "disorder," whereby the strong live on the blood of the weak, like vampires. We say an Islamic "No" to this constitution, which will only reinforce social insecurities already developing in Europe. . . .

(Collectif des musulmans de France [French Muslim Collective], May 26, 2005)
a. "A 'humane' no, a 'republican' no, and an 'Islamic' no."

Interview with Amar Lasfar [a]

I am favorable to the European Constitution because it will strengthen Europe's institutions. Muslims have everything to gain by European integration. We will be able to create links with residents of other European countries. I say this not as the rector of a mosque, but as a citizen. In any event, we cannot associate ourselves with the [nationalists] and racists who are voting "no."

a. Leader of the Union des Organisations Islamiques de France (UOIF) [Union of Islamic Organizations of France], in Xavier Ternisien, "Les organisations musulmanes de France en majorité pour le oui" ["The majority of Muslim organizations in France are for a 'yes' vote"], *Le Monde,* May 10, 2005.

---

flexed for them. Those occasions did not appear to represent a Muslim vote per se, but rather an immigrant or a *beur* vote—that is to say, the voice of those in the lower socioeconomic groups. Interestingly, in places where the popularity of Le Pen and his Front National (FN) (National Front) runs high, immigrant participation in elections is significantly higher than elsewhere: in 1995, 89 percent of the children of immigrant parents in those areas were registered to vote, compared with an average of 81 percent (see figures 8-1 and 8-2).[13] Racist pressure has actually led to higher civic integration. Associations

Figure 8-1. *Voter Registration and Participation among French Youth in the 1995 Presidential Election*[a]

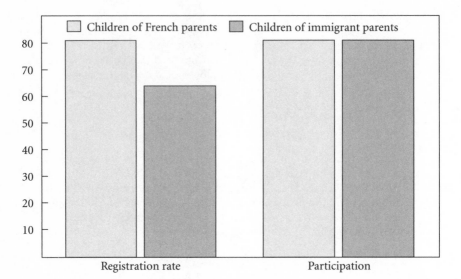

Source: Jean-Luc Richard, *Partir ou rester? Destinés des jeunes issus de l'immigration étrangère en France* [*Go or stay? The fate of young people of immigrant origin in France*] (Paris: PUF, 2004).
   a. Nineteen- to twenty-five years of age.

like the Forum Citoyen des Cultures Musulmanes (FCCM) (Forum for Citizens of Muslim Cultures) and even local authorities have led registration drives among younger generations to get them involved in civic life. In Vaulx-en-Velin, a heavily Muslim neighborhood outside Lyon, the proportion of voters among the young generations reached as high as 65 percent in 2001, whereas participation had been almost nonexistent before. That was the result of a registration drive begun in 1999 in Seine-Saint-Denis, with the backing of a national coalition of immigrant associations that were not religion-based organizations.[14] Since the end of the 1990s, other local initiatives have led to the involvement in local politics of many young *beurs,* such as that in Toulouse, where a political group called Motivé-e-s, based around the music band Zebda, has established itself as a force in local politics. The latest political mobilization efforts, mentioned above, followed the urban riots of November 2005, when thousands of young people of foreign origin flocked to the voter registration tables. But they will probably wind up having a greater impact on local than on national politics.

Figure 8-2. *Registration Rate for the 1995 Presidential Elections among Children of Immigrant Parents, by Origin* [a]

Percent

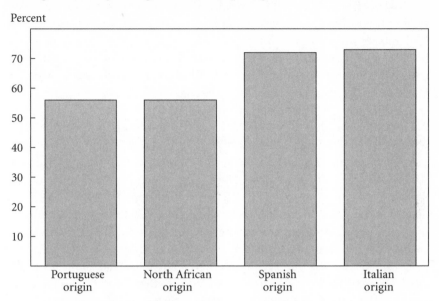

Portuguese origin — North African origin — Spanish origin — Italian origin

Source: Jean-Luc Richard, *Partir ou rester? Destinés des jeunes issus de l'immigration étrangère en France* [*Go or stay? The fate of young people of immigrant origin in France*] (Paris: PUF, 2004).
a. Nineteen- to twenty-five years of age.

In a bid for swing votes, both the Parti Socialiste (PS) (Socialist Party) and the UMP held recruitment meetings with hundreds of participants of immigrant origin during the 2004 regional election campaign. Jean-Paul Huchon (PS) held six such encounters across France, and Philippe Douste-Blazy (UMP) held one in Toulouse. Huchon aimed to put ten Socialist candidates of North African origin in regional elections in the Paris region alone, and nearly thirty in all of France.[15] The regional elections attracted a slightly more diverse slate of candidates than they had in previous years—and ten to twenty times more diverse than in national parliamentary elections. Of the 25,871 candidates fielded in 2001 by political parties on 500 first-round party tickets, 1,957 (7.6 percent) were of foreign origin and 1,200 (4.6 percent) were of North African origin.[16]

In Seine-Saint-Denis, where more than 8 percent of candidates in the 2004 local elections were members of minorities, nearly all of them ran on small party (or independent) tickets and did poorly. Only two candidates were lucky enough to be placed on a major party (PS or UMP) ticket.[17] Of the minority candidates in the 2004 regional elections, the parties placed very few in positions in which they could be elected: six from the UMP and just over twenty from the PS.[18] It is conceivable that the parties still feel a need to temper their openness, especially in electoral districts where the National Front makes a three-way race more competitive. In reaction, several Muslims resigned from the UMP to protest the party's consistent placement of minority candidates at the bottom of candidate lists after the promising steps the UMP government had taken in 2002 (see chapter 5).[19]

In Maubeuge, home of one of the CFCM vice presidents—Mohamed Bechari of the Fédération Nationale des Musulmans de France (FNMF) (National Federation of Muslims of France)—the incumbent mayor was defeated by his Socialist rival in March 2001 thanks in part to the challenger's strategy of appealing to voters of North African descent, who made up 28 percent of the town's population.[20] The Socialist opponent, Rémi Pauvros, had led an active campaign in poor neighborhoods (le Bastion, les Provinces françaises), and he was supported by organizations active in the community, such as Sambre-Avesnois, a network of community associations coordinated by Karim Hensal. After the election, Hensal claimed that "the *beur* votes made the difference." The mayor later downplayed any ethnic aspect of his election, vowing to represent the interests of all residents.[21] Mouloud Aounit, who headed up the Communist Party list in Seine-Saint-Denis, followed a strategy very similar to that of Pauvros and received 14.3 percent of the vote in 2004 (more than twice the figure for the last Communist Party candidate in 2002), including up to one-third of the vote in the heavily Muslim neighborhoods, which also are heavily Communist. It also has been surmised that George Frêche, the Socialist former mayor of Montpellier, lost his seat in parliament by a tiny margin thanks to a number of insensitive remarks he made about Muslims, who make up around 10 percent of Montpellier's population of 230,000. (Frêche was later suspended by the Socialist party in winter 2006 for disparaging comments that he made about the reflexive conservatism of *harkis,* Algerian refugees who had supported the French army in Algeria, in his electoral district.)[22]

The Euro-Palestine List (a list of candidates), another local initiative, ran candidates in the European Parliament elections in June 2004. The Euro-Palestine List's platform consisted of denouncing Israel's occupation of Palestinian territory and demanding Israel's respect for UN resolutions and the Geneva Convention. Led by a surgeon, Christophe Oberlin, and featuring a black comedian, Dieudonné M'Bala M'Bala (who has acquired notoriety for his baiting comments about Jews), Euro-Palestine candidates appeared on the ballot in only one electoral district: Ile-de-France, the belt around Paris.

(European parliamentary elections are decided on the basis of large regional districts.) The Euro-Palestine List garnered a community vote among the Arab and Muslim populations by playing on their deep identification with the Palestinians as underdog and victim.[23] The list received only 50,000 votes overall (or 1.83 percent), far short of the number required to secure a representative in Brussels, but it did much better in certain areas of Île-de-France, at times surpassing the Greens and the Communist Party in poor neighborhoods with a strong Arab presence. In its best showings, Euro-Palestine got 10.75 percent in the small city of Garges-lès-Gonesse (Val d'Oise, Département 95); 8.1 percent in Villetaneuse (Seine-Saint-Denis, Département 93); 19 percent in the Val-Fourré neighborhood in the Yvelines (Département 78), famous for urban unrest and riots in the 1990s and again in 2005; and 20.33 percent in the Luth neighborhood in Genevilliers (Hauts-de-Seine, Département 92).

The Right, the Left, and the Hunt for the White Whale

The absence of a national Muslim voting bloc has not stopped politicians from conjuring one up and courting it. On one hand, the extreme right conjures up the Muslim vote as a scare tactic: one National Front poster, for example, portrayed a diagram showing direct links between Muslims' "growing electoral power" and the caving in of political parties to Islamist pressures.[24] Sometimes, self-appointed representatives of the community may try to increase their own political weight by evoking the existence of a Muslim bloc. Finally, certain strategists of major political parties have espoused the idea that Muslims could become a political force at some point in the future, as exemplified by the "Boniface affair" in the Socialist Party (discussed below). As a result, parties do try to identify issues that could attract voters on the basis of their national origin or religious affiliation. There often are private discussions among the French political class about how to capture "the *beur* vote," but those discussions generally are closer to fantasy than reality, especially on the topic of foreign policy. Although the limited studies of Muslim electoral behavior have shown that Muslims do not vote as a bloc, they are nonetheless a constituency that is sought after like any other, and political parties appeal to this minority's sensibilities by addressing some of the issues that are important to them (see tables 8-2 and 8-3).

A Muslim Influence on French Foreign Policy?

During the 2002–03 debate about a possible military intervention in Iraq, many American commentators suggested that France's antiwar position was

Table 8-2. *Relative Importance of Selected Issues among French Catholics, Muslims, and the General Population*[a]

Issue	Overall French population Percent	Overall French population Rank	Self-identified Catholics Percent	Self-identified Catholics Rank	Self-identified Muslims Percent	Self-identified Muslims Rank
Security	48	1	56	1	40	3
Employment	36	2	38	2	55	2
Social inequality	33	3	30	3	60	1
Pensions	27	4	30	3	29	5
Education and training	22	5	22	6	31	4
Immigration	21	6	24	5	28	7
The environment	20	7	18	9	26	9
Maintaining the authority of the state	19	8	20	7	29	5
Keeping the French system healthy	16	9	17	11	17	14
Tax/fiscal policies	16	9	19	8	21	10
Corruption and business	16	9	16	12	21	10
The role of France in the world	16	9	18	9	20	12
Buying power	15	13	16	12	16	15
Working hours	12	14	12	14	27	8
Globalization	9	15	8	16	18	13
EU integration	9	15	9	15	10	16
No response	13		7		1	

Source: CSA/*La Vie* poll, April 21, 2002, "Analyse du vote au premier tour de l'élection présidentielle en fonction de la religion et de la pratique religieuse" ["Analysis of the vote in the first round of the presidential election as a function of religion and religious practice"] and "Le vote des Français d'origine étrangère au premier tour de l'élection présidentielle" ["The vote of French citizens of foreign origin in the first round of the presidential election"] (www.csa-fr.com).

a. Survey question: What issues are most important to you when you vote?

dictated by the country's 5 million Muslims, or at least that this population significantly limited the options available to President Jacques Chirac.[25] According to the commentators, had Chirac taken a pro-American stance, not only would he have run the risk of antagonizing a growing segment of the electorate—Muslim voters—he might also have even ignited riots and anti-state or anti-Semitic violence in the *banlieues*. More generally, they argue that as far as the Middle East is concerned, France's foreign policy is hostage to its Muslim population.

Such a portrait is inaccurate, in part because it implicitly projects a U.S. model—pressure group politics—onto French politics. But the issue is an important one that so far has not been adequately addressed by researchers.

Table 8-3. *First Round Voting in the 2002 French Presidential Election*
Percent

Candidate	Total French population	Self-identified Catholics	Self-identified Muslims	French with at least one foreign ancestor	
				Of European origin	Of North African or Turkish origin
Arlette Laguiller (Trotskyist)	6	5	6	8	9
Olivier Besancenot (Trotskyist)	4	3	9	6	9
Robert Hue (Communist)	4	3	1	6	1
Jean-Pierre Chevènement (Sovereigntist left)	5	4	9	6	7
Lionel Jospin (Socialist party)	16	13	39	18	29
Christiane Taubira (Multicultural left)	2	1	1	2	1
Noël Mamère (Green party)	5	3	11	6	13
François Bayrou (Center right, Europeanist)	7	8	1	6	3
Alain Madelin (Anti-state, free market right)	4	5	1	3	2
Jacques Chirac (Gaullist right)	20	24	11	15	12
Christine Boutin (Social conservative)	1	2	1	1	1
Bruno Mégret (Extreme right)	2	3	1	3	—
Jean-Marie Le Pen (Extreme right)	18	19	5	15	7

Source: CSA/*La Vie* poll, April 21, 2002, "Analyse du vote au premier tour de l'élection présidentielle en fonction de la religion et de la pratique religieuse" ["Analysis of the vote in the first round of the presidential election as a function of religion and religious practice"] and "Le vote des Français d'origine étrangère au premier tour de l'élection présidentielle" ["The vote of French citizens of foreign origin in the first round of the presidential election"] (www.csa-fr.com).

Several dimensions of the problem must be examined: the relevance of foreign policy in determining French Muslims' political behavior, foreign policy decisionmaking in France and French "Arab policy," and the relationship between domestic considerations and diplomatic grand strategy. As Bruno Etienne, a specialist on France and Islam, wrote, "France has always had an Arab—and Muslim—policy, even when there were no Muslims in metropolitan France. When France installed itself in North Africa, Syria, or Lebanon, it was not because there were Muslims in France. If France didn't go to war in Iraq, [it was] not to please French Muslims. What is happening in the Near and Middle East is the realignment of global forces, not something being done in order to please Dalil Boubakeur."[26]

French Muslims' Views on Foreign Policy

As noted, there are 5 million persons of Muslim origin and 500,000 to 600,000 Jews in France—in each case, the largest such communities in Europe. On foreign policy matters, these groups' opinions tend not to differ markedly from those of the rest of the population, except on the Israeli–Palestinian issue and other questions regarding the Middle East. As might be expected, people of Muslim origin tend to side with the Palestinians and people of Jewish origin tend to side with Israel (see figure 8-3).

Anti-Americanism does not elicit such a strong discrepancy between Muslims and non-Muslims in France. In the 1980s and 1990s, parts of the *banlieues* had a somewhat positive image of the United States, in part because of American popular culture but also because the United States, being far away, could be idealized, whereas the obvious failures of integration in France and pessimism about the future resulted in a negative image of France. Today, growing feelings of solidarity with the Palestinians among French youth of Muslim or Arab origin have undoubtedly contributed to tarnishing the image of the United States. Now, in the most negative perceptions, the United States is sometimes conflated with Israel because of the "Jewish lobby's" purported control of U.S. policy. In fact, according to a 2005 CEVIPOF survey, the image of the United States is more negative than that of Israel. A slight majority of French of African or Turkish background have a negative image of Israel (52 percent), but the percentage is actually lower than the French national average (55 percent) and much lower than the negative image that this subgroup has of the United States (67 percent, compared with 64 percent among the general population).[27] Some disaffected young people in the *banlieues* say that they support Osama bin Laden because he is challenging the U.S.–Israeli domination of Muslims throughout the world.[28] However, such extreme positions are rarely heard among people of Muslim origin, and in any case it is hard to generalize about their views.

There have been some explicit but symbolic and relatively minor manifestations of anti-Americanism among Muslims in France, such as U.S. conspiracy theories about September 11 and the campaign to promote a Coke substitute, *Mecca Cola*—"Don't drink like an idiot; drink Mecca." But the United States is not the object of economic boycotts, and any criticism of U.S. policy is accompanied by the rejection of terrorist methods (see figure 8-4). The Muslim representatives on the CFCM unanimously condemned the attacks on the United States, and the Union des Organisations Islamiques de France (UOIF) (Union of Islamic Organizations of France) sent a letter of

Figure 8-3. *Position on French and American Policies vis-à-vis the Israeli-Palestinian Conflict*

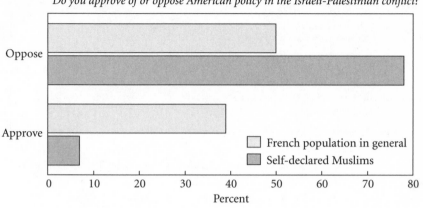

Do you approve of or oppose American policy in the Israeli-Palestinian conflict?

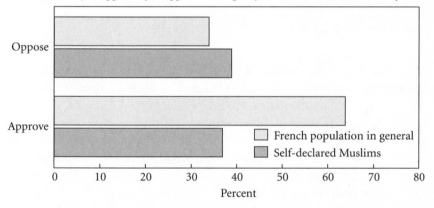

Do you approve of or oppose French policy in the Israeli-Palestinian conflict?

Source: IFOP–*Le Monde*/*Le Point*/Europe 1 poll, October 5, 2001, "L'Islam en France et les réactions aux attentats du 11 septembre 2001" ["Islam in France and the reactions to September 11, 2001"] (www.ifop.com/europe/sondages/OPINIONF/islam.asp).

condolences to the U.S. ambassador, saying that the organization "empathizes with the pain of the American people."[29]

There is no doubt that the Israeli–Palestinian conflict is an important issue in the eyes of many French Muslims, especially young people. Polls taken in high schools by Vincent Geisser and Khadija Mohsen-Finan showed a great deal of interest in this issue. The conflict was the first reason given by students of Muslim background for mobilizing politically, just followed by the issue of

Figure 8-4. *Opinions of French Self-Declared Muslims on 9/11*

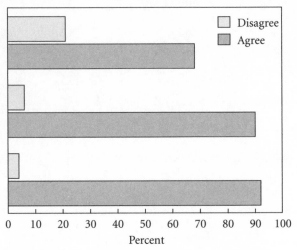

Source: IFOP–*Le Monde*/*Le Point*/Europe 1 poll, October 5, 2001, "L'Islam en France et les réactions aux attentats du 11 septembre 2001" ["Islam in France and the reactions to September 11, 2001"] (www.ifop.com/europe/sondages/OPINIONF/islam.asp).

legalizing undocumented residents: 41 percent said that they had already taken part in a demonstration about the conflict while the same was true for only 16.5 percent of other (non-Muslim) students.[30]

Among French Muslims, identification with the Palestinian cause seems stronger than with other Arab-Muslim issues, including the war in Iraq, or even with the homeland of their parents or grandparents. However, this identification is peculiar, at once obsessive and yet abstract. On one hand, the Palestinians epitomize the subordinate status of Arabs and Muslims in the world, particularly in Western societies. The issue creates and sustains a distinct identity, creating an enlarged *umma* that unifies a diverse group that includes Muslim believers, Arab nationalists, and sympathizers on the left (mostly from the extreme-left and antiglobalization movements). Only this subject could serve as the impetus for creating Euro-Palestine, the first "ethnic" list in elections for the European Parliament.

On the other hand, this identification does not have the characteristics of a deeply rooted belief. Supporters tend to know very little about Palestine or Palestinian politics, about the peace process, or about the diplomatic issues involved. Apart from a handful of militants (mostly of European descent) who went to Gaza to serve as human shields for Yasser Arafat in 2002–03, who was isolated in his headquarters, not many activists have traveled to the occupied territories. Intelligence services have not found a single instance in which a French radical Islamist went there to fight the Israelis, for example, although some went to fight in Afghanistan, Bosnia, Chechnya, and Iraq. When Arafat died in Paris in November 2004, only a handful of sympathizers gathered outside the hospital—most of them reportedly of Palestinian origin—and there was little public fervor, although representatives from the Great Mosque of Paris participated in the ceremonial convoy from the hospital to the airport.[31] The scapegoating of French Jews between 2001 and 2004 has indeed been linked with political developments in the Middle East—and with the televising of new images of Israeli crackdowns (see chapter 9). But the empathy of French Muslims for the Palestinians has not advanced into any clear political agenda—that is, no specific demands have been made of Israel or the French Ministry of Foreign Affairs. Leila Shahid, the former representative of the Palestinian Authority in France (who regularly condemned attacks on French Jews, saying that they did not further the Palestinian cause in any measure) was widely respected but not influential among French Muslims.

In general, persons of Muslim and Arab origin in France are wary of military intervention in the Middle East, and they tend to side reflexively with Middle East Arabs and Muslims. Figure 8-5 shows responses to a poll taken two weeks after September 11 that dealt with French policy options.

On most other foreign policy issues, the views of people of Muslim origin largely coincide with those of the rest of the French population. This was especially true of the war in Iraq. In March-April 2003, 94 percent of Muslims living in France disapproved of the U.S. intervention and 4 percent approved, not too different from the general French population, of whom 78 to 87 percent disapproved and 17 to 12 percent approved, depending on the date that they were surveyed.[32] The same percentage of self-identified Muslims (94 percent) supported the French position, whereas support among the general French population was around 92 percent.[33]

This convergence had a positive impact in terms of integration: the people in the *banlieues* had never felt more in sync with rest of the French people, and seeing eye to eye on Iraq revitalized the bond between them. People of immigrant origin discovered a certain pride in being French.[34] That newfound pride stands in partial contrast to the Gulf War in 1991—in which French troops took part in military operations—when a certain malaise was palpable in the *banlieues* and graffiti and clandestine circulation of audiocassettes supporting Saddam Hussein were widespread. (Support for President Mitterrand, however, remained high among immigrants.) After the U.S.-led

Figure 8-5. *Position on Possible French Policies after 9/11*[a]

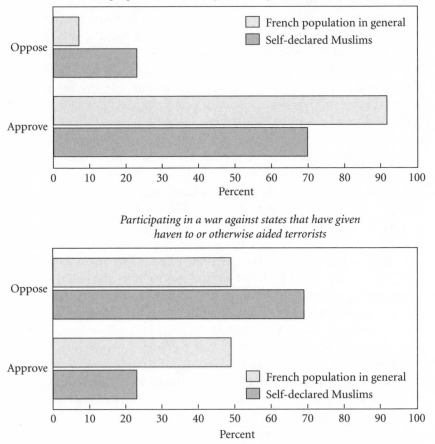

Helping the United States find the responsible terrorist network

*Participating in a war against states that have given
haven to or otherwise aided terrorists*

Source: IFOP–*Le Monde*/*Le Point*/Europe 1 poll, October 5, 2001, "L'Islam en France et les réactions aux attentats du 11 septembre 2001" ["Islam in France and the reactions to September 11, 2001"] (www.ifop.com/europe/sondages/OPINIONF/islam.asp).

a. Survey question: "Would you approve or disapprove of the following policy initiatives?"

invasion of Iraq on March 20, 2003, the French Council of the Muslim Religion issued a statement calling for "calm and dignity," and no incidents were reported.[35]

Foreign Policy as a Secondary Concern

That Muslims do not yet constitute a voting bloc in France does not mean that their preferences on certain issues are ignored by political parties. Yet for all its symbolic weight, foreign policy does not seem to rank high among their political concerns, as shown in table 8-2. In fact, self-identified Muslims rank foreign policy issues at the bottom of the list: the "role of France in the world" is twelfth, "globalization" is thirteenth, and "European integration" is sixteenth. Foreign policy may count in the political attitudes of French Muslims, but for most of them it does not appear to be a decisive electoral factor.

That does not stop politicians from honestly believing that they can still score points in this area. Nevertheless, Muslims' political attitudes are determined much more by domestic policy. In general, immigrants and their children tend to be wary of the political right, which they suspect of being excessively repressive in trying to ensure "security" and of being too tough on illegal immigrants and not tough enough on racism and discrimination—or even worse, of being Islamophobic.

Immigrants and their children thus tend to favor the left, although the Socialists disappointed many in the 1980s and 1990s by failing to deliver on their promises of greater advancement and integration of immigrants. In general terms, Muslims care about issues related to housing, medical services, education, and so forth; the fight against racism and discrimination; the institutionalization of Islam; and immigrant rights. The reform of the *double peine* (double jeopardy) law in 2003 (which subjected non-French criminals to deportation after time served, even if their family was settled in France) was especially popular among French people of Arab origin, and Nicolas Sarkozy, then the minister of the interior, benefited from having pushed the measure through Parliament. Indeed, Sarkozy's trips abroad while interior minister—especially to Muslim countries—often received more popular attention and media coverage than trips by then Foreign Minister Dominique de Villepin, in part because they were related to issues of basic importance—the number of visas issued for travel to France, the fight against terrorism, the institutionalization of Islam in France, and so forth.

These facts have done little to dampen politicians' fantasies of attracting the "Muslim vote" by virtue of their position on foreign policy issues. A revealing example is the private memo that a Socialist Party member, Pascal Boniface, sent to party leaders in April 2001.[36] In his memo, he reasoned that the primary victims of the Israeli-Palestinian conflict were the Palestinians, whose land was occupied, even if one took into account both their mistakes (corruption, suicide bombings, the opportunities missed by Arafat, and so forth) and the undeniable right of the state of Israel to exist. He stressed the importance of not confusing legitimate criticism of some policies of the state of Israel with anti-Semitism: the former was normal; the latter was reprehensible.

Boniface was most harshly attacked—so much so that he left the Socialist Party—for a related recommendation that he made with respect to French politics.[37] He suggested that the French Jewish community was using its political weight to shield Ariel Sharon from official criticism and that the growing Arab-Muslim community might consider doing the same for the Palestinians. Boniface reasoned that Muslims would count for more than Jews in the long run and that by aiming for a balanced policy with respect to the interests of both Israel and the occupied territories, the Jospin government was perceived as unfair by an increasing segment of the population. Struck by the growing number of students of Arab origin and of French Muslims generally who told him that they normally voted for the left but would not vote for the Socialists in the presidential election of 2002 because of the government's position on Israel, Boniface called for the Socialist Party to issue a stronger condemnation of Ariel Sharon's policies. In a question that sums up the memo's objective, he asked, "Does support for Sharon warrant losing in 2002?" With that memo, Boniface made a triple assumption regarding a supposed Arab or Muslim vote: that it existed, that it could be co-opted, and that foreign policy was the key to its capture. But to what extent can any of those assumptions be verified? Beyond the central fact already mentioned—that is, that even if Muslim voters were united, they would have little ability to express their unity because not enough Muslims can vote and they lack strong political organizations—polls and statistics simply do not seem to recommend a foreign policy–based strategy for capturing Muslim votes.

Another real-life test can be summoned here. How would a pro-Palestinian stance by the French government change French Muslims' voting behavior? During five years of political *cohabitation* (1997–2002), the Gaullist president, Jacques Chirac, shared power with the Socialist prime minister, Lionel Jospin. It could be argued that Chirac's foreign policy tilted slightly more toward the Palestinians than Jospin's, at least symbolically—a reflection of each party's traditional preferences.

Two striking media images from this period serve to illustrate the question. The first is of Chirac in East Jerusalem, on October 22, 1996, scolding the Israeli security guards who prevented him from greeting Palestinian passers-by and walking freely in the Old City to visit the holy places himself, as he had wished to do. "You want me to go back to my country?" Chirac shouted, angrily threatening to leave Israel if the guards did not relax their restrictions. Chirac's gesture was also symbolic of Paris's nonacceptance of Israel's annexation of Jerusalem's holy sites, although then Prime Minister Benjamin Netanyahu apologized to Chirac for the incident.

The second image is of Lionel Jospin, on February 26, 2000, being pelted by rocks and forced to flee under the protection of his bodyguards after a tense debate with students at Bir-Zeit University in the West Bank. Two days earlier, he had declared that Hezbollah was a terrorist movement, going beyond the French position at the time, including that of his own foreign minister, Hubert Védrine. Chirac used the incident to score political points and to remind Jospin—and the French public—that he, as head of state, was responsible for foreign policy and that it had to be at least a bipartisan exercise. Arafat later apologized for the rock-throwing incident.

The first image made Chirac something of a hero among French Muslims, and the second reflected negatively on Jospin, even though the debate was largely a symbolic, not substantive, event. Few young *beurs* knew what the incident was all about, having only seen Jospin being pelted with stones by angry Palestinian students without being fully aware of the context. Some Muslim leaders, nonetheless, claimed that it marked a turning point in the Socialists' fortunes: "Jospin paid a dear price for his behavior," said FNMF leader Mohamed Bechari, also vice president of the CFCM, in a debate on Al Jazeera. "The Arab community in France was betting on Chirac from the first round of the 2002 presidential elections; in addition, Jospin was being supported by the Zionist lobby."[38] A magazine article in fall 2003 counted 10,000 "Arab-sounding names" among the 150,000 enrolled UMP activists (about 8 percent), including some who claimed to have joined thanks to Chirac's foreign policy positions.[39] So, in the past the two main candidates in the presidential election of 2002 had taken slightly different stances on what was, in the eyes of French Muslims, the hottest foreign policy issue, producing strikingly different images on television. Did that have any impact on Muslims' choice of a candidate?

Three polls of French Muslims from 2001–02 suggest an answer. The first, taken in September 2001, showed Jospin tied with Chirac: 66 and 67 percent of self-declared Muslims held a positive opinion of Jospin and Chirac, respectively.[40] The second poll, taken in October 2001, showed that among young Muslims, Jospin was far ahead of Chirac. When asked for whom they would vote if they could, 39 percent of high school students of Muslim origin said that they would favor the Socialist leader over Chirac (17 percent favored Chirac), while their classmates favored neither (14 percent and 15 percent for Jospin and Chirac respectively).[41] The last poll was a 2002 election day exit poll that showed that self-identified Muslims gave Jospin 39 percent of their votes and Chirac only 11 percent.[42]

In other words, the positions taken by politicians on the most salient foreign policy issue—the Middle East conflict—did not seem to have had any significant impact on Muslims' voting behavior. That lack of significant impact seems to be true in a broader sense, too. Since de Gaulle presided over the birth of France's "Arab policy," Gaullists have been thought of as more pro-Arab, while Socialists have been considered more pro-Israeli. That, of course, is just a stereotype; French policy toward Israel has actually been bipartisan and extremely stable over the course of the last decades. It was Mitterrand, a Socialist, who declared during a speech to the Knesset in the early 1980s that Tel-Aviv needed to negotiate with the Palestine Liberation Organization (PLO) and who later received Yasser Arafat at the Elysée. And it was Chirac who recognized the responsibility of the French state in the deportation of Jews during World War II—an issue of importance to Israel's government—thereby reversing the historical fiction maintained by his mentor, de Gaulle, who claimed that the French state bore no responsibility for helping the Nazis persecute the Jews because during the war the legitimate government of the French Republic was not in Vichy but in exile in London. These stereotypes nonetheless persist in the public imagination—but how do French Muslims actually perceive the supposedly pro-Arab Gaullists and the pro-Israeli Socialists?

Opinion data are available on this topic, both for the self-identified Muslim population in general and for high-school students. Overwhelming identification with the left, not the right, is the most solid trend. There has been no massive shift to the right among self-identified Muslims out of exasperation with Socialist policies: the breakdown according to the 2002 election among actual Muslim voters (not the Muslim population at large) is more or less 76 percent for the left and 20 percent for the right.[43] The figures for the 1998–2001 period, according to Claude Dargent, were 47 percent for the left and extreme left, 12 percent for the center, 4 percent for the right, and 34 percent undecided.[44] The results for high school students showed a similar trend: those of Muslim origin felt closer to the left (13 percent), the Greens (6 percent), and the extreme left (24 percent) than the right (5 percent). Forty-one percent said that they did not know which party they preferred.[45]

Jacques Chirac himself offers an interesting case study. He has many sources of support among French of Arab origin, but his image remains complex. As president of the Republic, he is seen as a fatherly, protective figure for minorities. He was responsible for hiring the first cabinet ministers of Arab origin, Tokia Saïfi and Hamlaoui Mekachera. During the second round of the presidential elections of 2002, he was also the de facto champion of a multicultural vision of France against Jean-Marie Le Pen, the extreme-right populist leader, and his 82 percent victory on May 5, 2002, was celebrated in the

Place de la République by a huge crowd composed largely of people of Arab origin, some waving Palestinian and Algerian flags along with the French flag.[46] Polls demonstrate that he is even more popular in the Arab world, and huge cheering crowds greeted his arrival in Algeria and Morocco in spring 2003.[47] Chirac's popularity among Muslims abroad is partly explained by his foreign policy positions and his opposition to the U.S. intervention in Iraq. That is also somewhat true at home, although the spring 2004 regional elections, marked by a substantial defeat of Chirac's political party, UMP, showed how precarious his support was in terms of actual votes.

At the same time, French of Arab origin still suspect his center-right coalition of harboring an Islamophobic or borderline racist wing, and they feel that his government is excessively attached to a law-and-order agenda. Many also recall his words of June 1991, at a time when he was still pandering to that wing: "It may be true that there are fewer foreigners than before World War II, but they are not the same foreigners, and that makes a difference. Having Spaniards, Poles, and Portuguese working in our country poses less problems than having Muslims and blacks." He went on to relate an anecdote about a working French couple who earned far less than their neighbor of immigrant origin, who had many spouses and dozens of children and who loafed around on welfare, observing that "if you add the noise and the smells, the French worker can go crazy—and it is not racist to say that." Those unfortunate remarks help explain his somewhat blurred image. Chirac is popular, and his foreign policy stance is one source of popularity among others, but that does not necessarily mean that citizens of Arab or Muslim origin would vote for him.[48]

France's Bipartisan Arab Policy and the Setting of French Foreign Policy

Since the presidency of Charles de Gaulle (1958–69), France's foreign policy on the Middle East has been dubbed its "Arab policy" (*politique arabe,* although some officials and scholars reject that term).[49] France has a dense network of ties with the Arab and Muslim world dating back to François I in 1535. This complex relationship led to Napoleon's expeditions to Egypt in 1798–99 and then in the nineteenth century to the colonization of Algeria and other territories where Islam was the religion of the majority of the people.

France's so-called Arab policy originated in 1967, when France and Israel parted ways. The split came after the two states had been close allies since 1948, in that Paris was the first weapons supplier for the Jewish state and had even cooperated in providing the technological assistance that accelerated Israel's progress toward acquiring an atomic bomb. In June 1967, when the Six-Day War erupted, de Gaulle imposed an arms embargo on the warring countries, which affected Israel most (his successor, Georges Pompidou, later maintained that policy). De Gaulle stated his opposition to the occupation of Gaza, the West Bank, Golan Heights, and Sinai. His diplomatic stance reflected a French tendency after the tensions linked with colonization and decolonization to seek rapprochement with the Arab world and the third world in general, against the backdrop of his quest for a more sovereign French foreign policy.

In addition to the desire for French political influence in the region, economic considerations played an increasingly important role in France's Arab policy after instability in the oil supply appeared in the 1970s. Europeans first recognized their dependence on the Arab world following the Arab-Israeli conflict in October 1973, when the Organization of the Petroleum Exporting Countries (OPEC) placed an embargo on the United States and the Netherlands and threatened to embargo the rest of Europe.[50] The use of the "oil weapon," said one observer, had revealed the "capacity of the Arab states to change the terms of their relationship with external powers through their control of large supplies of a critical resource—oil."[51] This period saw increased European involvement in the Middle East, through not only France's *politique arabe* but also the European Community's adoption of "associative diplomacy" with regard to the Arab world and in its increased foreign aid to Arab countries. European efforts to guarantee an oil supply had led to greater openness to the concerns of Arab states and a desire for economic and cultural exchange. In the course of the 1970s, the European Community signed accords covering half of all European exports to the Arab world with governments representing 70 percent of the Arab population.[52]

France maintained a range of political, military, economic, and cultural ties with several of its former colonies in North Africa and the Middle East as well as with oil-producing states in the Persian Gulf, and its relations always incorporated what Paris considered a "balanced" view of the Israeli-Palestinian issue. Very early on, France had advocated a two-state resolution of the conflict under which the Israelis and the Palestinians would live peacefully side by side, even before the European Council endorsed the same approach in 1980. The important point is that French Arab policy predated the arrival in France of a sizable Muslim minority in the 1970s and 1980s, and even more to the point, it predated the expression of that minority's political identity, which began to take place in the 1990s and 2000s. In other words, the French stance vis-à-vis Middle Eastern affairs is rooted in history and geography, not political sociology.

It should also be noted that decisionmaking in the French executive branch is largely insulated from the political pressures of civil society and special interest groups. Political society in France is still based on Rousseau's "general will," not on U.S.-style Lockean pluralism. That means that in France the defense of private interests or minorities per se is not encouraged. Lobbies are perceived to be intrinsically illegitimate, a subversion of the regular political process, and that is especially true in the domain of foreign policy, where *raison d'Etat* is expected to reign unchallenged. That does not mean that lobbies do not exist, but they have no legal status (as they do in the United States), and they are not seen as legitimate actors. With no claim to the status of American political action committees (PACs), French lobbies cannot hope to weigh in on issues by delivering electoral votes or campaign funds as they do in Washington. French campaign finance laws make it difficult to wield a financial advantage, and few districts have enough voters of immigrant origin to elect a community representative in the National Assembly (indeed, there has not been any representative of Muslim background since colonial times). There is one slight exception to this description of France's aversion to lobbies in foreign policy: Armenian activist associations obtained recognition by both houses of Parliament in January 2001 of the genocide of the Armenian people by the Ottoman Turks (antagonizing the current Turkish state). That was rather exceptional, however, and the National Assembly, the lower house of Parliament, has very little influence over foreign policy. The executive branch dominates almost completely, in striking contrast to U.S. practice; Parliament, therefore, is not fertile ground for even a hypothetical Muslim lobby.

The sole factors emanating from civil society that carry weight in foreign policy debates are the personal popularity of candidates and the public opinion polls. As in other countries, foreign policy in France offers the head of state a chance to score political points outside the realm of domestic politics. The constitution of the Fifth Republic clearly reserves diplomatic and defense powers for the president. Thus, even if voters install an opposition government in mid-term elections (as they did in 1986, 1993, and 1997), the head of state still predominates in international relations and benefits from the political capital that accrues when citizens "rally around the flag."

Chirac's opposition to the U.S. intervention in Iraq made him very popular among the general population for a few months, at a time when the public had little other reason to be satisfied with the government Chirac had appointed after winning parliamentary elections in May 2002. But when it comes to electoral politics, foreign policy plays no significant role, or in any case much less than in the United States. Politicians do not try to score points on foreign policy differences in political campaigns. The 2002 confrontation in Germany of the competing "America" policies of Chancellor Schroeder and his opponent Edmund Stoiber, for example, has no equivalent in France. Though anti-Americanism is stereotypically a potent force in contemporary European electoral politics, it is simply not a factor in French elections. That is because of the bipartisan nature of French foreign policy and because foreign policy is not a high priority of French voters. Foreign affairs is thus just one part of the larger political context.

In any event, French foreign policy has for the most part been insulated from politics since the end of the Algerian war. Since foreign policy is largely conducted on a bipartisan basis, a change in government has never meant a radical change in policy. A good measure of that bipartisanship is the relative consensus on foreign policy during periods of "cohabitation," when the prime minister and a majority of the National Assembly belong to one political party and the president belongs to another. Such was the case during 1986–88 (Prime Minister Chirac under President Mitterrand); 1993–95 (Prime Minister Balladur under Mitterrand); and 1997–2002 (Prime Minister Jospin under President Chirac).

Fearing a Clash of Civilizations in the Middle East—and in France

Aside from electoral motivations, another possible explanation that commentators have given to explain Chirac's behavior in the Iraq crisis of 2002–03 was his fear of social disorder and violence in the *banlieues*. Ironically, the urban riots of November 2005 came at a time when there was a relative lull in foreign policy coverage in the news, which is further indication that the unrest was provoked by domestic, not international, factors. However, events in the Middle East have had an increasing impact on intercommunity relations in France, especially between Muslims and Jews, at least between 2001 and 2004. Young French Muslims tend to identify with young Palestinians and may take Middle Eastern events as a pretext to target French Jews and label them proxies of the Israeli government. That tendency has produced mini-waves of violence against Jewish symbols—and Jews themselves—that closely mirrored the dynamics of events in the Middle East.

In theory, this phenomenon could limit the policy options available on the Israeli-Palestinian issue if there were pro-Likud tendencies present in the

French political spectrum, which is not the case. If a French politician were to have delivered a strongly worded speech in favor of Ariel Sharon's policies, for example, or called him "a man of peace," as President George W. Bush did, it would almost certainly have sparked protests from the Arab-Muslim community—and from a large sector of the French public in general. In other words, although there are certain domestic concerns with regard to potentially alienating this subpopulation, they have never had the chance to manifest themselves because of the public's preexisting leanings and the common political line followed by the French government, left or right, since 1967.

The link between Muslims and other foreign policy issues that typically have been of interest to the Muslim community is even less clear. French Muslims have never mobilized on behalf of Chechnya, Kashmir, or even Bosnia as they have for Palestine. Even the Iraq debate of 2002–03 came in second to the Israeli-Palestinian conflict. Witnessing the U.S. overthrow of an Arab ruler was less likely to produce tensions than a burst of violence between the Palestinians and the Israelis, especially because Saddam Hussein's image was far less positive than it was in 1991 during the Gulf War. Still, polls suggest that France's direct military intervention in the Muslim world could lead to social unrest.

As the poll results in figure 8-6 show, there is actually some fear of social disorder and strife in the *banlieues* between the Muslim minority and the "majority society" in the event of French military intervention against a Muslim country. However, it should be noted that nothing of the sort happened following France's military contribution to the U.S. intervention in Afghanistan, which started in 2002 and included carrying out bombing missions and extensive special forces operations. In other words, this real fear has not, thus far, corresponded with reality on the ground.

Most important, there is no straightforward way in which that fear could percolate up to influence French foreign policy decisions. There are simply very few scenarios in which France would militarily intervene in the Muslim world without legitimate grievances and strong legal grounding. In other words, French people of Arab origin are unlikely to unanimously condemn a hypothetical French military action, because it is unlikely that such an action would be aggressive in nature. The historical record of French policy in the Arab world since Charles de Gaulle suggests that France's position on international affairs would not look much different even if there were no Muslim minority in France.

In 1991, during the Gulf War, the *banlieues* were generally supportive of Mitterrand, even if they did not favor French military participation and were

Figure 8-6. *Possible Outcomes of French Foreign Policies*

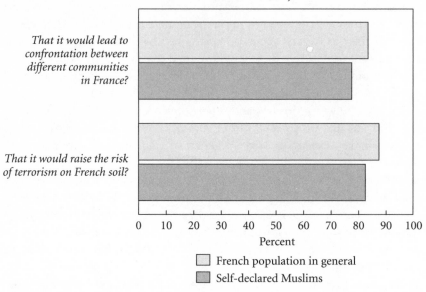

If France were to participate in military action against a Muslim state, do you think . . .

□ French population in general
■ Self-declared Muslims

Source: IFOP–*Le Monde*/*Le Point*/Europe 1 poll, October 5, 2001, "L'Islam en France et les réactions aux attentats du 11 septembre 2001" ["Islam in France and the reactions to September 11, 2001"] (www.ifop.com/europe/sondages/OPINIONF/islam.asp).

troubled by the events. There was some agitation, but there was no general strife or unrest, and public protest against "American imperialism" came from the left in general, not from the Muslim segment of the population in particular. It should also be noted that in the 2002–03 crisis over Iraq, Jacques Chirac did not make up his mind about French participation in the current Iraq intervention until mid-January 2003. He had contemplated the possibility of deploying up to 15,000 French troops in the region, to the point that he sent General Jean-Patrick Gaviard to the Pentagon to coordinate with U.S. armed forces on December 16, 2002.[53] Should Chirac have decided that the situation merited intervention, considerations about social order apparently would not have gotten in the way.

Government concern about social unrest is precisely where domestic politics and foreign policy intersect. As long as a French military intervention is seen as fully justified—implying, among other things, a solid grounding in international law, multilateral action, and the perception of international legitimacy—French authorities do not feel constrained by domestic factors. The entire French population, not just the Muslim segment, is sensitive to the principles of multilateralism and international law, which are presented as the hallmarks of French foreign policy. Had Saddam blatantly violated his commitments to the UN inspection regime—by refusing access to the inspectors or killing some of them, for example—it is reasonable to think that French troops would have joined U.S. troops in Iraq.

The French government fears unrest in the *banlieues* only inasmuch as it fears a clash of civilizations in the Middle East overall.[54] Chirac tried to avoid giving the impression of subscribing to the clash theory because he thought that the theory was bad for the Middle East and for French society—a stance that reflects his view of a continuum between the two. The electoral "shock" of April 21, 2002, when Le Pen edged out Jospin for second place in the first round of presidential elections, underscored for the president the fragility and fractured nature of French society and probably served to reinforce his insistence on international legitimacy and multilateralism in foreign affairs. But French Middle East policy is the result of myriad factors, including institutional considerations as well as the sense of a specifically French role in the Arab world, given France's complex history with much of it.

While there is no evidence of the Muslim minority's direct influence on French foreign policy, the presence of 5 million Muslims does have an indirect impact on diplomacy with respect to the Middle East. But it seems mostly to confirm France's preexisting policies toward this region and to reinforce the government's insistence on abiding by international law and obtaining a multilateral consensus before intervening there.

9

Anti-Semitism among Muslims
and the Rise of *Communautarisme*

France is home to 500,000 to 600,000 Jews, approximately 30 percent of whom are of Ashkenazi origin and 70 percent of whom are Sephardim.[1] A vast majority of the Sephardim trace their origins to the same countries as most of the 5 million Muslims in France: Algeria, Morocco, and Tunisia, from which they have emigrated since the 1960s. France's Jewish population is the third-largest in the world (after that of the United States and of Israel), and France has both the largest Muslim and the largest Jewish minority in Europe.[2]

The physical and political coexistence of French Muslims and French Jews, which was relatively peaceful in the last decades of the twentieth century, has since been strained. In the recent surge of anti-Semitic incidents in France, most incidents that can be attributed can be traced largely to the younger generations born in France of Muslim origin. The year 2000 was pivotal in this regard. According to figures published by the Commission Nationale Consultative des Droits de l'Homme (CNCDH) (National Advisory Commission on Human Rights), before 2000, racist (anti-Arab and anti-black) incidents in France were more numerous than anti-Semitic incidents, but over the subsequent five years, the converse became true (see figure 2-2 in chapter 2). In addition, before 2000 there were proportionally more anti-Semitic incidents in the United States than in France. However, the opposite was true for the 2000–04 period.[3]

The ties between the evolution of the Muslim community and the resurgence of anti-Semitism in France are complex. In general, however, French anti-Semitism can be traced to a combination of factors: problems related to the social and economic integration of Muslims, the importation of the Israeli-Palestinian conflict into France, competition among immigrant groups (occasionally giving rise to resentment of those who are seen as wealthy and well integrated), and even a slight reawakening of traditional, extreme-right anti-Semitism. Islam, as a religion, also seems to play a role, albeit limited. Identity issues stemming from the social and political status of French Muslims seem to offer a more powerful explanation. Nonetheless, anti-Semitism and the rise of "*communautarisme*"—which could be defined as group-based identity politics—are two of the most worrisome and negative aspects of the integration process, both in themselves and for the larger failures that they reveal.

The Old and New Faces of Anti-Semitism in France

It is difficult to analyze the rise of anti-Semitism since 2000 without evoking its various historical incarnations. Anti-Jewish sentiments and acts have appeared in France in different guises since the Middle Ages, in particular as Christian "religious" anti-Judaism (based on the blaming of the Jews for the death of Jesus) and extreme-right and populist "racial" anti-Semitism (based on the purported inferiority of the Semites to other races, especially the Aryans) between the end of the nineteenth century and the end of the Vichy regime. Recent years have witnessed a new incarnation, controversially referred to as "Judeophobia," the product of extreme anti-Zionist sentiments among leftist and Islamist groups.[4] Indeed, France has a long and troubled history with respect to anti-Semitism.

Not all aspects of Jewish history in France are negative, of course. In 1789, during the Revolution, France was the first country to emancipate Jews formally and offer them citizenship. Napoleon created the *Consistoire,* a representative body for the Jewish religion, in 1807. Almost a century later, the Dreyfus affair occasioned a resurgence of anti-Semitism—and indicated its persistence —in post-Revolution France. But the national debate over the Dreyfus trial also revealed the existence of a counterforce, notably among intellectuals, that eventually prevailed. France has had Jewish government ministers and even prime ministers for decades, including during the 1930s, when anti-Semitism was widespread. The Vichy regime (1940–44), in collaboration with the Nazis, implemented anti-Semitic policies, including the deportation of 75,000 Jews to death camps; however, after the end of World War II, anti-Semitism gradually receded in French society. As in many other countries, greater consciousness of the Holocaust emerged in France in the

1960s, and in the 1970s France began to face its complicity in crimes commit-ted against Jews during World War II, most notably through the new histories of the period that were being written.[5] In 1995, President Jacques Chirac—breaking with fifty years of Gaullist orthodoxy that refused to see the Vichy regime as the legitimate French state—recognized France's responsibility in the wartime deportation of what amounted to 25 percent of the Jews, French and non-French, living in France at that time.

For the most part, the level of anti-Semitism in French society as measured by polls (for example, through such questions as "Are Jews too powerful in France?") has been quite comparable to that in the United States over the last few decades: in both nations about 10 to 15 percent of the public espouse the worldview of hard-core anti-Semites. There are indeed national differences (Christian anti-Judaism does not play a significant role in France, for exam-ple), but the similarities are noteworthy. In both countries, anti-Semitic views are correlated with lower education and socioeconomic status. Racism, intol-erance, and ethnocentrism in general also are highly correlated with anti-Semitism: if someone is anti-Arab, anti-black, and Islamophobic, there is a good chance that he or she also is intolerant of Jews.

Two parallel developments have taken place in France in recent years. First, there has been a steady decline in declared antipathy toward Jews, similar to the decline registered for antipathy toward blacks and Arabs (see figure 2-1 in chapter 2). (The number of core-group anti-Semites, however, has stabilized at around 10 to 15 percent of the population.) An interesting long-term indi-cator of such attitudes is whether poll respondents would ever vote for a Jew-ish presidential candidate. Even when the question was asked in different forms, the negative responses clearly declined, from 50 percent in 1966 to 25 percent in 1978, before bottoming out at 10 percent in 1998 and rising slightly to 13 percent in 2000.[6]

The second development is the growing condemnation of racist and anti-Semitic acts. Nonna Mayer, a researcher specializing in anti-Semitism at the CEVIPOF research center at Sciences Po, points out that as the public became more aware of growing anti-Semitism between 2002 and 2004, people increasingly indicated their support for more drastic repression of anti-Semitic threats and acts. The proportion of survey respondents supporting judicial action against people who use the slur "dirty Jew," for example, jumped from 59 percent to 81 percent (and from 47 percent to 67 percent for "dirty Arab").[7] More generally, the French public is increasingly in favor of more severe crackdowns on racist and anti-Semitic behavior.

A revealing sign of the general trend is the changing behavior of Jean-Marie Le Pen, the leader of the extreme-right Front National (FN) (National

Front), who habitually relied on implicitly anti-Semitic remarks as a way of rallying his xenophobic constituency. Le Pen is an anti-Semite of the traditional mold, notorious for his trivialization of the Holocaust, his ethnocentric nationalism, and his claims that Chirac is "held hostage" by the Jewish organization B'nai B'rith.[8] In recent years, however, Le Pen has stopped telling jokes or tossing off one-liners with anti-Semitic undertones, indicating his diminishing insistence on the theme. He has instead turned his attention to another traditional pillar of the extreme right: anti-immigrant and anti-Arab rhetoric. One expert on the extreme right said that after September 11, a new school of thought emerged among FN adherents: Israel could be viewed as a "temporary tactical ally" in the fight against "the new enemy: the Arab world, the Arab-Muslim world, or Islam, depending on the formulation chosen."[9] When Le Pen won a surprising second place in the first round of the 2002 presidential election, several prominent French Jewish citizens, without going as far as endorsing him, declared that Muslims should heed his advance as a telling warning of how much intercommunity relations had been strained by Islam's emergence in France, the message being that Muslims should behave, especially regarding their relations with Jews, and that Muslims would suffer more than Jews from any advance of the extreme right.

In spite of the enduring tensions and stereotypes that had built up during the trauma of decolonization, the relationship between French Jews and French Arabs was not of much concern from the 1970s to the 1990s. There was even a degree of amicability and neighborliness between the two, as many recent immigrants moved to the same neighborhoods where Jews repatriated from North Africa in the 1960s resided. Arab immigrants sometimes preferred to patronize Jewish pharmacies or Jewish doctors rather than their "traditional French" counterparts, feeling more at ease with someone from their home country. In the political sphere, many French Jews on the left became militant members of groups opposed to the extreme right when the National Front began to rise. In 1984, for example, Julien Dray, a *pied-noir* (a French person born in Algeria and "repatriated" after Algeria's independence) of Jewish origin and now a member of the Socialist Party, cofounded the organization SOS Racisme with Harlem Désir.

But relations between the communities soured with the Gulf War in 1990–91 and the intensification of the Israeli-Palestinian conflict in the fall of 2000, and they grew more estranged with the accompanying surge in anti-Semitic violence in French cities. To some extent this dynamic can be compared with that between American Jews, who played a major role in the U.S. civil rights movement, and American blacks, whose relations were marked by mutual disenchantment and increasing tension at the end of the 1960s and during the following Black Power era (the Israeli-Palestinian conflict also played a role, though a less prominent one).[10]

A sudden spike in anti-Semitic incidents occurred over the last couple of days of September 2000, at the same time that the second intifada began. From September to October 2000, according to figures from the Ministry of the Interior (deemed by Jewish organizations to greatly underestimate the situation at the time), monthly anti-Semitic threats jumped from twelve to 418 and, more important, violent acts increased from none to 102 (see figure 9-1). The spike receded, but a new wave of anti-Semitic incidents occurred a year later, after 9/11. An even higher number of incidents occurred in April 2002, corresponding with the Israel Defense Force's Defensive Shield operation in the West Bank, and yet another wave—smaller but still significant— came during the U.S. invasion of Iraq (March-April 2003).

The level of anti-Semitic incidents in the last months of 2003 and through 2004 was persistently high, and the spikes were no longer clearly linked to events in the Middle East. The numbers greatly receded in 2005, falling by 48 percent for the entire year, from 974 to 504.[11] Moreover, synagogues and other Jewish sites were not targeted during the urban riots of November 2005. This trend continued in the first months of 2006, in spite of the horrific and well-publicized death in February of Ilan Halimi, a young Jew who was kidnapped and tortured before being killed when kidnappers failed to get the ransom they were looking for. Halimi's was the first anti-Semitic murder since another man was killed in 1995.[12]

There are two alternative explanations for the new, structurally higher level of anti-Semitism (which was still higher in 2004 than what it was before 2000, as can be seen in figure 9-1). The first one is technical: there was better record-keeping of anti-Semitic incidents starting in 2003 and 2004 than in the preceding years, meaning that the phenomenon was previously underreported. After the Conservative Party gained a majority in Parliament in spring 2002, the government increased the number of measures targeting anti-Semitism in general. Real efforts have been made by the government to improve collection of data on racist and anti-Semitic acts, whether by the Ministry of Education (the SIGNA database, which documents violence at school, was overhauled in January 2004), the Ministry of Justice (in February 2003, the Lellouche law made anti-Semitism an aggravating factor in determining sentences for crimes), or the Ministry of the Interior, whose officials have worked with Jewish organizations on implementing a common methodology for describing and classifying anti-Semitic incidents. Jewish organizations have since ceased complaining about statistical underestimation, although some still lend a

Figure 9-1. *Monthly Level of Anti-Semitic Incidents and Tentative Correlation with Events in the Middle East, 2000–04*[a]

Number

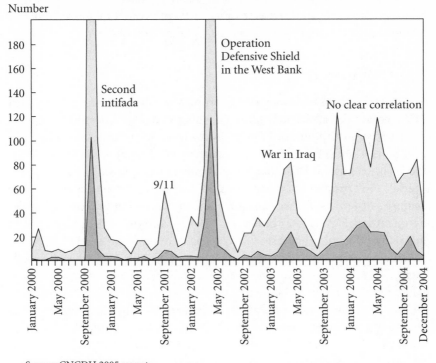

Source: CNCDH 2005 report.
a. In September 2000 the total number of incidents was 520; in April 2002, it was 566.

helping hand in reporting incidents. More generally, broader acceptance of the reality of resurgent anti-Semitism has meant that victims are more inclined to lodge formal complaints. Tensions between Jewish groups and the government have gradually disappeared, as officials have come to acknowledge the gravity of the situation and implement security measures to protect the community. Although Jewish groups are now satisfied with the official stance, there is still residual bitterness and uneasiness.

The second explanation—which does not preclude the first—is much more worrying. The absence of a correlation between anti-Semitic incidents and events in the Middle East may mean that a somewhat higher level of anti-Semitism has become the norm in France, independent of international events, even if the numbers dropped markedly in 2005. But how does the increase in the number of anti-Semitic acts fit in the picture sketched above, in which opinion polls show that France has become less anti-Semitic as a whole and more intolerant of racism and anti-Semitism? Conflicting interpretations of the increase in anti-Semitic incidents have arisen, and it is useful to review the controversies surrounding them in order to understand how the politics of the debate influences the reading of events.

Four Controversies

The first of four major controversies erupted in fall 2000, when the Conseil Représentatif des Institutions Juives de France (CRIF) (Representative Council of Jewish Institutions of France) voiced its concern that government figures grossly underestimated what was actually happening. More generally, the Jewish community felt that the government was ignoring its plight, with officials preferring to stick their heads in the sand and deny bad news. After centuries of Jewish efforts to integrate, the impression of government abandonment left French Jews bitter, and Jewish communitarianism increased markedly.[13] Neighborhood security groups were created, French emigration to Israel increased, and Jewish schools experienced a wave of new enrollments—from 16,000 in the late 1980s to 28,000 in 2002, accounting for one-quarter of Jewish schoolchildren.[14]

The seriousness of the reaction can be explained by the severity of the anti-Semitic incidents that have occurred: in 2004 for example, there were no fewer than 200 violent acts (seventy-four acts of serious vandalism; 117 physical attacks on individuals; eight arsons; and one bombing), leaving thirty-six French Jews injured. In some neighborhoods, wearing a yarmulke or a Star of David can be an invitation to aggression, and when discovered to be Jewish, the victim of a robbery or an assault has sometimes been treated even worse. The wave of anti-Semitic attacks since 2000 had not resulted in any deaths before the murder of Ilan Halimi in February 2006. There also were 770 "threats" in 2004, including 483 instances of anti-Semitic graffiti and 256 verbal attacks. And all of this took place in the context of greater protection of the Jewish community.

At least two reasons can be given for the government's undeniably lethargic reaction in 2000 and 2001. First, French officials did not consider their country anti-Semitic, and they could not believe that the situation had become so bad so quickly. The real victims of racist acts and discrimination, they thought, were Arab immigrants, not the well-integrated Jewish community that now fingered Arabs as the perpetrators. Second, officials worried that giving too much publicity to the acts would trigger more copycat incidents, just as media coverage of a cemetery desecration in Carpentras in 1990 led to a wave of desecrations in the following weeks. That particular point—to publicize or not to publicize—has remained a delicate question ever since. The Rufin report to the prime minister of October 2004, for example, notes that many perpetrators commit anti-Semitic attacks out of a desire for "stature" and media attention.[15]

That finding points to the second controversy, over the media's reporting of anti-Semitic incidents. The news media are accused by some of doing too much, of sounding the alarm too quickly and in a counterproductive way, thereby stigmatizing Jews and inspiring copycats. Critics believe that the media overdramatize anti-Semitic incidents to the point of rendering them banal. Others think that given France's past anti-Semitism, the media do too little and are guilty of downplaying the moral and historical significance of anti-Semitic acts. Jewish activists voiced the latter complaint in the first few years of the new wave of anti-Semitic acts, whereas worries that the public would be desensitized grew in 2004 because of a few highly publicized reports of attacks that were later revealed to be false.

In July 2004, for example, a young woman named Marie Leblanc claimed that she and her baby were attacked in a train on the outskirts of Paris; this would become the second major controversy. She alleged that six black and Arab teenagers harassed her, tossed the baby aside, and drew swastikas on her stomach with indelible markers. After a couple of days marked by intense emotion throughout the country and strong reactions from politicians and officials, including President Chirac, it turned out that the young woman had made the story up to persuade her parents to "take care" of her. One interpretation of the event was that anti-Semitism had become so common that nobody even questioned what was an unlikely story (blacks and *beurs* tend not to draw swastikas). But another reaction saw this as yet another instance in which immigrants and their children were falsely accused, another instance of exaggeration by the Jewish community. The Leblanc incident was coupled with several other false alarms during the same period, including the arson of a Jewish social center on rue Popincourt in Paris that was committed by a former employee, not an anti-Semite. Partly as a result of those events, 32 percent of the French public in 2004 thought that media coverage was likely to trigger more anti-Semitic acts, while a plurality (37 percent) thought that it made no difference; only 8 percent thought that media coverage would help deter such acts.[16]

Media coverage is sometimes faulted for focusing exclusively on confrontation when in fact the reality is more complicated and less dramatic. It is not uncommon for the principals in such stories to feel misrepresented, and controversies often erupt around supposed media distortion. Two 2004 television programs on anti-Semitism in French schools were accused of focusing only on tensions and problems and of ignoring the cooperation between public school principals and teachers with a local Jewish school. The well-known filmmaker Elie Chouraqui, who made one of the programs, was even suspected of cuing students to make anti-Semitic comments.[17] Such disagreement and mistrust have worrying aspects. More and more, it seems that anti-Semitism is in the eye of the beholder, with political opponents on both sides minimizing or dramatizing the same event. That is especially true with respect to the situation in schools, where it is often difficult to distinguish expressions of real anti-Semitism from adolescent provocation, bullying, or plain stupidity.

The third controversy, which was bound to surface, is the blame game between the Arab and Muslim community on one hand and traditional French anti-Semites on the other. The former resent being constantly charged by the latter with anti-Semitism. They claim first of all that the extreme right—the traditional "white" French anti-Semites—is responsible for the violence that is pinned on them. And more important, they point out, is the fact that not only are they free of prejudice against Jews (they are Semites themselves, and they had nothing to do with Vichy and the Holocaust), but they themselves are also victims of racism and xenophobia. They complain that Jews are better protected than vulnerable Muslims; even in victimhood, Jews remain "privileged" over Arabs.[18]

Facts do not support the first claim. While extreme-right violence accounted for 90 percent of anti-Semitic acts that could be attributed in the 1990s, the percentage of Arab and Muslim perpetrators jumped to more than 80 percent in 2000. Muslim/Arab involvement stabilized at about 25 to 40 percent of all acts (threats and actual physical assaults) in the following years, with approximately 50 percent of acts unaccounted for and 15 to 35 percent attributed to the extreme right.[19] The wave of anti-Semitic acts may have liberated a latent anti-Semitism in different sectors of French society, however, shattering some taboos and giving way to freer expression of anti-Semitic opinions. But if extreme-right violence sometimes targets the Jewish community, notably near the German border in Alsace, its favorite victims are still Arabs and blacks, not Jews, who are the targets of only 7 percent of violent acts perpetrated by the extreme right.

The second point raises the question of competition among victims and whether anti-Semitism should be considered separate from racism. Some in the Muslim community think that acts of racism and Islamophobia are underreported, and they deplore the lack of public mobilization against racism. Even worse, they charge, day-to-day discrimination is not properly acknowledged or punished. The accusation of a double standard translates into other claims. French history classes are thought to devote too much time to the Holocaust without adequately addressing other genocides, slavery, the Algerian war, or the situation in the Middle East. In other words, French universalism is being described as hypocritical, and it is the first casualty of recent developments, which reflect the distinct rise of "*communautarisme*."

The fourth controversy has an international dimension: it pits American Jewish groups—and occasionally the Israeli government—against the French government and sometimes even against French Jewish groups. American Jewish organizations have closely tracked the rise in anti-Semitism in France, and they have repeatedly voiced their preoccupations in private meetings with the French government as well as to the French embassy and consulates in the United States. French officials resented this intervention in their country's internal affairs, at first because they were in a state of denial about the problem and later—when they had a more balanced view—because of the exaggerations of American critics. These critics sometimes painted a portrait of a uniformly anti-Semitic France, where the Vichy past was resurfacing and where the "Final Solution, Phase 2," as one columnist put it, was under way.[20] The resurgence of anti-Semitism became an argument used by columnists like Charles Krauthammer, George Will, and the late Michael Kelly to bash France for its policies toward Iraq or the Israeli-Palestinian conflict. While French Jewish activists like Sammy Ghozlan credited alarmist articles (such as one devoted to his work in *Vanity Fair*) with having a positive impact on the French government, some French Jewish organizations, like the CRIF, at times felt overshadowed and bullied by the more powerful American organizations.[21]

Another aspect of the international controversy involved the Israeli government's harsh public criticism of France. Ariel Sharon's government appeared to combine genuine worry about anti-Semitism in France with a separate political agenda. In addition, Sharon seemed to want to dampen France's international influence (deemed to be too pro-Palestinian) and to attract new migrants to Israel, since the pool of Jewish migrants from the Soviet Union had begun to dry up.[22] At various points during his tenure, Sharon and his aides made comments stressing the danger for Jews of remaining in France amid the growing Muslim population, triggering angry protests from the French Jewish community's leadership as well as the French government.[23] The Israeli government substantially increased its economic aid for French migrants in 2002, making them eligible for the same migration incentives as Argentine Jews (which were primarily monetary).

French emigration to Israel did increase after the first wave of anti-Semitic acts. In 2004, 6 to 8 percent of French Jews (which amounted to about 40,000 individuals) declared that they were preparing for *aliyah* (immigrating to Israel), a figure that indicates the extent of the fear and trauma in the community since the rise in anti-Semitic acts.[24] The actual rate of *aliyah* doubled from 2001 to 2002, to around 2,000 a year, a level last attained in the aftermath of the Yom Kippur War thirty years before (the 2002 rate remained steady in 2003 and 2004). Figures on the rate of *aliyah* are controversial, however, since they do not take into account the rate of return to France ("failed *aliyah*"). Nor do they count French Jewish emigration to the United States or the French "commuters" who split their time evenly between France and Israel.

Eli Barnavi, the popular Israeli ambassador in Paris, put a temporary end to the French-Israeli and French-American debates by declaring at the end of his mission in 2002, "There is anti-Semitism in France.... But France is not an anti-Semitic country."[25] That defense left a central question: if France is not anti-Semitic, then why does it produce so many anti-Semitic acts? And what role, exactly, do Muslims play in them?

Is There a Specific Muslim Anti-Semitism?

Among the perpetrators of anti-Semitic acts who have been identified, people of Arab or Muslim origin constitute a large plurality. In 2004 and 2005, they committed respectively 34 and 41 percent of acts of anti-Semitic violence, versus 7 and 10 percent for the extreme right, while 59 and 48 percent of acts were either not attributed (and may have been perpetrated by either group) or were attributed to individuals without ties to either group (in 20 percent of cases).[26] The judiciary investigations revealed the following profile of perpetrators of Arab or Muslim background: they tended to be young, socially marginalized males with a low level of education who were generally unable to articulate a political rationale for their actions beyond their prejudice against Jews.[27] Many had already been arrested for other crimes (vandalism, theft, drug dealing, and so forth). Sometimes anti-Semitic vandalism against Jewish establishments was accompanied by theft.[28] In the case of Ilan Halimi, the gang of kidnappers, who called themselves "the barbarians," had previously targeted non-Jews for their extortion or kidnapping schemes, but they chose Halimi because "Jews have money . . . and they stick together."[29]

Both Muslims and non-Muslims were among "the barbarians"; some traced their roots to sub-Saharan Africa and the Maghreb, while others were of Portuguese or older French origin. What they shared, however, was a common background in the bleak *cités*, a pattern of violent behavior since childhood, and, for many of them, anti-Semitic stereotypes.

In the overwhelming majority of cases, anti-Semitic acts are not elaborate affairs. They are carried out by petty criminals, and there has not been any report of coordination with any community association or mosque. As the Rufin report points out, almost all perpetrators of anti-Semitic crimes, whether they are Muslim or from the extreme right or unconnected with either group, share the characteristics of "uprootedness, a lack of sense of their own identity, and social failure."[30] In other words, the same unaffiliated and disgruntled young man who engages in petty delinquent acts, behaves aggressively toward the neighbors, or targets the police or firefighters is the most likely perpetrator of anti-Semitic violence. The Muslim community is overrepresented in anti-Semitic violence, but it also is overrepresented in crime statistics in general (and in the prison population). This points to a predominantly social problem, namely a lack of integration, among the population living in the *banlieues.*

However, the correlation between anti-Semitic violence and events in the Middle East—at least between 2000 and 2003—also indicates a political basis for such violence. This leads to three questions: what is the link between anti-Israel sentiment and anti-Semitism? Is there, among persons of Muslim background, more anti-Semitism than in the rest of the population? And does the factor of religion—Islam per se—play a role?

Anti-Israel Sentiment and Anti-Semitism

Successive CNCDH reports have concluded that it is difficult to establish definitive proof that attacks on French Jews occur out of anger over or as revenge for Israeli policies or as a way of putting pressure on the Israeli or French governments.[31] That is in part because many perpetrators do not articulate any coherent rationale for their actions and also because those who do tend to mix several justifications: anti-Semitism, anti-Zionism, resentment against a better-off community, and, sometimes, Islamist calls for violence against Jews. Many of these perpetrators would have committed some act of vandalism or another offense, whatever its target, on the day that they committed an anti-Semitic act. In that sense, international events provide them with a political pretext for their actions to justify them and give them a higher meaning. The 2004 CNCDH report concludes that only a minority of perpetrators are specifically motivated by hatred for Jews or feelings of solidarity with Palestinians.[32]

Some scholars have argued that the perpetrators, whatever their level of political consciousness, have found cover in a permissive political atmosphere in which the general population is indifferent to anti-Semitism at best, or, at worst, French Jews and Israel are readily conflated. That is the thesis put forward by Pierre-André Taguieff, who sees a "new Judeophobia" emerging in France and elsewhere.[33] Taguieff argues that traditional anti-Semitism has been complemented by extreme anti-Zionism, in which the stigmatizing and targeting of Jews is a legitimate payback for the suffering of Palestinians. This Judeophobia emanates not from the extreme right, Taguieff writes, but rather from a combination of Islamists and extreme-left activists. Their views are characterized by anti-imperialist solidarity with the third world and reinforced by the antiracist movements that defend Palestinians as victims of Israeli racism and colonialism.

While it is clear that the perception of Israeli injustices against Palestinians figures more prominently than before in anti-Jewish feelings, it is less obvious that the new Judeophobia has definitively replaced traditional anti-Semitism, especially when France is analyzed as a whole. A specific strain of anti-Semitism has always existed among the extreme left that blends anti-Zionism (motivated by third-worldism and anti-imperialism) with anticapitalism (with capitalism seen as the domain of wealthy Jews of all nationalities), but it has traditionally been less vocal than right-wing anti-Semitism. Researcher Nonna Mayer argues that that is still the case.[34] Anti-Jewish feelings are more highly correlated with right-wing opinions and xenophobic attitudes in general than with a left-wing ideology, and that correlation has increased, not decreased, in the last decade. In 2002, poll respondents who mostly or completely agreed with the statement that "Jews have too much power in France" were still more likely to be on the extreme right (37 percent) than on the extreme left (18 percent, down from 21 percent in 1988). The figures have increased on the right in general, but not on the left.

As evidence of this development, Mayer uses the only poll that allows for cross-referencing of data on opinions about the Middle East with data on anti-Semitic stereotypes. Her study indicates that the correlations between respondents' opinions of Israeli and Palestinian leaders and anti-Semitic attitudes are complex. In 2002, one-third of those who expressed a dislike of Ariel Sharon and a positive view of Yasser Arafat agreed mostly or completely with the statement that "Jews have too much power in France." But rejection of that statement was still rather high (60 percent) among those who disliked

Sharon, and there were more anti-Semites among those who disliked Arafat (28 percent) than among those who liked him (24 percent). Sylvain Brouard and Vincent Tiberj reached similar conclusions in their study of French of African and Turkish origin in 2005: the most anti-Zionist respondents not only were those who were anti-Semitic—no surprise there—but also those who were less anti-Semitic. Therefore anti-Semitism and opposition to Israel did not completely correlate. In addition, 52 percent of French from an African or Turkish background had a negative view of Israel, compared with 55 percent of the general population, which was markedly less anti-Semitic. (As mentioned in chapter 8, negative views of the United States reached 67 percent and 64 percent for the African/Turkish group and for the general population, respectively.)[35]

Comparing attitudes toward the Israelis and the Palestinians with poll data on anti-Semitic attitudes provides a final useful indicator. Sympathy for the Palestinians has markedly increased in the recent years. The French public identifies more and more with the Palestinian side, reinforcing a tendency that began in 1967; thus, 18 percent of respondents declared themselves more sympathetic with the Palestinians in 2000, 30 percent in 2002, and 34 percent in 2004. Respondents more sympathetic to the Israelis constituted 14 percent, 16 percent, and 13 percent for those years respectively.[36] But as mentioned above, anti-Semitic opinions decreased during the same period, although there was a stable core of 10 to 15 percent of respondents who expressed "very anti-Semitic" views. That suggests an absence of correlation between attitudes toward the Israeli-Palestinian problem and general anti-Semitic views.

To conclude, the link between anti-Israel feelings and anti-Jewish attitudes in France is difficult to assess. But it is safe to say that anti-Zionism is not replacing traditional anti-Semitism as the primary source of anti-Jewish attitudes.[37] The "new Judeophobia" could, however, be reflected in the impassiveness of the general French population, as Taguieff and Rufin note in their recent work. In their view, the French are not becoming more anti-Semitic, but they may react less vigorously against anti-Semitic acts and tolerate the anti-Semitism of young French Arabs because of their own anti-Israel and antiracist sympathies.

The Extent of Muslim Anti-Semitism and the Influence of Islam

It is worth asking whether the French Muslim community is special in this regard—that is, whether French Muslims are more anti-Semitic or "Judeophobic" than the rest of the population. It is important to keep in mind that there is no such thing as "the Muslim community." The French Muslim population is quite diverse, hailing from many ethnic and national backgrounds and entertaining a wide range of political opinions. Statistics on Muslims' views on Jews are very scarce, because of both the traditional French aversion to identifying people by ethnic group in polling data and the political sensitivity of the topic. There are no polls comparable to American data showing, for example, that in 2005, 36 percent of African Americans fell in the "most anti-Semitic" category, versus 29 percent of Hispanics and 9 percent of whites.[38] There is one exception, however: in 2005 researchers Sylvain Brouard and Vincent Tiberj of CEVIPOF conducted an extensive study of French of African and Turkish background, whether Muslim or not. Their research reveals that the anti-Semitic statement that "Jews have too much power in France" was believed by 39 percent of respondents of African or Turkish background (versus 20 percent of the general population) and that 33 percent of respondents were categorized as anti-Semites (versus 18 percent of the general population) on the basis of giving three anti-Semitic answers on key questions.[39] However, large majorities of French Muslim respondents still reject the stereotype. The 2005 IFOP poll commissioned by the U.S. State Department found that 64 percent of French Muslims had a positive opinion of Jews, while 27 percent held a negative opinion (in the same poll, 88 percent of the general French public had a positive opinion of Jews).[40]

Brouard and Tiberj also note other interesting elements: anti-Semitism is strongest among French of African or Turkish origin who are between thirty-two and forty-one years of age, and it recedes greatly as the time spent in France increases. Among the three generations studied by Brouard and Tiberj, anti-Semitism was at its highest among naturalized immigrants (37 percent), it was lower in the first generation born in France (32 percent), and it dropped definitively in the second generation born in France (17 percent, which is lower than the figure recorded by Brouard and Tiberj for the general population).

Last, the two researchers show the importance of religion as a factor in anti-Semitism. Anti-Semitism declines with level of practice: it reached 46 percent among practicing Muslims, 40 percent among "infrequently" observant Muslims, 30 percent among nonpracticing Muslims, and 23 percent among those who declared that they had no religion. (There was still a gap with the rest of the French population.) Brouard and Tiberj therefore conclude that anti-Semitism is correlated with participation in social networks associated with the practice of the Muslim faith.

An Anti-Semitic Subculture?

There have been many qualitative studies and reports about a new anti-Semitic subculture in the *banlieues* that has sometimes found public expression, especially in schools with a large number of students of immigrant origin. In some student circles, anti-Semitic remarks are an accepted aspect of everyday life. For example, the slang term *"feuj"* (*juif,* or Jew, pronounced in reverse) is used to describe a nonfunctioning object—*"un stylo feuj"* (a broken pen)—or to describe a selfish or mean person. The scholar Michel Wieviorka of the Ecole des Hautes Etudes en Sciences Sociales (EHESS) (School of Advanced Studies in Social Sciences) found that in discussions with teenagers in the *banlieues,* Jews were sometimes described as "owning" the television, movie, and entertainment industries and the media in general. They also were represented as all-powerful in the clothing and fashion industry.[41] These anti-Semitic stereotypes have been adapted to fit the contemporary French environment, in which, for example, because Jews are believed to control the media, some anti-Semitic individuals decide whether they like or dislike popular TV and radio personalities depending on their Jewishness.

Anti-Semitic stereotypes in the *banlieues* may be bolstered by frustration with what some see as Jews' comparatively more successful integration in France. They may believe that Jews are richer; that they have better clothes and electronic gadgets, which they are more prone to showing off; and that they also benefit from a more cohesive community than the Arab or Muslim population. As explained above, that kind of stereotyping led to the targeting of Ilan Halimi for kidnapping. Jews have their own schools and their own institutions, and many French Muslims believe that Jewish community leaders enjoy privileged access to the government. They also believe that Jews are spared the daily discrimination and racism that young French Muslims encounter from the traditional French community and that even when Jews do suffer attacks, as in recent years, their plight is given more attention than the Muslims' experience of racism. In this view, anti-Semitic acts are better tracked and acted upon, while Muslims/Arabs are unfairly accused of being perpetrators when in fact they are the true victims of racist attitudes.

This *"banlieue* anti-Semitism" thus mixes feelings of injustice and resentment of the Jewish community with stereotypes. Jews become a scapegoat for the failures of integration, and traditional anti-Semitic stereotypes (Jewish power, wealth, greed, and so forth) reinforce Muslim feelings of solidarity with oppressed Palestinians—and, more generally, for all Muslims oppressed by Western society. Some media personalities, like the black comic Dieudonné M'Bala M'Bala, have poured oil on the fire by making anti-Semitic comments on television. Dieudonné, dressed as an Orthodox Jewish settler, ironically called on the young people of the *banlieues* to "join the American-Zionist axis" and finished by shouting "Isra-Heil!"and giving a Nazi salute. His comments and actions were unanimously condemned in the media and political sphere, which had the effect of reinforcing sympathy for him in disaffected areas. Dieudonné became an outcast with whom disaffected young *beurs* and blacks could identify. The comedian has combined his campaign for the recognition of the enslavement of Africans by Europeans from the sixteenth through the eighteenth century with other public anti-Semitic remarks, and he has become the symbol of a new competition among victims (Jews, Armenians, Algerians, and sub-Saharan Africans during colonialism and the wars of decolonization) that fuels *communautarisme* in contemporary France.

If the failures of integration provide a springboard to anti-Semitism, then nowhere is this relationship more evident than in public schools. The school system is where social ills are clear for all to see, but it is also the institution that is supposed to address those ills. One book published in 2002, *The Lost Territories of the Republic,* had a large impact on the debate over schools (see discussion in chapter 3).[42] This work, coauthored by a group of schoolteachers, painted a somber portrait of French schools in the *banlieues,* where anti-Semitism, racism, communitarianism, sexism, and the lack of respect for authority dominated classrooms. Even worse, the authors argued, the indifference of most teachers to those developments bordered on appeasement. The book had the merit of focusing attention on real problems and brought the issue of anti-Semitism in schools to the forefront. But the new awareness came at the expense of a more realistic assessment of the situation in schools and increased social stigmatizing of young Muslims.

More important, the book gave only one side of the story—that is, the provocations and communitarian attitudes of Muslim students. The authors made no mention of any positive developments or improvements in their attitudes or of the administrative resources and pedagogical tools available to teachers to fight stereotypes and anti-Semitism, sexism, racism, and so forth. In one case at least—the Jules Siegfried high school in northern Paris—the portrait painted in *Lost Territories* by a former teacher there was described by the principal (himself an activist in the campaign against anti-Semitism) as a crude, pessimistic caricature of what was really going on in the classrooms.[43]

Nonetheless, anti-Semitic behavior does exist in middle schools and high schools in *zones d'education prioritaire* (ZEPs) (priority education zones) in French *banlieues*. Between January and August 2004, officials recorded 235 anti-Semitic incidents and 1,040 racist incidents, which affected about 10 percent of all middle schools and high schools.[44] Between September 2004 and June 2005, the first full school year examined, these numbers increased to 330 anti-Semitic and 1,707 racist incidents, taking place in 15 percent of all middle schools and high schools; nonetheless, there was a slight downward trend in the first six months of 2005 compared with the same period in 2004.[45] Insults and threats constituted half of the anti-Semitic and two-thirds of the racist incidents in 2004–05, whereas physical violence was involved in 325 (19 percent) of the racist and 26 (8 percent) of the anti-Semitic incidents (none of the violence involved the use of weapons). The analytical difficulty has always been to distinguish between the effects of a genuinely anti-Semitic subculture and the routine provocations and bullying of teenagers. It is hard to classify instances of violence between students. Most sociologists would agree, for example, that the slur "dirty Jew" when uttered by an eleven-year-old does not have the same significance as it does when uttered by a seventeen-year-old—and that blurting it out in anger during a schoolyard fight does not carry as much weight as doing so in history class. The teaching of the Holocaust has indeed sometimes been disrupted by unruly students, and such behavior extends to other subjects too, such as religion, the Middle East, colonialism, or U.S. foreign policy; on occasion, even Darwinian evolution has been challenged (a rarity in France). A study conducted by the Fondation pour la Mémoire de la Shoah (Foundation in Memory of the Holocaust) and the Association des Professeurs d'Histoire-Géographie (History and Geography Teachers Association) in 2003 revealed that incidents related to the teaching of sensitive subjects (including, but not limited to, the Holocaust) had occurred in 15 percent of French schools.[46]

Though anti-Semitism at school is a genuine issue—confirmed by the decision of many Jewish families to enroll their children in Jewish schools—its prevalence and causes should be carefully assessed. It appears to be first and foremost a problem of disaffected neighborhoods, and as such it is just one among many symptoms of the failures of integration, especially among students with immigrant parents. Anti-Semitism at school is also a reflection of an anti-Semitic subculture that has gained ground in recent years, in part as a reaction to international events. Antiracism associations have argued that there is an educational mission to fulfill among the younger generations, whether Muslim, Jewish, or nonminority, and that the trick is to make them more sensitive to the issue of anti-Semitism and racism without stigmatizing a whole community. That was the position taken by SOS Racisme and the Union des Etudiants Juifs de France (UEJF) (Union of Jewish Students of France), the primary organization of Jewish students, in their coproduced book in 2002. The organizations emphasized the reasons to reject anti-Semitism (and racism) rather than argue that young Muslims were collectively responsible for the trend. But they issued a strong admonition: young people "may not know how easily the hands that have written 'death to the Jews' can also begin to kill Jews."[47]

The last question regarding anti-Semitism in the Muslim community is the weight of the religious—that is, specifically Islamic—factor. As mentioned above, no known perpetrators of anti-Semitic violence have been affiliated with a mosque or an organized Muslim group, but anti-Semitic opinions are more prevalent among practicing than nonpracticing Muslims. Some activists in the Jewish community, such as retired police chief Samy Ghozlan, have suggested that there might be a link between anti-Semitic incidents and the presence of a radical imam or preacher in a given neighborhood.[48] However, no study has yet tested that hypothesis.

Muslim officials from the main umbrella organizations—the Conseil Français du Culte Musulman (CFCM) (French Council of the Muslim Religion), the Union des Organisations Islamiques de France (UOIF) (Union of Islamic Organizations of France), and others—have always been very clear in their condemnation of anti-Semitism, and some have worked jointly with Jewish groups to increase mutual understanding and reduce hate crimes. Both the Grande Mosquée de Paris (Great Mosque of Paris) and the UOIF hold regular meetings with their Jewish counterparts from the CRIF. They also reacted unanimously and immediately to condemn the attacks of 9/11. Jewish groups, for their part, always condemn acts against mosques and desecration of Muslim graves. However, not all Muslim leaders have been irreproachable in that regard, especially some unofficial leaders. Tariq Ramadan, for example, who has always clearly condemned anti-Semitism and warned young Muslims against it, nonetheless wrote an op-ed that smacked of anti-Semitism in fall 2003.[49] In addition, a cassette tape from 2000 that was circulated among UOIF activists contained a strongly worded anti-Semitic speech by the popular preacher Hassan Iquioussen. He later apologized for it, and his organization, the UOIF, quickly dissociated itself from the incident and reiterated its condemnation of anti-Semitism both in the organization's "school of thought" and "model of behavior."[50] The Alsace-based Parti des Musulmans de France (Party of French Muslims), founded by Mohammed Latrèche—which organized a demonstration against the ban of headscarves in public schools—is unapologetically anti-Semitic, although its constituency is minuscule.

The main problem, then, appears not to be religious so much as cultural or even "civilizational" (according to Samuel Huntington's notion of Islam versus the West).[51] Some French Muslims choose to define their identity in global terms—"in solidarity with other Muslims in the world"—and that stance sometimes includes the geopolitical aspect of being anti-Jewish and anti-American. Satellite television also plays a role, as many networks from the Middle East can be seen in France, and they convey images of the Israeli-Palestinian conflict and the war in Iraq that tend to inflame public opinion. An extreme example of this tendency was given by al-Manar, the Lebanese-based Hezbollah network, which broadcast anti-Semitic soap operas and appeals for the "death of Israel." The channel was eventually banned, in 2004, from the French satellite network Eutelsat (and later banned by the United States) although the station can still be received on the Internet and, in certain parts of France, through outside satellite providers. Such links with "international anti-Semitism" reinforce the identification of some French Muslims—when they understand Arabic, which is actually rare among those born in France—with a larger Islamist, and sometimes anti-Semitic, *umma*.

In conclusion, caution should be exercised when assessing anti-Semitism among French Muslims. Anti-Semitic incidents increased dramatically between 2000 and 2004, and a large number of the incidents can be traced to disaffected members of the Arab and Muslim community. Two hundred or so individuals attacking synagogues, Jewish schools, and French Jews have been enough to create the impression of widespread anti-Semitism in France. Since it has been argued that some of them act in a permissive environment created by the importation of the intifada into the heart of France, the French government has put policies in place to try to change that environment.

Government Reactions

After an initially slow reaction and a tendency to minimize the seriousness of events, the French government has vigorously pursued policies to combat anti-Semitism since 2002, even earning the praise of American Jewish organizations and the Israeli government.[52] France has been at the forefront of some measures, such as one to prevent hate speech on the Internet. There is no equivalent of the U.S. First Amendment in France, and both Holocaust denial (referred to as "negationism") and racist and anti-Semitic comments can be prosecuted under two statutes: the Gayssot law of 1990 and the Lellouche law of 2003, which makes anti-Semitism an aggravating factor in sentences handed down for acts of violence. For the last two years, a special interministerial commission on anti-Semitism has gathered each month in the prime minister's office and issued a press release on a practical agenda to be accomplished before its next meeting.

President Chirac has spoken out forcefully and repeatedly against anti-Semitic acts, saying that any attack on French Jews is an attack on all France and the very idea of the Republic. Nicolas Sarkozy, the former interior minister, publicly condemned the rationale of attacking a French Jew out of anger over Israeli policies. The government increased security around synagogues and Jewish schools and community centers, and, through special administrative memorandums, it has instructed the police and judges to be tougher in cases of anti-Semitism. "The best policy against the ugly beast of anti-Semitism is to identify infractions, arrest suspects, and sentence the guilty," Sarkozy told a regional CRIF meeting.[53]

Confronted with the rise in anti-Semitism and communitarianism, in 2005 the government created a new agency called the Haute Autorité de Lutte contre les Discriminations et pour l'Egalité (HALDE) (High Authority to Combat Discrimination and Promote Equality), charged with combating discrimination of all kinds (anti-Semitism and racism, homophobia, sexism, and so forth). The creation of the HALDE, however, had been scheduled by the government, right and left, since the 1990s; it was not a direct response to the rise in anti-Semitic acts. A special effort has been made to better record and study anti-Semitic incidents. As mentioned above, the Ministry of Education modified its database on violence in schools to keep track of racist and anti-Semitic acts in 2004, and the Ministry of the Interior worked with Jewish groups to standardize their record-keeping. And the Ministry of Justice used the Lellouche law to create a new database of anti-Semitic acts. Last, each year the CNCDH collects and analyzes data that it publishes in a report that serves as an indispensable resource in the fight against anti-Semitism.

One weak spot has been in the realm of justice, first because too few cases of anti-Semitism are resolved. In 2004, the Ministry of Justice examined 387 cases; in 295 of them, the perpetrator had not been identified. Furthermore, many observers think that the sentences issued are too light and that judges are too complacent with young perpetrators of immigrant origin. The result, in the words of the CNCDH, is that "the productivity of the repression [of anti-Semitism] has been low."[54] In fall 2003, however, courts in Chambéry and Lyon handed down prison sentences of three years and six months for anti-Semitic violence and synagogue desecration, respectively, and in January 2004, an assailant was sentenced to six months for having thrown a rock at a Jewish man.[55] A French man of North African origin was sentenced in December 2004 to two months in prison (plus a suspended sentence of six months) and forced to pay €4,000 ($4,855) in damages to a rabbi whom he had physically attacked in October 2003; he had already served four months in preventive detention by the time his trial ended. In addition, civil lawsuits have been filed in French courts against allegedly anti-Semitic statements made by Tariq Ramadan (for his polemic against a pro-Israel group of "Jewish intellectuals"), the comedian Dieudonné M'Bala M'Bala (for the comedy routine in which he impersonated an Orthodox Jewish settler using Nazi phrases and gestures), and Party of French Muslims leader Mohammed Latrèche (for making negative generalizations about Jews).[56]

At the end of the day, the deeper cause of anti-Semitism—especially in disaffected areas where Muslims are numerous—is lack of socioeconomic integration. In the face of such a huge challenge, the government can do only so much to help forge a more confident self-image among Muslims, but there is evidence that at least it is beginning to do what its own experts have recommended. The Stasi Commission's 2003 report on secularism in schools suggested that as a way of officially recognizing France's complex relationship with this population, the national school curriculum should take into account the history of colonialism and slavery—particularly as experienced by colonized and enslaved peoples—which currently receives scant mention in official texts. Meetings between commission members and officials of the Ministry of Education have begun to discuss how to implement the commission's recommendations. When the documentary filmmaker Claude Lanzmann went to the Département 93 *banlieue* to screen an educational version of his celebrated Holocaust film *Shoah* in spring 2004, he was surprised to find a highly receptive audience among the children of Arab immigrants. "It is necessary to go talk to these young people," he told *Le Monde*. "We have to keep talking to them."[57]

10 | *The Threat of Terrorism and the French Response*

Islamist terrorism in France—as well as French anti-Semitism and French Muslims' impact on French foreign policy—is an example of the nexus of local integration problems and global affairs. Starting in the 1990s, transnational Islamist networks have sought, with some success, to recruit followers among disaffected Muslims in Europe. Their efforts have been especially apparent in France, where integration problems and close immigrant links with Algeria—the theater of a bloody civil war between the secular government and Islamist groups—made the issue of terrorism more salient. That fact, incidentally, gave French authorities a head start in devising tactics for monitoring and dismantling these networks, tactics that proved valuable in the years after 9/11.

The current situation is mixed. On one hand, Islamist networks are still active. Recent international developments, such as events in Iraq and the continuing Israeli-Palestinian conflict, have been exploited by skilled preachers and recruiters, ensuring a small but constant trickle of recruits to wage holy war. The U.S. intervention in Iraq has been described in several official documents as a particular boon for Islamist recruitment efforts.[1] Exemplified by the "Buttes-Chaumont" cell, which sent several young French Arabs from Paris's nineteenth arrondissement to fight American soldiers in Iraq in 2004, radical networks steadily recruit and radicalize young Muslims who have not found their place in European society. Such global jihadists are all the more dangerous for other countries, including the United States, because they hold regular European passports.

On the other hand, the phenomenon is marginal, numbering just a few dozen cases a year out of a population of around 5 million Muslims. Muslim associations, from the Conseil Français du Culte Musulman (CFCM) (French

Council of the Muslim Religion) on down, condemn violent jihad in strong terms, as does an overwhelming majority of French Muslim respondents to public opinion polls.[2] Furthermore, the radical Islamist milieu is closely monitored by the French government, which is recognized as the most effective in Europe against this threat.[3] French police and justice officials have worked steadily to reduce terrorist activities on national territory. The head of the domestic intelligence service, the Renseignements Généraux (RG) has estimated that there are around 5,000 salafists in France, of whom approximately 500 are considered potentially dangerous. The counterterrorism unit of the Direction du Surveillance du Territoire (DST) (Directorate of Territorial Surveillance) made fifty-five arrests in the first half of 2005, compared with seventy-six for all of 2004 and fifty-eight for 2003.[4] As of December 31, 2004, a total of 361 individuals were in jail on terrorism-related charges: 153 for Basque terrorism, seventy-nine for Corsican terrorism, and 103 for Islamist terrorism.[5] The Ministry of the Interior has created regional centers to encourage administrative cooperation among police, gendarmes, domestic intelligence, counterterrorism, and other officials through regular meetings, in addition to establishing special regional offices for the fight against radical Islamism.[6]

One way that the government has combated extremists' influence at the neighborhood level has been to expel any imams who have praised terrorist violence, called for assassinations, or otherwise expressed "hatred."[7] Interior Minister Sarkozy announced that thirty-five imams had been expelled between fall 2003 and fall 2005, and that another dozen were in the process of being deported.[8] In addition, in the space of a few months in 2005, French courts finally handed down convictions to Djamel Beghal for his plot against the U.S. embassy, to the Parisian accomplices of "shoe bomber" Richard Reid, and to the accomplices of the assassins of Afghanistan's Northern Alliance commander Massoud.

The precise link between Islam and terrorism—and, more specifically, between terrorism and the re-Islamization of French youth of Muslim background—deserves close examination in order to understand what combination of factors—integration failure, identity crisis, and political and religious motives—may result in a person's involvement with terrorist networks. To convey a more concrete sense of these realities, this chapter gives one "real-life" example, that of Zacarias Moussaoui.

France: A Recruiting Ground for Islamic Terrorists?

The birth of an Islamist terrorist in the West, particularly in France, should be seen as the result of a complex set of factors. Religion is one such factor, but it is insufficient to explain the radicalization of an individual. Cultural and psychological conditions play a background role, as do social and economic conditions. Political considerations, especially the feeling of solidarity with other victimized Muslims in the world and the desire to attack Western domination, are often decisive. Whatever the mix, the personal encounter between "re-Islamized" French youth and recruiters for terrorist networks is, of course, the single most important step in their drift toward violent action. Terrorism is thus predicated on three separate steps: favorable preconditions, political awareness mixed with religious awakening or conversion, and an invitation to radical action by recruiters who provide youths with military training and give the orders to act.

There is no automatic link between an individual's lack of socioeconomic integration and subsequent involvement in terrorism. It is paradoxically observed that the most "Westernized" of Muslims, who are culturally—if not always economically—"integrated," are in fact more likely to become prey for recruiters of radical Islam. (Indeed, even the perpetrators of 9/11, most of them Saudis, were not the products of madrasas, but rather of their own experience, outside the Muslim world, which involved Westernization, religious conversion, political awareness, and radicalization.) The case of Mohammed Bouyeri, the assassin of the filmmaker Theo Van Gogh in Amsterdam, suggests that successful social and linguistic integration is indeed quite compatible with a process of radicalization and the drift toward violence. The same holds true for the perpetrators of the London bombings of July 7, 2005. The few French-born terrorists generally have not come from the lowest social classes (some, however, are working-class dropouts or juvenile delinquents). Rather, they usually are educated young men of Arab origin who hail from the lower middle class. "We have not yet detected in France the profile of a terrorist with a higher education, like the Saudis from September 11," the director of the DST said in May 2005. "The French jihadi has rougher edges, is younger, but also is more radicalized and engaged than in previous years."[9] Tarek Ouinis, for example, who killed himself in Iraq in 2004, was from an apparently solid family of the lower middle class. His father lived in Paris and held a stable job, and his five brothers had no police record.[10] In the summer of 2003, Ouinis traveled to Syria with his friend Abdel Halim Badjoudj "to learn Arabic" and to get an Islamic education. He returned to Paris for a few months in the winter of 2004 and then flew back to Syria and traveled by land to Iraq, where he joined an armed resistance group. Ouinis had been in contact with the El-Hakim brothers (he reported Boubakeur El-Hakim's arrest in Syria to the French consulate) as well as with Badjoudj.[11]

Badjoudj, who grew up in Seine-Saint-Denis, just outside Paris, apparently was the first suicide bomber of French origin: he blew himself up in a car bomb attack on U.S. troops near Falluja on October 20, 2004.[12]

A common characteristic of known terrorists often is a personal identity crisis that precedes radicalization. To that extent, violent radicalization is similar to the politically neutral process of re-Islamization. In each individual terrorist's trajectory, a recruiter precipitates the arrival of a young man at a "tipping point" that leads him to radical action. Some aspects of the recruitment process vary by case: speed, religious content, promoters, and geography, but the general itinerary has been from France to London and then to "lands of jihad." The sociologist Farhad Khosrokhavar has studied the factors that lead up to this so-called tipping point.[13] He describes common feelings of humiliation and victimhood—especially on encountering racism—and finds, unsurprisingly, a general hatred of "Western arrogance." Embracing Islam also is a way for some young men to reject a Britishness or a Frenchness that has always eluded them, offering them dignity, moral grounding, and a sense of belonging. "Because society excludes me," goes the logic, "I reject it and thereby become an actor in my own life, gaining the initiative."[14]

These men establish a clear link between their own status as victims of an unfair system and the political conditions of Muslims around the world; to them, it appears that there is oppression everywhere, from Palestine to Chechnya to Europe. They gradually redefine themselves around Islam—both locally (through membership in the local mosque) and globally (through membership in the *umma,* or borderless Muslim community)—and protest Western domination of "our people."[15] Identity is not rediscovered but constructed anew, and that is one reason why would-be terrorists generally are not interested in their parents' or grandparents' native countries but in the land of jihad *du jour* (Bosnia, Chechnya, Afghanistan, or Iraq, for example).

Political awareness is an important precondition for adherence to radical Islam. Kamel Daoudi (who was born in 1974 in Algeria and arrived in France in 1979) wrote essays and kept a diary in his cell after he was arrested for involvement in the planned bombing of the U.S. embassy in Paris by a cell linked to al Qaeda. Daoudi's writings show that he was bright and educated: "Just as I came close to achieving my dream [graduating from the University of Paris in science and engineering] I started to worry about religious and political questions. The context at the time was the civil war in Algeria, where they were about to set up a regime based on Islamic law. The West hated us because we were Arabs and Muslims."[16] In the case of the radicalization of

Zacarias Moussaoui, who pled guilty to belonging to an al Qaeda cell in the United States and claimed to be an alternate pilot for the September 11 attacks, racism and personal failures were key factors, but similarly, political awareness—of the Gulf War, the Algerian civil war, and Bosnia—also acted as triggers (Moussaoui's biography is discussed in greater detail below).

The move from political awareness to violent action can take place very quickly. Lionel Dumont, a French man of Catholic origin who had attended medical school, sympathized with the plight of Bosnia's Muslims, which he had read about in the media. He traveled to Bosnia as a humanitarian aid worker, and there he met foreign jihadists. Almost immediately, he converted to a radical brand of Islam and turned to violent action, fighting with the Arab Legion and eventually organizing a weapons-smuggling network called the "Roubaix gang" (after a suburb of Lille). The religious factor is often secondary in such cases of rapid conversion. Dumont, for example, explained that he joined Islam because "the Muslims are the only ones to fight the system."[17] Radical Islam is often viewed by its adherents as the only real political protest movement, the only true militancy of the *banlieues,* which they feel have been deserted by the traditional parties of the left, especially the Communist Party.[18] That was made clear during the urban riots of November 2005, when no political agenda emerged from the violence. The riots were not carried out on the orders of any organized political force, and Islamists stayed clear of them.[19] The unrest did not serve their aims in any way: why burn cars and play hide-and-seek with French cops when one can fight a real jihad in Iraq? Religion is, of course, ever-present in the terrorist framework, but Islam often serves as a pretext to fight "Western oppression" worldwide.

The process of religious awakening or conversion is, of course, a factor in an individual's drift toward radical action. It is important to note, however, that the phenomenon of re-Islamization (discussed in chapter 3), does not, in most cases, pave the way for political radicalization and enrollment in a jihadist movement. In fact, as Olivier Roy noted, "A necessary condition of radicalization is re-Islamization. . . . But this is not a sufficient condition. . . . Re-Islamization can take on a humanist and even a liberal mode, such as that form advocated by the imam of the Ad-Dawa mosque in Paris. Nevertheless, re-Islamization can also lead to radicalization."[20] As descendants of immigrants lose contact with the country and politics of their ancestors, radicalization takes on an ideological form that is divorced from a specific national culture or diaspora, whether Algerian, Moroccan, Turk, or any other. It is instead defined by adherence to a transnational or "globalized Islam," as political as it is religious, in strict communal terms (us versus them). This powerful combination provides a strong dose of group identity, meaning, and purpose to young and often educated but jobless and alienated second- or third-generation immigrants.[21]

In the rare instances in which re-Islamization leads to terrorism, the first contact with Islam has generally been through a rigorous and puritanical version of the religion: Salafism. This ideological religious movement combines a rejection of Western culture with deracination from one's own traditional or native Muslim culture. The combined effect is to create an appetite for a global, fundamentalist, and "pure" Islam. As discussed in chapter 3, some salafists are "sheikhist" (that is, they respect the edicts of Saudi sheikhs and do not challenge the political authorities in their host country), but others are "jihadists" and defend violent action (organizations like al Qaeda, Hizb-ut-Tahrir, and, with greater ambiguity, the Muslim Brotherhood and Tabligh).[22] Of approximately 1,600 prayer spaces in France, the Renseignements Généraux reported in 2005 that seventy-five had recently been subject to "destabilization attempts" by radicals; half resisted and the other half were "conquered by radicals."[23] The Ministry of the Interior had about thirty-three salafist-controlled prayer spaces under observation in 2004, mostly in the Paris and Lyon regions.[24]

The conversion of many French youth is inspired by the proselytizing activities of Tabligh, during the organization's "*tours de France,*" which take place in the summertime. A group of ten missionaries, usually including some recent converts, tour popular campgrounds and the poor neighborhoods that are home to disaffected young men. They often use conventional gestures of hospitality to gather an audience in prayer spaces and social centers, offering a bite to eat in exchange for the attendees' time. Once a young man has converted, he may be encouraged to travel to Pakistan for religious training in a madrasa. This type of conversion generally leads to a fairly puritanical, rigorous brand of Islam, creating an environment in which jihadists can sometimes recruit future militants. Indeed, many young French jihadists of the 1990s were first converted or re-Islamized by Tabligh (Khaled Kelkal, David Courtailler, Djamel Beghal, Hervé Djamel Loiseau, and others). Tabligh is not a terrorist or even an extremist organization—it has a representative on the French Council of the Muslim Religion—but it is nonetheless the movement through which the evolution toward radicalization has occurred most often.

There are two categories of recruits: young men of Muslim origin who turn to Islam, and French converts, of European and generally Catholic origin. Native French conversions from Catholicism or a nonreligious background to

Islam are sometimes simply the result of adoption of the local culture where the future convert resides, that is, the *banlieues*. Recent converts (other than the wives of Muslim men who convert to Islam for the purpose of marriage) often try to compensate for their lack of "ethnic" legitimacy by adopting fundamentalist or radical views—the zeal of the convert. Because they are French and white and therefore able to cross borders, rent apartments, and buy equipment with less scrutiny than re-Islamized young men of Arab background, these converts are valued by terrorist recruiters.[25] Pierre Robert, a convert, was sentenced to life in prison in September 2003 for his role in suicide bombings a year earlier in Morocco. David Courtailler, born in 1976, was converted at age eighteen by Tabligh, after which he frequented the Baker Street mosque in London and then traveled to Afghanistan. He was arrested in 1999 for abetting terrorists, and in 2001 he was joined in jail by his brother Jérôme.

The last step in the would-be terrorist's path is actual recruitment by a global terrorist network and the active pursuit of violent jihad. Two common ways of coming into contact with radical Islam have been through the obligatory French military service (which was abolished in 2001) and in French prisons. Hervé Djamel Loiseau, born in France in 1973 to a French mother and an Algerian immigrant father, converted during his military service through contacts with Tabligh in the 1990s. He then made several trips to London and Saudi Arabia, traveled to Pakistan in 2000, and went on to join the Taliban. Loiseau was ultimately found dead (from cold and starvation) by U.S. soldiers in a cave in Tora Bora. The other source of Islamist militants has been the prison system: a recent report by the Renseignements Généraux estimated that 175 inmates across the country actively seek to proselytize others in French prisons.[26] In some prisons that are located close to the *banlieues*, up to 70 percent of inmates were either born in North Africa or have parents from the Maghreb.[27] Islamic proselytizing has occasionally led to the re-Islamization of juvenile delinquents, as in the case of Khaled Kelkal (also by way of Tabligh). Kelkal carried out several deadly bombings on behalf of the Algerian Groupe Islamique Armé (GIA) (Armed Islamic Group) before being killed in a shootout with French police in 1995.

The prison connection also appears in more recent cases. In his survey of Muslim inmates, Farhad Khosrokhavar observed a modest degree of three kinds of proselytizing.[28] First there is the discreet variety, in which observant Muslims lend prayer books or religious literature to their Muslim, but nonobservant, cellmates—or, occasionally, to non-Muslim inmates (known as "lost sheep," or *brebis perdues*). Jose Padilla, an American once suspected of planning a "dirty bomb" attack in 2002, had undergone conversion to radical Islam in a U.S. prison, and Richard Reid, the would-be "shoe bomber" aboard a Paris-Miami flight in December 2001, converted in a British prison. Then there is the apolitical or puritanical variety of proselytizing, such as that carried out by Tabligh. Finally, there is what Khosrokhavar calls the "radical Islamist" variety: in one prison, the Muslim chaplain reported the presence of 200 radical Islamists in 1995, including ten women. Many of them were subsequently deported or transferred to separate prisons.

In addition to the army and the prisons, another important site of radicalization has been the city of London, which played a decisive role in the trajectory of re-Islamized young men who turned to violent action from the late 1980s until as recently as 2002–03. The city earned the nickname "Londonistan," the "capital of political Islam"—a place where Islamism could be preached, organized, and financed.[29] Almost all of the known Islamist terrorists of the 1990–2005 period passed through London. The city was the hub of radical Islamists linked to Osama bin Laden, and many of them gravitated toward imams like Abu Hamza al-Masri at Finsbury Park mosque, who is now fighting the denaturalization process; Abu Qutada, who preached at the Baker Street mosque, among other places, and was arrested in October 2002 for involvement with al Qaeda; Abu Doha, who recruited volunteers for Afghanistan and Chechnya from his London apartment; and Omar Bakri, who founded the U.K. branch of Hizb-ut-Tahrir—in addition to the now defunct Jama'at Al-Muhajirun, another extremist group—and who is currently in exile in Lebanon following the British government's toughening of regulations on foreign clerics.[30] This concentration of individuals can be explained by the long-time tolerance of the British authorities vis-à-vis jihadists and radical preachers, many of whom claimed political asylum from repressive regimes in the Arab world. The United Kingdom was thought of as a sanctuary, unlike France, which was viewed as repressive because of its close surveillance of extremist preachers and its backing of the Algerian government against the Islamists.[31]

The case of Djamel Beghal illustrates the role of the United Kingdom. Born in 1965 in Algeria, Beghal was arrested in July 2001 while preparing to bomb the U.S. embassy in Paris. In 1994, while studying business administration in France, where he was a citizen, he discovered Islam through Tabligh-run activities, but it was the political struggle of Muslims around the world, rather than a purely religious awakening, that inspired him to wage jihad. Beghal traveled to the United Kingdom in 1998, visiting the Al Taqwa mosque in Leicester and then the Al Islkah mosque in Birmingham, where he underwent further radicalization. Then he went on to London, where he met frequently with Abu Qutada. He traveled to Jalalabad, Afghanistan, for military training in 2000, bringing along his wife and children. When he returned to France, he was given the task of bombing the U.S. embassy by Abu Zubaida, a close partner of bin Laden who was himself arrested in Pakistan in April 2002.

The most common destination of radical Islamic terrorists since the 1990s has been Jalalabad and the training camps of Afghanistan, Bosnia, Chechnya, and, more recently, Iraq. Some have suggested that as many as 200 French citizens or former French residents went to train in Afghan camps. In 2002, in a rare interview, Pierre de Bousquet, the director of the DST, remarked that "several dozen young men left France to spend time in various Afghan camps or to fight in the former Yugoslavia. Others returned and their whereabouts are currently unknown."[32] Up to seven French citizens have been held at the U.S. detention center in Guantanamo: Mourad Benchellali, Khaled Ben Moustapha, Imad Kanouni, Redouane Khalid, Mustaq Ali Patel, Nizar Sassi, and Brahim Yadel. The dead bodies of five young French jihadists were found in Falluja after the U.S. intervention there in November 2004. Bousquet estimated that another four or five French citizens are being held in Syrian or Iraqi prisons, and that ten others who are known to have joined the Iraqi resistance remain unaccounted for.[33]

The Revealing Case of Zacarias Moussaoui

Zacarias Moussaoui, the French citizen detained in the United States and sentenced in May 2006 by a federal judge to life in prison for being part of the broad 9/11 terrorist plot, presents an interesting case study. His brother, Abd Samad Moussaoui, wrote a book in which he described their upbringing, how Zacarias came into contact with Islam, and, beginning with his stay in London, how he later became a radical.[34] Zacarias Moussaoui's childhood, as recounted by his brother—however subjectively—exemplifies the experience of many second-generation immigrants, although very few of them ever radicalize to the extent that Moussaoui did.[35]

Moussaoui was born in 1968 to Moroccan parents in St. Jean de Luz, France. His mother, Aïcha, a strong, independent woman, divorced her husband in 1971 and raised their four children alone. When Moussaoui was four years old, he was taken with his brother into foster care for more than a year because his mother could not afford to care for them. But their mother improved her situation by finding a job as a cleaning woman in the Mulhouse post office, and she eventually moved her family into a housing project in

Bourtzwiller, a somewhat rough neighborhood. There, Moussaoui confronted racism for the first time: his skin is dark, and he was called a "dirty Negro." His mother eventually saved enough money to buy a small house, a sign of upward social mobility. She did not pass on much in the way of religious or Moroccan culture to her children (the family celebrated both Christian and Islamic holidays at home);[36] however, the two brothers did visit Morocco twice before the age of ten, where they witnessed their mother do a complete turnabout: whereas she usually complained bitterly about living conditions in France, in Morocco she would describe a bountiful promised land to her family. While on vacation, the two Moussaoui brothers accompanied their cousins to a Qur'an school, themselves barely aware of the existence of the holy book.

Back in France, Moussaoui discovered a passion at which he excelled: handball. But his mother decided to move to the South of France, forcing Moussaoui to quit the handball league and leaving him with the lost hope of a fantasy life as a handball champion. The new move forced a return to the "*cité*," the difficult neighborhood of Razimbaud in Narbonne. It was a hostile environment, although he had friends, including some French Jews.[37] Moussaoui and his brother were considered "black" (their skin is dark by Arab standards), and they spoke with Alsatian accents. Moussaoui tried his hand at rugby, but encountered racism on the field and quickly gave up. He was admitted to the local high school but preferred to study for a vocational degree in mechanical repair. Over the years that followed, however, he did everything possible to pursue higher education in another area of study.

Family life, marked by frequent and violent arguments, became more and more unpleasant, although Moussaoui's mother again succeeded in saving up enough to build a small house just outside of Narbonne, marking another step up on the social ladder for the family. The two brothers, teenagers at the time, were very well integrated in this bourgeois milieu, where they had access to swimming pools and tennis courts. Moussaoui had a girlfriend named Fanny, a pretty blond girl with pale skin and light eyes; together they won dancing contests, and they even lived together briefly. Their relationship lasted six years, over the objections of Fanny's racist father, who called Moussaoui a "dirty Arab."[38] At the time, his brother writes, Moussaoui still imagined that racists were "educable" and that they could be changed. Nonetheless, Moussaoui confronted discrimination on two fronts: the French mainstream and the North African community, since neither he nor his brother spoke any Arabic. Their mother later explained: "I discouraged them from hanging out with Arabs."[39]

The two brothers would sometimes ask their mother how to pray, but she never responded to their queries. Abd Samad Moussaoui explained that in their adolescent quest for identity and religion, he and his brother, like many other children whose North African parents declined to pass on any religious tradition, had two choices: overly complex theological teachings or simplified Islamist discourse. "The result," the brother writes,

> is that a void insidiously grows within us. An abyss which Zacarias and I seek to fill, both of us, though not in the same way. Like many children of our generation, we know that we do not know our native culture. We are ignorant of almost all the social codes of the Arab world. What's more, we are not truly accepted by the country we were born in. The native French rarely go out of their way to make us feel as though we're just like them. This vague feeling eats away at you. And just when you've forgotten it, one word is unrelenting in its ability to make it come back: the famous "integration." Throughout our childhood, our ears were beaten with this word. At first, we just didn't understand what it was about. We were born here, on this land, in this country. We've grown up here. So what then is the meaning of our "integration"?[40]

Racial discrimination was the other essential factor in the Moussaoui brothers' self-definition; this also formed a component of Moussaoui's defense in his U.S. trial, and several jurors found his experience of racism as a youngster to be a factor mitigating against the death penalty.[41] The two brothers suffered at the hands of a racist schoolteacher in Mulhouse, and they found no reprieve on the city streets, where during village festivals the brothers often had to run to escape local toughs. Once when Abd Samad was beaten up, the police refused to intervene or even to take a report of the incident. Furthermore, Abd Samad reports, the brothers had difficulty finding internships because of widespread racism in the workplace. Abd Samad writes that their only supporters were schoolteachers who sympathized with their plight.[42]

When they were about twenty years old, the two brothers moved in together. Their relationship with their mother remained strained. Moussaoui got his vocational degree with little difficulty, earned some money as a hall monitor at a *lycée* on the outskirts of Montpellier, and bought a Ford Fiesta. He enrolled at the University of Montpellier for a degree in economic and social administration. But left to himself, no longer under the watchful guidance of his teachers, Moussaoui soon became overwhelmed by the schoolwork. He lost motivation, and he suspected that each job rejection was motivated by racism.

The Gulf War was an important wake-up call: the national mood was tense at the time, and it became increasingly complicated for *beurs* and their French peers to find common ground for discussions. The war crystallized the brothers' wariness of U.S. imperialism, and they criticized France's decision to send troops. Conversations between Moussaoui and his brother began to take on broader dimensions, turning from the Gulf War to the situation in Palestine and the civil war in Algeria. The Bosnian crisis would soon follow, further enhancing Muslims' sense of solidarity with fellow Muslims. Moussaoui's view of the world became increasingly pessimistic, and he saw racism everywhere he looked. At the college cafeteria in Montpellier, he ate his meals almost exclusively with foreigners: Moroccans, Algerians, Tunisians, Malians, Senegalese, Syrians, and Palestinians. It was during that period that he discovered a radical, political vision of Islam.

At the end of 1991, Moussaoui had saved enough money to study English in London, and he enrolled at South Bank University to pursue a master's degree in international business. His living conditions were poor, and he slept in a homeless shelter. Moussaoui told his brother that he did not respect the way British society was organized; in England, he said, all communities were tolerated but they never mixed with one another. He decided to stay in London, broke off his relationship with Fanny, and began distancing himself from his brother. Abd Samad noticed a change in behavior: during his visits home, Moussaoui started making comments that revealed sexism and intolerance.[43] In 1995, Moussaoui returned to London, ostensibly to pick up his university diploma, and that was the last time Abd Samad saw his brother until Moussaoui's mug shot was published after September 11, 2001.

In 1996, Abd Samad was told about an earlier incident at the Narbonne mosque, where Moussaoui had been castigated by the imam for having defended Wahhabi ideals without really knowing what he was talking about. Soon thereafter, Moussaoui immersed himself in the Islamist network that recruited him: he was sent to Pakistan and Afghanistan, where his poor performance got him dismissed from a training camp. It is not known what became of him afterward, but it is assumed he aspired to carry out a mission for al Qaeda without ever actually having been a member of the September 11 cell, perhaps because he was ultimately deemed unreliable by his recruiters; this mystery was at the crux of the sentencing phase of Moussaoui's federal trial.[44]

While this narrative presents a rare instance of Islamist radicalization, it also reveals some characteristics commonly found among second- and third-generation immigrants: an uprooted family, parents' reluctance to pass on cultural and religious traditions, the sense of not belonging to any community, the search for identity, the experience of racism, the difficulty of finding internships or jobs. In the case of Zacarias Moussaoui, such factors ultimately converged to prey upon a mind susceptible to indoctrination (his two sisters and his father all suffer from psychotic illnesses, and his American defense lawyers argued that he was mentally unstable). His ambitions to "make it" in France were constantly cut down to size by reality, and he wound up falling head first into the "Londonistan" of radical mosques, which at the time was still the operational base of Islamist terrorism in Europe.

The French Antiterrorism Apparatus and the Surveillance of Islamic Radicals

When one considers the strengths and weaknesses of France's antiterrorism capabilities, it is interesting to compare Moussaoui's trajectory with that of his "predecessor," Khalid Kelkal, a French-Algerian operative of the Armed Islamic Group.[45] On the night of September 29, 1995, Kelkal, a twenty-four-year-old born in Algeria and raised in a heavily Muslim suburb of Lyon, was shot to death by the French police. Kelkal was the prime suspect in a series of terrorist bomb attacks across France that had begun in July, and, despite his death, continued into October. The attacks, a spillover of the Algerian civil war into France, prompted severe security measures, triggered massive roundups, and delayed the scheduled removal of French border controls along with those of other European parties to the Schengen Agreement.[46]

Kelkal became a suspect when a train driver, alerted by the government's campaign to encourage vigilance, spotted an unexploded bomb on the TGV high-speed train line between Paris and Lyon. Special antiterrorism investigators were called, and rather than exploding the bomb immediately, they carefully lifted a fingerprint off the bomb, passed the print through a multitude of databases, and established that it belonged to Kelkal, who had once been arrested for burglary. Through a prearranged system, a nationwide manhunt began on September 27. Within two days, an elite paramilitary squad trained in antiterrorist operations found and killed Kelkal in a bus station a few miles from his home.

Kelkal's death was a national sensation in France. The bombings had terrorized France for months, plunging the country into a state of mobilization of its civil and military forces that had no post–World War II precedent. The manhunt took place under such intense media scrutiny that a camera crew accompanied the antiterrorism squad on the operation and caught much of it on film, including cries from unidentified voices, presumably those of police officers, to "finish him off" as he lay wounded.[47] His killing sparked riots in the Muslim communities of Paris and Lyon.

The Kelkal episode not only was the most dramatic moment in the wave of terrorism that overtook France in 1995–96, it also neatly encapsulates both the strengths and the weaknesses of France's approach to counterterrorism. That the bomb was found before it exploded, despite being poised innocuously beside a stretch of monotonous train tracks, speaks to the effectiveness of the government's campaign to encourage vigilance, part of the so-called *Vigipirate* plan to mobilize society against terrorism. The special investigators that were dispatched to the bomb site immediately found that the bomb fit the pattern already established by previous attacks elsewhere in France. The manhunt demonstrated how coordinated the myriad of internal security agencies had become in the fight against terrorism, and its finale, orchestrated by a squad specifically established for antiterrorist interventions, spoke to the firmly repressive bent of French policy, a fairly marked shift since the early 1980s.

At the same time, French security agencies had been unable to stop the attacks before they happened. Their massive sweeps and intense intelligence work had failed to identify Kelkal as a suspect before his fingerprint was found, and the attacks continued after he died. Moreover, the reaction in France's economically and politically disenfranchised Muslim community to Kelkal's very public death demonstrated the risks of implementing a repressive policy in a divided society.

It should be noted when assessing the French government's policy response to the homegrown terrorist threat that Paris has had long and bitter experience with terrorism. Indeed, France has faced nearly all of the modern incarnations of terrorism: anticolonial terrorism intended to force France to disengage from Algeria in the 1950s; right-wing terrorism intended to prevent France from doing just that in the 1960s; left-wing terrorism aimed at undermining the capitalist system during the 1970s and 1980s; international terrorism aimed at French policy in the Middle East in the 1980s; separatist terrorism in Brittany and the Basque region and throughout Corsica; and finally, the spillover of the Algerian civil war and radical Islamist terrorism beginning in the 1990s. In response to those various challenges and to key dramatic events in particular, France has evolved a complex government apparatus specifically aimed at the problem of terrorism. Since the 1980s and especially since 1995, France has been a leader in the international fight against terrorist networks. To take only one example, France's role in the

Alliance Base—a multilateral operation based on a French-U.S. partnership and located in Paris that was disclosed in July 2005—has been singled out by Islamists as another reason for making France a high-priority target.[48]

Many features of France's antiterrorism system stem from reforms undertaken in the mid-1980s in response to a wave of terrorist attacks of Middle Eastern origin. The attacks generated an overwhelming public outcry for increased security and confirmed the view of many that the French state had little capacity to combat terrorism. The system was uncoordinated, it was rife with political and institutional rivalries, and officials lacked understanding of terrorists. A new center-right government took power during the wave of attacks and resolved to reform the French internal security apparatus to meet the challenge.

The main response was embodied in the antiterrorism legislation of September 1986.[49] The legislation codified into French law the idea that terrorism was a special crime and that combating it required special laws, procedures, and institutions. For these purposes, terrorism was defined as "acts committed by individuals or groups whose goal to gravely trouble public order by intimidation or terror."[50] In such cases, normal restrictions on length of detention and investigation were relaxed, courts could mete out longer jail terms, and special procedures were put in place for protecting sources of evidence and even for non-jury trials. Nonetheless, rather than creating an entirely new court for terrorism, as France had done in the 1960s, the legislation called for centralizing proceedings related to terrorism in the existing Trial Court of Paris and left it to conventional judges to decide the ultimate outcome of the cases. This combination of special and routine procedures reflected an attempt to balance the unique requirements of fighting terrorism with the long-established and therefore broadly legitimate procedures of the French legal system.

The legislation also centralized all investigative proceedings related to terrorism. Previously, local prosecutors and investigators in the vicinity of the attacks handled terrorism cases. Unfortunately, terrorist attacks were rarely isolated incidents, and the specific location of the attack was of little relevance in its investigation or prosecution. With little contact between the prosecutors in different jurisdictions who were working on related cases, there was little capacity to integrate information and thereby to discover patterns. Centralization created within the Trial Court of Paris a small section of prosecutors and investigating magistrates who dealt only with terrorism cases and who eventually became established as the lead actors in the French struggle against terrorism.[51]

The investigating magistrate, something of a cross between a prosecutor and a judge, has no precise analog in the Anglo-Saxon system of justice. An investigating magistrate (the term is an inexact translation of *juge d'instruction*) is not an advocate for the prosecution or the defense, but rather is charged with conducting an impartial investigation to determine whether a crime worthy of prosecution has been committed. Magistrates are, at least in theory, not answerable to any political authority and are granted fairly wide powers to open judicial inquiries, authorize search warrants and wiretaps, and issue subpoenas (powers that in the United States would usually require specific judicial authorization).

The 1986 legislation also created a new specialized coordinating body within the Ministry of Justice, the Service pour la Coordination de la Lutte Anti-Terroriste (SCLAT) (Service for Coordination of the Fight against Terrorism), to complement a similar preexisting organization within the Ministry of the Interior, the Unité de Coordination de la Lutte Anti-Terroriste (UCLAT) (Coordination Unit of the Fight against Terrorism).[52] The purpose of these organizations is to establish connections among and coordinate all the activities of the various intelligence and police services with their ministries that bear on terrorism, as well as to establish solid channels of communication between the ministries. Previously, no single service, even within a ministry, had been responsible for coordinating activities in the fight against terrorism. No one, therefore, was responsible for assembling a complete picture of the information available from various institutional sources, ensuring information flow among the various agencies, or providing coordinated direction to the intelligence and police services for the prevention of terrorism.[53]

The system was further modified in response to the series of terrorist bomb attacks across France that began in July 1995 and continued into October, eventually killing eight and wounding as many as 200 others. The threat that violence from Algeria would spill over into France had been widely anticipated, and indeed the security services had engaged in a series of operations to break up Algerian networks within France beginning in 1993. They were partially successful in disrupting potential terrorist networks, but they failed to prevent all of the attacks, in part because most of the incidents were small and relatively easy to plan and carry out.

The lesson learned was that stopping such attacks requires not just intelligence about terrorist networks but also surveillance of entire communities,[54] including the more than 1,600 mosques and prayer spaces as well as the several hundred other Islamic organizations within France.[55] That job falls primarily to the intelligence agencies, particularly Renseignements Généraux, the intelligence agency specifically intended and empowered to conduct domestic surveillance. The RG is dispersed in fairly small cells throughout France and has reputedly achieved a great deal of penetration of the various Muslim subcultures in France through extensive knowledge of local communities, informants, relationships with community leaders, and electronic listening devices. Another domestic intelligence agency, the Direction du Surveillance du Territoire, is responsible for threats emanating from abroad, a distinction that becomes less and less useful as France's borders become increasingly porous. The DST therefore also finds it necessary to maintain an extensive network of informers within the Muslim community, many of whom are convicted felons who receive reduced sentences for their cooperation. The DST monitors immigrants entering France, particularly those of Muslim or North African background, and attempts to track their movements within France.[56]

The problem, however, beyond the obvious issues of overlap and sheer volume of information, is that anticipating the types of very simple attacks that occurred in 1995 requires thinking less in terms of terrorist organizations and more about the community support mechanisms on which operatives might rely. French intelligence had tended to focus its surveillance on organizations that had a history or background of violence, such as the Front Islamique du Salut (FIS) (Islamic Salvation Front), which was establishing networks to send aid to the guerillas fighting in Algeria. That provided the intelligence necessary for the roundups that preceded the 1995 bomb attacks, but it also meant that theretofore dormant, yet ideologically more radical groups had not been disabled and may even have been relatively empowered in the Muslim community by the roundups.

The lack of focus on community support networks reflected not only an intelligence failure but also the lack of institutional powers inherent in French law. The essential problem was that terrorism, particularly as practiced in France in the mid-1990s, did not require the maintenance of substantial operational or planning capacity. Operatives could drop in from abroad or be quickly recruited from within the French Muslim community. Rather, it required the maintenance of logistics networks that, while not directly involved in terrorist activities, could supply false papers, financing, or simply safe lodging to potential operatives. In order to support themselves financially, the logistics networks of the diverse armed Algerian groups (including some reputedly established by the Algerian government's security services) set up legitimate businesses, conducted armed robberies, and trafficked in stolen credit cards and false documents such as forged passports.

Under French law, such activities were either not illegal or did not fall under the purview of the antiterrorism magistrates, who therefore could not invoke their special powers or the attention of the various specialized antiterrorism units within France. Normal intelligence or police organizations, more interested in gathering information or stopping crime than in recognizing specific patterns of activity preceding a terrorist act, failed to react appropriately to what would appear to them as fairly mundane criminal or even noncriminal activity.

As a result, new legislative initiatives in 1995 and 1996 specifically targeted the logistics networks by codifying the notion that "the participation in any group formed or association established with a view to the preparation, marked by one or more material actions, of any of the acts of terrorism provided for under the previous articles shall in addition be an act of terrorism."[57] Thus, conspiracy to commit terrorism could invoke the whole special cadre of laws and procedures established for terrorism.

The new law dramatically widened the types of investigations that antiterrorism magistrates and the specialized antiterrorism sections within the intelligence and law enforcement agencies could undertake. In that way, they gained the capacity not just to punish terrorist attacks after they took place, but also to disrupt logistics networks and to prevent attacks from happening in the first place.

The basic French system has changed only slightly since the mid-1990s, despite a lot of apparent activity after September 11. Although France passed new antiterrorism legislation very soon after the attacks, the legislation in fact contained only minor updates to the power of the French police, as well as a lot of regulations not related to terrorism.[58] Yet another antiterrorism law was approved in December 2005, with an emphasis on video surveillance, maintenance of telephone and e-mail records for several years, monitoring of travel by French youth to sensitive countries, and lengthening of preventive detention from four to six days in case of suspected terrorist activity.[59] French officials seem broadly satisfied with the system, but they emphasize that France is hardly invulnerable to terrorist attack, even large-scale attack. The current focus for improvement is on international cooperation, as exemplified by the Alliance Base, mentioned earlier, both to make up for the loss of border security implicit in the free movement of people in the enlarged European Union and to cut off financing for terrorist organizations.

There is also some concern about how the counterterrorism system affects civil liberties—in particular, how it affects those of the large French Muslim community. The action of the counterterrorism apparatus in the 1990s was often fiercely criticized by the media and by human rights groups. Two areas in particular have been the object of acerbic criticism: the preventive roundups and the associated indiscriminate detention of suspects; and the broad powers given to the magistrates to conduct the sweeps and detentions with very little oversight.

In the wake of the 1995 attacks, some 32,000 soldiers and police and customs officials were mobilized. They checked the identities of nearly 3 million people and detained some 70,000 people for questioning.[60] A variety of media outlets, as well as the Fédération Internationale des Ligues des Droits de l'Homme (FIDH) (International Fédération of Human Rights Organizations), labeled the sweeps "media spectacles" that were "destructive of liberty."[61] The roundups often swept up people for whom there was no evidence of wrongdoing and people who had nothing to do with the networks but happened to be present on the day of the sweep. The decision after the 1995 attacks to go after logistics and support networks has only increased the breadth of the sweeps.

For civil liberties groups, the introduction into law of language regarding conspiracy to commit terrorism opened the door to arbitrary enforcement because a number of acts that basically are not illegal become illegal when a magistrate decides that they occurred in the context of intent to commit terrorism. Thus the definition of criminal conspiracy contravenes the principle of French law according to which laws must be certain and precise.[62]

Interestingly, such criticisms of the specialized system of antiterrorism enforcement in France generally have not emanated from Muslim civil groups. And indeed there has been very little talk about how much this cadre of special antiterrorism legislation contributes to frictions between the Muslim community and the state—a debate that is almost glaring in its absence.[63] On the most mundane level, that appears to be because the Muslim community in France has bigger issues with which to contend. Cultural integration and economic opportunity, the plague of "normal" criminal activity in Muslim areas, and the debate over public expression of religious faith are the issues that dominate the French domestic political agenda. In this highly contentious environment, neither occasional counterterrorism actions that affect the Muslim population nor the associated constant state surveillance—usually quite discreet and part of a long French tradition of domestic surveillance—generates much public outcry from within the Muslim community.

The public protests that followed the antiterrorism squad's killing of Khalid Kelkal in 1995 reflected a general frustration that had built up in the French Muslim community over its treatment by the police and by society.

That tension could accumulate again in the course of the enhanced surveillance and arrest sweeps associated with the French counterterrorism apparatus. Many Muslim associations objected to the unceremonious deportation of imams accused of radical preaching in 2004, and some brought a lawsuit against the "arbitrary detention" of French returnees from Guantánamo. Future dramatic episodes along the lines of the Kelkal shooting have the potential to loosen a torrent of social discontent that might find expression in opposition to the special cadre of antiterrorism laws and methods that, in effect, target the North African community.

Moreover, the domestic and international association of Islam and terrorism in the eyes of the general population is taking a heavy toll in the realm of integration. As seen in chapter 2, the fear of terrorism has added another layer of negative stereotypes about Muslims. And the forces of the extreme right emphasize the connection between Islam and terrorism while saying nothing of the "family Islam" practiced by an overwhelming majority of French Muslims. A good example of this strategy is found in the rhetoric of Philippe de Villiers, a politician who offers a lighter version of the ideas of Jean-Marie Le Pen that may be more palatable to a large electorate (he has no connection to anti-Semitism or to the defense of the Vichy regime). On July 16, 2005, on TF1, the most widely watched French television channel, he declared: "We cannot be passive witnesses to the growing islamization of France. . . . I believe that Islam is a breeding ground for Islamism and Islamism is a breeding ground for terrorism, so we should beware."[64] There is no doubt that such remarks reinforce negative views about Islam in general and make it more difficult to improve the situation of French Muslims.

11 | Conclusion

This book has aimed to fill the large gaps in common knowledge about Muslims living in France and how France has addressed the policy challenge of integrating Islam. These lacunae tend to reinforce the misgivings of the United States about the progress of Islam's coexistence with French institutions as well as those regarding French goals in the Arab-Muslim world. Our study has attempted to portray the more complex reality of integration's successes and failures in French politics and society. We have argued that the importance of religion in the lives of Muslims should be considered alongside the political, social, and economic aspects of integration. The recent policies developed by successive French governments to encourage integration (and to discourage religious extremism) reveal a methodical and sometimes dramatic approach, from the controversial 2004 French law banning headscarves in public schools to the new French Council of the Muslim Religion.

There is a disconcerting degree of official pessimism in Washington regarding the integration of Muslims in France. Much of that pessimism is due to ignorance of readily available information about the everyday experience of Islam in France, which this book attempts to convey. When information does trickle through the American news media, the focus is often on the prospect of a Muslim Europe—"Eurabia"— or the danger of European governments falling prey to radical lobbies or "parallel societies." The book hopes to have challenged the gloomy and alarmist view of France's (and Europe's) inevitable "Islamization." The evidence presented here runs counter to the general impression that Muslim populations are uniformly impoverished and disgruntled, on the verge of revolt and ready to take over the French Republic. It is true that the concept of a globalized *umma* is present among French Muslims. But their sectarian, ideological, and national diversity cannot be glossed over. That is especially true because community organizations in France both reflect this diversity and engage in healthy competition with one another—for the first time, in a Western, democratic context.

France's relations with the Arab world, furthermore, are not black and white. Policy decisions regarding Islam at home have not shied away from confrontation with the very regimes that the government is suspected of coddling. The creation of the French Council of the Muslim Religion, for example, has begun to wean local associations and federations from the influence of homeland governments and foreign donors. On the other hand, the ban on headscarves and other religious symbols in public schools has sparked debate over the meaning of French citizenship and inadvertently alienated the very "Arab street" to which the French president is often accused of pandering by domestic as well as foreign critics.

Islam in France is, above all, a question of internal French politics. When the United States can help to address the challenges that arise, in terms of cooperating on intelligence operations or sharing the insight of experts on Islam, it should, of course, do so. Within the context of general U.S. outreach programs to the "Muslim world"—broadcasting efforts, public diplomacy, and so forth—the importance of Muslim minorities in the West itself and of European Muslims in particular should not be overlooked. For example, to improve U.S. understanding of French Islam, especially where its potential influence on French foreign policy is concerned, the U.S. government could enlarge the staff at the U.S. embassy to cultivate links with the Muslim community. Other public relations initiatives also could have important effects on smoothing the process of integration, such as exchange programs between French and American imams and guided visits of Muslim community leaders to the two countries so that they can become acquainted with the political process and state-religion relations in both. In 2005, the U.S. State Department's International Visitor Leadership Program (IVLP) brought its first all-Muslim European contingent of NGO leaders, government officials, journalists, and academics for a three-week visit with U.S. officials and opinion leaders, and in 2006, the State Department's Bureau of European and Eurasian Affairs and its Bureau of Educational and Cultural Affairs developed a "Muslim incentive program" to encourage selected European consulates and embassies to nominate more Muslims for the IVLP.[1] The Fulbright Commission has also sought to increase applications from Muslims to come to the United States from the Netherlands and the United Kingdom. And the U.S. embassies in Brussels and Rome held conferences in 2005 and 2006 that brought together American and European Muslims and other specialists to discuss social and political integration. Such efforts should be encouraged and expanded to other countries, since they open a dialogue about U.S. domestic politics and foreign policy goals with European Muslims, which could help, for example, to mitigate negative Muslim opinion of current U.S.-led military interventions in the Middle East or to educate them about religious diversity and minority politics in the United States.[2]

Although France and the United States have often failed to see eye to eye, the banning of the Hezbollah television station al-Manar on both sides of the Atlantic in December 2004 and subsequent Franco-American cooperation regarding Syria in the United Nations Security Council provide good examples of how the two nations can cooperate with regard to developments in the Muslim world. Most of the work to be done in integrating Islam in France, however, is for France to do alone, and it will be a long-term, not a short-term, process.

It is true that European governments generally tolerated religious proselytizing and Islam's organizational implantation during the initial expansion of the Muslim population in the 1970s and 1980s. Since around 1989, however, Muslim organizations and actors no longer operate in an institutional vacuum. European governments' approaches to the complex network of Muslim associations have changed drastically, from tolerating an Islam "in" Europe (1974–89) to creating the institutional conditions for the emergence of an Islam "of" Europe from 1989 to the present. European governments have put in place institutional mechanisms to limit the influence of political Islam and to assert the state's authority and sovereignty over its own territory.

Not just France, but all European nations with sizable Muslim minorities (for example, Belgium, Germany, Italy, Netherlands, Spain, and Austria) have been trying to fit Islam within special legal entities designed to govern educational, associational, and church-state relations. To that end, they have initiated dialogue with a broad swath of Muslim religious organizations and prayer spaces and pursued the institutionalization of state-Islam relations, as they have done with other major religious communities. The United Kingdom and Holland subsidize Islamic schools as well as Catholic, Protestant, and Jewish schools. They also are home to dozens of independent Muslim schools, which are especially highly attended in Britain. German courts have granted Muslim federations the right to conduct Islamic education during religion class in public schools.

These institutionalized interactions have improved the mutual acquaintance—and recognition—of Muslims and the state, and they have reduced the degree of formal foreign control over prayer spaces and religious personnel in Europe. Subsequent state-led accommodations of Islam—in terms of mosque funding, cemeteries, halal slaughter facilities, religious education, and so forth—fulfill genuine material needs for religious practice as well as undercut Islamists' claims that Europe is inhospitable or hostile to Muslims, claims that may otherwise be used to gain potential followers. State-Islam forums and emergent Muslim councils are quite young, but they provide a blueprint for participation and interaction with the major civil organizations and the religious leadership of the Muslim minority.

The French government's interventionism in its relations with Muslim organizations active in its territory should not be viewed as a threat to the secular order. On the contrary, it is in the interest of both Muslims and the state that the government acknowledge and welcome the cultural and religious diversity of its society. And the emergence of French and European Islam can have many potentially salutary effects on homeland countries too. The birth of a tolerant, moderate, and "modern" Islam in France and Europe offers an opportunity to reverse the flow of Islamic ideas, customs, theology, books, imams, and so forth, which until now has come from Muslim countries, and so broaden the discourse on what it means to be Muslim.

It should be recalled that new institutions like the French Council of the Muslim Religion have been established to ensure religious, not political, representation. The latter will take place over a longer period of time, and indicators of integration suggest that in the near future, Muslims will be able to find their place in French politics without creating any unprecedented rifts or ruptures.

Insofar as the European Union is concerned, Brussels does not have jurisdiction over its members' state-church affairs, and there is no planned harmonization within the EU of state policies on religion. The guiding EU principle of "subsidiarity," which calls for policies to be made at the lowest possible level of government, means that for the most part religion is the province of national or local governments. However, European states share many of the same objectives with respect to their Muslim populations, and they sometimes have coordinated their diplomatic relations with immigrants' countries of origin—for example, on matters of asylum and immigration control. And some cross-border learning has taken place with respect to nations' policies toward Islam, but the EU itself has not pursued policies specifically related to Muslim integration or state-Islam relations.[3] Beyond limited cooperation on counterterrorism goals, no coordinated EU policies on "Muslim minorities" have emerged thus far—and any attempt to form such policies would be even further complicated by the entry into the EU of new members that also have sizable (and historical) Muslim populations.

Though there is no such thing as an EU religion policy, small symbolic milestones have been reached in the acknowledgment of Europe's Muslim populations. The European Commission—the Brussels-based executive branch and "motor" of EU integration—has recognized the importance of nurturing Europe's religious heritage in efforts to further a common identity. The Forward Studies Unit (FSU)—an in-house think tank attached to the office of the commission's president—serves as a semiofficial liaison between the EU and European religious communities. In a 1998 report, the FSU asked the interior ministers of member states to reconsider "the place of Islam," in the hope that a new generation of moderate Muslims—and all people—"can return . . . to their own cultural and religious roots." "There is no longer a dominant culture in Europe," the report said, and the "excesses" of modern nations' separation of religion and politics must be "corrected."[4] In 1999, the EU Commission's president, Romano Prodi, commissioned a study on the spiritual contribution of different faiths and communities toward a new European identity and also sponsored the production of a book on Muslims in Europe.[5]

Following the terrorist attacks of September 2001, Prodi also created a "council of sages" to regularly meet and to inform and advise the office of the president on Islam-related issues. The European Parliament, the representative body with the greatest number of deputies of non-European immigrant origin, has also sought to enhance the image of Muslims and Islam in Europe. In December 1998, the parliament created a day in honor of Averroës, a twelfth-century Spanish-Arab philosopher and classicist who sought to reconcile Islam with Western philosophy.[6] In addition, the Italian interior minister took advantage of his government's six-month EU presidency in 2004 to propose a debate on "interreligious dialogue as a factor in social cohesion and an instrument of peace in the Mediterranean area," and the European Commission is planning a European Year of Intercultural Dialogue for 2008.[7]

Members of the EU's Convention for a European Constitution, chaired by former French president Giscard d'Estaing, had their own ideas of how to promote a cohesive European identity. Some members of the European Parliament expressed their opposition to Turkey's EU candidacy by attempting to include a reference to Europe's Christian heritage in the European Constitution, an effort that was strongly supported by the Vatican and vigorously opposed by humanist groups. Although in the midst of the debate the *Osservatore Romano* blared the headline "Either Europe is Christian or it is not Europe!" members of the convention backed down, and Giscard stated that the constitution would protect "private and public expression of religion" as well as "spiritual values" rather than mention any specific faith.[8]

The EU has exercised some control over policy areas that have an impact on Europe's Muslims, although not in terms of religious expression: for example, since the 1980s there has been extensive cooperation on security issues among a core group of national interior ministers; in the 1990s a number of antidiscrimination measures were passed; and finally, since 2000 there has been a search among EU members to find common ground for developing migration, asylum, and family unification policies. Some European Commission bureaucracies occasionally draft directives that might concern Muslim communities—for example, antidiscrimination legislation—and the European Monitoring Center on Racism and Xenophobia in Vienna investigates issues that concern Muslim minorities, but the lack of a single Muslim interlocutor at the supranational level has left Brussels without a Muslim counterpart.[9]

Therefore the most important developments in state relations with formal Muslim communities will continue to evolve at the level of national politics. The emergence of a significant Muslim minority in France and Europe is a historic demographic shift. The legacy of French colonialism in the Arab world and of large-scale immigration—that legacy's most tangible consequence in France—has permanently changed the face of France. Indeed, this book ends up telling as much about France as about its Muslim minority. Islam had always been kept outside of modern French institutional and political life, through nearly 130 years of colonial relations. Muslim subjects of the French empire were not full citizens, and Islam was exempted from the 1905 law separating church and state. This encounter has now entered the phase of permanent integration of colonialism's children—and their religion.

Compared with other European countries with large immigrant minorities, France has the advantage of familiarity and experience with the population at hand. The centuries-long French encounter with Islam, however checkered its past, could amount to an institutional advantage in efforts to integrate Muslims into national politics. Nevertheless, the government has discovered that France needs to fine-tune the self-proclaimed universalism of its citizenship model. The reforms under way in the education system are a good start: the rigid system of recruitment of the elite for high-level administrative and political jobs in the Fifth Republic is starting to show some flexibility and encouraging signs of ethnic and socioeconomic intermingling.

One French commentator recently found meaning in the fact that the youth of the *banlieues* and the youth of the universities took to the streets separately and "one season apart"—the former in the fall 2005 riots and the latter during the spring 2006 anti–labor law reform demonstrations: "Being the same age doesn't create commonalities between those who have no diploma and are looking for a job and others who are at university looking for a diploma."[10] As the riots made clear, improvements are still needed in many areas for the entire population of immigrant origin, whether of Muslim background or not: from antidiscrimination policy and job training and creation programs to public dialogue on the colonial past. But there is encouraging evidence that a sustained effort to achieve social and political integration and to begin resolving the fragmentation of French society is well under way. Perhaps most important, politicians have come at last to the sobering realization that the stability and success of the Republic depend on its ability to live up to its motto: "Liberté, égalité, fraternité."

Notes

Introduction

1. Or 63 million, if the populations of French overseas territories are included. See "France in Facts and Figures," Institut National de la Statistique et des Études Économiques [National Institute of Statistics and Economic Studies] (www.insee. fr/en/ffc/pop_age4.htm).

2. Eugen Weber, *From Peasants to Frenchmen: The Modernization of Rural France, 1870–1914* (London: Chatto and Windus, 1977).

3. Nonna Mayer and Pascal Perrineau, eds., *Le Front national à découvert* [*Behind the National Front*] (Paris: Presses de Sciences Po, 1996).

4. French politicians have demonstrated sensitivity to "Anglo-Saxon" bias in media coverage of social unrest in France, from the 2005 riots to the 2006 demonstrations against the government's proposed employment reforms. See Katrin Bennhold, "French Find the Villain in Protests: The Media," *International Herald Tribune*, March 30, 2006.

5. See Patrick Haenni, "France and Its Muslims: Riots, Jihadism, and Depoliticisation," *Europe Report* no. 172 (Brussels: International Crisis Group, March 2006).

6. Frank Gaffney and Alex Alexiev, "Farewell to Europe?" *Washington Times*, November 10, 2005.

7. Daniel Pipes, "Reflections on the Revolution in France," *New York Sun*, November 8, 2005.

8. There have been exceptions to this general observation, however: see, for example, U.S. Senate, "Islamist Extremism in Europe: Testimony of Daniel Fried, Assistant Secretary of State for European Affairs, before the Senate Foreign Relations Committee," Subcommittee on European Affairs, April 5, 2006; and Department of State, "French Muslims Favor Integration into French Society," Opinion Analysis M-58-05, Office of Research, May 24, 2005.

9. House Committee on International Relations, Subcommittee on Europe and Emerging Threats, *Islamic Extremism in Europe,* April 27, 2005, testimony of Claude Moniquet.

10. George Weigel, "Europe's Two Culture Wars," *Commentary,* May 2006.

11. Christopher Caldwell, "Islamic Europe? When Bernard Lewis Speaks," *Weekly Standard,* October 4, 2004.

12. Niall Ferguson, "Eurabia?" *New York Times,* April 4, 2004; Caroline Fourest, "The War for Eurabia," *Wall Street Journal,* February 2, 2005; Bruce Bawer, *While Europe Slept: How Radical Islam Is Destroying the West from Within* (New York: Doubleday, 2006).

13. Thomas L. Friedman, "Divided We Stand," *New York Times,* January 23, 2005, p. A17.

14. Robert Leiken, "Europe's Angry Muslims," *Foreign Affairs,* July-August 2005, pp. 120–135.

15. See, for example, Steven Pfaff and Anthony Gill, "Will a Million Muslims March?" paper presented at Conference on Islam in the West, University of Washington at Seattle, April 2005; Carolyn Warner and Manfred Wenner, "Organizing Islam for Politics in Western Europe," CFIA Working Paper, Harvard University, 2002; Christopher Soper and Joel Fetzer, *Muslims and the State in Britain, France, and Germany* (Cambridge University Press, 2005).

16. "Pour Nicolas Sarkozy, la menace terroriste est à 'un niveau très élevé'" ["For Nicolas Sarkozy, the terrorist threat is at 'a very high level'"], *Le Monde,* September 26, 2005.

17. Olivier Roy, *Globalized Islam* (Columbia University Press, 2004).

18. Department of State, "French Muslims Favor Integration into French Society."

19. Rémy Leveau and Catherine Wihtol de Wenden, *La Beurgeoisie: les trois âges de la vie associative issue de l'immigration* [*The Beurgeoisie: Three phases of immigrant civil society*] (Paris: CNRS, 2001); Vincent Geisser and Scherhazade Kelfaoui, "Trois generations de militantisme politique sous la Vème republique: l'activiste immigré, le beur civique, et l'électeur musulman" ["Three generations of political activism under the Fifth Republic: The immigrant activist, the civic beur, and the Muslim voter"] *La Médina,* December 12, 2001; see also Vincent Geisser, *L'éthnicité républicaine: les élites d'origine maghrébine dans le système politique Français* [*Republican ethnicity: Elites of North African origin in the French political system*] (Paris: Presses de Sciences Po, 1997).

20. Tariq Ramadan, *Être musulman européen* [*To be a European Muslim*] (Lyon: Tawhid, 1999).

21. Sylvain Brouard and Vincent Tiberj, *Français comme les autres? Enquête sur les citoyens d'origine maghrébine, africaine, et turque* [*French like the rest? A study of citizens of North African, African, and Turkish origin*] (Paris: Presses de Sciences Po, 2005), pp. 110–11.

22. See Marcel Gauchet, "L'Occident est aveugle sur les effets de la mondialisation de l'économie et des moeurs" ["The West is blind to the effects of globalization of the

economy and of customs"], *Le Monde*, March 11, 2006; and Gauchet, *The Disenchantment of the World: A Political History of Religion* (Princeton University Press, 1997).

23. "Les autres religions" ["The other religions"], *Teo*, École supérieure de journalisme [School of Journalism], Lille, May 2002 (www.esj-lille.fr/atelier/magan2/teo/reperes/stats2.html).

24. Unemployment among immigrants in sensitive urban zones rose from 26.2 percent in 1990 to 35.3 percent in 1999. See Hervé Viellard-Baron, "Les quartiers sensibles de banlieue: entre disqualification visible et réseaux mondialisés invisibles" ["Sensitive neighborhoods in the *banlieue:* Between visible exclusion and invisible global networks"], paper presented at the Festival International de Géographie [International Festival of Geography], Saint-Dié-des-Vosges, 2002.

25. Angel M. Rabasa and others, eds., *The Muslim World after 9/11* (RAND, 2004); Cheryl Benard, *Civil Democratic Islam: Partners, Resources, and Strategies* (RAND, 2003); and Timothy M. Savage, "Europe and Islam: Crescent Waxing, Cultures Clashing," *Washington Quarterly* 27 (Summer 2004): 25–50.

26. House Committee on International Relations, Subcommittee on Europe and Emerging Threats, *Islamic Extremism in Europe*, April 27, 2005, testimony of Peter Bergen; Robert Leiken, "Europe's Mujahideen: Where Mass Immigration Meets Global Terrorism," Center for Immigration Studies, Washington, April 2005 (http://www.cis.org/articles/2005/back405.html [March 15, 2006]).

27. Although the state school system is secular, not all schools are fully representative of the nation's diversity because some students opt out of the system. Fully one-fourth of Jewish children in France, for example, attend state-subsidized private Jewish schools. Therefore, while France may be seen as somewhat hostile to religion, that view does not tell the full story.

Chapter 1

1. Sylvain Brouard and Vincent Tiberj, *Français comme les autres? Enquête sur les citoyens d'origine maghrébine, africaine, et turque* [*French like the rest? A study of citizens of North African, African, and Turkish origin*] (Paris: Presses de Sciences Po, 2005), p. 27–30.

2. Ibid.

3. Neal Robinson, "France," in *Islam outside the Arab world,* edited by David Westerlund and Ingvar Svanberg (Richmond, England: Curzon, 1999).

4. Ibid.

5. Spaniards, Portuguese, and Italians accounted for most family reunification until around 1970, after which North and West Africans steadily increased their share to about half of all immigration through this method. See Laetitia van Eeckhout, "Immigration familiale: les faits" ["Family immigration: The facts"], *Le Monde*, January 5, 2006.

6. See Erik Bleich, *Race Politics in Britain and France: Ideas and Policymaking since the 1960s* (Cambridge University Press, 2003); and Adrian Favell, *Philosophies of*

Integration: Immigration and the Idea of Citizenship in France and Britain (New York: St. Martin's Press, 1998).

7. It is known, however, that 134,500 immigrants were naturalized in 2005, compared to 80,268 in 1998 (when 44 percent hailed from the Maghreb, a decrease from previous years). See "La politique de la nationalité en 1998: données, chiffrées, et commentaires" [Nationality policy in 1998: Numerical data and commentary], Ministère de l'emploi et de la solidarité, Direction de la population et des migrations [Ministry of Employment and Solidarity, Directorate of Population and Migration], Paris 1998; and Cécilia Gabizon, "Vautrin veut généraliser la cérémonie d'acceuil des nouveaux français," ["Vautrin wants to standardize the welcome ceremony for new French citizens"], *Le Figaro*, April 19, 2006.

8. Michèle Tribalat, "Une estimation des populations d'origine étrangère en France en 1999" ["An estimate of populations of foreign origin in France in 1999"] *Populations*, no. 1 (2004), p. 51.

9. Michèle Tribalat, "Le nombre de musulmans en France: qu'en sait-on?" ["The number of Muslims in France: What do we know?"] *Cités*, hors-série [special issue] (2004).

10. Claude Dargent, "Les musulmans déclarés en France: affirmation religieuse, subordination sociale, et progressisme politique" ["Self-declared Muslims in France: Religious affirmation, social subordination, and political progressivism"], *Cahier du CEVIPOF*, no. 34 (February 2003), p. 4.

11. Ibid.

12. Turks are a slight majority in Alsace and Algerians in Marseille. Agence pour le développement des relations interculturelles [Agency for the Development of Intercultural Relations] (ADRI), *Le point sur l'Islam en France [All you need to know about Islam in France]* (Paris: La Documentation française, 2000).

13. "L'accueil des immigrants et l'intégration des populations issues de l'immigration," Rapport au président de la République ["Welcoming immigrants and integrating populations of immigrant origin," Report to the president of the Republic], Cour des Comptes, November 2004.

14. Timothy Savage, "Europe and Islam: Crescent Waxing, Cultures Clashing," *Washington Quarterly* 27, no. 3 (Summer 2004): 25–50.

15. "L'accueil des immigrants et l'intégration des populations issues de l'immigration ["Welcoming immigrants and integrating populations of immigrant origin"], p. 457.

16. See André Lebon, Report of the Directorate of Population and Migration, Ministry of Social Affairs, April 2004; Sylvia Zappi, "La dernière version du projet de 'contrat d'intégration' inquiète les associations" ["The last version of the 'integration contract' worries the associations"], *Le Monde*, April 7, 2003; Sylvia Zappi, "M. Fillon concentre son plan d'intégration sur les nouveaux arrivants" ["Mr. Fillon focuses his integration plan on new arrivals"], *Le Monde*, April 10, 2003.

17. See Van Eeckhout, "Immigration familiale: les faits" ["The facts on family immigration"].

18. There were 52,204 first-time requests. Sylvia Zappi, "La France, première destination des demandeurs d'asile en Europe" ["France, the first destination of asylum seekers in Europe"], *Le Monde*, April 20, 2004; Laetitia van Eeckhout, "L'hébergement d'urgence est démuni face à l'afflux d'étrangers" ["Emergency housing is unprepared for the influx of foreigners"], *Le Monde*, April 16, 2005; See Lebon, Report of the Directorate for Population and Migration.

19. EU cooperation on illegal immigration is relatively robust. Projected annual net immigration to western Europe over the next half-century is steady at 350,000. Tobias Just and Magdalena Korb, "International Migration: Who, Where, and Why?" *Deutsche Bank Research* (Frankfurt: August 2003), chapter 5.

20. Based on the number of undocumented illegal aliens who have applied for residency during recent amnesties. See Lebon, Report of the Directorate for Population and Migration.

21. "Nicolas Sarkozy fixe un objectif de 25,000 immigrés en situation irrégulière expulsés en 2006" ["Nicolas Sarkozy aims to deport 25,000 illegal immigrants in 2006"], *Le Monde*, November 29, 2005.

22. "Les députés suppriment la regularisation des sans-papiers au bout de dix ans" ["Parliamentary deputies end the naturalization of *sans papiers* after ten years"], *Le Monde*, May 5, 2006.

23. See Laurent Toulemon, "La fécondité des immigrées: nouvelles données, nouvelle approche" ["Immigrant fertility: New data, new approach"], *Population et Société*, no. 400 (April 2004) ; and Lucile Richet-Mastin, "Bilan démographique 2005: En France, la fécondité des femmes augmente toujours" ["2005 demographic balance sheet: In France, the fertility of women is still rising"], *La France en faits et chiffres* [*France in Facts and Figures*] (INSEE, January 2006) (www.insee.fr/fr/ffc/docs_ffc/ IP1059.pdf [February 8, 2006]).

24. See U.S. Senate, "Islamist Extremism in Europe: Testimony of Daniel Fried, Assistant Secretary of State for European Affairs, before the Senate Foreign Relations Committee," Subcommittee on European Affairs, April 5, 2006: "Muslims in Western Europe comprise only about 5 percent of the total population. However, that number has tripled over the last thirty years, and it is expected to double again by 2025." Another expert has estimated that the Muslim population in the European Union will triple to around 40 million by 2035 (not including Turkey). See Bassam Tibi, *Euro-Islam. L'integrazione mancata* [*Euro-Islam: The missing integration*] (Venice: Marsilio, 2003).

25. Another study, by Laurent Toulemon of the Institut Nationale d'Etudes Démographiques (INED), criticized the INSEE data in figures 1-2 and 1-3 on two accounts. First, an age factor is hidden in the data. Girls who migrate to France before they turn thirteen have, on average, only 0.4 more children in their lifetime than their French-born peers. And those between twenty-five and thirty are on average *less* fertile on arrival than French women because they have waited to have children until they arrive. Their subsequently higher rate of fertility occurs when, in effect, they make up for lost time, thereby raising the average fertility of their subgroup. Second, Toulemon

argues, the data exclude women who are naturalized French citizens. Because foreign women must wait several years before becoming citizens, the data reflect only the period between their arrival and naturalization, which is when they are most fertile. See Toulemon, "La fécondité des immigrées" ["Immigrant fertility"].

26. Data in figures 1-2 and 1-3 were taken from Françoise Legros, "La fécondité des étrangères en France: une stabilisation entre 1990–1999" ["Immigrant fertility: Stabilization between 1990 and 1999"], Cellules statistiques et études sur l'immigration [Office for Statistical Analysis and the Study of Immigration], *INSEE Première* no. 898 (May 2003).

27. On the history of immigration, see Gerard Noiriel, *The French Melting-Pot: Immigration, Citizenship, and National Identity* (University of Minnesota Press, 1996). On policy questions, see Patrick Weil, *La France et ses étrangers: l'aventure d'une politique de l'immigration, de 1938 à nous jours* [*France and its foreigners: The adventure of immigration policy from 1938 to the present*] (Paris: Calmann-Lévy, 1991), and on the question of citizenship, see Patrick Weil, *Qu'est-ce qu'un Français? Histoire de la nationalité française depuis la revolution* [*What is a French citizen? The history of French nationality since the Revolution*] (Paris: Grasset, 2002).

28. There is one encouraging sign that the state still provides some opportunities for this population, however: 17 percent of all French schoolteachers have at least one foreign parent, of whom 42.6 percent are from North Africa (mostly Algeria). Martine Laronche, "À l'école de la République" ["At the school of the Republic"], *Le Monde*, January 8, 2005.

29. Jean-Paul Fitoussi, "La France européenne" ["European France"], *Le Monde*, May 7, 2005; Jean-Paul Fitoussi, "Les banlieues, loin de l'emploi" ["The suburbs, far from jobs"], *Le Monde*, December 30, 2005.

30. Dominique Andolfatto and others, *L'état de la France 2002* [*The state of France: 2002*] (Paris: La Découverte, 2001).

31. Michel Glaude and Catherine Borrel, "Immigrés et marché du travail: regard statistique" ["Immigrants and the job market: A statistical look"] in *Immigration, marché du travail, intégration* [*Immigration, the job market, integration*], edited by François Héran (Paris: La Documentation française, 2002).

32. For example, the rate at which high school graduates found a job within seven months of graduation fell from 70 percent to 58 percent between 2002 and 2003. Luc Bronner, "L'insertion professionnelle des jeunes peu diplômés se dégrade" ["Professional integration of youth without diplomas gets worse"], *Le Monde*, August 10, 2004.

33. Glaude and Borrel, "Immigrés et marché du travail."

34. Ibid.

35. According to the Institut Nationale d'Etudes Démographiques, cited in Gilbert Charles and Jean-Sébastien Stehli, "Où en sont les beurs?" ["How are the *beurs* doing?"] *L'Express*, November 8, 2001.

36. Data from 1995, 1998, and 2001: *Enquêtes emploi* [*Employment Studies*] (Institut National de la Statistique et des études économiques/CES, March 2001); Mouna

Viprey, "L'insertion des jeunes d'origine étrangère" ["The integration of youth of foreign origin"] (Paris: Conseil économique et social, November 2002), p. 63.

37. The categories were information technology, financial accounting, financial regulation, sales, marketing, and office administration/management. See Samuel Thomas, "Rapport d'analyse des affaires récentes de discriminations à l'embauche poursuivies par SOS Racisme" ["SOS Racisme report on recent instances of discrimination in hiring"] (Paris: SOS Racisme, March 21, 2005).

38. Hakim El ghissassi, "Entretien avec Jean-Louis Borloo" ["Interview with Jean-Louis Borloo"], *La Médina*, no. 18 (January 2003).

39. Olivier Roy, "Get French or Die Trying," *New York Times*, November 9, 2005, p. A27.

40. The strict geographical limits of the unrest were not generally appreciated abroad, as many European and American newspapers reported that "Paris is burning."

41. Data from Ministère de l'Equipement des Transports et de l'Aménagement du Territoire, du Tourisme, et de la Mer [Ministry of Equipment for Transportation and for Development of Land, Tourism, and Sea] (METATTM), 2003.

42. 1996 INSEE housing survey in Andolfatto and others, *L'état de la France 2002*; Viprey, "L'insertion des jeunes d'origine étrangère" ["Integration of youth of foreign origin"], p. 92.

43. Julien Boëldieu and Catherine Borrel, "La proportion d'immigrés est stable depuis 25 ans" ["The proportion of immigrants has been stable for twenty-five years"], Cellules statistiques et études sur l'immigration [Office for Statistical Analysis and the Study of Immigration], INSEE, 1999.

44. Marie-Christine Tabet, "197 nationalités dans le creuset du '93'" ["197 different nationalities in the melting pot of '93'"], *Le Figaro*, May 6, 2004.

45. Eric Taïeb, *Immigrés: l'effet générations. Rejet, assimilation, intégration d'hier à aujourd'hui* [*The generational effect on immigrants: Rejection, assimiliation, and integration, yesterday and today*] (Paris: Éditions de l'Atelier, 1998).

46. Marie-Christine Tabet, "93: radiographie d'une banlieue symbole" ["'93': Analysis of an emblematic *banlieue*"], *Le Figaro*, May 5, 2004.

47. Piotr Smolar, "Les RG constatent un phénomène de repli communautaire dans la moitié des quartiers sensibles surveillés" ["The RG observes community isolationism in half of 'sensitive neighborhoods' under their watch"], *Le Monde*, July 6, 2004.

48. "Ghettos, Danger!" *Le Monde*, July 6, 2004.

49. Jean-Philippe Moinet, "Plan d'action et d'information civique pour la cohésion sociale" ["Plan of action and civic information for social cohesion"], *Rapport du Haut Conseil à l'Intégration*, December 2004.

50. Hakim El ghissassi, "Entretien avec Jean-Louis Borloo," *La Médina*, no. 18, January 2003.

51. Roxane Silberman, "Les enfants d'immigrés sur le marché du travail: les mécanismes d'une discrimination sélective" ["The children of immigrants in the job market: Mechanisms of selective discrimination"] in *Immigration, marche du travail, integration* [*Immigration, the job market, integration*], edited by Héran; and

Dominique Schnapper, *La France de l'intégration* [*The France of integration*] (Paris: Gallimard, 1991).

52. Martine Laronche, "Comment les stratégies des lycées pèsent sur la réussite des éleves" ["How the strategies of high schools affect student success"], *Le Monde,* March 31, 2004.

53. "Le directeur de Sciences Po Paris veut créer un lycée d'élite pour les élèves des banlieues," *Le Monde,* December 1, 2005.

54. Luc Bronner, "L'académie de Créteil concentre les maux de l'école en banlieue" ["The Creteil school district concentrates the ills of education in the banlieue"], *Le Monde,* April 23, 2003.

55. Laronche, "Comment les stratégies des lycées pèsent sur la réussite des éleves" ["How the strategies of high schools affect student success"], *Le Monde,* March 31, 2004.

56. Michèle Tribalat, *Faire France: une grande enquête sur les immigrés et leurs enfants* [*Making France: A large-scale study of immigrants and their children*] (Paris: La Découverte, 1995).

57. Dargent, "Les musulmans déclarés en France" ["Self-declared Muslims in France"].

58. Renaud Fillieule, *Sociologie de la délinquence* [*The sociology of delinquency*] (Paris: PUF, 2001), cited in Farhad Khosrokhavar, *L'islam dans les prisons* [*Islam in the prisons*] (Paris: Balland, 2004).

59. Study by Sebastian Roché and Monique Dagnaud, sociologists at the Centre Nationale de la Recherché Scienifique (National Center of Scientific Research), reported by Nathalie Guibert, "Selon une étude menée en Isère, deux tiers des mineurs délinquants sont d'origine étrangère" ["According to a study in Isère, two-thirds of juvenile delinquents are of foreign origin"], *Le Monde,* April 16, 2004. Of 325 cases, 41.8 percent were classified as assault, 25.2 percent as sexual assault, 17.5 percent as armed robbery, 7 percent as rape, 6.2 percent as violent rape, and 2.2 as homicide; the perpetrators were 95 percent male, with an average age of fifteen and a half years. Isère does not have a particularly high rate of immigration: only 6.1 percent within the larger Rhône-Alpes region, which itself has an immigrant population of 7.5 percent.

60. Farhad Khosrokhavar, *L'islam dans les prisons* [*Islam in the prisons*]. These estimations are based on several data points: the place of birth of a prisoner's father, the number of prisoners requesting meals without pork (subtracting the relatively few Jewish prisoners), and the number attending Friday prayers. Comparing other European countries, Khosrokhavar reports that the percentage of Muslims in German prisons varies between 8 and 25 percent. In Denmark, where Muslims represent just 3 percent of the general population, they make up between 10 to 15 percent of inmates.

61. There are ninety-nine prisoners for every 100,000 inhabitants in France, compared with 135 in Great Britain and more than 700 in the United States. Fifteen years ago, the French number was only seventy-eight, but between September 2001 and

September 2002, it grew 14 percent. If this trend continues, then the prison population will double in the next five years; at 63,444 prisoners, it is already at its highest since the end of World War II. Nathalie Guibert, "La situation dans les prisons est 'explosive,' selon les surveillants" ["The situation in prisons is 'explosive,' according to guards"], *Le Monde*, July 18, 2003; U.S. Department of Justice, "Prison and Jail Inmates at Midyear 2002" (www.ojp.usdoj.gov/bjs/abstract/pjim02.htm).

62. Khosrokhavar, *L'islam dans les prisons* [*Islam in the prisons*], p. 280.

63. Compiled from data in Khosrokhavar, *L'islam dans les prisons* [*Islam in the prisons*], p. 280.

64. Study by Roché and Dagnaud, reported by Guibert in "Selon une étude menée en Isère, deux tiers des mineurs délinquants sont d'origine étrangère" ["According to a study in Isère, two-thirds of juvenile delinquents are of foreign origin"].

65. "Vers une haute autorité unique contre toutes les discriminations" ["Toward a single anti-discrimination agency"], *Le Monde*, February 16, 2004.

66. Commission Nationale Consultative des Droits de l'Homme [National Advisory Commission on Human Rights], *2002: La lutte contre le racisme et la xénophobie* [*2002: The fight against racism and xenophobia*], Rapport d'activité (Paris: La Documentation française, 2003).

67. Tribalat, *Faire France* [*Making France*].

68. Francis Fukuyama, "Voile et contrôle sexuel" ["The veil and sexual control"], *Le Monde*, February 3, 2004.

69. "La fréquence des mariages forcés pose la question de la pénalisation" ["The frequency of forced marriage raises the question of making it a crime"], *Le Monde*, April 11, 2005.

70. Department of State, "French Muslims Favor Integration into French Society," Opinion Analysis M-58-05, Office of Research, May 24, 2005.

71. Brouard and Tiberj, *Français comme les autres?* [*French like the rest?*], p. 91.

72. In the United States, in contrast, figures showed that while roughly 40 percent of Asian Americans married whites in the late 1990s, only 6 percent of blacks did. Nicholas D. Kristof, "Love and Race," *New York Times*, December 6, 2002.

73. Emanuel Todd, *Le destin des immigrés* [*The destiny of immigrants*] (Paris: Seuil, 1994), pp. 366–67.

74. Tribalat, *Faire France* [*Making France*]; Brouard and Tiberj, *Francais comme les autres?* [*French like the rest?*], p. 142.

75. While those between a non-Algerian and an Algerian mother rose from 6.2 percent to 27.5 percent (the statistics do not distinguish between married and single mothers); See also Todd, *Le destin des immigrés* [*The destiny of immigrants*].

76. Glaude and Borrel, "Immigrés et marché du travail" ["Immigrants and the job market"].

77. Tribalat, *Faire France* [*Making France*], p. 126.

78. Department of State, "French Muslims Favor Integration into French Society."

79. Of course, the preparation of ethnic dishes is not a sure sign of lack of integration. See, for example, Mary Waters, *Ethnic Options* (University of California Press, 1990).

80. Dargent, "Les musulmans déclarés en France" ["Self-declared Muslims in France"], pp. 71 and 72.

81. Brouard and Tiberj, *Francais comme les autres?* [*French like the rest?*], p. 124.

82. See, for example, Vincent Geisser and Khadija Mohsen-Finan, "L'islam à l'école" ["Islam at school"], Institut des Hautes Etudes de la Sécurité Intérieure (IHESI) (Institute of Higher Studies in Internal Security), Paris, 2001.

Chapter 2

1. Ernest Renan, *Dialogues philosophiques* [*Philosophical dialogues*], 1877, cited in Claude Liauzu, *Immigration et intégration: l'état des savoirs* [*Immigration and integration: What we know*] (Paris: La Découverte, 1999).

2. Gérard Noiriel, *Atlas de l'immigration en France* [*Atlas of immigration in France*] (Paris: Autrement, 2002).

3. Thomas Deltombe, *L'islam imaginaire: la construction médiatique de l'islamophobie en France, 1975–2005* [*An imaginary Islam: The media's construction of Islamophobia in France, 1975–2005*] (Paris: La Découverte, 2005).

4. Louis Chevalier, *Classes laborieuses et classes dangereuses à Paris pendant la première moitié du XIXe siècle* [*The working classes and the dangerous classes in Paris during the first half of the nineteenth century*] (Paris: Plon, 1958).

5. Mohamed Sifaoui, *La France malade de l'islamisme: menaces terroristes sur l'hexagone* [*France's Islamist sickness: Terrorist threats against the homeland*] (Paris: Le Cherche-midi, 2002); Christophe Deloire and Christophe Dubois, *Les islamistes sont déjà là: enquête sur une guerre secrète* [*The Islamists are already here: Investigation of a secret war*] (Paris: Albin Michel, 2004).

6. Marc d'Anna (also known as Alexandre del Valle), interview with former prime minister Pierre Messmer on the website Nouvelle Liberté. See also Jamie Glazov, "The Death of France?" *FrontPageMagazine.com*, June 9, 2003; Theodore Dalrymple, "The Barbarians at the Gates of Paris," *City-journal.org* 12, no. 4 (Autumn 2002); and the report by Mouvement contre le Racisme et pour l'Amitié entre les Peuples (MRAP) (Movement against Racism and for Friendship among Peoples), "Racisme anti-arabe: nouvelle évolution" ["Anti-Arab racism: A new evolution"], August 6, 2003 (www.mrap.asso.fr/dossiers/doc-94.pdf [February 15, 2006]).

7. For example, the former actress and animal rights activist Brigitte Bardot has been convicted and fined in court three times for having denounced "the Islamization of France," "the underground and dangerous infiltration of Islamism," "the hordes of young people who terrorize the population," and, echoing the Italian polemicist Oriana Fallaci, the illegal immigrants who "profane our churches by transforming them into human pig sties" (as she alleged immigrants had done in a church where they had taken refuge that had inadequate sanitary facilities).

8. Department of State, "French Muslims Favor Integration into French Society," Opinion Analysis M-58-05, Office of Research, May 24, 2005.

9. See Mary Lewis, "L'histoire ne s'écrit pas comme on compose une majorité parlementaire" ["History is not written in the same way as a parliamentary majority is made"], *Le Monde*, January 29, 2006

10. See Roger Hewitt, *White Backlash and the Politics of Multiculturalism* (Cambridge University Press, 2005).

11. See Commission Nationale Consultative des Droits de l'Homme (CNCDH), "La lutte contre le racisme et la xénophobie" ["The fight against racism and xenophobia"].

12. Philip H. Gordon and Sophie Meunier, *The French Challenge: Adapting to Globalization* (Washington: Brookings, 2001). The Tobin tax is a scheme originally conceived (and later disavowed) by Nobel Prize–winning economist James Tobin to tax international financial speculation. ATTAC is a left-wing, anti–free trade, antiglobalization grass-roots organization.

13. Olivier Roy, *La laïcité face à l'Islam* [*Laïcité confronts Islam*] (Paris: Stock, 2005).

14. Alain Finkielkraut, "Un certain sens de l'honneur" ["A certain sense of honor"], *L'Arche* no. 573 (January 2006).

15. Dror Mishani and Aurelia Smotriez, "What Sort of Frenchmen Are They?" *Haaretz*, November 17, 2005.

16. Béatrice Jérôme, "La Seine-Saint-Denis, chouchoutée, reste sous tension" ["Seine-Saint-Denis, coddled by the government, is still tense"], *Le Monde*, May 7, 2006.

17. For a militant point of view of the antitotalitarian tendency, see Caroline Fourest, *La tentation obscurantiste* [*The temptation of obscurantism*] (Paris: Grasset, 2005).

18. See, for example, the German interior ministry report on Islamism: Guido Steinberg, "Der Islamismus im Niedergang? Anmerkungen zu den Thesen Gilles Kepels, Olivier Roys und zur europäischen Islamismusforschung" [*The decline of Islamism? Comments on the theses of Gilles Kepel and Olivier Roy and European research on Islamism*], in *Islamismus* (Berlin: Bundesministerium für Inneres, 2004).

19. Catherine Wihtol de Wenden, "Les 'jeunes issus de l'immigration': entre intégration culturelle et exclusion sociale" [*Youth of immigrant origin: Between cultural integration and social exclusion*], in Liauzu, *Immigration et intégration* [*Immigration and integration*].

20. Jean-Michel Aphatie, "Entretien avec Nelly Olin," RTL, June 16, 2004 (www.rtl.fr).

21. Jean-Philippe Moinet, "Plan d'action et d'information civique pour la cohésion sociale"["Plan of action and civic information for social cohesion"], Haut Conseil à l'Intégration, December 2004.

22. The source for all figures about racism and anti-Semitism is the Commission Nationale Consultative des Droits de l'Homme (CNCDH) and its annual reports, notably the 2004 report, "La lutte contre le racisme et la xénophobie 2004" ["The

fight against racism and xenophobia 2004"] (hereafter referred to as "CNCDH [year] report"). The full report is available at http://lesrapports.ladocumentationfrancaise. fr/BRP/054000193/0000.pdf.

23. BVA opinion poll in CNCDH 2004 report.

24. BVA polls in CNCDH 2004 and 2003 reports.

25. See CNCDH 2005 report.

26. Y. B., *Allah Superstar* (Paris: Grasset, 2003), p. 31.

27. See chapter on discrimination by SOS Racisme in the CNCDH 2004 report.

28. In May 2006, three youths of Turkish origin were shot at by the security staff of a nightclub in Garchizy (Nièvre), prompting the departmental prefect to hold a meeting with nightclub owners on security and anti-discrimination policies; see "Trois agents de sécurité d'une discothèque écroués après avoir tiré sur des jeunes" ["Three nightclub security agents are held after firing on youth"], *Le Monde*, May 2, 2006.

29. See "Discriminations: un projet de loi au Parlement avant la fin de l'année" ["Discrimination: A draft bill to Parliament before the end of the year"], February 16, 2004 (www.premier-ministre.gouv.fr).

30. See report on the future antidiscrimination agency by Bernard Stasi, "Vers la Haute Autorité de Lutte contre les Discriminations et pour l'Egalité: Rapport au Premier ministre" ["Toward the High Authority to Combat Discrimination and Promote Equality: Report to the prime minister"] (http://lesrapports.ladocumentationfran-caise.fr/BRP/044000074/0000.pdf).

31. Pierre Bourdieu, "Forms of Capital," in *Handbook of Theory and Research for the Sociology of Education,* edited by J. C. Richards (New York: Greenwood Press, 1983).

32. Roxane Silberman, "Les enfants d'immigrés sur le marché du travail: les mécanismes d'une discrimination selective" ["Children of immigrants in the job market: Mechanisms of selective discrimination"] in *Immigration, marché du travail, integration [Immigration, job market, integration]*, edited by François Héran (Paris: Documentation française, 2002).

33. CSA opinion poll, "L'entreprise: est-elle raciste?" ["Are business firms racist?"] June 3, 2004 (www.csa-fr.com/dataset/data2004/opi20040507b.htm).

34. Samuel Thomas, "Rapport d'analyse des affaires récentes de discriminations à l'embauche poursuivies par SOS Racisme" ["SOS Racisme report on recent instances of discrimination in hiring"] (Paris: SOS Racisme, March 21, 2005).

35. "Les handicapés et les Maghrébins sont les premières victimes des discriminations à l'embauche" ["Handicapped citizens and North Africans are the first victims of discrimination in hiring"], *Le Monde*, May 21, 2004.

36. See chapter on discrimination in CNCDH 2004 report.

37. Philippe Bernard, "On nous qualifie sans cesse 'd'Arabes' et on prétend nous empêcher de nous situer par rapport à l'islam" ["We are always called 'Arabs' and people try to prevent us from aligning ourselves with Islam"], *Le Monde,* July 6, 2004.

38. Ibid. For more on this topic, see the discussion of Tariq Ramadan in chapter 4.

39. Piotr Smolar, "Les étrangers sont les premières victimes des violences policières" ["Foreigners are the first victims of police violence"], *Le Monde*, December 4, 2004.

40. Ibid.

41. CNCDH 2003 report and other polls for 2002 and 2004; "L'opinion des Français musulmans" ["The opinions of French Muslims"], IPSOS poll, April 7, 2003.

42. In a February 2005 CSA poll, 57 percent of respondents who were registered to vote were opposed (www.csa-fr.com/dataset/data2005/opi20050203b.htm), and 60 percent were opposed in a September 2005 IFOP poll (http://www.ifop.com/europe/sondages/opinionf/turquie.asp).

43. Pierre-André Taguieff, *La nouvelle judéophobie* [*The new Judeophobia*] (Paris: Mille et une Nuits, 2002); Vincent Geisser, *La nouvelle islamophobie* [*The new Islamophobia*] (Paris: La Découverte, 2003). On Islamophobia, see also Jytte Klausen, *The Islamic Challenge: Politics and Religion in Western Europe* (Oxford University Press, 2005).

44. "Les responsables musulmans déplorent le temps de réaction des politiques après l'incendie de deux lieux de culte" ["Muslim leaders decry politicians' delayed reactions to arson in two prayer spaces"], *Le Monde*, March 8, 2004.

45. Michel Houellebecq, interview with Didier Sénécal, *Lire*, September 2001. For the complete interview, see http://www.lire.fr/entretien.asp/idC=37437/idTC=4/idR=201/idG.

46. Xavier Ternisien, "Trouble au Haut conseil à l'intégration à la suite des propos de Claude Imbert" ["Trouble at the High Council for Integration after the remarks of Claude Imbert"], *Le Monde*, November 5, 2003.

47. Pascal Santi and Xavier Ternisien, "Le conseil du culte musulman veut poursuivre *Charlie Hebdo*" ["Muslim religious council wants to file suit against *Charlie Hebdo*"], *Le Monde*, February 7, 2006; "Le CFCM attaque en justice" ["The CFCM goes to court"], *Nouvel Observateur*, February 13, 2006.

48. Xavier Ternisien, "Un collectif tente de dénombrer les actes 'islamophobes'" ["An association tries to count the number of 'Islamophobic' incidents"], *Le Monde*, October 21, 2004.

49. Nonna Mayer and Guy Michelat, "Analyse du racisme et de l'antisémitisme en France en 2004" ["Analysis of racism and anti-Semitism in France in 2004"], in the CNCDH 2004 report.

50 IFOP poll (http://www.ifop.com/europe/sondages/opinionf/islam.asp).

51. BVA poll in CNCDH 2004 report.

52. CNCDH 2004 and 2005 reports.

53. Sylvain Brouard and Vincent Tiberj, *Français comme les autres? Enquête sur les citoyens d'origine maghrébine, africaine, et turque* [*French like the rest? A study of citizens of North African, African, and Turkish origin*] (Paris: Presses de Sciences Po, 2005).

54. Sophie Fay, "Un club va promouvoir la réussite des Français d'origine étrangère" ["A new club will promote the success of French of foreign origin"], *Le*

Monde, November 25, 2004, and Mustapha Kessous, "L'élite beur tisse son propre réseau" ["The *beur* elite develops its own network"], *Le Monde*, December 17, 2005.

55. Laurent Blivet, "Ni quotas, ni indifférence: l'entreprise et l'égalité positive" ["Neither quotas nor indifference: Business and 'positive equality'"], *Note de l'Institut Montaigne*, October 2004, and Laurence Méhaignerie and Yazid Sabeg, "Les oubliés de l'égalité des chances: Participation, pluralité, assimilation . . . ou repli?" ["Those left behind by equal opportunity: Participation, plurality, assimilation . . . or isolation?"] *Note de l'Institut Montaigne*, January 2004.

56. Erik Bleich, *Race Politics in Britain and France* (Cambridge University Press, 2003).

57. Catherine Coroller, "Le MRAP maintient le cap contre l'islamophobie" ["The MRAP stays the course against Islamophobia"], *Libération*, December 6, 2004.

58. Pascal Blanchard and others, *Le Paris Arabe: deux siècles de présence des orientaux et des maghrébins* [*Arab Paris: Two centuries of "oriental" and North African presence*](Paris: La Découverte, 2003).

59. Noiriel, *Atlas de l'immigration en France* [*Atlas of immigration in France*].

60. The only publicly financed French schools named after Arabs are the Lycée Al-Jabr in Morocco and the Lycée Ibrahim Nahr and Lycée Abdelkader, both in Lebanon. See Xavier Ternisien, "Un college de Nanterre portera-t-il un nom arabe?" ["Will a middle school in Nanterre have an Arab name?"], *Le Monde*, April 15, 2006. Bouzar, a trained anthropologist, served on the Conseil Français du Culte Musulman, and Cherifi and Arkoun served on the Stasi Commission on religious symbols in public life (see chapters 5 and 6). See Burhan Schawi, "Mohammed Arkoun, A Modern Critic of Islamic Reason," *Qantara.de*, April 27, 2005; and Xavier Ternisien, "Dounia Bouzar, la voix des jeunes musulmanes de France" ["Dounia Bouzar, the voice of young French Muslims"], *Le Monde*, March 11, 2003. On Hanifa Cherifi, see Charles Fleming and John Carreyrou, "In France, Policy on Muslims Comes to a Head on Scarves," *Wall Street Journal*, June 26, 2003. On Malek Chebel, see Nathalie Szerman, "Algerian Reformist Malek Chebel: 27 Propositions for Reforming Islam," MEMRI Analysis no. 273, May 5, 2006.

Chapter 3

1. Vincent Geisser, "Qui parle de 'lobby'? Lettre ouverte aux apprentis sorciers de la République" ["Who speaks of a 'lobby'? An open letter to the sorcerers' apprentices of the Republic"], April 13, 2004 (*www.oumma.com*).

2. Department of State, "French Muslims Favor Integration into French Society," Opinion Analysis M-58-05, Office of Research, May 24, 2005; Vincent Geisser and Khadija Mohsen-Finan, "L'islam à l'école" ["Islam at school"], Institut des Hautes Etudes de la Sécurité Intérieure (IHESI) [Institute of Higher Studies in Internal Security], Paris, 2001.

3. Sylvain Brouard and Vincent Tiberj, *Français comme les autres? Enquête sur les citoyens d'origine maghrébine, africaine, et turque* [*French like the rest? A study of citizens of North African, African, and Turkish origin*] (Paris: Presses de Sciences Po, 2005), p. 27.

4. See "Les Français et leurs croyances" ["The French and their beliefs"], Sondage exclusif [Exclusive poll], *CSA/La Vie/Le Monde*, March 2003 (www.csa-tmo.fr).

5. Authors' interview with Ministry for Foreign Affairs official; "Villepin contrôle la quête pour les mosquées" ["Villepin is overseeing the search for mosques"], *Libération*, December 8, 2004.

6. See "Les français et la religion" [The French and religion"], Sondage de l'Institut CSA, December 2004 (http://www.csa-tmo.fr/dataset/data2004/0401664.pdf); Danièle Hervieu Léger, "L'état des religions en France" ["The state of religions in France"], Embassy of France, Washington, D.C., July 31, 2002.

7. Geisser and Mohsen-Finan, "L'islam à l'école" ["Islam at school"]. This study on Islam in schools in several French cities—Lille, Montbéliard, and Marseille—was conducted in 2001 on behalf of the Ministry of the Interior from a sample of 494 middle-school and high-school students, 42 percent of whom were Muslim.

8. Brouard and Tiberj, *Français comme les autres?* ["French like the rest?"].

9. Michel Wieviorka, "La grande mutation des juifs de France ou l'impossible retour au modèle républicain" ["The great transformation of French Jews, or the impossibility of returning to the republican model"], October 2003 (*www.proche-orient.info*).

10. Philippe Bernard, "Foulard à l'école: la réalité cachée derrière les chiffres officiels" ["The headscarf at school: The hidden reality behind the official numbers"], *Le Monde*, December 10, 2003.

11. Claude Dargent, "Les musulmans déclarés en France: affirmation religieuse, subordination sociale, et progressisme politique" ["Self-declared Muslims in France: Religious affirmation, social subordination, and political progressivism"], *Cahier du CEVIPOF*, no. 34, February 2003, p. 31.

12. Ibid., p. 24.

13. Ibid.

14. Piotr Smolar, "Les RG constatent un phénomène de repli communautaire dans la moitié des quartiers sensibles surveillés" ["The RG observes community isolationism in half of 'sensitive neighborhoods' under their watch"], *Le Monde*, July 6, 2004.

15. Bernard, "Foulard à l'école" ["The headscarf at school"]; Vianney Sevaistre, "Les relations entre le Conseil Français du Culte Musulman et l'état: Quelle nature?" ["Relations between the French Council of the Muslim Religion and the state: Of what nature?"], *French Politics, Culture, and Society* 23, no. 1 (Spring 2005); see also interview with Hanifa Cherifi, "La guerre du voile n'aura pas lieu" ["There will be no war over the headscarf"], *Nouvel Observateur Hebdo*, no. 1671, November 14, 1996; "Il n'y a que 150 cas conflictuels, selon la médiatrice de l'éducation nationale" ["There were only 150 cases of conflict, according to the national educational mediator"], *Le Monde*, May 9, 2003.

16. Patrick Weil, "Why French Secularism Needs to Adapt: The Experts' Recommendations and the Ban of Religious Symbols in Schools," Harvard University, Minda de Gunzburg Center for European Studies, May 10, 2004.

17. Michel Gurfinkiel, "The French Way of Life Is in Danger," *Middle East Quarterly*

4, no.1 (March 1997); Jean-Marc Leclerc, "Ces banlieues du non-droit" ["The lawless banlieues"], *Valeurs Actuelles*, March 4, 1995.

18. "Des écoles confessionnelles commencent à voir le jour" ["Religious schools begin to open"], *Le Monde*, May 12, 2002.

19. *100 ans de laïcité* [*One hundred years of laïcité*], Conseil d'Etat, March 2004, part 2, p. 96; testimony to the Stasi Commission suggested that some of these students' parents hoped to spare their daughters the peer pressure to wear the headscarf that might exist in some public schools.

20. Wieviorka, "La grande mutation des Juifs de France" ["The great transformation of French Jews].

21. Dalil Kenz, "Le premier lycée musulman à Lille en 2003" ["The first Muslim high school in Lille in 2003"], *Le Figaro*, December 11, 2002.

22. Haydée Saberan, "Le lycée musulman de Lille autorisé à ouvrir ses portes" ["The Muslim high school in Lille is authorized to open its doors"], *Libération*, July 11, 2003.

23. The schools were in Antony (Hauts-de-Seine), Fontenay-aux-Roses (Val-de-Marne), and Argenteuil (Val-d'Oise).

24. Dounia Bouzar, "Etude de 12 associations à référence musulmane: l'islam entre mythe et religion—le nouveau discours religieux dans les associations socio-culturelles musulmanes" ["A study of twelve Muslim associations: Islam between myth and religion—The new religious discourse in socioculturally Muslim associations"], *Les Cahiers de la Sécurité Intérieure*, no. 54, 2004, Institut des Hautes Etudes de la Sécurité Intérieure (IHESI) [Institute of Higher Studies in Internal Security].

25. There are 4 to 5 million American Muslims. Philip Jenkins, "Islam in America," *Watch on the West* 4, no. 4 (July 2003) (Foreign Policy Research Institute) (http://www.fpri.org/ww/0404.200307.jenkins.islaminamerica.html).

26. "Les Grandes Mosquées de France" ["The great mosques of France"], *Le Monde*, October 13, 2001; "La plupart des salles de prière n'ont pas été construites pour cet usage" ["Most prayer rooms were not built for that purpose"], *Le Monde*, January 26, 2002; Xavier Ternisien, "Le temps des 'mosquées cathédrales' semble révolu" ["The time of 'cathedral mosques' seems to be over"], *Le Monde*, June 18, 2004.

27. Interview with Idriss Elouanali in Catherine Coroller, "Les caves sont maintenant très minimes, il doit en rester une trentaine" ["There are only a few basement prayer rooms left, perhaps only thirty"], *Libération*, December 8, 2004.

28. Thierry Tuot, interview with authors, June 2000.

29. Interview in Coroller, "Les caves sont maintenant très minimes."

30. Nicolas Sarkozy, "Les musulmans ne doivent pas avoir plus de droits. Veillons à ce qu'ils n'en aient pas moins" ["Muslims should not have more rights than others, but we must ensure they don't have fewer"], *Le Monde*, October 26, 2004.

31. Christophe Dubois, "Plongée chez les ultras de l'Islam en France" ["A look at extremists within Islam in France"], *Le Parisien*, April 19, 2004.

32. Interview with Dominique de Villepin, *Le Parisien*, December 6, 2004.

33. Xavier Ternisien, "Les représentants des musulmans de France se sont mobilisés pour renouveler leurs dirigeants" ["The representatives of French Muslims mobilize to reelect their leaders"], *Le Monde,* June 19, 2005.

34. Michèle Tribalat, "Pouvoirs publics et islam: la tentation d'un nouveau concordat" ["Public authorities and Islam: The temptation of a new concordat"], France-Mail-Forum, 2004.

35. Interview in Coroller, "Les caves sont maintenant très minimes."

36. Dalil Boubakeur, interview with the authors, July 2000.

37. Haut Conseil à l'Intégration, *L'Islam dans la République* ["Islam in the Republic"], November 2000, p. 63.

38. See Jean-Louis Debré, *En mon for intérieur* [*In my heart of hearts*] (Paris: Jean-Claude Lattès, 1997).

39. Fouad Alaoui, interview with the authors, June 2002. See Habib Affes, "La mosquée: lieu d'enseignement et d'éducation" ["The mosque: A place of teaching and education"], in *La mosquée dans la cite,* Hakim El ghissassi, ed. (Paris: Editions la Médina, 2002); Cécilia Gabizon, "Ahmed Boubeker: de nouvelles mosquées sur le mode des églises paroissiales" ["Ahmed Boubeker: new mosques are modeled on parish churches"], *Le Figaro,* December 7, 2004.

40. Fouad Alaoui, interview with the authors, June 2002.

41. Alain Boyer, "Le droit des religions en France," *Administration,* no. 165, October-December 1994.

42. Fouad Alaoui, interview with the authors, June 2002.

43. Nicolas Sarkozy, *La République, les religions, l'espérance* [*The Republic, religions, and hope*] (Paris: Cerf, 2004).

44. See Nicolas Weill, "Cent ans après, la loi sur la laïcité est l'enjeu de nouveaux débats" ["One hundred years later, the law on laïcité is the subject of new debates"], *Le Monde,* February 14, 2005.

45. Hakim El ghissassi, "La fondation des œvres de l'islam de France: aménagement, entretien, et construction des lieux de cultes musulmans" ["French Foundation for Muslim Works: Development, maintenance, and construction of Muslim prayer spaces"], March 20, 2005 (www.sezame.info).

46. Agence pour le Développement des Relations Interculturelles [Agency for the Development of Intercultural Relations], *Le point sur l'Islam en France* [*All you need to know about Islam in France*] (Paris: La Documentation française, 2000); Xavier Ternisien, *La France des mosquées* [*The France of mosques*] (Paris: Albin Michel, 2002).

47. Half of all Algerian Berber respondents said that they eat pork and two-thirds said that they drink alcohol. The figures for Arabs were 25 percent and 33 percent, respectively. Michèle Tribalat, *Faire France: Une enquête sur les immigrés et leurs enfants* [*Making France: A study of immigrants and their children*] (Paris: La Découverte, 1995).

48. Ibid., pp. 94–96. That was true of 48 percent of Algerians overall.

49. Ibid. While 41 percent of Moroccans answered that they had no religion or did

not practice it, the figure for Moroccan Berbers was only 33 percent. Roughly 22 percent of Moroccans are of Berber origin.

50. Bureau of Democracy, Human Rights, and Labor, "International Religious Freedom Report 2003: France," U.S. Department of State, 2003.

51. Hakim El ghissassi, interview with the authors, June 2000; Ternisien, *La France des mosquées* ["The France of mosques"].

52. Hakim El ghissassi, interview with the authors, June 2000. See "La viande halal: la face cachée" ["The hidden side of halal meat"], a special issue of *La Médina*, no. 5, October 2000; Besma Lahouri and Boris Thiolay, "L'argent de l'islam" ["The money of Islam"], *L'Express*, November 21, 2002.

53. "Le Franprix 'halal' d'Evry, qui ne vend ni porc ni vin, provoque la colère du maire" ["The halal Franprix store in Evry, which sells neither pork nor wine, provokes the anger of the mayor"], *Le Monde*, December 12, 2002.

54. Rémy Léveau and Catherine Wihtol de Wenden, *La Beurgeoisie: Les trois âges de la vie associative issue de l'immigration* [*The Beurgeoisie [sic]: Three phases of immigrant association life*] (Paris: CNRS, 2001); Catherine Wihtol de Wenden, "Civic Associationism among Franco-Maghrebians in France: New Trends,"New York University, Center for European Studies, 2002; and Vincent Geisser and Scherhazade Kelfaoui, "Trois generations de militantisme politique sous la Vème republique: l'activiste immigre, le beur civique, et l'electeur musulman" ["Three generations of political activism in the Fifth Republic: The immigrant activist, the civic *beur*, and the Muslim voter"], *La Médina*, December 12, 2001. See also Vincent Geisser, *Ethnicité républicaine* [*Republican ethnicity*] (Paris: Presses de Sciences Po, 1997).

55. Leveau and Wihtol de Wenden, *La Beurgeoisie* [*The beurgeoisie* [sic]], p. 22.

56. Geisser, *Ethnicité républicaine* [*Republican ethnicity*].

57. Brouard and Tiberj, *Français comme les autres?* [*French like the rest?*], p. 31.

58. Interview in *Le Nouvel Observateur*, October 14, 2003.

59. See Jonathan Laurence, "Managing Transnational Islam," in *Immigration and the Transformation of Europe*, edited by Craig Parsons and Timothy Smeeding (Cambridge University Press, 2006); Laurie Brand, *Citizens Abroad: Emigration and the State in the Middle East and North Africa* (Cambridge University Press, 2006); and Vincent Geisser, "L'islam consulaire: Le rôle des etats d'origine dans la gestion de l'islam de France" ["Consular Islam: The role of states of origin in the administration of French Islam"], June 2004 (*www.oumma.com*).

60. Confidential interviews with the authors, June 2002.

61. Farhad Khosrokhavar, *L'islam dans les prisons* [*Islam in the prisons*] (Paris: Balland, 2004), p. 222.

62. Olivier Bertrand, "La tentation salafiste" ["The salafist temptation"], *Libération*, December 8, 2004.

63. Smolar, "Les RG constatent un phénomène de repli communautaire" ["The RG observes community isolationism"].

64. Olivier Roy, *Globalized Islam: The Search for a New Umma* (Columbia University Press, 2004).

65. Dounia Bouzar, "Etude de 12 associations à référence musulmane: l'islam entre mythe et religion—le nouveau discours religieux dans les associations socio-culturelles musulmanes" ["A study of twelve Muslim associations: Islam between myth and religion—the new religious discourses in socioculturally Muslim associations"], Institut des Hautes Etudes de la Sécurité Intérieure (IHESI) (Institute of Higher Studies in Internal Security), *Les Cahiers de la Sécurité Intérieure*, no. 54, 2004.

66. Interview with Dounia Bouzar in Cécilia Gabizon and Jean-Marc Leclerc, "L'inquiétant repli identitaire des jeunes musulmans" ["The worrisome identity crisis among young Muslims"], *Le Figaro*, May 28, 2004.

67. Dounia Bouzar, *L'islam des banlieues: Les prédicateurs musulmans—nouveaux travailleurs sociaux?* [*Islam of the banlieues: Muslim preachers—the new social workers?*] (Paris: Syros, 2001).

68. Philippe Bernard, "On nous qualifie sans cesse d' 'Arabes' et on prétend nous empêcher de nous situer par rapport à l'islam" ["We are always called 'Arabs' and people try to prevent us from aligning ourselves with Islam"], *Le Monde*, July 6, 2004.

69. Smolar, "Les RG constatent un phénomène de repli communautaire" ["The RG observes community isolationism"].

70. Dounia Bouzar, *Monsieur Islam n'existe pas* (Paris: Hachette, 2004).

71. Gabizon and Leclerc, "L'inquiétant repli identitaire des jeunes musulmans" ["The worrisome identity crisis among young Muslims"]; Jean-Pierre Obin, *Rapport de l'inspection générale de l'éducation nationale sur les signes et manifestations d'appartenance religieuse dans les établissements scolaires* [*National education inspector general's report on signs and manifestations of religious belonging in schools*] (Paris: Ministry of Education, Higher Learning, and Research, June 2004).

72. See Fouad Imarraine, "De Villepin l'a rêvé, Dounia l'a fait!!!" ["De Villepin dreamed it and Dounia did it!"], June 3, 2004 (www.saphir-info.net).

73. Philippe Bernard, "Entretien avec Didier Lapeyronnie, professeur de sociologie à l'université Victor-Segalen de Bordeaux" ["Interview with Didier Lapeyronnie, sociology professor at Victor-Segalen University in Bordeaux"], *Le Monde,* July 6, 2004.

74. Ibid.

75. Dargent, "Les musulmans déclarés en France" ["Self-declared Muslims in France"].

76. Cécilia Gabizon and Thierry Portes, "Les musulmans laïques veulent faire entendre leur voix" ["Lay Muslims want to make their voice heard"], *Le Monde,* May 15, 2003.

77. Hakim El ghissassi, "Organiser le pèlerinage de 21,000 citoyens français musulmans" ["Organizing the pilgrimage for 21,000 French Muslims"], January 12, 2005 (*www.sezame.info*); and Ternisien, *La France des mosquées*, p. 104. That number, which included 8,000 French citizens, dwarfs the 4,500 Saudi visas granted annually to U.S. residents or the 1,500 granted to British residents.

78. Eighty-four percent of those fifty-five years of age and older and 74 percent of those twenty-four and younger claim to observe Ramadan—"a perfect U" (shape of

the line when the data are graphed). Thirty-eight percent of Turkish youth in France pray occasionally, and 35 percent never do, but 60 percent celebrate Ramadan. Alain Boyer, *L'Islam en France* [*Islam in France*] (Paris: PUF, 1998), p. 30.

79. Geisser and Mohsen-Finan, "L'islam à l'école" ["Islam at school"].

80. Ibid.

Chapter 4

1. Peter Hall and John Keeler, "Interest Representation and the Politics of Protest," in *Developments in French Politics 2,* edited by Alain Guyomarch and others (London: Palgrave, 2001).

2. Jonah Levy, *Tocqueville's Revenge: State, Society, and Economy in Contemporary France* (Harvard University Press, 1999).

3. Stanley Hoffmann and others, *In Search of France* (New York: Harper & Row, 1963), p. 62.

4. The actual number of associations in each federation is not always verifiable; some members may be branches of the same organization, that is, local affiliates of a national organization. The numbers given in table 4-1 are based on claims of the associations' leadership and Ministry of the Interior estimates.

5. "La question cruciale de la formation des imams en France" ["The crucial question of training imams in France"], *Le Monde*, May 4, 2004.

6. Jacques Berque, *Il reste un avenir: Entretiens avec Jean Sur* [*There is still a future: Interviews with Jean Sur*] (Paris: Arlea, 1993), p. 203; Hakim El ghissassi, "Un islam Gallican: Entretien avec Bruno Etienne" ["A Gallic Islam: Interview with Bruno Etienne"], September 14, 2004(www.sezame.info).

7. The law passed by Prime Minister Pierre Mauroy (under President Mitterrand) removed the requirement that foreigners first receive special permission to charter an association, which had been established by a 1939 decree aimed at limiting the activities of pro-Nazi groups and was preferred by the Socialists' Gaullist rivals.

8. See Bruno Etienne, *La France et l'Islam* [*France and Islam*] (Paris: Hachette, 1989).

9. The current board of directors includes members of Algerian, Moroccan, Senegalese, Egyptian, Tunisian, and French origin. See Alain Boyer, *L'Islam en France* [*Islam in France*] (Paris: PUF, 1998); Jocelyne Cesari, *Etre musulman en France* [To be a Muslim in France] (Paris: Karthala, 1994), p. 138; Gilles Kepel, *Les banlieues de l'islam* [*The banlieues of Islam*] (Paris: Seuil, 1991), p. 64–94; and Chems-eddine Hafiz, "Quel rôle joue la Grande Mosquée de Paris au CFCM?" ["What role does the GMP play in the CFCM?"], July 13, 2005 (www.saphirnet.info).

10. It briefly held a monopoly on halal certification under Minister of the Interior Charles Pasqua (1993–97).

11. Boyer, *L'Islam en France* [*Islam in France*].

12. Michel Gurfinkiel, "The French Way of Life Is in Danger," *Middle East Quarterly* no. 24 (1997); see also Chems-eddine Hafiz and Gilles Devers, *Droit et religion musulmane* [*Law and the Muslim religion*] (Paris: Dalloz, 2005). Hafiz is general counsel of the GMP.

13. *Caffé Europa*, numero speciale, July 19, 2003.

14. "Les appels à la 'guerre sainte' n'ont aucune chance d'être entendus en France" ["Calls to Holy War have no chance of being heeded in France"], *Le Monde*, October 14–15, 2001.

15. Hakim El ghissassi, "Entretien avec Dr. Dalil Boubakeur" ["Interview with Dr. Dalil Boubakeur"], *L'Economiste* (Morocco), March 1, 2005.

16. "Pour un rapprochement judéo-musulman" ["For a Judeo-Muslim rapprochement"], *Tribune Juive*, March 28, 2003.

17. Roland Jacquard, *Fatwa contre l'occident* [*A Fatwa against the West*] (Paris: Broché, 1998), p. 105.

18. Jo Johnson, "Lunch with the FT: Dr. Dalil Boubakeur," *Financial Times*, March 28, 2003.

19. Quoted in Marie-France Etchegoin and Serge Raffy, "La vérité sur l'islam en France" ["The truth about Islam in France"], *Nouvel Observateur,* February 2–8, 2006.

20. El ghissassi, "Entretien avec Dr. Dalil Boubakeur" ["Interview with Dr. Dalil Boubakeur"].

21. "Islam des banlieues, islam des excités" ["The Islam of the *banlieue* is the Islam of the overexcited"], *Vingt minutes,* October 18, 2002.

22. *Caffé Europa*, numero speciale, July 19, 2003.

23. Hafiz, "Quel rôle joue la Grande Mosquée de Paris au CFCM?" ["What role does the GMP play in the CFCM?"].

24. Jacques Fortier, "Elections du CFCM: Dalil Boubakeur en campagne" ["CFCM elections: Dalil Boubakeur on the campaign trail"] *Dernières Nouvelles d'Alsace*, June 17, 2005.

25. Patrick Haenni, "France and Its Muslims: Riots, Jihadism, and Depoliticisation," *Europe Report no. 172* (Brussels: International Crisis Group, March 2006).

26. The UOIF emerged from the Groupement Islamique de France (Islamic Group of France), itself a result of splintering with the Association des Etudiants Islamiques de France (AEIF) (French Association of Islamic Students).

27. "Islam de France, a savoir" ["Things to know about Islam in France"], *Libération*, December 8, 2004.

28. Abdallah Ben Mansour (Iraq) and Mahmoud Zouheir (Tunisia); Ben Mansour is still active and now represents the "conservative wing" of the movement. Xavier Ternisien, "Les leaders viennent davantage de l'étranger que des cités" ["More leaders come from abroad than from the neighborhood"], *Le Monde*, December 12, 2002; and Xavier Ternisien, "Islam: l'UOIF conserve une ligne modérée" ["Islam: The UOIF keeps its moderate line"], *Le Monde*, September 26, 2005.

29. Ternisien, "Islam: l'UOIF conserve une ligne modérée" ["Islam: The UOIF keeps its moderate line"].

30. Xavier Ternisien, "Les associations de jeunes musulmans prennent leurs distances avec Tariq Ramadan" ["Associations of young Muslims distance themselves from Tariq Ramadan"], *Le Monde*, May 23, 2005.

31. Interview with Fouad Alaoui by the authors, June 2002.

32. See Nicolas Mombrial, "L'UOIF et l'organisation de l'Islam de France" ["The UOIF and the organization of French Islam"], April 14, 2003 (www.saphirnet.info); Xavier Ternisien, "Un budget encore très dépendant des 'généreux donateurs' du Golfe" ["A budget still very dependent on 'generous donors' from the Gulf"], *Le Monde*, December 12, 2002; "Nous ne comprenons pas pourquoi l'islam devrait se doter d'une fondation" ["We do not understand why Islam needs a foundation"], *Le Monde*, December 12, 2004; Fabrice Maulion, *L'organisation des frères musulmans: évolution historique, cartographie, et éléments d'une typologie* [*The organization of the Muslim Brotherhood: Historic evolution, cartography, and basis of a typology*] (Paris: Université Panthéon-Assas, 2004), pp. 47–48.

33. Ternisien, "Un budget encore très dépendant des 'généreux donateurs'" ["A budget still very dependent on 'generous donors'"].

34. "Islam des banlieues, islam des excités" ["The Islam of the *banlieue* is the Islam of the overexcited"].

35. "La laïcité en actes," *Le Monde*, November 25, 2003.

36. Christine Garin and Hervé Gattegno, "Bertrand Delanoë: 'Au lieu de faire des choix clairs, M. Raffarin esquive'" ["Delanoë: 'Instead of making clear choices, Raffarin dodges them'"], *Le Monde*, December 2, 2003.

37. Michel Abu Nujum, "After a Fiery Session: Election of the CFCM," *Al-Sharq Al-Awsat* (a London-based Arabic language daily), May 5, 2003; Maulion, *L'organisation des frères musulmans* [*The organization of the Muslim Brotherhood*].

38. Ternisien, "Un budget encore très dépendant des 'généreux donateurs'" ["A budget still very dependent on 'generous donors'"].

39. *Le Parisien*, February 12, 2003.

40. Hani Ramadan, "La Charia incomprise" ["The misunderstood shari'a"], *Le Monde*, September 10, 2002; the UOIF 2006 convention program is available at www.uoif-online.com/bourget2006/ramf2006.pdf.

41. Interview with Fouad Alaoui by the authors, June 2002.

42. Roger Cukierman and Fouad Alaoui, transcript of Jean-Pierre Elkabbach's radio talk show on Europe 1, June 13, 2004 (http://72.14.203.104/search?q=cache: zbq33sXR30AJ:www.upjf.org/documents/showthread.php%3Fs%3D%26thread-did%3D6879+l'émission+de+Jean-Pierre+Elkabbach+(Europe1&hl=en&gl= us&ct=clnk&cd=2&client=safari [March 21, 2006]).

43. Bechari remains president of the FNMF, but a caretaker administrator was appointed to organize an election of the administrative council while the leadership struggle continued in the courts; see Hakim El ghissassi, "Un administrateur judiciaire au sein du Conseil français du culte musulman" ["A judicial administrator at the heart of the CFCM"], April 4, 2006 (www.sezame.info).

44. Amara Bamba, "La justice condamne le président de la FNMF" ["A court finds the FNMF president guilty"], October 5, 2005 (www.saphirnet.info).

45. Bechari later announced plans to establish a theological seminary, the Institut Avicenne des Sciences Humaines (Avicenna Institute of Human Sciences) in Lille; Marie Lemonnier, "Université islamique de Lille: info ou intox ?" ["The Islamic University of Lille: Information or intoxication?"], March 23–29, 2006.

46. Xavier Ternisien, "Mohamed Bechari: VRP de l'islam de France à l'étranger" ["Mohamed Bechari: Roving ambassador of French Islam abroad"], *Le Monde,* September 22, 2004.

47. Abdallah Naanaa, "Cinq questions à Mohamed Bechari" ["Five questions for Mohamed Bechari"], *La Gazette du Maroc,* April 21, 2003.

48. El ghissassi, "Un administrateur judiciaire" ["A judicial administrator"].

49. Ayoub Lesseur was the first president and Youssef Leclerc the second.

50. Younès Alami, "L'Etat parie sur les musulmans d'origine marocaine" ["The state bets on Muslims of Moroccan origin"], *Tel Quel,* no. 101, November 15, 2003.

51. Hakim El ghissassi, "Un islam algérien 'modéré' face à un islam marocain 'intégriste'" ["A 'moderate' Algerian Islam faced with a 'fundamentalist' Moroccan Islam"], *L'Economiste,* September 19, 2004.

52. Bechari was reinstated in January 2006; Hakim El ghissassi, "France: la guerre des mosquées" ["France: Mosques at war"] March 26, 2006 (www.sezame.info); Xavier Ternisien, "L'instance représentative des musulmans est minée par de violentes querelles"["The representative body for Muslims is fraught with serious disputes"], *Le Monde,* November 24, 2005.

53. See El ghissassi, "Un islam algérien 'modéré' face à un islam marocain 'intégriste'" ["A 'moderate' Algerian Islam faced with a 'fundamentalist' Moroccan Islam"].

54. "Seule une réforme de fond de la Moudawana: Entretien de Madame Nadia Chekrouni" ["There is only one substantial reform in the Moudawana: An interview with Mrs. Nadia Chekrouni"], *La Gazette du Maroc,* July 21, 2003.

55. However, interior ministry officials have singled out FFIAAC prayer spaces in public housing for eluding association regulations and allowing their prayer rooms to be infiltrated by informal salafist groups. See Xavier Ternisien, "Mille et un jours: Chroniqe des Islams de France" ["A thousand and one days: A chronicle of the Islams of France"], *Le Monde,* June 14, 2005.

56. Xavier Ternisien, "Disparition : Mohammad Hamidullah, une figure de l'islam en France" ["Obituary for Mohammad Hamidullah, an Islamic figure in France"], *Le Monde,* December 20, 2002.

57. Thomas Lemmen, *Islamische Organisationen in Deutschland [Islamic organizations in Germany]* (Bonn: Friedrich Ebert Stiftung, 2000).

58. Dilek Zaptcioglu, "Turkey's Religion Council: Setting Guidelines for Islam and Politics," October 5, 2004 (www.qantara.de).

59. Valérie Amiraux, *Acteurs de l'islam entre Allemagne et Turquie [Islamic actors between Germany and Turkey]* (Paris: L'Harmattan, 2001).

60. Although not officially a ministry, its budget is larger than that of some ministries.

61. Brigitte Maréchal, "Mosquées, organisations, et leadership," in *Convergences Musulmanes: aspects contemporains de l'islam dans l'Europe élargie* [*Muslim convergences: Contemporary aspects of Islam in an enlarged Europe*], edited by Felice Dassetto and others (Louvain-la-Nueve: Bruylant Academia, 2001), p. 32.

62. Christiane Schlötze, "Die Türkei zwischen Islam und westlicher Moderne" ["Turkey between Islam and Western modernity"], *Frankfurter Allgemeine Zeitung*, December 19, 2001; Lemmen, *Islamische Organisationen in Deutschland* [*Islamic organizations in Germany*].

63. Antonio Missiroli and Walter Posch, "Turkey and/in the EU: The Security Dimension," Paris, EU Institute for Security Studies, September 2004.

64. Nils Feindt-Riggers and Udo Steinbach, *Islamische Organisationen in Deutschland* [*Islamic organizations in Germany*] (Hamburg: Deutsches-Orient-Institut, 1997); Dale Eickelman, "Trans-State Islam and Security," in *Transnational Religion and Fading States,* edited by Susanne Hoeber Rudolph and James Piscatori (Penn.: Westview Press, 1997), p. 33 ; Udo Ulfkotte, *Der Krieg in unseren Staedten* [*The war in our cities*] (Frankfurt: Eichborn Verlag, 2003).

65. Mustafa Yeneroglu, deputy secretary general of IGMG, interview with authors, October 2003.

66. See Ruba Salih, "The Backward and the New: National, Transnational, and Post-National Islam in Europe," *Journal of Ethnic and Migration Studies* 30 (2004).

67. Dalil Boubakeur, interview with the authors, June 2002.

68. Patrick Weil, *La France et ses étrangers: l'aventure d'une politique de l'immigration, de 1938 à nous jours* [*France and its foreigners: The adventure of immigration policy from 1938 to the present*] (Paris: Calmann-Lévy, 1991); Jocelyne Césari, *When Islam and Democracy Meet* (Basingstoke: Palgrave-Macmillan, 2006).

69. Laurie Brand, *Citizens Abroad: Emigration and the State in the Middle East and North Africa* (Cambridge University Press, 2006).

70. Zoubir Chatou and Mustafa Belbah, *Double nationalité en question* [*Double nationality under investigation*] (Paris: Karthala, 2002).

71. Adil Hmaity, "Les MRE tiennent à la politique" ["Politics is important to Moroccans residing abroad"], *La Gazette du Maroc*, August 16, 2004.

72. Chatou and Belbah, *Double nationalité en question* [*Double nationality under investigation*].

73. Ibid.; Brand, *Citizens Abroad.*

74. Besma Lahouri and Boris Thiolay, "L'argent de l'islam" ["The money of Islam"], *L'Express*, November 21, 2002.

75. "L'Algérie enquête sur le Centre Technique d'Evry" ["Algeria investigates the Technical Center at Evry"], *Africa Intelligence Maghreb Confidentiel*, no. 398, December 17, 1998.

76. "La mosquée de Paris restaurée grâce aux deniers de la France, de l'Algérie et

de l'Arabie saoudite" ["The mosque of Paris restored thanks to French, Algerian, and Saudia Arabian funds"], *La Médina*, December 2003.

77. "Enfin une mosquée à Clichy" ["Finally, a mosque in Clichy"], *Le Parisien*, May 26, 2004.

78. Sarkozy's interview in *Le Figaro*, April 30, 2003.

79. The CIF regroups between 100 and 500 imams active in France. Quotation cited in Frédéric Antoine, "Sarkozy à la rencontre des imams au Mureaux" ["Sarkozy attends meeting of imams at Mureaux"], *Le Courrier de Mantes*, April 2, 2003. On the CIF, see Frank Peter, "Training Imams and the Future of Islam in France," *ISIM Newsletter* no. 13, October 2003 (Leiden: Institute for the Study of Islam in the Modern World).

80. Ibid.

81. See Bernard Godard, "Formation des imams: état des lieux" ["The state of imam training in France"], February 16, 2005 (www.sezame.info/index.php?action=article&id_article=120635 [March 22, 2006]).

82. Etchegoin and Raffy, "La vérité sur l'islam en France" ["The truth about Islam in France"].

83. Ibid.

84. See Hakim El ghissassi, "La sécularisation de l'Islam en France" ["The secularization of Islam in France"], May 15, 2004 (www.sezame.info).

85. Xavier Ternisien, *La France des mosquées* [*The France of mosques*] (Paris: Albin Michel, 2002), p. 98.

86. Haut Conseil à l'Intégration, "L'Islam dans la République" ["Islam in the Republic"], November 2000, pp. 78–79; and Maryvonne Monfeuillard, "Migrations intérieures et extérieures et paysages religieux: le cas de la France" ["Internal and external migration and religious landscapes: The case of France"] (FIG, 2002); confidential interview with the authors, April 2006.

87. According to an RG source quoted in Etchegoin and Raffy, "La vérité sur l'islam en France" ["The truth about Islam in France"].

88. Xavier Ternisien, "Les imams de France prêchent un islam moralisateur et non belliqueux" ["French imams preach a moralizing, not a bellicose, Islam"], *Le Monde*, February 8, 2002.

89. "Pour Nicolas Sarkozy, la menace terroriste est à 'un niveau très élevé'" ["For Nicolas Sarkozy, the terrorist threat is at 'very high level'"], *Le Monde*, September 26, 2005.

90. Hadi Yahmid, "French Muslims 'Abort' Imam Deportation," August 7, 2005, *Islamonline.net*.

91. For more on the Bouziane affair, see Gilles Kepel, *Fitna: Guerre au coeur de l'Islam* [*Fitna: War at the heart of Islam*] (Paris: Flammarion, 2004).

92. His parent organization, the UOIF, issued condemnations of his speech and noted that the cassette had been immediately pulled from circulation when its contents had first become known several years earlier. See chapter 9 for further discussion.

93. "Le ministre de l'intérieur veut des imams français parlant français" ["The minister of the interior wants French imams who speak French"], *Agence France-Presse*, December 6, 2004.

94. "Dominique de Villepin évoque la formation des imams avec Dalil Boubakeur" ["Dominique de Villepin raises the issue of imam training with Dalil Boubakeur"], Yahoo News, August 1, 2005 (http://fr.news.yahoo.com/050801/5/4iw73.html).

95. Hadi Yathmid, Islam on-line, December 19, 2004 (www.islam-online.net).

96. Lemonnier, "Université islamique de Lille" ["The Islamic University of Lille"].

97. Hakim El ghissassi, "Les bizarries musulmanes" ["Strange Muslim Happenings"] May 9, 2004 (www.sezame.info). The IIIT was founded in 1981 and is headed by Taha Jaber Al Alwani. Its Saint-Ouen office is run by Mohamed Mestiri, a Tunisian with a Ph.D. from the Sorbonne who was earlier consulted by Daniel Rivet for his 2003 report on imam training for education minister Luc Ferry. For the past five years, the IIIT has held an annual dinner that is well attended by political élites. Nicolas Mom and Assmaâ Rakho Mom, "Dîner débat annuel de l'IIIT sous le signe de la laïcité" ["Annual dinner-debate of the IIIT under the banner of *laïcité*"], October 30, 2005 (www.oumma.com).

98. Adel Abdel Halim, "France Seeks Azhar Help for 'Qualifying' Imams," September 30, 2005, *Islamonline.net*.

99. Xavier Ternisien, "Enquête sur ces musulmans qui inquiètent l'islam de France" ["An investigation of the Muslims who worry French Islam"], *Le Monde*, December 13, 2002.

100. Cécilia Gabizon, "Des imams bientôt formés à Assas et à la Sorbonne" ["Imams soon will be trained at Assas and at the Sorbonne"], *Le Figaro*, December 7, 2004.

101. Hakim El ghissassi, "Un islam Gallican" ["A Gallic Islam"].

102. Berque, *Il reste un avenir*.

103. Samir Amghar, "L'UOIF et les enjeux d'une représentation nationale de l'Islam de France" ["The UOIF and the issues at stake for a national representation of French Islam"], *Eurorient*, no.12, 2002.

104. John R. Bowen, "Does French Islam Have Borders? Dilemmas of Domestication in a Global Religious Field," *American Anthropologist* 106, no. 1(2004).

105. Confidential interview with the authors, June 2002.

106. Quoted in *Le Monde*, October 14, 2003.

107. Dounia Bouzar, "Bilan et perspectives du CFCM" ["An assessment of the CFCM's past and future"], June 17, 2005 (www.saphirnet.info).

108. Jocelyne Césari, *Musulmans et Républicains* [*Muslims and Republicans*] (Paris: Complex, 1998). His brother, Hani Ramadan, was director of the Geneva Islamic Cultural Center.

109. His books include *How to Be a European Muslim* (1999); *L'Islam en Questions* [*Islam in Questions*] (2002); *Les Musulmans d'Occident et l'avenir de l'islam* [*Western Muslims and the Future of Islam*] (2003)].

110. Tariq Ramadan, *Les Musulmans dans la Laïcité* [*Muslims in a Secular Society*] (Lyon: Tawhid, 1994).

111. Tariq Ramadan,"Europeanization of Islam or Islamization of Europe?" in *Islam, Europe's Second Religion*, edited by Shireen Hunter (Washington: CSIS/ Praeger, 2002), pp. 209–10.

112. Shahanaaz Habib, "Dr. Tariq Ramadan: Viewing Islam from All Angles," *The Star* (Malaysia), July 27, 2003.

113. Bénédicte Suzan and Jean Marc Dreyfus, "Muslims and Jews in France: Communal Conflict in a Secular State," U.S.-France Analysis Series, Brookings, March 2004.

114. Bruno Jeudy and Myriam Lévy, "Le débat Sarkozy-Ramadan irrite l'Elysée" ["The Sarkozy-Ramadan debate irritates the Elysée"], *Le Parisien*, November 19, 2003.

115. Boyer, *L'islam en France* [*Islam in France*].

116. Ibid., p. 202.

117. Ian Hamel, "Tariq Ramadan: 'J'ai reçu le soutien du PEN American Center présidé par Salman Rushdie'" ["Tariq Ramadan: 'I've received the support of the PEN American Center led by Salman Rushdie'"], January 30, 2006 (www.oumma.com).

118. Tariq Ramadan, "Who is responsible for the attacks of July 7?" *Al-Sharq al-Awsat* (London-based Arabic language daily), July 21, 2005; see also "Tariq Ramadan zu Muslimen in Europa und den Anschlägen in London" ["Tariq Ramadan on Muslims in Europe and the attacks in London"], MEMRI Special Dispatch, August 3 2005.

119. Habib, "Dr. Tariq Ramadan: Viewing Islam from All Angles."

120. Tariq Ramadan, "Réponse à Alexandre Adler" ["Response to Alexandre Adler"], *Le Figaro*, October 29, 2003.

121. See, for example, Caroline Fourest, *Frère Tariq* [*Brother Tariq*] (Paris: Grasset, 2004).

122. Bouzar, "Bilan et perspectives du CFCM" ["An assessment of the CFCM's past and future"].

123. Nina Fürstenberg, "Soheib Bencheikh: Primo, separare Islam e politica" ["Soheib Bencheikh: First, separate Islam and politics"] Caffe Europa, *Reset*, no. 76, July 19, 2003.

124. Ternisien, *La France des mosquées* [*The France of mosques*].

125. Henri Tincq, "Soheib Bencheikh: 'Ou l'islam marche avec son siècle, ou il reste à la marge de la société moderne'"["Soheib Bencheikh: 'Either Islam marches in step with the century or it stays on the margins of modern society'"], *Le Monde*, November 20, 2001.

126. Soheib Bencheikh, *Marianne et le Prophète* [*Marianne and the Prophet*] (Paris: Bernard Grasset, 1998).

127. Caffe Europa, *Reset*, no. 76.

128. Soheib Bencheikh, "Ceux qui ne comprennent ni l'islam ni la liberté" ["Those who understand neither Islam nor freedom"], *Le Monde*, February 10, 2006.

129. Ternisien, *La France des mosquées* [*The France of mosques*].

130. The IAMS was created in July 2004, with Al Qaradawi as president; the founding statement described the associations' objectives as follows: "to preserve the identity

of the Islamic nation . . . to counter the destructive currents that want to change the identity of the nation and also to counter even the inner currents that seek to change the nature of Islam and make of it a religion of violence." See Ali Al Halawani, "Scholars launch pan-Islamic body," July 12, 2004 (http://www.islamonline.net/English/News/2004-07/12/article01.shtml).

131. See "Six enseignements à tirer des derniers événements subis par la communauté" ["Six lessons to learn from the recent events experienced by the community"], June 27, 2003 (www.islamiya.info/).

132. Jean-Marie Montali and others, "L'histoire secrète d'une libération," *Le Figaro*, December 24, 2004.

133. Ian Hamel, "Yusef Al Qaradawi: 'le ministre français des Affaires étrangères m'a félicité après la libération de Florence Aubenas" ["Yusef Al Qaradawi: 'The French foreign minister congratulated me after the liberation of Florence Aubenas'"], September 26, 2005 (www.oumma.com).

134. "Leading Sunni Sheikh Yousef Al-Qaradawi and Other Sheikhs Herald the Coming Conquest of Rome," MEMRI Report No. 447, December 6, 2002.

135. Alexandre Caero, "The European Council for Fatwa and Research," Fourth Mediterranean Social and Political Research Meeting, European University Institute, Florence, 2003; Ahmed Jaballah, "Le Conseil européen de la fatwa: Adapter la pratique musulmane au contexte occidental" ["The European Council for Fatwa and Research: Adapting Muslim practice to the Western context"], in *L'avenir de l'Islam en France et en Europe*, edited by Michel Wieviorka (Paris: Balland, 2003), p. 210. Jaballah is a member of the ECFR.

136. European Council for Fatwa and Research, *Recueil de fatwas* [*Collection of fatwas*] (Lyon: Tawhid, 2002), with a preface and commentary by Tariq Ramadan.

137. Martin van Bruinessen, "Making and Unmaking Muslim Religious Authority in Western Europe," Fourth Mediterranean Social and Political Research Meeting, Florence, March 2003.

138. Ibid.

139. "L'UOIF dément s'être opposée à la parution d'un recueil de fatwas" ["The UOIF denies having opposed the publication of a collection of fatwas"], May 24, 2005 (www.saphirnet.info); "La souveraineté sur Jérusalem doit être islamique" ["Sovereignty over Jerusalem must be Islamic"], *Le Monde*, May 24, 2005.

140. John R. Bowen, "Does French Islam Have Borders? Dilemmas of Domestication in a Global Religious Field," *American Anthropologist*, 106, no. 1 (March 2004): 43–55.

141. Olivier Roy, *Globalized Islam* (Columbia University Press, 2004), p. 21.

Chapter 5

1. Didier Beyens, *L'alchimie de la médiation musulmane* [*The alchemy of Muslim representation*] (Paris: La Médina, 2001).

2. See Jonathan Laurence, "Knocking on Europe's Door: Islam in Italy," *Europe Analysis Brief* (Brookings, March 2006).

3. The history of political negotiations and the institutional design of Islamic councils that took shape during the second period of incorporation (1989–2004) are reconstructed in this chapter using material from forty-eight interviews with bureaucrats, politicians, and religious community leaders conducted by the authors in France from 2000 to 2003.

4. Jacques Berque, *Il reste un avenir: entretiens avec Jean Sur* [*There is still a future: Interviews with Jean Sur*] (Paris: Arléa, 1993), p. 203.

5. Angel M. Rabasa and others, eds., *The Muslim World after 9/11* (RAND, 2004); Cheryl Benard, *Civil Democratic Islam: Partners, Resources, and Strategies* (RAND, 2003); Timothy M. Savage, "Europe and Islam: Crescent Waxing, Cultures Clashing," *Washington Quarterly* 27 (Summer 2004): 25–50.

6. Cited in Guilain Denoeux, "The Forgotten Swamp: Navigating Political Islam," *Middle East Policy* 9 (June 2002): p.80.

7. The law did not apply to France's overseas departments and territories. The French colonial administration in Algeria used religion as an instrument of social control, selecting friendly imams and withholding support from unofficial prayer spaces, a practice not unlike that of the Turkish system today. A decree issued in the *départements* of Algeria (two years after the 1905 law) put imams under state training and employment, viewing them as foot soldiers of France's secularization project and overall "civilizing"mission. Later on, the French created a Conseil Supérieur Islamique and even put religious organizations in charge of some aspects of civil administration. See Haut Conseil à l'intégration, "L'Islam dans la République" ["Islam in the Republic"], November 2000, p. 17.

8. See Alain Boyer, *L'Islam en France* [*Islam in France*] (Paris: Presses Universitaires de France, 1998).

9. See "Discours de Jacques Chirac" ["Speech by Jacques Chirac"], July 3, 2003 (www.elysee.fr).

10. Edgar Morin, "Le trou noir de la laïcité" ["The black hole of laïcité"], *Le Débat*, no. 58 (1990), p. 38.

11. See U.S. Department of State, Bureau of Democracy, Human Rights, and Labor, "International Religious Freedom Report: France" (2002) (www.state.gov/g/drl/rls/irf).

12. Marie-Claude Decamps and Henri Tincq, "Jacques Chirac assure le pape de la fidélité de la France" ["Jacques Chirac assures the pope of France's loyalty"], *Le Monde*, January 25, 1996; William Safran, "Ethnoreligious Politics in France: Jews and Muslims," *West European Politics* 27 (May 2004): 423–51.

13. "La mise en berne des drapeaux en France pour la mort du pape crée un début de polémique" ["The flying of French flags at half mast for the death of the pope creates a debate"], *Le Monde*, April 4, 2005.

14. Marie-France Etchegoin and Serge Raffy, "La vérité sur l'islam en France" ["The truth about Islam in France"], *Nouvel Observateur,* February 2–8, 2006.

15. This region was annexed by Germany between 1871 and 1918 and again from 1940 to 1944; it thus escaped the effects of the 1905 law. Only three administrative departments—Haut Rhin, Bas Rhin, and Moselle—retain the Napoleonic Concordat of 1801.

16. Ridha Kéfi, "Dieu, la femme, et le cadi" ["God, woman, and the Cadi"], *Jeune Afrique l'Intelligente*, July 13, 2003.

17. Patrick Weil, *La France et ses étrangers: L'aventure d'une politique de l'immigration de 1938 à nos jours* [*France and its foreigners: The adventure of immigration policy from 1938 to the present day*] (Paris: Gallimard, 1995).

18. Boyer, *L'Islam en France* [*Islam in France*].

19. Interview with Mouloud Aounit, president of the MRAP and a member of the French Communist Party, in *Le Nouvel Observateur*, October 15, 2003.

20. Olivier Roy, *L'Islam Globalisé* [*Globalized Islam*] (Paris: Seuil, 2002), p.117.

21. Alain Billon, "Les fondements idéologiques et les choix de la consultation" ["The ideological foundation and the choices made in the consultations with Islam"], *French Politics, Culture, and Society* 23, no.1 (Spring 2005).

22. See chapter 3. Jean-Marc Leclerc, Guillaume Tabard, and Jean de Belot, "Interview: Corse, sécurité, islam, les vérités de Sarkozy" ["Interview: Corsica, security, Islam, Sarkozy's truths], *Le Figaro*. September 18, 2003

23. Josette Alia and Carole Barjon, "Le ministre de l'Intérieur intervient dans le débat sur le voile: 'Ce que les intégristes réfusent de voir'" ["The interior minister weighs in on the headscarf debate"], *Nouvel Observateur*, October 14, 2003.

24. See Boyer, *L'Islam en France* [*Islam in France*], and Thomas Deltombe, *L'Islam imaginaire* [*Imaginary Islam*] (Paris: La Découverte, 2006).

25. Glenn R. Simpson and John Carreyrou, "Saudi Rulers Were Told of Extremism Funding," *Wall Street Journal*, January 13, 2004; Nicolas Beau, *Paris: Capitale Arabe* [*Paris: An Arab capital*] (Paris: Seuil, 1995), p. 241.

26. See Boyer, *L'Islam en France* [*Islam in France*].

27. The total number of members eventually reached twenty; the CORIF had fifteen.

28. Billon, "Les fondements idéologiques et les choix de la consultation" ["The ideological foundation and the choices made in the consultations with Islam"].

29. Yannick Blanc, speaking at a conference on "Droits, libertés, et obligations du culte musulman en France à l'aube du XXIe siècle" ["Rights, freedoms, and obligations of the Muslim religion in France at the dawn of the twenty-first century"], Les amis de La Médina et Institut de l'Islam et des Sociétés du Monde Musulman, Ecole des Hautes études en Sciences Sociales, Paris, December 2004.

30. Prayer spaces were assigned one "grand elector" per hundred square meters (area of the sanctuary plus 20 percent of the rest of the space), except great mosques and prayer spaces larger than 800 square meters, which received fifteen grand electors each; the Great Mosque of Paris was assigned eighteen grand electors. In 2005, there were 5,219 delegates representing 1,221 prayer spaces; see Martine de Sauto, "Le Conseil du culte musulman mûrit" ["The Council of the Muslim Religion matures"], *La Croix*, June 20, 2005.

31. Xavier Ternisien, "Dalil Boubakeur a été réélu président du CFCM" ["Dalil Boubakeur has been reelected president of the CFCM"], *Le Monde*, June 26, 2005; Amara Bamba, "CFCM: le faux suspense présidentiel" ["CFCM: The fake suspense over the president"], June 26, 2005 (www.saphirnet.info).

32. Xavier Ternisien, "La Grande Mosquée de Paris demande un nouveau report des élections au Conseil français du culte musulman" ["The GMP asks for another postponement of CFCM elections"], *Le Monde*, May 11, 2002.

33. Interview with Nicolas Sarkozy in *La Médina*, October 2002.

34. Interview with Nicolas Sarkozy in *Le Nouvel Observateur*, October 14, 2003.

35. Xavier Ternisien, "Accord sur la composition du futur Conseil du culte musulman" ["Agreement on the composition of the future CFCM"], *Le Monde*, December 20, 2002.

36. Xavier Ternisien, "Les représentants des musulmans de France se sont mobilisés pour renouveler leurs dirigeants" ["The representatives of French Muslims mobilize to reelect their leaders"], *Le Monde*, June 19, 2005.

37. Catherine Coroller, "Redistribution des cartes au Conseil du culte musulman" ["Reshuffing the cards at the Council of the Muslim Religion"], *Libération*, June 20, 2005.

38. Xavier Ternisien, "Tractations secrètes avant la formation des bureaux régionaux" ["Secret negotiations before the formation of the CRCM"], *Le Monde*, May 21, 2003; Catherine Coroller, "Election contestée au conseil du culte musulman d'Alsace" ["Contested election at the CRCM of Alsace"], *Libération*, June 29, 2005; Hakim El ghissassi, "Conseil français du culte musulman: les véritables enjeux" ["The real issues in the CFCM"], June 27, 2005 (www.sezame.info).

39. In 2005, the number of seats won by the UOIF decreased from thirteen to ten. See Martine de Sauto, "Le Conseil du culte musulman mûrit" ["The Council of the Muslim Religion matures"].

40. Interview with Nicolas Sarkozy, *La Médina*, October 2002; "Islam's secret diplomacy in France," *Africa Intelligence*, no. 556, April 16, 2002.

41. See Hakim El ghissassi, "Un islam Gallican: Entretien avec Bruno Etienne" ["French Islam: Interview with Bruno Etienne"], September 15, 2004 (www.sezame.info).

42. Marie-Christine Tabet and others, "Entretien: Le ministre de l'Intérieur dévoile le projet présenté ce matin en Conseil des ministres" ["Interview: The interior minister unveils the project presented this morning in the Council of Ministers"], *Le Figaro*, April 30, 2003.

43. Michèle Tribalat and Jeanne-Hélène Kaltenbach, *La République et l'Islam* [*The Republic and Islam*] (Paris: Gallimard, 2002).

44. Aslam Timol and others, "L'imposition de l'état?" ["Imposed by the state?"], *French Politics, Culture, and Society*, vol. 23, no. 1 (Spring 2005).

45. Tabet and others, "Entretien: Le ministre de l'Intérieur dévoile le projet" ["Interview: The interior minister unveils the project"].

46. Interview with Bernard Godard in *France–Pays Arabes*, no. 274, (October 2001).

47. Interview with Nicolas Sarkozy, *La Médina*, October 2002.

48. Hakim El ghissassi, "La fondation des œvres de l'islam de France: aménagement, entretien, et construction des lieux de cultes musulmans" ["French Foundation for Muslim Works: Development, maintenance, and construction of Muslim prayer spaces"], March 20, 2005 (www.sezame.info).

49. "La Fondation des oeuvres de l'islam de France reconnue d'utilité publique" ["The French Foundation for Muslim Works recognized as a public entity"], Agence France-Presse, July 27, 2005.

50. Jean-Louis Debré, *En mon for intérieur* [*In my heart of hearts*] (Paris: Jean-Claude Lattès, 1997).

51. Hakim El ghissassi, "Viande halal: un gros marché en Europe" ["Halal meat: A large market in Europe"], *L'Economiste*, December 16, 2004.

52. Xavier Ternisien, "Trois responsables régionaux critiquent le CFCM et déplorent les divisions" ["Three regional representatives criticize the CFCM and denounce its divisions"], *Le Monde*, June 19, 2005.

53. Hakim El ghissassi, "Le CFCM, un an après: quel bilan des commissions thématiques?" ["The CFCM one year later: What are the results of the thematic working groups?"], May 13, 2004 (www.sezame.info).

54. There are just sixty-nine chaplains in place for Muslims—who are thought to account for more than half of France's (relatively small) prison population of 60,000 (see chapter 1)—compared with 513 Catholic chaplains, 267 Protestant chaplains, sixty-four Jewish chaplains, and three Orthodox Christian chaplains. Conseil d'Etat, *Rapport Public: Réfléctions sur la laïcité* [*Public Report: Reflections on laïcité*] (Paris: March 2004), p. 315.

55. Craig S. Smith, "Islam in Jail: Europe's Neglect Breeds Angry Radicals," *New York Times*, December 8, 2004.

56. Xavier Ternisien, *La France des mosquées* [*The France of mosques*] (Paris: Albin Michel, 2002), p. 95.

57. Xavier Ternisien, "Deux aumôniers musulmans des prisons au lieu d'un seul" ["Two Muslim chaplains in the prisons instead of just one"], *Le Monde,* March 17, 2006.

58. Hakim El ghissassi, "Viande halal" ["Halal meat"]; also Hakim El ghissassi, "La viande halal: la face cachée" ["The hidden side of halal meat"], special issue of *La Médina*, no. 5, October 2000; Besma Lahouri and Boris Thiolay, "L'argent de l'islam" ["The money of Islam"], *L'Express*, November 21, 2002.

59. Hadi Yahmid, "France Issues Hajj Guide, Media Showing Interest," December 17, 2005 (http://islamonline.net/English/News/2005-12/17/article06.shtml); Hakim El ghissassi, "Organiser le pèlerinage de 21,000 citoyens français musulmans" ["Organizing the pilgrimage for 21,000 French Muslims"], January 12, 2005 (www.sezame. info); Ternisien, *La France des mosquées*, p. 104.

60. El ghissassi, "Un islam Gallican."

61. Xavier Ternisien, "Vingt mille musulmans de France s'apprêtent à partir pour le traditionnel pèlerinage de La Mecque" ["Twenty thousand French Muslims get

ready to leave for the traditional pilgrimage to Mecca"], *Le Monde*, December 29, 2004; Yahmid, "France Issues Hajj Guide."

62. Luc Bronner and Piotr Smolar, "Quand les 'frères' musulmans tentent de ramener le calme" ["When Muslim 'brothers' try to bring calm"], *Le Monde*, November 2, 2005; Catherine Coroller, "Le silence assourdissant du CFCM dans les banlieues" ["The deafening silence of the CFCM in the banlieue"], *Libération*, November 19, 2005; Patrick Haenni, "France and Its Muslims: Riots, Jihadism, and Depoliticisation," *Europe Report* no. 172 (Brussels: International Crisis Group, March 2006).

63. Amélie Gautier, "Jean-Pierre Raffarin charge le Conseil français du culte musulman d'un 'rôle modérateur auprès des jeunes'" ["Raffarin gives the CFCM a 'moderating role among young people'"], *Le Monde*, May 5, 2003.

64. See Aurore Vidal and Houda Bouali, "Elections aux enjeux locaux" ["Elections on local issues"], April 14, 2003 (www.saphirnet.info).

65. Interview with Nicolas Sarkozy, *Le Figaro*, September 10, 2003.

66. Catherine Coroller, "Sarkozy presse l'islam de s'unir avant l'été" ["Sarkozy presses Muslims to unite before summer"], *Le Figaro*, January 10, 2003.

67. Catherine Coroller, "Clash au sein du futur Conseil du culte musulman" ["Clash in the heart of the future Council of the Muslim Religion"], *Le Figaro*, February 7, 2003.

68. Debate at conference on "Le Conseil Français du Culte Musulman: Quel rôle pour l'état et la société civile?" ["The French Council of the Muslim Religion: What role for the state and civil society?"], Institut d'Etudes Politiques, November 24, 2003.

69. Xavier Ternisien, "Les représentants musulmans appellent au 'calme' et à la 'dignité'" ["Muslim representatives appeal for 'calm and 'dignity'"], *Le Monde*, March 21, 2003.

70. Jean-Pierre Chevènement, interview with the authors, November 23, 2003.

71. Cécilia Gabizon, "Islam de France: le chantage de l'UOIF avant les élections de juin" ["French Islam: The UOIF's blackmail before June's elections"], *Le Figaro*, May 23, 2005; Cécilia Gabizon, "Le gouvernement recule sur l'aumônier musulman des prisons" ["The government takes a step back on the Muslim chaplain in prisons"], *Le Figaro*, May 12, 2005.

72. Xavier Ternisien, "Islam: l'UOIF conserve une ligne modérée" ["Islam: The UOIF keeps its moderate line"], *Le Monde*, September 26, 2005.

73. *Islam Hebdo*, no.10, October 2004.

74. Coroller, "Redistribution des cartes" ["Reshuffling the cards"].

75. "En France, 'Charlie Hebdo' s'engage dans la polémique sur les caricatures de Mahomet" ["In France, the magazine *Charlie Hebdo* gets involved in the debate over the caricatures of Mohammed"], *Le Monde*, February 8, 2006; see "Petition Nationale" at http://www.contre-islamophobie.com/.

76. Cécilia Gabizon, "Tokia Saïfi: 'Donner des gages à la société française'" ["Tokia Saïfi: 'Make pledges to French society'"], *Le Figaro*, October 25, 2003.

77. Rabah Ait-Hamadouche, "La nouvelle instance, dont on ignore souvent le fonctionnement, est un sujet qui fâche parmi les fidèles" ["The new organization,

whose workings are unknown by many, is a touchy subject among the faithful"], *Le Figaro*, November 4, 2003.

78. Interview with Nicolas Sarkozy in *Le Nouvel Observateur*, October 14, 2003.

79. Dounia Bouzar, "Démission de Dounia Bouzar au CFCM" ["Dounia Bouzar's resignation"] (www.oumma.com, January 3, 2005 [www.oumma.com/article.php3?id_article=1331]).

80. Piotr Smolar and Xavier Ternisien, "Le ministre de l'intérieur souhaite faire émerger une instance représentative d'un 'islam laïque'" ["The interior minister would like to help create a representative organization for 'lay Islam'"], *Le Monde*, December 6, 2004.

81. Hamlaoui Mekachera, "A propos de l'islam français" ["On French Islam"], *Le Monde*, October 23, 2001.

82. *Islam*, no. 4, February 2003.

83. See Mohammed Colin, "Jacques Chirac a fait le mauvais choix" ["Jacques Chirac made the wrong choice"], December 19, 2003 (www.saphirnet.info).

84. IPSOS poll of 523 Muslims, April 1–3, 2003, commissioned by *Le Figaro*.

85. Department of State, "French Muslims Favor Integration into French Society," Opinion Analysis M-58-05, Office of Research, May 24, 2005 (conducted by French polling firm IFOP in February 2005).

86. Interview with Hakim El ghissassi, "Il y a une institutionnalisation des differents cultes" ("There is an institutionalization of several religions"], *Libération*, May 29, 2004.

Chapter 6

1. The final text of the law (Loi no. 2004-228) was adopted on March 15, 2004 (www.senat.fr/dossierleg/pjl03-209.html).

2. See John R. Bowen, *Why the French Don't Like Headscarves* (Princeton University Press, 2006, forthcoming).

3. Pierre Bourdieu, "Un problème peut en cacher un autre" ["One problem can hide another"], in *Interventions, 1961–2001: Science sociale et action politique* [*Interventions, 1961–2001: Social science and political action*] (Marseille: Agone, 2002).

4. Eugen Weber, *From Peasants into Frenchmen* (Stanford University Press, 1976).

5. Pierre-Henri Tavoillot, quoted in Nicolas Weill, "Les relations états-églises convergent en Europe" ["State-church relations converge in Europe"], *Le Monde*, February 14, 2005.

6. See Ministère de l'Education Nationale, Jeunesse, et Sports [Ministry of National Education, Youth, and Sports], *Circulaire* of December 12, 1989; and Conseil d'Etat [Council of State], *Décret* no. 91-173 of February 18, 1991, "relatif aux droits et obligations des élèves dans les établissements publics locaux d'enseignement du second degré"["concerning the rights and obligations of students in public secondary schools"].

7. Robert O'Brien and Bernard Stasi, *The Stasi Report: The Report of the Committee of Reflection on the Application of the Principle of Secularity in the Republic* (Buffalo, N.Y.: Hein, 2004).

8. Vianney Sevaistre, "Les relations entre le Conseil Français du Culte Musulman (CFCM) et l'état: Quelle nature?" ["Relations between the CFCM and the state: Of what nature"], *French Politics, Culture, and Society* 23, no.1 (Spring 2005).

9. Interview with Hanifa Cherifi, "La guerre du voile n'aura pas lieu" ["There will be no war over the headscarf"], *Nouvel Observateur Hebdo*, no. 1671, November 14, 1996; "Il n'y a que 150 cas conflictuels, selon la médiatrice de l'éducation nationale" ["There were only 150 conflict cases, according to the national educational mediator"], *Le Monde*, May 9, 2003.

10. Patrick Weil, "Why French Secularism Needs to Adapt: the Experts' Recommendations and the Ban of Religious Symbols in Schools," Harvard University, Minda de Gunzburg Center for European Studies, May 10, 2004.

11. Dounia Bouzar, *L'Islam des banlieues: Les prédicateurs musulmans: nouveaux travailleurs sociaux?* [Islam of the banlieue: Are Muslim preachers the new social workers?] (Paris: Syros, 2001).

12. Comuniqué du CFCM [CFCM press release], October 11–12, 2003; see Sévaistre, "Les relations entre le CFCM et l'état ["Relations between the CFCM and the state"]; Amélie Gautier, "'Pas de conflit inutile' sur le foulard" ["'No futile conflict' over the headscarf"], *Le Monde*, May 6, 2003.

13. See Commission de Reflexion sur l'Application du Principe de Laïcité dans la République [Stasi Commission], *Rapport au President de la République* [*Report to the President of the Republic*], December 11, 2003 (http://lesrapports.ladocumentation-francaise.fr/BRP/034000725/0000.pdf).

14. The government, however, was not insensitive to potential repercussions in the Muslim world: Nicolas Sarkozy met with Sheikh Mohamed Sayyed Tantawi of Cairo's Al Azhar University in December 2003 to receive the sheikh's tacit approval for the French legislation. Subhy Mujahid, "French Women Can Remove Hijab if Forced: Tantawi," December 30, 2003, *Islamonline.net*.

15. Several members have since announced their partial regrets, and even the commission's defenders acknowledged its faults, such as lack of time and resources and the imposition of a politically determined timeline. For an example of the latter, see Patrick Weil, "Lifting the Veil," *French Politics, Culture, and Society* 22, no. 3 (Fall 2004).

16. Christine Garin, "La Ville de Paris embarrassée par le cas d'une assistante sociale voilée" ["The city of Paris embarrassed by the case of a veiled social worker"], *Le Monde*, October 14, 2004.

17. Thierry Portes, "Juppé: 'La force d'une loi sera nécessaire'" ["Juppé: 'The force of a new law will be necessary'"], *Le Figaro*, October 28, 2003.

18. Claire de Galembert and Nikola Tietze, "Institutionalisierung des Islam in Deutschland" ["The institutionalization of Islam in Germany"], *Mittelweg* 36 (January 2002).

19. Patrick Weil, "Lifting the Veil."

20. Laetitia van Eeckhout, "L'exclusion de trois élèves Sikhs devant le tribunal administrative" ["The expulsion of three Sikh students comes before the administrative tribunal"], *Le Monde*, March 14, 2005; Luc Bronner, Xavier Ternisien, and Jacques Fortier, "Les signes religeux ostensibles ont pratiquement disparu des écoles" ["Conspicuous religious symbols have practically disappeared from schools"], *Le Monde*, September 29, 2005.

21. Xavier Ternisien, "Des organisations musulmans évoquent 806 'victimes'" ["Muslim organizations evoke 806 'victims'"], *Le Monde*, March 14, 2005.

22. Bronner, Ternisien, and Fortier, "Les signes religeux ostensibles ont pratiquement disparu des écoles" ["Conspicuous religious symbols have practically disappeared from schools"].

23. Ternisien, "Des organisations musulmans évoquent 806 'victimes'" ["Muslim organizations evoke 806 'victims'"].

24. "Une délégation du CFCM reçue par les oulemas à Bagdad" ["The Ulema in Baghdad receives a CFCM delegation"], Agence France-Presse, September 3, 2004.

25. Bruno Etienne, "La France en Otage" ["France held hostage"], *Le Monde*, September 6, 2004.

26. Simon Schwarzfuchs, *Napoleon, the Jews, and the Sanhedrin* (Boston: Routledge and Kegan Paul, 1979).

27. Haydée Saberan, "Le lycée musulman de Lille autorisé à ouvrir ses portes" ["The Muslim high school in Lille is authorized to open"], *Libération*, July 11, 2003; Dalil Kenz, "Le premier lycée musulman à Lille en 2003" ["The first Muslim high school in Lille in 2003"], *Le Figaro*, December 11, 2002.

28. See Muhammad Mahdi Othman, "Akef," MEMRI Brief no. 655, February 4, 2004 (www.alwihdah.com/view.asp?cat=3&id=50).

29. Thierry Portes, "Sarkozy consulte le Cheikh d'al Azhar" ["Sarkozy consults the sheikh of Al Azhar"], *Le Figaro*, December 24, 2003.

30. "Le Préfet de Seine-Saint-Denis exclut les femmes voilées de la cérémonie de remise des décrets de naturalization" ["The prefect of Seine-Saint-Denis excludes veiled women from a naturalization ceremony"], *Le Monde*, December 21, 2004. Catherine Coroller, "Une barbe en trop à la piscine de Villemomble" ["One beard too many at the Villemomble city pool"], *Libération*, March 22, 2004.

31. Hakim El ghissassi, "'Ce n'est pas aux autres de réfléchir à notre place': Entretien avec Fouad Alaoui" ["'It is not up to others to think in our place': Interview with Fouad Alaoui"], February 15, 2005 (www.sezame.info).

32. Fouad Alaoui, "Des conditions de l'intégration de l'Islam dans le cadre républicain" ["Conditions for the integration of Islam in a republican framework"], Discours au Vingt-deuxième Rencontre Annuelle des Musulmans de France [Speech at the Twenty-Second Annual Meeting of French Muslims], March 26, 2005.

33. Gérard Courtois, "Les blessures de la colonisation" ["The wounds of colonization"], *Le Monde*, January 20, 2006.

Chapter 7

1. One exception was the creation of the Fonds d'Action Social (FAS) (Social Action Fund) in 1959 and its subsidiary agencies, whose cultural activities were actually aimed at facilitating the eventual "return" of migrant families to their homelands. The FAS is now known as the Fonds d'Action et de Soutien a l'Intégration et à la Lutte contre les Discriminations (FASILD) (Support Fund for Integration and the Fight against Discrimination).

2. See Dominique Decherf, "French Views of Religious Freedom," U.S-France Analysis, Brookings, July 2001, and Erik Bleich, "Race Policy in France," U.S.-France Analysis, Brookings, May 2001 (www.brook.edu/fp/cusf/analysis/).

3. Michèle Tribalat, *Immigration et intégration: L'état des savoirs* [*Immigration and integration: What we know*] (Paris: Institut national d'études démographiques, 1992); François Héran, *Immigration, marché du travail, intégration* [Immigration, the job market, and integration] (Paris: La Documentation française, 2002).

4. Xavier Serre, "Le recensement est reporté" ["The census is postponed"], *Les Nouvelles Calédoniennes,* July 28, 2003.

5. Jonah Levy, *Toqueville's Revenge: State, Society, and Economy in Contemporary France* (Harvard University Press, 1999), p. 10.

6. Béatrice Gurrey, "Jacques Chirac a choisi son 'préfet issu de l'immigration'" ["Jacques Chirac has selected his 'prefect of immigrant origin'"], *Le Monde,* January 10, 2004.

7. However, faced with inadequate funding, Saïfi eventually resigned in June 2004 and reclaimed her seat in the European Parliament (in Strasbourg and Brussels), where she had previously been elected in 1999 as a member of the Liste Madelin, a small political party under the leadership of Alain Madelin, a member of Parliament. One year later, Prime Minister Dominique de Villepin named Azouz Begag, a novelist and sociologist born in Lyon to Algerian parents, as deputy minister for promotion and equal opportunity in his June 2005 cabinet.

8. Jean-Pierre Raffarin, *Pour une nouvelle gouvernance* [*For a new governance*] (Paris: L'Archipel, 2002).

9. Christophe Deloire, "Enfants de l'immigration: Des élites à fleur de peau" ["Children of immigration: The new elites"], *Le Point* (www.lepoint.fr/france/document.html?did=159284).

10. Previous leaders of SOS Racisme, like Harlem Désir and Fodé Sylla, had been sent to the European Parliament on Socialist Party lists in the 1990s.

11. Jean-Pierre Raffarin, interview with Radio Orient on the occasion of Aïd el-Fitr, December 5, 2002 (www.radioorient.com/audio.html?open=raffarin_20021206).

12. François Mitterrand, the Socialist Party president of France from 1981 to 1995, had avoided such an acknowledgment; however, Lionel Jospin, the Socialist Party prime minister from 1997 to 2002, oversaw a large-scale effort through the Mattéoli Commission to indemnify French Jews and the Jewish community for their losses.

13. Prime minister's speech at the inauguration of the High Council for Integration (www.premier-ministre.gouv.fr/fr/p.cfm?ref=36457 [October 24, 2002]).

14. Interview with Jacques Chirac by the Association des Amis d'Alexandre Dumas, April 10, 2002 (www.elysee.fr/elysee/elysee.fr/francais/interventions/interviews_articles_de_presse_et_interventions_televisees./2002/avril/interview_de_m_jacques_chirac_president_de_la_republique_par_des_membres_des_amis_d_alexandre_dumas.1584.html).

15. Speech by Jacques Chirac upon the transfer of Alexandre Dumas's ashes into the Pantheon, Paris, November 30, 2002 (www.elysee.fr/documents/discours/2002/021130DU.html).

16. Patrick Roger, "Une République métissée" ["A mixed Republic"], *Le Monde*, July 12, 2003.

17. This built on two earlier laws: the Pleven law (1972), against racism, and the Gayssot law (1991); see Erik Bleich, *Race Policies in France and Britain* (Cambridge University Press, 2003); and Erik Bleich, "Antiracism and Policy in a 'Color-Blind' State," *French Politics, Culture, and Society* 18, no. 3 (2000).

18. Known as the Parcours d'Accès à la Fonction Publique Territoriale, Hospitalière, et d'Etat (PACTE) [The path to public employment in land management, hospitality, and the state]. See "Entretien avec Mme. Catherine Vautrin, secrétaire d'Etat à l'intégration et à l'égalité des chances" ["Interview with Catherine Vautrin, state secretary for integration and equal opportunity"], September 2004 (www.sezame.info); "Le plan Borloo" ["The Borloo plan"], *Le Monde*, June 30, 2004.

19. For a short-term assessment of these policies, see Luc Bronner, "L'après-crise des banlieues: six mois après les promesses de M. de Villepin" ["After the crisis of the banlieues: Six months after Mr. Villepin's promises"], *Le Monde*, May 7, 2006.

20. Daniel Cohen, "Banlieues, chômage, et communautés" ["Banlieues, unemployment and communities"], *Le Monde*, January 10, 2006; Jean-Paul Fitoussi, "La France européenne" ["European France"], *Le Monde*, May 7, 2005; Jean-Paul Fitoussi, "Les banlieues, loin de l'emploi" ["The banlieues, far from jobs"], *Le Monde*, December 30, 2005.

21. Laurence Méhaignerie and Yazid Sabeg, "Les oubliés de l'égalité des chances: Participation, pluralité, assimilation . . . ou repli?" ["Those forgotten by equal opportunity: Participation, plurality, assimilation . . . or isolation?"], Institut Montaigne, January 2004.

22. "Des CV anonymes pour éviter les discriminations à l'embauche des 'minorités visibles'" ["Anonymous resumes to avoid discrimination against 'visible minorities'"], *Le Monde*, November 23, 2004.

23. "Recruteurs et employeurs sont perplexes face au CV anonyme" ["Recruiters and employers are confused by the anonymous resume"], *Le Monde*, December 2, 2004.

24. "Des initiatives pour favoriser l'égalité à l'embauche" ["Initiatives to promote equality in hiring"], *Le Monde*, October 26, 2004.

25. The first event was called the Carrefour Maghrébin au Forum Rhône-Alpes,

held in Lyon, March 8–9, 2005; the second event, called "Les Journées de la Jeunesse Marocaines" ["Moroccan Youth Days"], was organized by the Association des Marocaines aux Grandes Ecoles (Association of Moroccans at Elite Universities) and was held at the Institut du Monde Arabe [Institute of the Arab World] in Paris, April 18–20, 2006. See Salma Belabes, "Le Maroc de demain, que les compétences retournent au pays" ["The Morocco of tomorrow: May professional expertise return home"], April 22, 2006 (www.sezame.info).

26. See Dominique Versini, "Rapport sur la diversité dans la fonction publique" ["Report on diversity in public service"], presented to Renaud Dutreil, minister of public service and state reform (December 2004) (www.social.gouv.fr/htm/pointsur/discrimination/rapp_versini.htm).

27. Azouz Begag, *La République à ciel ouvert* [*The Republic in the open air*], Ministry of the Interior, December 14, 2004.

28. Patrick Weil, "Un plan pour l'égalité" ["A plan for equality"], *Le Monde*, December 13, 2004.

29. Interview with Jean-Pierre Chevènement by the authors, November 25, 2003.

30. Commission Départementale d'Accès à la Citoyenneté (CODAC) (Regional Commission for Access to Citizenship) monitored racial discrimination but with very limited means. Social Affairs Minister Martine Aubry also created the Group d'études et de lutte contre les discriminations (GELD) (Task Force on Fighting Discrimination). More important, in 1999 Chevènement rekindled the government's discussions with French Muslims to adopt a church-state framework to meet their religious needs (see chapter 5).

31. Interview with Jean-Pierre Chevènement by the authors, November 25, 2003.

32. Gurrey, "Jacques Chirac a choisi son 'préfet issu de l'immigration'" ["Jacques Chirac has selected his 'prefect of immigrant origin'"].

33. Interview with Nicolas Sarkozy in *Nouvel Observateur*, October 14, 2003.

34. Interview with Nicolas Sarkozy, *Le Parisien*, January 7, 2004.

35. Half of the board members of the Fondation pour la Mémoire were appointed by Jewish community bodies, the other half by the state.

36. Interview with Philippe Séguin, former president of the National Assembly, by the authors, December 1999.

37. See, for example, Mona Viprey, *L'insertion des jeunes d'origine étrangère* [*The integration of youth of foreign origin*] (Paris: Conseil Economique et Social, July 2002), available at www.ces.fr/rapport/doclon/02070912.PDF.

38. The law was proposed by Education Minister Alain Savary.

39. This extra subsidy amounted to 1.2 percent of the national school budget in 2004; see "Nicolas Sarkozy provoque un tollé en proposant le 'dépôt de bilan' des ZEP" ["Nicolas Sarkozy provokes a reaction by proposing an end to ZEPs"], *Le Monde*, November 30, 2005; "1,000 professeurs expérimentés dès 2006 pour les ZEP" ["One thousand experienced teachers for ZEPs beginning in 2006"], *Le Monde*, December 13, 2005.

40. Bernard Toulemonde, "La discrimination positive dans l'éducation: des ZEP à Sciences Po" ["Positive discrimination in education: From the ZEPs to Sciences Po"], *Pouvoirs*, no. 111, 2004.

41. "L'essor du '93' passe par ses écoles" ["The rise of '93' comes through its schools"], *Le Figaro*, May 10, 2004.

42. Bernard Salanié, "The Riots in France: An Economist's Perspective," Social Science Research Council Forum on Riots in France, December 15, 2005 (http://riotsfrance.ssrc.org/).

43. Toulemonde, "La discrimination positive dans l'éducation" ["Positive discrimination in education"].

44. Martine Laronche, "La violence dans les ZEP ne serait pas plus importante qu'ailleurs" ["Violence in ZEPs is no greater than elsewhere"], *Le Monde*, March 28, 2005.

45. Gwenaele Calvès, "Les politiques francaises de lutte contre le racisme, des politiques en mutation" ["French antiracism policies in transformation"], *French Politics, Culture, and Society* 18, no. 3 (2000); Gwenaele Calvès, "The Introduction of Indirect Discrimination into French Law: A Skeptical Note," in *Discrimination and Antidiscrimination Policies in Britain and France*, edited by D. Middleton and Jeanne-Pierre Révauger (Ashgate: Aldershot, 2002).

46. Interview with Richard Descoings, *Le Figaro*, November 25, 2003.

47. Toulemonde, "La discrimination positive dans l'éducation" ["Positive discrimination in education"].

48. Ibid.

49. Nathalie Savary, "Les conventions d'éducation prioritaire de Sciences Po: de la polémique aux premiers effets" ["Educational priority agreements at Sciences Po: From polemics to first results"], *Esprit*, November 2004.

50. "Conventions d' Education Prioritaire (CEP): Bilan synthétique après 4 années de mise en oeuvre" ["Educational priority agreements: The full report after four years of activity"], Sciences Po, September 2004.

51. Savary, "Les conventions d'éducation prioritaire de Sciences Po" ["Educational priority agreements at Sciences Po"].

52. The Education Ministry announced 10,000 merit scholarships and said that 15,000 students had already participated in the employment programs: see "Intervention de M. François Fillon à l'Assemblée nationale" ["Speech by François Fillon to the National Assembly"], Ministère des Affaires Sociales, du Travail, et de la Solidarité [Ministry of Social Affairs, Labor, and Solidarity], March 11, 2004.

53. "Vu dans *Le Monde*: Des beurs dans l'armée" ["Seen in *Le Monde*: Beurs in the army"], *Le Monde*, October 1, 2003.

54. "Les beurs dans l'armée, un nouveau documentaire de Yamina Benguigui" ["*Beurs* in the army: A new documentary by Yamina Benguigui"] (www.kelma.org/lesnews/news/islam_de_france.htm). Once in the army, however, many *beurs* report

discriminatory treatment at the hands of superiors: see Christophe Bertossi and Catherine Wihtol de Wenden, *Les militaires français issus de l'immigration* [*French soldiers of immigrant origin*] (Paris: Les documents du C2SD, 2005).

55. See also "L'armée s'ouvre timidement aux beurs" ["The army timidly opens its doors to *beurs*"], *Le Monde Diplomatique*, September 2001; "L'armée peine à faire une place aux recrues issues de l'immigration" ["The army is still trying to make room for recruits of immigrant origin"], *Le Monde*, October 27, 2005.

56. *Aïcha, Mohamed, and Chaïb: Enlisted for France,* a documentary film by Yamina Benguigui on second-generation immigrants in the French army, was broadcast September 30, 2003, on France 3; "Liberté, égalité . . . armée" ["Liberty, equality . . . army"], *Le Monde*, September 27, 2003; "Chez moi, la France" ["France, my home"], *L'Humanité*, September 27, 2003.

57. "M. Sarkozy veut promouvoir l'égalité des chances par la loi" ["Mr. Sarkozy wants to promote equality through the law"], *Le Monde*, October 27, 2005; "Nicolas Sarkozy teste l'accueil de jeunes venus de ZEP au sein de la 'fac Pasqua'" ["Nicolas Sarkozy proposes hosting young people from ZEPs on the 'Pasqua campus'"], *Le Monde*, November 26, 2005.

58. "Jacques Chirac s'oppose à la discrimination positive et promeut la diversité" ["Jacques Chirac opposes positive discrimination and promotes diversity"], *Le Monde*, June 23, 2005.

59. Michel Wieviorka, "Equité à babord" ["Port-side equality"], *Libération*, December 10, 2004.

60. Patrick Weil, "Un plan pour l'égalité" ["A plan for equality"], *Le Monde*, December 13, 2004.

61. Agence Nationale de l'Accueil et des Migrations (ANAM). For further reading, see Sylvia Zappi, "French Government Revives Assimilation Program," October 2003 (www.migrationinformation.org/Feature/display.cfm?ID=165).

62. "Nicolas Sarkozy fixe un objectif de 25,000 immigrés en situation irrégulière expulsés en 2006" ["Nicolas Sarkozy fixes a goal of expelling 25,0000 illegal immigrants in 2006"], *Le Monde*, November 29, 2005.

63. See Laetitia van Eeckhout, "Immigration familiale: les faits" ["Family integration: The facts"], *Le Monde*, January 5, 2006.

64. Christophe Jakubyszyn, "Le premier ministre appelle à 'éviter certains amalgames' sur la crise des banlieues" ["The prime minister calls for 'avoiding certain misconceptions' about the crisis of the banlieues"], *Le Monde*, November 20, 2005.

65. Patrick Roger, "M. Sarkozy plaide pour les quotas . . . qui ne sont pas dans son projet de loi" ["Mr. Sarkozy argues in favor of quotas . . . which are not in his immigration bill"], *Le Monde*, May 4, 2006.

66. Sophie Huet, "Immigration: droite et gauche s'apprêtent à une bataille sur le projet Sarkozy" ["Immigration: The right and the left prepare for a battle over the Sarkozy project"], *Le Figaro*, April 20, 2006.

67. Philippe Ridet, "Pour Nicolas Sarkozy, 'l'immigration choisie est un rempart contre le racisme'" ["For Nicolas Sarkozy, 'selective immigration is a rampart against racism'"], *Le Monde*, April 27, 2006.

68. *Jus sanguinis*, "law of blood," is a legal principle whereby citizenship is granted solely on the basis of the citizenship of one's parents, as opposed to *jus soli*, "law of the land," which grants citizenship on the basis of the place of one's birth. Both the United States and France grant citizenship according to the latter principle.

69. "M. Sarkozy: 'Il ne serait pas anormal qu'un étranger puisse voter'" ["Mr. Sarkozy: 'It would not be strange for a foreigner to be able to vote'"], *Le Monde*, October 24, 2005.

70. Arnaud Leparmentier, "Philippe Séguin: 'Le modèle canadien ou anglais est plus efficace que le modèle français non appliqué'" ["The Canadian or British model is more efficient than the unapplied French model"], *Le Monde*, February 22, 2006.

Chapter 8

1. See, for example, Jamie Glazov, "The Death of France?" *FrontPageMagazine.com*, June 9, 2003.

2. See Pierre Khalfa, "L'islam, l'enjeu de l'intégration" ["Islam: The issue of integration"], *Libération*, November 11, 2004.

3. L'Agence Panafricaine de Presse [Pan-African Press Agency], "123 candidats d'origine africaine aux législatives françaises" ["One hundred twenty-three candidates of African origin in the French legislative elections"], June 6, 2002 (www.panapress.com).

4. Yves Bordenave, "A l'UMP, Kacim Kellal tente de faire entendre la voix des Français d'origine étrangère" ["At the UMP, Kacim Kellal tries to give voice to the French of foreign origin"], *Le Monde*, May 13, 2003.

5. Interview, *Le Nouvel Observateur*, October 15, 2003.

6. Pascal Ceaux, "Nicolas Sarkozy souhaite 'être compris' des Français vivant dans les quartiers difficiles" ["Nicolas Sarkozy wishes to 'be understood' by those French living in bad neighborhoods"], *Le Monde*, March 25, 2004 .

7. "Un collectif appelle les jeunes à s'inscrire sur les listes électorales" ["A group calls for young people to register to vote"], *Le Monde*, December 20, 2005.

8. Christophe Jakubyszyn, "L'inscription sur les listes électorales séduit les 'quartiers'" ["Voter registration drives are successful in bad neighborhoods"], and "Record d'affluence dans plusieurs villes" ["Record turnout in many cities"], *Le Monde*, December 29, 2005.

9. See Romain Garbaye, "Ethnic Minorities, Cities, and Institutions: A Comparison of the Modes of Management of Ethnic Diversity of a French and a British City," in *Challenging Immigration and Ethnic Relations Politics*, edited by Ruud Koopmans and Paul Statham (London: Oxford University Press, 2000).

10. Interview with Tokia Saïfi in *Le Figaro*, October 24, 2003.

11. Bordenave, "A l'UMP, Kacim Kellal tente de faire entendre la voix des Français

d'origine étrangère" ["At the UMP, Kacim Kellal tries to give voice to the French of foreign origin"].

12. Xavier Ternisien, "Les organisations musulmanes de France en majorité pour le oui" ["Most French Muslim organizations are for a 'yes' vote"], *Le Monde*, May 10, 2005.

13. Jean-Luc Richard, *Partir ou rester? Destinées des jeunes issus de l'immigration étrangère en France* [*Go or stay? The fate of young people of immigrant origin in France*] (Paris: PUF, 2004).

14. Eder Lizi, "Vote maghrébin: naissance d'une force politique" ["The North African vote: Birth of a political force"], *La Médina*, December 12, 2001.

15. Besma Lahouri, "Des beurs très courtisés" ["*Beurs* in high demand"], *L'Express*, January 15, 2004.

16. Vincent Geisser and Paul Oriol, "Les Français 'd'origine étrangère' aux élections municipales de 2001" ["French of 'foreign origin' in 2001 municipal elections"], *Migrations-Societe*, vol. 13, no. 77 (September-October 2001), p. 44.

17. Malika Ahmed, "Les arabes et le référendum sur l'Europe" ["Arabs and the referendum on Europe"], *L'économiste*, May 18, 2005.

18. Lahouri, "Des beurs très courtisés" ["*Beurs* in high demand"].

19. Ahmed, "Les arabes et le référendum sur l'Europe" ["Arabs and the referendum on Europe"].

20. Lizi, "Vote maghrébin: naissance d'une force politique" ["The North African vote: Birth of a political force"].

21. Ibid.

22. Xavier Ternisien, "Existe-t-il un vote musulman?" ["Is there a Muslim vote?"], *Le Monde*, April 19, 2004; and Xavier Ternisien, "L'oecuménisme selon Georges Frêche" ["Ecumenicalism according to Georges Frêche"], *Le Monde*, April 20, 2004; "Suspension de Georges Frêche dans les instances nationales du PS" ["George Frêche is suspended from the national institutions of the PS"], *Agence France-Presse*, February 28, 2006.

23. François Capelani, "Les animateurs de la liste Euro-Palestine fêtent leur percée électorale en banlieue parisienne" ["The leaders of the Euro-Palestine list celebrate their electoral success in the banlieue outside Paris"], *Le Monde*, June 22, 2004; and Didier Hassoux, "La Courneuve: Europalestine dans les urnes et les coeurs" ["Courneuve: Euro-Palestine in their ballot boxes and in their hearts"], *Libération*, June 15, 2004. See "Résultats complets de la liste Euro-Palestine: la mobilisation paye!" ["Complete results of the Euro-Palestine list: Mobilization pays!"], communiqué from Euro-Palestine, June 15, 2004 (www.oumma.com).

24. http://france-islamique.tripod.com/ (May 2003).

25. See, for example, Francis Fukuyama, "Voile et contrôle sexuel" ["The head-scarf and sexual control"], *Le Monde*, February 3, 2004.

26. Dalil Boubakeur is the head of CFCM (see chapter 5). Bruno Etienne, "La France en Otage" ["France held hostage"], *Le Monde*, September 6, 2004.

27. Sylvain Brouard and Vincent Tiberj, *Français comme les autres? Enquête sur les citoyens d'origine maghrébine, africaine, et turque* [*French like the rest? A study of citizens of North African, African and Turkish origin*] (Paris: Presses de Sciences Po, 2005), p. 105.

28. Michel Wieviorka, *La tentation antisémite: Haine des juifs dans la France d'aujourd'hui* [*The anti-Semitic temptation: Hatred of Jews in today's France*] (Paris: Robert Laffont, 2005), p. 159. Pierre-André Taguieff, "La nouvelle judéophobie: une menace planétaire" ["The new Judeophobia: A global menace"], *Arche*, no. 535, September 2002.

29. Xavier Ternisien, *La France des mosquées* (*The France of the mosques*) (Paris: Albin Michel, 2002).

30. Vincent Geisser and Khadija Mohsen-Finan, "L'islam à l'école" ["Islam at school"], Institut des Hautes Etudes de la Sécurité Intérieure (IHESI), 2001.

31. Chems-eddine Hafiz, "Quel rôle joue la Grande Mosquée de Paris au CFCM?" ["What role does the GMP play in the CFCM?"], July 13, 2005 (www.saphirnet.info).

32. IFOP (Institut Français d'Opinion Publique), *Le Figaro* poll, March 21, 2003; IPSOS, *Le Figaro* poll, April 7, 2003.

33. IPSOS, *Le Figaro* poll, April 7, 2003.

34. Xavier Ternisien, "Les maghrébins de France se sentent en phase avec l'opinion" ["French North Africans and public opinion are in harmony"], *Le Monde*, March 22, 2003.

35. Xavier Ternisien, "Les représentants musulmans appellent au 'calme' et à la 'dignité'" ["Muslim representatives call for 'calm' and 'dignity'"], *Le Monde*, March 22, 2003.

36. Pascal Boniface, *Est-il permis de critiquer Israël?* [*Is it permissible to criticize Israel?*] (Paris: Robert Laffont, 2003).

37. PS leader Dominique Strauss-Kahn's denunciation of the "unauthorized memo" at an Israeli solidarity march on June 22, 2003, was followed by Boniface's resignation from the Socialist Party.

38. Joseph Macé-Scaron, editorial, *Le Figaro*, September 28, 2004.

39. Hakim El ghissassi, "Les arabes de France sortent petit à petit du discours sur la citoyenneté" [French Arabs are slowly leaving the discourse of citizenship behind"], *La Médina*, November 2003.

40. See "L'Islam en France et les réactions aux attentats du 11 septembre 2001" ["Islam in France and reactions to the attacks of September 11, 2001"], IFOP–*Le Monde/Le Point/Europe 1* poll, October 5, 2001 (www.ifop.com/europe.sondages/OPINIONF/islam.asp).

41. Geisser and Mohsen-Finan, "L'islam à l'école" ["Islam at school"].

42. CSA–*La Vie* election day polls, April 21, 2002.

43. Ibid.

44. Claude Dargent, "Les musulmans déclarés en France: affirmation religieuse, subordination sociale, et progressisme politique" ["Self-declared Muslims in France:

Religious affirmation, social subordination, and political progressivism"], *Cahier du CEVIPOF,* no. 34 (February 2003).

45. Geisser and Mohsen-Finan, "L'islam à l'école" ["Islam at school"].

46. In first-round voting, Lionel Jospin came in a close third, due to the scattering of votes from the left among many candidates.

47. Pew Research Center for the People and the Press, "Views of a Changing World 2003," June 3, 2003 (http://people-press.org/reports/display.php3?ReportID=185 [April 4, 2006]).

48. Vincent Geisser, "Les musulmans de France: Un lobby électoral en marche?" ["French Muslims: An electoral lobby on the move?"], *La Médina,* 2002.

49. On French Arab policy, see Rémy Leveau, "France's Arab Policy," in *Diplomacy in the Middle East: The International Relations of Regional and Outside Powers,* edited by Carl Brown (New York: Palgrave McMillan, 2001), and Maurice Vaïsse, "Enquête sur la politique arabe de la France"["A study of French Arab policy"], *L'Histoire* no. 282, December 2003.

50. Mustapha Benchenane, *Pour un dialogue euro-arabe* [*In favor of a Euro-Arab dialogue*] (Paris: Berger-Levrault, 1983), p. 79; Shireen Hunter, *The Future of Islam and the West: Clash of Civilizations or Peaceful Coexistence?* (Westport: Praeger, 1998), p. 125.

51. Cary Fraser, "In Defense of Allah's Realm: Religion and Statecraft in Saudi Foreign Policy Strategy," in *Transnational Religion and Fading States,* edited by Susanne Hoeber Rudolph and James P. Piscatori (Boulder, Colo.: Westview Press, 1997), p. 221.

52. Benchenane, *Pour un dialogue euro-arabe* [*In favor of a Euro-Arab dialogue*], p. 267.

53. Philip Gordon and Jeremy Shapiro, *Allies at War: America, Europe, and the Crisis over Iraq* (New York: McGraw-Hill, 2004), p. 142.

54. Samuel Huntington, *The Clash of Civilizations and the Remaking of World Order* (New York: Touchstone, 1996).

Chapter 9

1. Erik Cohen, *Les juifs de France: valeurs et identités* [*The Jews of France: Values and identities*] (Paris: Fonds social juif unifié, 2002), gives 535,000 Jews in 1980 and 500,000 in 2002.

2. The U.S. Jewish population is 5.3 million and that of Israel is 5.1 million. David Singer and Lawrence Grossman, eds., *American Jewish Yearbook 2003* (New York: The American Jewish Committee, 2003).

3. Before 2000, with a Jewish population ten times more numerous, the United States usually had between fifteen and twenty-five times more incidents than France. After 2000, there were between 1.7 and 6.6 times more incidents in the United States than in France. French figures are taken from the Commission Nationale Consultative des Droits de l'Homme (CNCDH), "La lutte contre le racisme et la xénophobie 2004"

["The fight against racism and xenophobia 2004"] (www.//lesrapports.ladocumenta-tionfrancaise.fr/BRP/054000193/0000.pdf), hereafter referred to as "CNCDH 2004 report." Figures for the United States were taken from the Anti-Defamation League's report for 2004 (www.adl.org/PresRele/ASUS_12/4680_12.htm).

4. According to Pierre-André Taguieff, *La nouvelle judéophobie* [*The new Judeo-phobia*] (Paris: Mille et une Nuits, 2002).

5. See Diana Pinto, "The Jewish Challenges in the New Europe," in *Challenging Ethnic Citizenship: German and Israeli Perspectives on Immigration,* edited by Daniel Levy and Yfaat Weiss (New York: Berghahn Books, 2002).

6. Quoted in Nonna Mayer, "Nouvelle judéophobie ou vieil antisémitisme?" ["New Judeophobia or old Anti-Semitism?"], *Raisons Politiques,* November 16, 2004.

7. Nonna Mayer, "Les opinions antisémites en France après la seconde Intifada" ["Antisemitic opinions in France after the second intifada"], *Revue internationale et stratégique*, no. 58 (Summer 2005). However, the most recent poll, which happened to be taken during the socially strained environment of the urban unrest of November 2005, points to a decrease in that support: 68 percent of respondents support judicial action against people who use the slur "dirty Jew," and 60 percent support judicial action against people who use the slur "dirty Arab." Commission Nationale Consultative des Droits de l'Homme (CNCDH), "La lutte contre le racisme et la xénophobie 2005" ["The fight against racism and xenophobia 2005"] (http://lesrapports.ladocu-mentationfrancaise.fr/BRP/064000264/0000.pdf), hereafter "CNCDH 2005 report."

8. Jean-Marc Dreyfus and Jonathan Laurence, "Anti-Semitism in France," CUSE US–Europe Analysis Series (http://brookings.edu/fp/cuse/analysis/dreyfus_20020514. htm).

9. Jean-Yves Camus, "Le nouvel ennemi: le monde arabo-musulman ou l'islam?" ["The new enemy: The Arab-Muslim world or Islam?"], *Le Monde*, January 22, 2005.

10. The comparison is also made by Michel Wieviorka, *La tentation antisémite: haine des juifs dans la France d'aujourd'hui* [*The anti-Semitic temptation: Hatred of Jews in today's France*] (Paris: Robert Laffont, 2005), p. 29.

11. CNCDH 2005 report.

12. Alexandre Levy, "La justice retient le motif de 'crime raciste' pour le meurtre d'Ilan Halimi" ["Prosecutors suspect a 'racist crime' in the murder of Ilan Halimi"], *Le Monde*, February 21, 2006. Some observers, however, doubted the centrality of anti-Semitism in the kidnapping plot: see Piotr Smolar, "L'affaire Halimi ou l'adieu à la nation" ["The Halimi affair, or the end of the nation"], *Le Monde*, March 3, 2006; and Fatiha Benatsou and Nourdine Cherkaoui, "Halte au masochisme national" ["Stop the national masochism"], *Le Monde,* March 8, 2006.

13. Cohen, *Les juifs de France* [*The Jews of France*].

14. Ibid.

15. Jean-Christophe Rufin, "Rapport au premier minister," Chantier sur la lutte contre le racisme et l'antisémitisme ["Report to the prime minister," Working group on the fight against racism and anti-Semitism] (www.interieur.gouv.fr/rubriques/c/c2_le_ministere/c21_actualite/2004_10_19_rufin/rapport_Rufin.pdf).

16. BVA poll in CNCDH 2004 report.

17. Elie Chouraqui, "La haine ordinaire" ["Ordinary hatred"], broadcast in *Envoyé Spécial*, France 2, April 15, 2004; also Cyril Denvers and Stéphane Tirchard, "Quand la religion fait la loi à l'école" ["When religion makes the rules at school"], broadcast on France 3, March 27, 2004.

18. See Wieviorka, *La tentation antisémite* ["The anti-Semitic temptation"], chapter 1.

19. CNCDH 2004 and 2005 reports.

20. George Will, "Final Solution, Phase 2," *Washington Post*, May 2, 2002.

21. Marie Brenner, "France's Scarlet Letter," *Vanity Fair*, June 2003; Marc Perelman, "Community Head: France No More Antisemitic than U.S.," *The Forward*, August 1, 2003.

22. See, for example, Gilles Paris, "Le premier ministre israélien souhaite faire venir un million de juifs d'ici dix ans" ["The Israeli prime minister would like to have 1 million Jews from here arrive in the next ten years"], *Le Monde*, July 19, 2004.

23. Mouna Naïm, "Le président français met le holà aux accusations israéliennes d'antisémitisme" ["The French president puts a stop to Israeli accusations of anti-Semitism"], and "Les récriminations d'Israël" ["Israel's recriminations"], *Le Monde*, May 13, 2002; Henri Hajdenberg, "Les juifs de France entre deux feux" ["French Jews between two fires"], *Le Monde*, May 16, 2002.

24. Wieviorka, *La tentation antisémite* [*The anti-Semitic temptation*], p. 128.

25. See Elie Barnavi, quoted by Daniel Vernet, "Un peu de raison dans la passion judéo-française" ["A bit of reason in the French-Jewish passion"], *Le Monde*, Novembre 15, 2002; see also Elie Barnavi, *La France, les Juifs, et Israël* [*France, Jews, and Israel*] (Paris: Perrin, 2002), and *Lettre ouverte aux juifs de France* [*An open letter to the Jews of France*] (Paris: Stock, 2002).

26. CNCDH 2004 and 2005 reports.

27. Wieviorka, *La tentation antisémite* [*The anti-Semitic temptation*], p. 25.

28. CNCDH 2004 report.

29. Quoted in Gérard David and Piotr Smolar, "Meurtre d'Ilan Halimi: le récit des geôliers" ["The murder of Ilan Halimi: his jailers speak"], *Le Monde*, March 22, 2006.

30. The same characteristics are found among the authors of "false alarms," whether Jewish or not. See Rufin, "Rapport au premier ministre" ["Report to the prime minister"].

31. CNCDH reports, various years (http://lesrapports.ladocumentationfrancaise.fr/).

32. CNCDH 2004 report.

33. Taguieff, *La nouvelle judéophobie* [*The new Judeophobia*]; Rufin, "Rapport au premier ministre" ["Report to the prime minister"].

34. Mayer, "Nouvelle judéophobie ou vieil antisémitisme?" ["New Judeophobia or old anti-Semitism?"] and "Les opinions antisémites en France" ["Anti-Semitic opinions in France"].

35. Sylvain Brouard and Vincent Tiberj, *Français comme les autres ? Enquête sur les citoyens d'origine maghrébine, africaine, et turque* [*French like the rest ? A study of*

citizens of North African, African, and Turkish origin] (Paris: Presses de Sciences Po, 2005), p.105.

36. BVA poll quoted by Nonna Mayer in "Les opinions antisémites en France" ["Anti-Semitic opinions in France"].

37. Except, in limited instances, in the professional milieux of universities; see Robert Solé, "De l'index au pilori" ["From censorship to burning at the stake"], *Le Monde*, January 11, 2003.

38. Figures from the Anti-Defamation League (www.adl.org/PresRele/ASUS_12/ 4680_12.htm).

39. Brouard and Tiberj, *Français comme les autres?* [*French like the rest?*], p. 100.

40. Department of State, "French Muslims Favor Integration into French Society," Opinion Analysis M-58-05, Office of Research, May 24, 2005.

41. Wieviorka, *La tentation antisémite* [*The anti-Semitic temptation*], p. 160.

42. Emmanuel Brenner (pseudonym for Georges Bensoussan, ed.), *Les territoires perdus de la République. Antisémitisme, racisme, et sexisme en milieu scolaire* [*The lost territories of the Republic: Anti-Semitism, racism and sexism in schools*] (Paris: Mille et une Nuits, 2002).

43. Interview by the authors with Theo Battistella, principal of Jules Siegfried technological high school, tenth arrondissement of Paris, March 23, 2005.

44. CNCDH 2004 report, p. 61.

45. This second period (9/2004–6/2005) included more active school days than the first period (racist and anti-Semitic incidents have been recorded by SIGNA only since January 2004). See Ministère d'Education Nationale [National Education Ministry], "Les actes de violence à l'école recensés dans SIGNA en 2004–2005" ["Acts of violence in school counted by SIGNA in 2004–2005"], *Note d'information* [*Information note*], no. 05.30, November 2005 (www.education.gouv.fr/stateval).

46. Quoted in Wieviorka, *La tentation antisémite* [*The anti-Semitic temptation*], p. 36.

47. Malek Boutih and Patrick Klugman for SOS Racisme–UEJF, *Les antifeujs* [*The anti-Jews*] (Calmann-Lévy, 2002).

48. Authors' interview with Samy Ghozlan, March 25, 2005

49. Tariq Ramadan, "Critique des (nouveaux) intellectuels communautaires" ["A critique of the new community intellectuals"], October 3, 2003 (www.oumma.com).

50. Marc Blachère, "Islamisme: Iquioussen ou la culture de la haine antijuive" ["Islamism: Iquioussen and the culture of anti-Jewish hatred"], *L'Humanité*, January 2004.

51. Samuel Huntington, *The Clash of Civilizations and the Remaking of World Order* (New York: Touchstone, 1996).

52. "Shoah Film Plays Role in French Anti-Hate Drive," Reuters, September 15, 2004; "Foreign Jews Praise France," Reuters, January 20, 2005; "Israel Takes in 200 French Jews," BBC News, July 28, 2004.

53. Speech by Nicolas Sarkozy, then interior minister, at a dinner of the CRIF of Toulouse, February 2, 2004.

54. CNCDH 2004 report, page 12.

55. See "Récapitulatif des procédures judiciaires closes et en cours concernant les poursuites engagées auprès des tribunaux contre les auteurs d'actes et de menaces antisémites pour les années 2002 et 2003" ["A summary of completed and continuing judicial proceedings concerning cases opened by courts against perpetrators of anti-Semitic acts and threats in 2002 and 2003"], a report issued by CRIF (www.crif.org).

56. In March 2006, Dieudonné was fined €5,000 for having compared Jewish people to "négriers" (slave owners): "Dieudonné, condamné pour propos racistes" ["Dieudonné convicted for racist remarks"], *Libération,* March 10, 2006.

57. Virginie Malingre, "Claude Lanzmann explique 'Shoah' à des élèves avant sa distribution dans les lycées" ["Claude Lanzmann explains *Shoah* to pupils before its distribution in the schools"], *Le Monde,* September 15, 2004.

Chapter 10

1. Piotr Smolar, "L'argumentaire islamiste contre le France" ["The Islamist argument against France"], *Le Monde,* December 23, 2005.

2. See "Discours de Lhaj Thami Brèze à l'AG de l'UOIF" ["Lhaj Thami Brèze's speech to the general assembly of the UOIF"], September 30, 2005 (www.uoif-online.com/modules.php?op=modload&name=News&file=article&sid=403); see also "Condamnation des attentats de Londres" ["Condemnation of the London attacks"], Grande Mosquée de Paris, July 8, 2005 (www.mosque-de-paris.net/cgi-bin/news/exec/search.cgi?cat=21&start=6&perpage=5&template=index/default.html).

3. See, for example, Robert Leiken, "Europe's Angry Muslims," *Foreign Affairs* 84, no. 4 (July-August 2005).

4. "Le djihadiste français est plus fruste, plus jeune, plus radicalisé" ["The French jihadi is rougher, younger, and more radical"], *Le Monde,* May 24, 2005; "Neuf personnes proches des islamistes algériens ont été interpellées" ["Nine people close to Algerian Islamists have been arrested"], *Le Monde,* September 26, 2005.

5. Frédéric Veaux (chief of the DNAT, National Antiterrorist Division), "Lutter efficacement contre le terrorisme" ["Fighting terrorism effectively"], in *Un an après Madrid: L'europe face au terrorisme* [*One year after Madrid: Europe faced with terrorism*] (Paris: Institut de relations internationales et stratégiques [Institute of International and Strategic Relations], 2005).

6. Jean Chichizola, "L'islam radical dans la mire de tous les services de l'état" ["Radical Islam in the cross-hairs of all state agencies"], *Le Figaro,* March 27, 2005; "Le djihadiste français est plus fruste, plus jeune, plus radicalisé" ["The French jihadi is rougher, younger, and more radical"].

7. "M. Sarkozy veut expulser les imams 'radicaux'" ["Mr. Sarkozy wants to deport 'radical' imams"], *Le Monde,* July 16, 2005.

8. "Pour Nicolas Sarkozy, la menace terroriste est à 'un niveau très élevé'" ["For Nicolas Sarkozy, the terrorist threat is at 'a very elevated level'"], *Le Monde,* September 26, 2005.

9. "Le djihadiste français est plus fruste, plus jeune, plus radicalisé" ["The French jihadi is rougher, younger, and more radical"].

10. Jean Chichizola, "De La Villette aux combats en Iraq: le mortel itinéraire de Tarek" ["From La Villette to fighting in Iraq: Tarek's deadly itinerary"], *Le Figaro*, December 9, 2004.

11. The French El-Hakim brothers traveled to Syria with the intention of fighting in Iraq; one was killed in the U.S. bombardment of Falluja, and the other was arrested by the Syrians. Gérard Davet, "Les filières de recrutement de la 'guerre sainte' sont en place" ["The recruitment network for the 'holy war' is in place"], *Le Monde*, December 15, 2004.

12. Ibid.

13. Farhad Khosrokhavar, *Les nouveaux martyrs d'Allah* [Allah's new martyrs] (Paris: Flammarion, 2002).

14. Olivier Bertrand, "La tentation salafiste" ["The salafist temptation"], *Libération*, December 8, 2004, and "Les proies du salafisme" ["Salafism's prey"], *Libération*, December 9, 2004.

15. Olivier Roy, *Globalized Islam: The Search for a New Ummah* (Columbia University Press, 2004).

16. Elaine Sciolino, "Portrait of the Arab as a Young Radical," *New York Times*, September 22, 2002.

17. Quoted by Olivier Roy, "EuroIslam: The Jihad Within?" *National Interest* 71 (Spring 2003).

18. Interview with Olivier Roy, "Musulmans dans la modernité" ["Muslims in modernity"], *Mouvements*, November 2004 (http://www.yodawork.com/websp/SW2_consult_ref?F_refid=22682&F_nom=SOGDECNEW).

19. See Patrick Haenni, "France and Its Muslims: Riots, Jihadism, and Depoliticisation," *Europe Report* no. 172 (Brussels: International Crisis Group, March 2006).

20. Roy, "EuroIslam: The Jihad Within?" Indeed, in the fall of 2004, the French secret service identified a "neighborhood" jihadist network operating on the margins of the same Ad-Dawa mosque, which the local imam could not control. The group sent several French youth to Iraq from Paris's nineteenth arrondissement. See Davet, "Les filières de recrutement de la 'guerre sainte' sont en place" ["The recruitment network for the 'holy war' is in place"].

21. Roy, *Globalized Islam: The Search for a New Ummah*.

22. Gilles Kepel, *Jihad: The Trail of Political Islam* (Harvard University Press, 2002).

23. "L'antiterrorisme, selon le Patron des RG" ["Counterterrorism, according to the head of domestic intelligence"], *Le Monde*, November 24, 2005.

24. Xavier Ternisien, "Enquête sur le salafisme, principale cible du ministère de l'intérieur" ["An investigation of Salafism, the principal target of the interior ministry"], *Le Monde*, May 5, 2004.

25. Jean-Marc Leclerc, "Le rapport des R.G. sur les convertis à l'islam" ["The RG's report on Muslim converts"], *Le Figaro*, October 7, 2003.

26. Quoted in Marie-France Etchegoin and Serge Raffy, "La vérité sur l'islam en France" ["The truth about Islam in France"], *Nouvel Observateur,* February 2–8, 2006.

27. Khosrokhavar, *L'islam dans les prisons* [*Islam in prisons*].

28. Ibid.

29. Dominique Thomas, *Londonistan: la voix du djihad* [*Londonistan: The voice of jihad*] (Paris: Michalon, 2003).

30. See Alan Cowell, "Britain Considers Lengthening Time for Holding Terror Suspects," *New York Times,* August 10, 2005; "Rachid Ramda a été extradé vers la France" ["Rachid Ramda has been extradited to France"], *Le Monde,* December 1, 2005.

31. Gilles Kepel, *Fitna: Guerre au coeur de l'islam* [Fitna: War at the heart of Islam] (Paris: Gallimard, 2004).

32. Jacques Amalric and Patricia Tourancheau, "Des réseaux terroristes très mobiles et autonomes" ["Terrorist networks are very mobile and autonomous"], *Libération,* December 6, 2002.

33. Interview with Pierre de Bousquet, *Le Monde,* May 24, 2005.

34. Abd Samad Moussaoui and Florence Bouquillat, *Zacarias Moussaoui, mon frère* [*My brother, Zacarias Moussaoui*] (Paris: Denoël, 2002).

35. Much of the brother's account was corroborated by defense witnesses from Zacarias Moussaoui's childhood who testified during the sentencing phase of the trial. See Richard Hétu, "Avant-dernier acte du procès moussaoui: retour sur une enfance 'fracassée'" ["Next-to-last act of the Moussaoui trial: A return to his 'shattered' childhood"], *La Presse* (Canada), April 16, 2006; Guillemette Faure, "Une carrière de terroriste jalonnée de multiples ratés" ["A terrorist career marked by multiple failures"], *Le Figaro,* April 25, 2006; and Michael J. Sniffen, "Defense: Traumatic Childhood Left Moussaoui Vulnerable to Recruitment by Radical Isam," *Associated Press,* April 17, 2006.

36. Sniffen, "Defense: Traumatic Childhood Left Moussaoui Vulnerable."

37. Pascal Riché, "Moussaoui au plus près de la mort" ["Moussaoui getting closer to the death penalty"], *Libération,* April 25, 2006.

38. Witnesses in Moussaoui's federal trial said the girl was named Karine B.; it is probable that Abd Samad Moussaoui changed her name in his book in order to protect her identity. Abd Samad Moussaoui also writes that the relationship lasted ten years. See Hétu, "Avant-dernier acte du procès moussaoui" ["Next-to-last act of the Moussaoui trial"], and Sniffen, "Defense: Traumatic Childhood Left Moussaoui Vulnerable"].

39. Stéphane Thepot, "La lente dérive intégriste de Zacarias Moussaoui" ["The slow fundamentalist drift of Zacarias Moussaoui"], *Le Monde,* September 27, 2001.

40. Moussaoui and Bouquillat, *Zacarias Moussaoui.*

41. Special verdict form for the second phase of *United States of America* v. *Zacarias Moussaoui,* U.S. District Court for the Eastern District of Virginia, available at http://notablecases.vaed.uscourts.gov/1:01-cr-00455/docs/72434/0.pdf.

42. One of these teachers testified during the sentencing phase of Moussaoui's trial

on behalf of the defense; see Guillemette Faure, "Une carrière de terroriste jalonnée de multiples ratés" ["A terrorist career marked by multiple failures"].

43. Moussaoui's sister Aïcha also testified to that effect in his federal trial; see Sniffen, "Defense: Traumatic Childhood Left Moussaoui Vulnerable."

44. Neil A. Lewis, "Prosecutors Concede Doubts about Moussaoui's Story," *New York Times*, April 21, 2006.

45. The authors are indebted to Jeremy Shapiro, a specialist at the Brookings Institution on the French antiterrorism apparatus, for his aid in drafting this section. See Jeremy Shapiro and Bénédicte Suzan, "The French Experience of Counter-terrorism," *Survival* 45, no. 1 (Spring 2003).

46. The Schengen Agreement—originally signed in 1985 in Luxembourg by Germany, France, Belgium, Luxembourg, and the Netherlands—involved the gradual abolition of checks at the common borders of the participating countries. It evolved into the Schengen Protocol to the Treaty of European Union of Amsterdam in 1997, allowing citizens of implementing countries (EU member states plus Norway and Iceland, with special arrangements for Britain, Ireland, and Denmark) to cross the borders of implementing countries at any point without border checks.

47. Andrew Jack and Roula Khalaf, "Row over Shooting of French Suspect," *Financial Times*, October 4, 1995, p. 2.

48. Dana Priest, "Help from France Key in Covert Operations," *Washington Post*, July 3, 2005; Piotr Smolar, "L'argumentaire islamiste contre la France" ["The Islamist argument against France"], *Le Monde*, December 23, 2005.

49. Loi no. 86-1020 du 9 septembre 1986 relative à la lutte contre le terrorisme et aux atteintes à la sûreté de l'Etat [Law 86-1020 of September 9, 1986, concerning the fight against terrorism and attacks on the security of the state].

50. Ibid., article 1.

51. An investigation by Jean-Louis Bruguière foiled a bomb attack on Strasbourg's Christmas market in 2000. Sentences of varying length (eighteen months to ten years) were handed down four years later to ten cell members by the Tribunal Correctionnel de Paris.

52. UCLAT was created in October 1984. SCLAT was later renamed the Fourteenth Section of the Public Prosecutor's Office of Paris.

53. French official, interview with the authors, October 2002.

54. Irène Stoller, interview with the authors, October 2002.

55. Nathalie Cettina, *L'Antiterrorisme en question* [*Counterterrorism in question*] (Paris: Michalon, 2001).

56. Peter Chalk and William Rosenau, *Confronting the "Enemy Within": Security, Intelligence, and Counterterrorism in Four Democracies* (RAND, 2004).

57. Article 421-2-1 of the French Penal Code (www.legifrance.gouv.fr/html/codes_traduits/code_penal_textan.htm [July 22,1996]).

58. For one review, see Dirk Haubrich, "September 11, Anti-Terror Laws, and Civil Liberties: Britain, France, and Germany Compared," *Government and Opposition* 38,

no. 1 (2003): 3–28. See also Shaun Gregory, "France and the War on Terrorism," *Terrorism and Political Violence* 15, no. 1 (Spring 2003), pp. 140–41.

59. Jacky Durand, "Prudences sur la future loi antiterroriste" ["Cautions on the future antiterrorism law"], *Libération*, September 27, 2005.

60. Bruce Hoffman, "Intelligence and Terrorism: Emerging Threats and New Security Challenges in the Post–Cold War Era," *Intelligence and National Security* 11 no. 2 (April 1996): 207.

61. "France: la porte ouverte à l'arbitraire" ["France: An open door for arbitrary treatment"], Rapport d'une mission internationale d'enquête en France sur l'application de la législation anti-terroriste [Report of an international board of inquiry on the application of antiterrorism legislation], January 1999, no. 271, Fédération Internationale des Ligues des Droits de l'Homme (www.fidh.imaginet.fr).

62. Ibid.

63. For an exception, see Didier Bigo, "Reassuring and Protecting: Internal Security Implications of French Participation in the Coalition against Terrorism," in *Critical Views of September 11,* edited by Eric Hershberg and Kevin W. Moore (New York: New Press, 2002), p. 72–94.

64. "Le Mrap dénonce des propos de M. de Villiers sur l'islam et saisit la Halde" ["The MRAP denounces Mr. Villier's speech about Islam and asks the HALDE to intervene"], Agence France-Presse, July 18, 2005.

Chapter 11

1. See U.S. Senate, "Islamist Extremism in Europe: Testimony of Daniel Fried, Assistant Secretary of State for European Affairs, before the Senate Foreign Relations Committee," Subcommittee on European Affairs, April 5, 2006.

2. For the reactions of one IVLP participant upon his return to Europe, see Aiman Maziyek, "Innenpolitisch von den USA lernen" ["Learning from domestic politics in the USA"], April 25, 2006 (www.islam.de).

3. Except for the Council of Europe, which has thirty-five members, but it is not the same thing as the European Council and it is not an EU institution. In 2006, however, European Union officials developed an official lexicon to use when publicly discussing Islam and terrorism, as part of their security strategy to combat radicalization and terrorist recruitment; see Peter Ford, "Fighting Terrorism One Word at a Time," *Christian Science Monitor*, April 24, 2006.

4. "Our Symposia: Governance and Civilisations," European Commission, Forward Studies Unit, Brussels, May 14–17, 1998; Carrefours Newsletter no. 9, November 1998 (Brussels: European Commission, Forward Studies Unit).

5. Félice Dassetto, Brigitte Maréchal, and Jørgen Nielsen, eds., *Convergences musulmanes: aspects contemporains de l'islam dans l'Europe élargie* [*Muslim convergences: Contemporary aspects of Islam in enlarged Europe*], Cellule de Perspective/Commission Européene, Academia Brulant (Louvain-La-Neuve: L'Harmattan, 2001).

6. European Parliament Resolution on Islam and the European Averroës Day, no.1.3.76 (December 1998).

7. Giuseppe Pisanu, interview in Magdi Allam, "L'Italia dialoga con l'Islam: No ai maestri del terrorismo" ["Italy dialogues with Islam and says no to the masters of terrorism"], *La Repubblica*, May 23, 2003; Benita Ferrero-Waldner, "Islam in Europe: From Dialogue to Action," speech at the Conference of European Imams, Vienna, April 7, 2006.

8. *Europe et Laïcité* newsletter, April 2005, published by the association of the same name.

9. Interview by the authors with Adam Tyson, European Commission, 2000.

10. Daniel Cohen, "Comment réformer la France?" ["How to reform France?"], *Le Monde,* May 5, 2006.

Index

Acculturation and changing social practices, 43–46

Adulterers, defense of stoning of, 107

The Adventures of Amélie Poulain (film), 73

AEIF. *See* Association des Etudiants Islamiques en France

Affirmative action: and educational system, 38, 182–89; and public employment, 9, 62–63, 182–89; rejection of, 175–76; and religion, 55

Africa and African immigrants: and anti-Semitism, 236; and attitudes toward French institutions and identity, 47; and re-Islamization, 90; religious observance among, 76; unemployment rate of, 34. *See also specific countries*

Against Ghettos and for Equality, 179

Age distribution of population of Muslim origin, 22, 23

Agence Nationale de Lutte contre l'Illetrisme (ANLCI) (Agency for the Fight against Illiteracy), 180

Aïd al-Adha, 73, 110, 143, 153

Al-Adl wa Al-Ihsan (Justice and Development Party) (Morocco), 107, 109

Alaoui, Fouad, 105, 106, 107, 159, 174

Al Azhar University (Egypt), 119, 122

Algeria and Algerian immigrants, 15, 16, 17; Berbers, 21, 87; fertility rates of, 27, 28; French language usage by, 43; funding religious needs of immigrants, 114, 117–18, 136; historical viewpoint, 57; and housing problems, 36, 37; and imams, 118, 119, 120; and intergroup socializing, 45–46; intermarriage rates of, 44; monitoring of organizations from, 260; and negative stereotypes, 53; and religious observance, 87, 91, 142; and school gap, 39; unemployment rate of, 33–34; war in, 50–52, 53, 218, 231. *See also* Grande Mosquée de Paris; Union des Organisations Islamiques de France

Al Haramayn foundation, 117

Al-Houweidi, 107

Al-Istîchara, 147, 150

Alliot-Marie, Michèle, 178

al-Manar (television network) (Lebanon), 241, 266

Al-Masri, Abu Hamza, 251

al Qaeda, 51, 127, 247, 248, 249, 255

Al Qaradawi, Yusef, 107, 113, 125, 126, 129–31

Al-Qarawiyyin (Morocco), 119

Al Rabita al Islamiya al-Alamiya. *See* Muslim World League